Dawn at Mineral King Valley

DAWN AT MINERAL KING VALLEY

THE SIERRA CLUB, THE DISNEY COMPANY, AND THE RISE OF ENVIRONMENTAL LAW

Daniel P. Selmi

The University of Chicago Press
Chicago and London

The University of Chicago Press, Chicago 60637
The University of Chicago Press, Ltd., London

Published 2022
Paperback edition 2024
Printed in the United States of America

33 32 31 30 29 28 27 26 25 24   1 2 3 4 5

ISBN-13: 978-0-226-81619-7 (cloth)
ISBN-13: 978-0-226-83340-8 (paper)
ISBN-13: 978-0-226-81628-9 (e-book)
DOI: https://doi.org/10.7208/chicago/9780226816289.001.0001

Library of Congress Cataloging-in-Publication Data

Names: Selmi, Daniel P., author.
Title: Dawn at Mineral King Valley : the Sierra Club, the Disney company, and the rise of environmental law / Daniel P. Selmi.
Description: Chicago : University of Chicago Press, 2022. | Includes bibliographical references and index.
Identifiers: LCCN 2021038211 | ISBN 9780226816197 (cloth) | ISBN 9780226816289 (e-book)
Subjects: LCSH: Environmental law—United States—History. | Environmental protection—United States—History. | Environmental policy—United States—History. | Actions and defenses—United States—History. | Nature conservation—Law and legislation—Sierra Nevada (Calif. and Nev.)—History. | Mineral King Valley (Calif.) | Sierra Club. | Walt Disney Company. | Mineral King Valley (Calif.)
Classification: LCC KF3817.S45 2022 | DDC 344.7304/6—dc23
LC record available at https://lccn.loc.gov/2021038211

♾ This paper meets the requirements of ANSI/NISO Z39.48-1992 (Permanence of Paper).

To Ann

Contents

Principal Participants

The Sierra Club

John Harper, club member
Will Siri, President (1964–1966)
Michael McCloskey, Conservation Director,
later Executive Director
Phil Berry, President (1969–1971)
Leland (Lee) Selna, principal lawyer for the Mineral King litigation

Walt Disney Productions

Walt Disney, President
Robert (Bob) Hicks, head of Mineral King planning
Roy Disney, Chair, Chief Executive Officer, and President
Donn Tatum, President and Chairman of the Board
E. Cardon Walker, Executive Vice-President and President

Mineral King Recreational Development Company

Robert (Bob) Brandt, President
Janet Leigh, actress

The Forest Service

Wilfrid ("Slim") Davis, Chief of Division of Recreation
(Western Division)
Lawrence Whitfield, Supervisor, Sequoia National Forest
Charles Connaughton, Regional Forester
Edward Cliff, Chief, Forest Service
Peter (Pete) Wyckoff, Mineral King Staff Specialist

The Department of Agriculture

Orville Freeman, Secretary of Agriculture

Thomas (Tom) Hughes, Executive Assistant to the Secretary of Agriculture

Clifford Hardin, Secretary of Agriculture

The National Park Service

George Hartzog, Director

Frank Kowski, Superintendent, Sequoia National Park

The Department of the Interior

Stewart Udall, Secretary of the Interior

Stanley Cain, Assistant Secretary of the Interior

U.S. Department of Justice

Irwin Griswold, Solicitor General

Elected Officials

Harlan Hagen, Congressman

Edmund G. "Pat" Brown, Governor of California

John Krebs, Congressman

Ronald Reagan, Governor of California

Phil Burton, Congressman

Prologue

IN THE SUPREME COURT

As the clock approached 11 a.m. on November 17, 1971, in Washington, DC, lawyers and observers in the United States Supreme Court awaited the oral argument in the case of *Sierra Club v. Morton*. The press had extensively covered the case, and individuals seeking to watch the argument queued in a line stretching from inside the courtroom out to a street abutting the court building. At issue in the appeal was the fate of Mineral King, a spectacularly scenic valley nestled high in the Sierra Nevadas of California. The United States Forest Service, the principal defendant in the case, had awarded the right to build a large ski facility there to a company bearing a legendary name: Walt Disney. The plaintiff, the Sierra Club, was the country's best-known conservation group, founded eighty years earlier by the famous apostle of wilderness, John Muir.

The Sierra Club had filed suit in the tumultuous year of 1969. The Vietnam War raged, and the country still reeled from the assassinations the previous year of Robert Kennedy and Martin Luther King Jr., and from riots following King's death. However, 1969 was also the year in which concern over environmental degradation grew so rapidly that, some opined, it now rivaled the Vietnam War as a political issue.[1]

In January of that year, a blowout on a production platform off Santa Barbara, California, released oil that fouled ocean waters and splattered the coast.[2] The public recoiled at pictures of dying birds and marine mammals covered with the tar-like substance, and of rescuers attempting to save them. Several months later, an oil-slicked stretch of the Cuyahoga River caught fire in Cleveland, Ohio, and transfixed television viewers throughout the nation watched video of a river burning.[3]

An explosion of media attention addressed environmental issues. *Time* magazine named the environment as the issue of the year, terming it a "national obsession,"[4] and *Fortune*, the widely read business magazine, devoted an entire special issue to environmental problems.[5] An estimated twenty million individuals participated in the first Earth Day, held that year.[6] The Environmental Protection Agency was created to centralize environmental regulation in one federal agency, a landmark in efforts to address pollution. While the fervor would cool slightly by 1972, the environment would remain of great concern to the public.

The Supreme Court case on Mineral King exemplified one important response to this concern: lawsuits challenging actions that harmed the environment. When the Sierra Club had sued over Mineral King in 1969, environmental lawsuits were rare. But the suits soon multiplied, as environmentalists sought to stop projects and hold government officials accountable for environmentally damaging decisions.[7]

The history of the fight over Mineral King typified the new environmental consciousness that led to such litigation. After endorsing a ski development in the valley in 1949, the Sierra Club reversed its position sixteen years later. Citing the project's massive size and inevitable damage to Mineral King Valley, the club sought to incorporate the valley into the adjacent Sequoia National Park. Even within the government, the ski development approved by the Forest Service for the valley was fiercely contested. Secretary of the Interior Stewart Udall refused to approve a road across Sequoia National Park needed to access the ski development; he capitulated only after officials in the White House intervened.

At first the Sierra Club's lawsuit succeeded when a federal judge granted a preliminary injunction stopping the development. By the time the case reached the Supreme Court, however, the key issue had become one of overriding importance to the developing body of environmental law in the United States. That issue concerned a doctrine known as "standing," an arcane legal term that boiled down to a fundamental question: What organizations would the law allow to challenge environmental violations?

To have standing and bring an environmental case, a plaintiff had to show the type of injury that the courts would recognize. In the Mineral King case, however, a lower court of appeals in 1970 had ruled that, despite the Sierra Club's long-term involvement with the Sierra Nevadas, the club lacked standing to sue for the alleged environmental damage to the valley. If the Supreme Court upheld that ruling, lower courts would reject many lawsuits brought by the developing class of "environmental lawyers," thus stifling the emerging use of litigation to prevent environmental damage.

Closely watching the case was Walt Disney Productions, a name at this point synonymous with the proposed Mineral King ski development. The Disney company chose not to participate in the litigation, fearing that a court fight over the environmental effects of its project would tarnish Disney's public image. Despite that strategy, however, the company had been swept into the controversy. Two 1969 *New York Times* editorials attacked the Mineral King project as scandalous and a folly,[8] while a *Ramparts* magazine cover depicted Walt Disney digging up the mountains and leading "Disney's War against the Wilderness."[9] At the same time, an adamant *Los Angeles Times* vigorously supported the Disney project,[10] castigating the Sierra Club as "wilderness purists," and ski groups rallied behind the project.

To its frustration, the Disney company found itself embroiled in a raging public dispute that it could never have anticipated in 1965, when it submitted its bid to develop Mineral King. The company was furious at being labeled an environmental villain and often defended itself by citing Walt Disney's thirteen nature films about the animal world made between 1948 and 1960, eight of which won Academy Awards.[11] Those groundbreaking movies, set in locales ranging from the desert to the Arctic, had led the Sierra Club in 1955 to award Walt Disney an honorary lifetime membership for his "magnificent contributions to a widespread appreciation of our wildlife."[12] An article in the club's bulletin had extolled, "We need Disney, an army of Disneys, to tell the world what we have found, what we are fighting for, the glory of creation with the bloom on it."[13] Disney had also received awards from the National Wildlife Federation and the National Audubon Society, among other groups.[14] However, much had changed since then.

At 11 a.m. the Sierra Club's lawyer stepped to the podium. He faced a wooden bench behind which the justices sat against an impressive background of marble pillars and red drapes that ran floor to ceiling. The bench had been altered within the past year so that it now curved rather than ran straight across. The chief justice, Warren Burger, had ordered the change so all nine justices would have eye contact with each other—and thus perhaps interrupt each other less.[15] In a strange development, however, only seven justices now took the bench; two had recently resigned. And, unknown to the lawyers, a third justice was seriously considering not participating in the important case.

The issue that the Supreme Court was considering, standing to bring environmental cases, would determine whether federal courts could hear many legal disputes about environmental issues. However, the controversy over Mineral King that culminated in this courtroom showdown was broader. It arose from a complex interplay of legal principles, politics, corporate plans, public agency ambitions, and disputes over claims of environmental damage. This mix of forces had produced a unique, decade-long series of events over Mineral King's future.

The origins of the dispute over Mineral King, however, went back much further than ten years. The relevant history began in the nineteenth century with a classic tale of the American West: hordes of miners rushing to file claims in a mountainous valley after reports about mineral riches there had spread like wildfire.

A SKI DEVELOPMENT AT MINERAL KING

1: A Resort in the American Alps

The twenty-five-mile road to the Mineral King Valley begins by branching off State Route 198 near the town of Three Rivers, California, in the foothills of the Sierra Nevadas. The road is treacherous. Winding and unpaved in many parts, it ascends the steep canyon of the East Fork of the Kaweah River. It then passes through an eleven-mile stretch of Sequoia National Park, home to the gigantic and world-famous redwood trees for which it is named.

Exiting the park, the road enters Sequoia National Forest. It proceeds to bisect a small development on privately owned land known as Silver City and located four miles west of the Mineral King Valley. Soon, several small clusters of summer cabins appear. Finally, having climbed nearly 7,000 feet, the road ends inside the Mineral King Valley.

The valley extends about two miles in length and spreads a quarter of a mile in width. It sits on the southernmost flank of the Sierra Nevadas, "form[ing] a balcony high along the Great Western Divide."[1] The valley floor lies 7,300 feet above sea level. From it, mountains rise sharply into the sky, and the names of their peaks and passes reflect the rugged grandeur: Timber Gap, Empire Mountain, Farewell Gap, and Sawtooth Peak. Several summits are near or surpass 12,000 feet. Above the valley, twenty-one lakes are sprinkled throughout the area.[2]

The Mineral King Valley is spectacular and awe-inspiring. As one guidebook extolled, the valley is "rimmed by cliffs and cirques from which streams and freshets explode and cascade and tumble."[3] The East Fork of the Kaweah River surfaces in the valley, rushing down steep ravines toward the adjacent Sequoia National Park. From the high peaks above the valley the vistas are breathtaking; hikers can view Mount Whitney to the east, the highest summit in the contiguous United States at 14,505 feet. A visitor to the valley would immediately recognize the valley's potential for skiing. In the winter, the snow is deep, and avalanches periodically thunder downhill.

In the late spring, as the snow melts, the valley emerges and wildflowers burst forth in bright colors. Over the years, many visitors reached the same conclusion as a Sierra Club writer who enthused in 1903, "There is nothing in the whole Sierra Range more beautiful than the valley of Mineral King in June; nothing more like an upper valley in the Swiss Alps."[4]

In 1864, miner Harry O'Farrell, who later changed his name to "Harry Parole" after serving a prison term, became the first white male to see the Mineral King Valley.[5] Two years later, a gold rush began when James Crabtree entered Mineral King. Crabtree, a devoted spiritualist, told others of his dream that an indigenous chief, white as the cliffs, would guide him to veins of gold. So he filed a claim in the Mineral King Valley on what became known as the White Chief lode, while O'Farrell returned to also file a claim. The fever spread as miners "saw through eyes of gold and silver."[6]

A small town grew called Beulah, a name with Biblical origins meaning "land of promise" or "the border of heaven."[7] The heavenly town soon included earthly necessities such as a saloon and a store, with some businesses housed in a two-story structure built by the proprietor, one "Whiskey" Smith. The miners voted to change the town's name to Mineral King,[8] a choice reflecting their optimism about huge deposits of ore.

That hope quickly vanished. A company with the geographically counterintuitive name of the New England Tunnel and Smelter Company was incorporated but encountered financial difficulty within two years, labeling the area's ore "rebellious." The first phase of the Mineral King boom ended when a large snow slide slammed into a workers' bunkhouse.[9] No one died, but the event seemed to symbolize the valley's refusal to yield riches.

The dream resurrected a mere nine months later. Thomas Fowler, a wealthy and well-respected farmer and cattle rancher, purchased the Empire Mine, located high on a steep mountainside in Mineral King. Fowler may have been enticed by an analysis of an ore sample at Columbia College in New York City which indicated a value of $1,400 per ton—a thousand dollars higher than in any previous report. Fowler poured funds into the mine at Mineral King, and more claims by others followed.[10] However, the valuable minerals could not be easily separated from the ore, so the miners' efforts were doomed.

During this period the Mineral King Wagon and Toll Road Company was formed to build a road from the town of Three Rivers in the foothills of the San Joaquin Valley up to Mineral King. Intended to supply the needs of the miners, the road followed the twisting path of the East Fork of the Kaweah River, a remarkable engineering feat over a short time given the steep terrain. It opened on August 20, 1879, with a hundred wagons supposedly loaded and awaiting transport. The town in the Mineral King Valley grew, adding among other establishments more saloons, which by one count totaled fourteen by fall 1879.[11] George Washington Boone, allegedly a grandson of the famous frontiersman Daniel Boone, hunted meat and sold it to buyers in the town.[12]

Thomas Fowler's judgment about potential wealth in Mineral King proved mistaken, and the boom collapsed by spring 1880. While Fowler remained a believer—at one point he waved around what he said was a 105-pound brick of silver—he ran out of money. Avalanches continued to thunder down. One took off the roof of a boiler room and crushed cabins, while another knocked a bunkhouse at the Empire Mine off its foundation. The defeat was so complete that by 1924, only abandoned relics of the short-lived boom years—ore mills, miners' cabins, and smelting equipment—lay scattered in the valley, serving as ghostly reminders of its lost potential.

The short-lived mineral rush, however, shaped the future of Mineral King in two crucial ways. First, the 1879 road to Mineral King continued to serve as the only vehicular access to the valley. The County of Tulare would purchase it in 1885,[13] declare it a public highway, and minimally upgrade it over the years. However, the twisting road could not accommodate significant amounts of automobile traffic and was impassable during winter, and the lack of access isolated Mineral King. As a 1963 article in an automobile magazine put it, the road has "enough steep narrow and dusty spots to discourage many of the casually interested explorers."[14]

Second, while the federal government owned nearly all the land in Mineral King, title to some mineral claims and to small parts of the valley transferred into private hands.

Meanwhile, important developments were affecting nearby areas of the Sierra Nevadas.

John Muir, the founder of the Sierra Club, was heavily involved in the formation of national parks in California. After Congress created Yosemite National Park in 1890, Muir turned his attention to other areas of the Sierra Nevadas. Muir had personal knowledge of Mineral King; he had hiked there in 1875 and would do so again in 1908, six years before his death. He advocated for broad protection for much of the high Sierras, visualizing a single large park with "natural boundaries."[15] However, political compromises drove the park-making, so it proceeded in a piecemeal fashion.

Concern had spread about the loss of giant sequoia trees. Since 1862, logging had been destroying them until the groves were about one-third of their original size.[16] In response, President Benjamin Harrison in 1890 signed legislation establishing Sequoia National Park.

The park was primarily intended to protect the visually spectacular "Giant Forest" of redwood trees from logging. The forest includes the General Sherman, the largest tree on earth by volume, extending almost 275 feet in height. Concern over the fate of other giant redwoods, however, continued to grow. The chief mover seeking protection for the big trees, George Stewart, argued that they "deserved a better fate than being converted into fence posts and shingles."[17]

Mineral King was excluded from the new Sequoia National Park, although the park was situated directly to the north and west of the valley. The focus was on preserving the big trees, and none of them grew in Mineral King. But the road to Mineral King, originating in the town of Three Rivers, now crossed the new Sequoia National Park before reaching Mineral King.

Almost simultaneously, Congress established the much smaller General Grant National Park to the northwest of Sequoia National Park. This new park also contained a spectacular set of sequoia trees, including the second largest known tree in the world, the General Grant, 267 feet in height and over 1,500 years old. The same legislation that created General Grant National Park also tripled the area of Sequoia National Park. The legislative process was hectic and mysterious; this second bill trailed the first by little more than a week.[18]

Congress also addressed public lands issues in other ways. It authorized the president to withdraw selected public lands from sale and retain them in federal ownership, a radical change in policy for the time. Urged on by Muir, who sought to preserve the area known as Kings Canyon, President Harrison signed a proclamation creating the Sierra Forest Preserve in 1893. It covered an area that included the Mineral King Valley. Later, in 1908, another proclamation carved out part of the preserve—including Mineral King—to form Sequoia National Forest.[19]

The decision to protect some lands as a national park and retain others as a national forest raised a question: Who would administer those lands? Congress answered this question in two pieces of legislation that designed a governing structure still in effect today. A February 1905 law created the United States Forest Service, a new agency within the Department of Agriculture that would manage national forests. Eleven years later, Congress established the National Park Service within the Department of the Interior to oversee the national parks. So, while the National Park Service administered Sequoia National Park, the Forest Service managed the adjacent Sequoia National Forest, including Mineral King.

Preservationists continued to press for more protection of the southern Sierra Nevadas. These efforts culminated in a 1926 law greatly enlarging Sequoia National Park by incorporating lands from Sequoia National Forest located east of the park, an addition that included towering Mount Whitney in the eastern Sierra. However,

Congress excluded one important area from this expansion of Sequoia National Park: the Mineral King Valley.[20] A Sierra Club representative testifying before Congress dismissed the valley as "not of national park character" because of existing mining claims and private land holdings.

In the end, these legislative efforts resulted in a peculiar and consequential geographic arrangement. The Mineral King Valley remained in Sequoia National Forest under the control of the Forest Service, while Sequoia National Park, managed by the Park Service, now surrounded it on three sides. But Congress did not entirely ignore Mineral King. When it enlarged Sequoia National Park in 1926 but excluded Mineral King, it also created a game refuge out of a twenty-five-square-mile area within the valley, naming it the Sequoia National Game Refuge.[21]

Then, as skiing grew popular after World War II, the future of Mineral King became a center of attention.

By the end of the 1930s, use of Mineral King had settled into a consistent pattern. Heavy snows virtually shut down the valley for the winter. Then the road became impassable; its winding turns, narrow width, and uneven surface precluded plowing it. Located on that road were cabins on privately owned land in an area called Silver City, four miles west of Mineral King.[22] Closer to Mineral King, individuals began to build and use cabins as summer homes. The cabins, almost all on public land, were authorized by permits issued by the Forest Service.

However, forces seeking change were growing. Throughout the 1930s, winter recreation had slowly become an industry. By 1935, California had two ski resorts, including Yosemite's Badger Pass. As economic conditions improved after World War II, skiing grew nationally at a 15 percent annual clip in the 1950s and 1960s, doubling the skiing population every five or six years.[23]

An important factor influencing this growth originated in World War II. The United States Army had established the 10th Mountain Division, which trained for mountain warfare and included expert skiers. After the war, some who had served in the famed division saw the potential to make a living in the field of skiing. As one history of modern American skiing explained, "It has long been an item of faith that veterans of the U.S. Army's 10th Mountain Division established the ski industry."[24] These members scattered after the war but remained in touch.

Another major force in the development of skiing was the United States Forest Service. Many new ski facilities, particularly in the western United States, were situated on federal land managed by the service. Unlike the National Park Service, which was dedicated to preserving areas within the national parks, the Forest Service's goal was to find the highest and best use of the federal land it managed, which was usually the one that benefited the most people. Skiing fell into that category.

As skiing joined timber cutting as a primary use of the national forests, specialists in the Forest Service championed the development of new ski areas.[25] Relationships developed between private individuals interested in building these areas and managers in the Forest Service. Many shared a history of service in the 10th Mountain Division. In the late 1940s, these forces coalesced around the idea of developing Mineral King as a ski area, bolstered by a crescendo of boosterism from local businesses.

Famous names in the skiing world sought the development of Mineral King. One was Alex Cushing, a lawyer from a monied East Coast family who had started the ski area at Squaw Valley (renamed Palisades Tahoe by the owner in 2021). He would later be the prime mover behind Squaw Valley's successful hosting of the 1960 Winter Olympics, a watershed event for American skiing. Another was André Roch, a European mountaineer who would help design the ski slopes at Aspen, Colorado. A third, Courtland Hill, was related to one of most well-known railroad names in America: James J. Hill, founder of the Great Northern Railroad. Last was broadcaster Lowell Thomas, renowned for filming T. E. Lawrence, the legendary Lawrence of Arabia, during World War II. On his nationwide radio program, Thomas proclaimed the Mineral King Valley's skiing "the finest in America."[26]

But the most enthusiastic promoters of Mineral King were local.

One was the county Chamber of Commerce, whose members envisioned an influx of economic prosperity from a ski area. Another was Tulare County itself, the local government unit that included Mineral King. The county demonstrated its support by paying the large sum of $5,000 in 1947 to fund a study of Mineral King that would investigate the valley's suitability as a winter sports area.[27] The study concluded that Mineral King "has superlative ski terrain, equal to some of the best to be found at the well-established winter sports centers of Europe."[28]

In January 1949, the Chamber of Commerce hosted a large gathering at Mineral King designed to spread the word about the "majestic winter wonderland."[29] Enthusiastic endorsements poured forth. A ski magazine envisioned a "Picturesque Skitropolis" and suggested that the name "Mineral King" would be "more fittingly termed (for skiers) 'King of Ski Areas!'"[30] The director of the ski school at Aspen, Colorado, enthused that Mineral King "matches or even surpasses the world's foremost potential ski area."[31] More pragmatically, another supporter stressed the benefits of skiing for youth: "You don't find juvenile delinquents among the skiing youth of the nation."[32]

The Sierra Club also evaluated Mineral King's future at this time, and the conclusions of that evaluation would haunt the club. Traditionally, many club members engaged in mountain sports such as climbing, hiking, and skiing. One member of the skiing group was David Brower, the executive director of the Sierra Club. Club literature and outings emphasized outdoor sports, and it had a very active Winter Sports Committee.

In September 1947, the Sierra Club board of directors discussed Mineral King. Although no vote was taken, the minutes reported that the club "cannot as a matter of principle oppose the development of Mineral King or any other non-wilderness area."[33] During the following May, twelve members of the club's Winter Sports Committee traveled to Mineral King to explore its potential for skiing. They concluded that "this region affords some of the finest ski-touring terrain in the country."[34]

In September 1949 the club's board of directors met at Atwell Mill, five miles below Mineral King. The Forest Service allowed the club to review a prospectus it was preparing that would authorize a lodge and two ski lifts in the valley. At its meeting, the board of directors adopted a resolution that would often be cited in the future. The Sierra Club, the resolution stated, "finds no objection from the standpoint of its policies to the winter sports development in Mineral King as proposed by the U.S. Forest Service."[35]

In November 1949, the Forest Service issued a "Prospectus for a Proposed Resort and Ski Area at Mineral King."[36] A press release declared that the "[p]ossibilities of developing Mineral King into one of the finest ski areas in the United States are so good" that the Forest Service was inviting private investors. They would build a hotel, a ski lift, and other facilities.[37] However, the prospectus drew only a single bid[38] that was ultimately voided.[39]

The setback was temporary. Within two years boosterism for developing Mineral King returned. The local enthusiasm for a ski area there reached a crescendo in 1953 at a two-day convocation held in Visalia, California. Like the Sierra Club's approval of skiing at Mineral King four years earlier, this event would have important ramifications in the future.

After the Tulare County Board of Supervisors passed a "board order authorizing" the Tulare Chamber of Commerce to hold a "public hearing,"[40] the chamber organized a meeting and sent out invitations. In essence, the event was intended to gather those who sought Mineral King's development, and the chamber "invited people of importance from all over the State."[41] The convocation took the form of a quasi-public hearing. Presiding over it were Congressman Harlan Hagen, the newly elected representative of the area, several state and local officials, and the president of the chamber.[42] Testimony was transcribed.

Except for a handful of individuals who voiced some concerns, all participants favored a ski resort in Mineral King. Among those, two made statements that would become more important in later decades. E. T. Scoyen, the superintendent of Sequoia National Park, was queried about his agency's attitude toward the construction of a new road to Mineral King that would have to cross the park. Scoyen would not commit to a toll road but otherwise was quite positive: "[W]e are officially on record that we would agree to a road being built."[43] Indeed, Scoyen, a skier, was cited as a chief supporter of the new ski area.[44] Moreover, previous internal communications from the regional director of the Park Service in 1947 indicated that "[u]ndoubtedly the Park Service would concur in a proposal to run a new road to Mineral King through a portion of the park."[45]

A representative of the Sierra Club, Dr. Leslie Gould, also appeared at the event. Introduced by Congressman Hagen as a member of a "group of public-spirited citizens interested in this area," Dr. Gould made a short statement that did not oppose the development:

> The Sierra Club was organized in 1892 to preserve and enjoy natural beauty. Its interest has been in the preservation and best use of wilderness areas. We are especially interested in the Mineral King development. We recognize that there is already a road into the Mineral King area, and therefore, we don't take any particular stand on this development, either in favor, or against it. We would, however, be satisfied with the development program, if it were to provide a sensible development, making skiing possible to more California residents, with the area easily accessible.[46]

In the end, however, this second wave of enthusiasm also foundered. The problem of improving the road to Mineral King remained unsolved, and interest in the area would not return for another seven years. By then, however, circumstances would change dramatically, as two new individuals entered the scene. One was world famous; the other was married to Hollywood motion picture royalty.

2 : An Invitation from the Forest Service

By the late 1950s, Walt Disney was not just a household name; he would later be labeled a "secular saint" of that period.[1] His productions had screened in theaters since the 1928 release of the cartoon *Steamboat Willie* with its main character, Mickey Mouse. In 1937, Disney released the groundbreaking and phenomenally successful *Snow White and the Seven Dwarfs*, the first animated feature film.[2]

With the advent of television, in 1954 Disney began hosting a serial featuring the legendary frontiersman, Davy Crockett, that exploded into national popularity.[3] Finally, in 1955 Disney opened his theme park, Disneyland, in Anaheim, California. This venture added to Disney's fame and brought financial security to his entertainment empire.[4] By then, Disney, who projected a friendly, grandfatherly image on television, had become a national treasure.

Walt Disney had caught the skiing bug early. He skied in the 1930s with his family at Badger Pass, California, where he met an Austrian skier named Hannes Schroll.[5] In 1938, Schroll attempted to start a ski resort, called Sugar Bowl, in the Sierra Nevadas near the place where the infamous Donner Party had become stranded, with some resorting to cannibalism.[6] When Schroll ran into difficulty raising money, Walt Disney contributed $2,500. The grateful Schroll changed the name of a mountain at his Sugar Bowl resort to Mount Disney, and features of the resort reflect the Disney imprint today, including the Donald Duck Ski Run.[7] Disney and his family skied at Sugar Bowl, and he once tended bar in the lodge for two hours, "almost incognito."[8]

Walt Disney's productions reflected his love of skiing. In 1941, Disney released a cartoon, *The Art of Skiing*, in which the animated dog Goofy offered "ski tips" at the "Sugar Bowl Lodge."[9] Two decades later, a Disney motion picture, *Third Man on the Mountain*, was filmed largely at Zermatt, Switzerland, where the Disney family had skied.[10] The picture chronicles a young man's attempt to climb an alpine peak that later became the model for the Matterhorn ride at Disneyland.[11]

Given his interest in skiing, Walt Disney seemed the perfect choice to work on the 1960 Winter Olympic Games at what was then known as Squaw Valley, California, and he was appointed Chief of Olympic Pageantry. The position placed him in charge of the opening and closing ceremonies, the victory ceremonies after each event, and the Olympic torch relay.[12] While working on the Olympics, Disney germinated an idea for a new project. His premise was simple: "I can build a better ski resort than Squaw Valley."[13] He "would show how it could be done right," as he had already done for the "attraction business" at Disneyland.[14]

To begin planning for a ski area, Walt Disney turned to Harrison "Buzz" Price, a trusted collaborator. Price had undertaken work for Disney since 1953 and had carried out much of the analytical calculations on the economics of Disneyland. In turn, Price tapped another person, Robert Hicks, to carry out the day-to-day work. Bob Hicks hailed from Visalia, California, near Mineral King, and knew the area well. He had trained to be a flight inspector before World War II and, after the war, flew as a copilot with William Lear during the period in which Lear developed his famous Learjet. Hicks would pilot the jet in the air, while Lear would handle takeoffs and landings. Hicks had met Disney in 1953, when Hicks had piloted a plane that was scouting locations for Disneyland.[15]

Another key member of the Disney team was Willy Schaeffler, a nationally known skier and coach of champion ski teams at the University of Denver. Schaeffler was a German native who, before coming to the United States, had been seriously wounded during the German invasion of Russia during World War II.[16] He was later credited with teaching General George Patton how to ski.[17] Schaeffler had met Walt Disney at Squaw Valley, where Schaeffler had designed the alpine runs for the 1960 games.[18]

In the meantime, the Forest Service's interest in developing Mineral King had rekindled, largely due to one person. In 1958, Wilfred "Slim" Davis became chief of the Division of Recreation in the Forest Service's western region. Davis was an avid skier with contacts throughout the burgeoning national ski industry, many originating with his military service with the 10th Mountain Division.[19] He had been supervisor of Inyo National Forest, where he became friends with Dave McCoy, who started the Mammoth Mountain ski area there.[20] He had also worked on the Arapahoe Basin ski area in Colorado, where a ski run was named after him.[21] Davis, a forceful personality, would provide the entrepreneurial energy for the Mineral King project within the Forest Service.

Davis encouraged the Disney team to examine Mineral King,[22] and it became the focus of their efforts. Hicks flew Willy Schaeffler and Buzz Price to survey Mineral King by air in May 1960, followed by a field trip to the valley.[23] Schaeffler wrote an extremely positive report for Disney documenting his conclusions: "Having skied and visited the best ski areas in Europe and North and South America, I am of the very honest opinion that the Mineral King area, as proposed, is equal to the best anywhere to be found."[24] He predicted that the development could be "a tremendous success," citing the need for an access road as the only drawback.

On June 7, 1960, Walt Disney and his team met with Slim Davis. The group reviewed Schaeffler's Mineral King report, "but the access road situation and other matters contributed to tabling the matter."[25] The Disney momentum stalled.

Then, in 1963, the situation abruptly changed again, apparently after Walt Disney had flown over the Mineral King Valley with his son-in-law, Ron Miller. Buzz Price "suddenly got an alert to activate [the] program of analysis and evaluation on Mineral King."[26] Disney took a serious step toward implementing the project; he ordered

Price to begin buying privately held lots located in the Mineral King Valley.[27] The purchases, Disney thought, would give him a strong argument for why the Forest Service should award him the right to develop the valley.[28]

By the end of 1964, Disney had successfully bought some land in the Mineral King Valley. In the meantime, however, a significant competitor had emerged.

Robert Brandt had founded a stock brokerage company in Los Angeles and moved in wealthy circles. He was personable and, as an outdoorsman, enjoyed activities such as off-road motorcycle riding and skiing.[29] In 1962, he married actress Janet Leigh, one of the brightest film stars in Hollywood. She had gained worldwide fame by starring in the 1960 Alfred Hitchcock film *Psycho*, where she portrayed the victim in the well-known "shower" murder scene. She had worked with screen legends, including Jimmy Stewart, Charlton Heston, Elizabeth Taylor, John Wayne, and Frank Sinatra.[30]

Most important for a development proposal soon to be immersed in politics, Leigh was active in the Democratic Party. She and her previous husband, actor Tony Curtis, had hosted a large fundraiser at their home for John F. Kennedy during the 1960 election.[31] Later, Leigh would have close ties to President Lyndon Johnson.

Recognizing the potential of Mineral King, Brandt had—like Disney—undertaken a preliminary investigation and decided that he wanted to build a ski development there. He talked to Forest Service personnel, who may have encouraged him and, Bob Hicks thought, led him to "believe that he would be awarded the permit."[32] Brandt hired American Resort Consultants to study Mineral King's potential as a ski area. The company's comprehensive report concluded that "an all-year outdoor development at Mineral King is feasible, and in fact, has a high probability of success." The report envisioned a very large facility in the valley and the surrounding mountains, recommending "a continuing program of expansion in order to develop the area to its maximum potential."[33] Bob Hicks heard reports that Brandt had spent $100,000 on this preliminary work.[34]

Brandt was poised to seek the skiing concession in the valley from the Forest Service.

Approving a ski resort in Mineral King was an easy decision for the Forest Service. In 1905 the first head of the agency, Gifford Pinchot, had articulated a principle that governed Forest Service decisions: public lands should provide "the greatest good for the greatest number in the long run."[35] A ski resort would open Mineral King to use by a great number of people, thus readily satisfying this principle. Since the late 1940s, the Forest Service had assumed that skiing was the best use of Mineral King, and its view never wavered.

With a Brandt application seeking permits for a Mineral King ski resort imminent, the Forest Service faced an important choice. It could negotiate just with Brandt and determine whether or not to grant the necessary permits to him. Alternatively, it could release a prospectus soliciting applications from the general public, as it had done in 1949. Slim Davis discussed the options with Lawrence Whitfield, the supervisor of Sequoia National Forest, and they settled on a prospectus. Before issuing it, the Forest Service would need to complete its recreation management plan for the area, the planning document utilized by the service for such decisions.[36] But that plan would simply reflect the prior decision to develop Mineral King.

On January 22, 1965, Davis informed Bob Brandt that the regional forester would issue a prospectus for a winter-summer recreation development at Mineral King.[37] Davis then accelerated the timetable by convincing the Chief Forester's Office in Washington, DC, that no new approval of the prospectus was necessary. The approval granted by the chief forester for the 1949 prospectus would suffice.[38]

Why the rush? If Brandt convinced the Forest Service to grant him a permit, other bidders—in particular, Walt Disney—would be shut out. As Davis's later actions showed, he favored Disney, and the prospectus would ensure that Disney could bid on the project.

Davis then addressed one final issue that would reverberate for over a decade: how would the National Park Service react to the proposed development of Mineral King? The Park Service would have to approve the road upgrade needed for that development, since the road would have to cross about eleven miles of Sequoia National Park. On February 5, 1964, Davis wrote to the regional director of the National Park Service in San Francisco, asking for "general agreement with our approach as far as the access road angle is concerned."[39]

Davis anxiously awaited a reply while Park Service officials in Washington debated the request.[40] Finally, on February 26, the regional director of the Park Service called and told Davis that the service did not object to the issuance of the Mineral King prospectus.[41] A confirming letter arrived two weeks later, and its content would play a central role in the dispute that would soon arise over the ski area. The regional director carefully chose his language:

> We are in sympathy with your proposal. Our only concern, and it is a vital one, is that any improvements to the . . . Mineral King access road which may have to be made within Sequoia National Park to accommodate winter traffic be accomplished in such manner as will not damage the giant Sequoia trees or other values for which the Park was established.[42]

Read closely, the letter did not object, but it preserved the Park Service's discretion to determine whether an upgraded road would damage the "values" of Sequoia National Park.

Davis, however, had not waited for the letter. The day after receiving the telephone call from the Park Service, the Forest Service released to the public a prospectus for the development of Mineral King.[43]

The prospectus called for lifts or tramways with a capacity of 2,000 persons per hour from the valley floor and parking for 1,200 automobiles. Also, a resort must provide overnight accommodations for at least a hundred individuals and would need to arrange power, water, and sewage treatment.[44] The Forest Service would receive a percentage of receipts.

The Forest Service would issue a preliminary permit for a three-year period "during which time a development program with layout and construction plans is to be prepared." After the Forest Service approved this final program, a thirty-year permit would be granted plus an annual, terminable permit for the ski slopes, trails, and parking areas, among others. This annual permit, explained the prospectus, was needed because federal law limited the size of long-term permits to eighty acres.[45]

Finally, the prospectus addressed the road. Improving access to Mineral King "is an essential first step in the design of the area." Accordingly, the prospectus was released "with the understanding that the successful applicant will find sufficient incentive . . . to solve the winter access problem." The Forest Service "is not committed to participate in financing the improvement of the access road."[46]

The prospectus brought to a head the question of Mineral King's future use. At this point, the Sierra Club began to reevaluate its attitude toward a ski development in Mineral King.

At the 1953 public gathering on Mineral King sponsored by the local Chamber of Commerce, the Sierra Club's representative had not opposed a ski area in the valley. Since then, the club had increasingly focused on environmental issues, a change that might have foretold reconsideration of its position on Mineral King. One overriding factor, though, militated against a change: the club was consumed with fighting national battles over other prized areas. By 1965, it was seeking congressional legislation to create a national park that would preserve giant redwood trees rapidly being logged in Northern California. It was likewise championing the creation of a new national park in the North Cascades mountains of Washington state.

Another factor affecting the situation was the fallout if the Sierra Club changed positions. For example, the board of directors had earlier agreed to construction of a dam in Grand Canyon National Park but later reversed that position.[47] Reversals like this greatly damaged relations with public agencies. Thus, in a dispute in the late 1950s about a new road through the Sierra Nevadas, the club's president had recognized that many board members "feared the Club would be accused of going back on its word, of lacking moral principle."[48] An ethical component thus underlay such reversals: when was the club's word good?

In the first half of the twentieth century, the Sierra Club had forged close bonds with both the Forest Service and the National Park Service, whose officials regularly consulted the club for guidance. By the mid-1960s, however, the club's relationship with the Forest Service had changed, even though the club's board of directors still periodically met in the offices of the regional forester in San Francisco.[49] After World War II, the Forest Service had greatly increased logging in the national forests.[50] The agency saw its role as promoting "multiple use" rather than protecting forests, and it viewed the increase in timber cuts as needed to meet the post–World War II housing boom. This view, however, resulted in the logging of areas that the Sierra Club sought to preserve, and relations between the two entities grew tense.

Conflict between the Sierra Club and the National Park Service was less likely, since park status by definition called for protecting the lands in the parks. But even here the club had disagreed with the Park Service on some recent issues. For example, the club was greatly concerned about a proposed road through Yosemite National Park, the so-called Tioga Pass Road.

The Sierra Club's foundational principles committed it to "explore, enjoy and render accessible the mountain regions of the Pacific Coast."[51] But the club had begun objecting to access roads that would impact wilderness or environmentally sensitive areas. In 1951, the club had repealed the "render accessible" goal and changed it to "explore, enjoy, and preserve the Sierra Nevada and other scenic resources of the United States." Ultimately, the Park Service built the Tioga Pass Road, blasting through rock walls within Yosemite National Park. The rift between the Sierra Club and the Park Service over the road led Park Service Director Conrad Wirth to characterize the club "as an organization looking for a fight."[52]

As the Sierra Club's relations with public agencies frayed, its internal dynamics evolved. By 1965, members of the club's board of directors held contradictory attitudes on both the club's use of resources and its relations with public agencies. Some long-time members still generally favored accommodation with Park and Forest Service officials. Increasingly, however, new board members viewed those agencies as insufficiently concerned about environmental protection.

The varied attitudes on the board reflected an important societal development: the emergence of what would become the environmental movement of the late 1960s. The ascendance of that movement profoundly impacted the Sierra Club, which had originated as an organization that celebrated the marvels of nature, largely through excursions into the Sierra Nevadas. Sierra Club members were generally outdoor enthusiasts who, in addition to enjoying hiking, would also engage in mountain climbing and skiing. As the club's historian observed, "Many members . . . believed that a ski resort improved the landscape on which it was built."[53]

The new environmental movement challenged that viewpoint. It suggested that the club should focus on avoiding damage to public lands. By 1965, the Sierra Club's board of directors had split, with traditional members clashing with newer ones who emphasized environmental protection. Fueling this dispute over organizational goals was a sharp increase in Sierra Club membership from fewer than 7,000 members in 1952 to 25,000 in 1964, growth that soon transformed a California-based organization into a national one.[54] The club also changed from an elite organization into a more democratic body by discarding its requirement that two existing members had to sponsor any new member.[55]

Finally, the Sierra Club was immersed in a major dispute over its leadership. The name most publicly associated with the club was David Brower, its executive director. Brower had originally gained a reputation as a mountaineer, receiving national attention for climbing the famous Shiprock mountain in New Mexico. He was also an excellent skier and had served—like Slim Davis of the Forest Service—in the army's 10th Mountain Division during World War II.[56] After becoming executive director of the club, he brilliantly led opposition to the construction of dams in Dinosaur National Monument and the Grand Canyon (although he later regretted agreeing to a dam in Glen Canyon). He was probably the most well-known conservationist in America.

Brower, however, was a headstrong administrator who increasingly acted without the approval of the club's board of directors. The club's finances were in disarray, and board members were concerned.[57] Complaints over Brower's leadership would come to a head in 1969, but the issue was simmering as early as 1965.

Thus, when the Forest Service released its prospectus on Mineral King in early 1965, forces of change swirled around and within the Sierra Club. No board member or high administrator in the club was paying any attention to Mineral King. One new Sierra Club member, however, would single-handedly change that situation.

In 1961 John Harper moved from Nebraska to Bakersfield, California, in the San Joaquin Valley, to work as a geologist with Standard Oil Company.[58] Harper liked the outdoors and quickly joined the Kern-Kaweah Chapter of the Sierra Club. Traditionally, many club members, like Harper, worked in industries related to the extraction of natural resources.

Harper soon discovered the Mineral King Valley, a slightly less than three-hour drive from his new home. He hiked out of the valley to higher elevations in the Sierras during the summer of 1961 and concluded it was "truly an extraordinary place." Where else in the Sierra Nevadas, enthused Harper, "could one penetrate so easily into the depths of genuine alpine country, and feel so totally removed from the demands of daily routine?"[59]

During trips to Mineral King, he started hearing rumors about plans to develop the valley into a ski area, and he began to pass information up the Sierra Club's loose organizational structure. Harper first reported a "fairly fantastic 'rumor'" that Walt Disney planned a monorail transit system to transport individuals into Mineral King. In alarmist tones, he wondered whether Mineral King "may become a winterized, alpine version of Dizzyland" and whether the monorail idea would "open other wilderness thresholds to commercialization."[60] A month later, Harper walked back his concern; a forest ranger had told him that Disney had only conducted a preliminary survey of the terrain.[61]

Within the Sierra Club, the response to Harper's concerns was indifference. The Southern California chapters of the club were occupied with opposing a strong effort to rescind the wilderness status of the San Gorgonio Wilderness Area near Los Angeles and to allow skiing there. The area contained San Gorgonio Mountain, which rose to over 11,500 feet above sea level. Club members in Southern California knew little about Mineral King and, if anything, viewed it as a possible alternative location for a ski area that could thus preserve the San Gorgonio Wilderness.

By mid-summer 1963, concern over Mineral King's future led Harper to undertake a detailed study of the valley and make recommendations about it. Methodical to the point of drawing a diagram indicating where to stow all his outdoor equipment in his Volkswagen van, and an excellent writer, Harper examined all aspects of Mineral King. The result was a summer 1964 report bureaucratically titled *The Mineral King Basin: A Preliminary Report on the Character and Uses of This Portion of the Sierra Nevada, Tulare County, California*.[62] Harper's report would play a pivotal role in deciding the future of Mineral King.

The report detailed the valley's physical characteristics, history, means of access, current and foreseeable uses, and what the report termed its "overlooked values." While generally scientific in approach, some of the report's language veered into poetic prose, as Harper could not mask his love for the valley:

> Through the 85 years since the momentary mining flourish the Mineral King basin has maintained its identity as a high mountain retreat owing to its exquisite beauty. Fisherman, hikers, campers, camping families—all sorts of people seeking recreation have visited the basin. Many have become devoted pilgrims who return often to savor the offerings of the East Fork of the Kaweah, its family of timberline lakes, and the forest carpet.[63]

Cognizant of the Sierra Club's 1949 position supporting skiing in the valley, Harper explored a potential way around it. He wrote to the superintendent of Sequoia National Park, raising the possibility of incorporating Mineral King into the park. The superintendent's response flatly rejected the idea, giving Harper "numerous and significant" reasons militating against such action.[64]

Concluding that the superintendent's "disinterest" meant that annexation to the park "promises almost no hope of succeeding," Harper urged "Interim Watershed Protection" for the valley and the establishment of a "Geological Area" that would include all lands in the basin above 8,000 feet. Harper had researched the Forest Service Policy Manual and found it promised that such areas "will be preserved as nearly as possible in an undisturbed condition" and "will be protected from the encroachment of roads or other improvements."[65]

Finally, the report cautiously raised the possibility of a ski resort, warning that only the "most humble of skiing establishments there" would be tolerable. Any elaborate development would "destroy . . . recreational, conservational, scenic, and educational values," and an improved access road created the possibility of "[e]ventual desecration of the entire basin." Commercial skiing, concluded Harper, "is definitely not recommended."[66]

Harper completed the report in February 1964 and, following Sierra Club policy, sent it off to a committee made up of members from the club's six Southern California chapters. These representatives, however, viewed the report as a nuisance. The chairman of the club's Southern California Conservation Committee, Robert Marshall, bluntly informed Harper that his recommendations "will be controversial." Marshall cited some sentiment that the club should not object to a ski development at Mineral King because it would relieve pressure to develop other areas.[67] To Marshall, Mineral King was a mere bargaining chip.

But the valley was important to Harper, who grew increasingly frustrated at the inaction on his report as more rumors about possible ski proposals percolated down from Mineral King. The logjam in the club's bureaucratic machinery was finally broken from the top. Harper was allowed to speak at a gathering that included Sierra Club President Will Siri, a biophysicist and mountaineer, and another member of the board of directors. Harper later reported that the two were "aghast at the suppression of the report for eight months."[68]

Perhaps they were not quite as aghast as Harper thought, for they certainly understood the importance to the Sierra Club of the battle over San Gorgonio. Nonetheless, the subject of Mineral King now had their attention. On November 16, 1964, Siri wrote Harper acknowledging the "excellent report." He promised that the club's Conservation Committee and board of directors would "take whatever action is required" once they received confirmation that the Kern-Kaweah Chapter committee had formally approved the report and its recommendations.[69] In a longer letter to Harper, the second board member pointed out that the report was not clear about why it had excluded the possibility of annexing Mineral King into Sequoia National Park.[70]

This letter correctly identified Harper's ambivalence about what action was possible. Harper thought Mineral King was physically unsuited for a large ski facility and told the Sequoia National Forest supervisor, Lawrence Whitfield, that the Kern-Kaweah Chapter of the club, a small group that included future club president Joe Fontaine, would oppose the "dreaded development."[71] Harper undoubtedly preferred incorporating the valley into Sequoia National Park but thought that solution unachievable.

Then, on February 27, 1965, the Forest Service released its prospectus for a ski development in Mineral King. The issue of the valley's future "became a brushfire."[72] Time was running out.

The question of the Sierra Club's position on Mineral King's future came to a head when the matter was placed on the agenda for the May 1965 meeting of the club's board of directors. The club was struggling as it evolved into a more environmentally protective organization, and the issue of Mineral King erupted into a cauldron of clashing forces. It took a rancorous debate that spread over two days for the board to resolve the club's position.

The board initially considered a resolution that would "uphold its earlier Mineral King policy" while requesting that the Forest Service implement measures to mitigate the ski development's impacts. One such measure was that "[a]ccess to the Mineral King Basin should be modernized only to the extent deemed absolutely necessary."[73] The board's debate revolved around the ethics of changing the board's previous position, with longer-serving members concerned that the Forest Service would perceive a change of position after the issuance of the prospectus as exhibiting bad faith.

A motion to uphold the earlier policy lost. Thereupon ensued a "verbal melee"[74] for which "nobody was prepared."[75] The unfamiliarity of most board members with the Mineral King Valley became obvious.[76] Martin Litton, the travel editor of *Sunset* magazine and a two-year member of the board, strongly opposed a ski area in Mineral King. Litton had brought maps of the area to the meeting. During a discussion of road access to Mineral King, the famed photographer and board member Ansel Adams stated that he "didn't know [the road] was going to be in the national park." Litton later recalled his response to the renowned Adams: "All you have to do is look at the map, dumbhead."[77]

Situated at the core of the debate was the relationship between the Sierra Club and the Forest Service. Regional Forester Charles Connaughton, who supervised all the national forests in California, was attending the board meeting,[78] and the Forest Service was well aware of the long-existing Sierra Club policy of nonopposition to the development of Mineral King. As Sierra Club President Will Siri later observed, the service "felt that there would be no serious objection to the development of Mineral King for winter sports."[79]

The debate seesawed back and forth. The board rejected a resolution that would oppose the type of development described in the Forest Service prospectus. Some board members argued that, realistically, it was too late to oppose a ski facility. Another concern centered on whether an improved road to Mineral King would damage Sequoia National Park and, in the end, might lead to a trans-Sierra highway. The board also debated the availability of alternative locations for a ski area.[80]

The turning point was an impassioned speech by Martin Litton in which he "raised hell."[81] Litton's argument opposing the ski development centered on Mineral King's beauty, of which he had first-hand knowledge "by the square inch," and on what he saw as the wilderness qualities of the area.[82] Litton was deeply suspicious of the Forest Service and never inclined to compromise.[83] He thought that the board's principal goal should be to adopt the most environmentally correct position, and he dismissed any need to be "realistic" about the situation.[84] Many would later recall Litton's fiery speech, including David Brower, who credited it with changing his mind on the issue.[85]

The new forces on the board prevailed. The final board vote was nine to four to approve a resolution declaring that "The Sierra Club opposes any recreational development in the Mineral King Area as contemplated" in the Forest Service's February 1965 prospectus. The resolution requested the Forest Service to conduct a public hearing on its management plan for Mineral King before accepting any bid.[86] Of the nine members favoring the resolution, only three, including Ansel Adams, had been board members before 1955. The four opponents of the resolution began serving on the board in 1933, 1938, 1948, and 1957,[87] and they were unhappy over the outcome.[88]

The board's change of position was unexpected, and some of the local chapters in Southern California were also very upset about it. They worried that the board's new resolution would harm their opposition to the San Gorgonio ski proposal. The chapters passed resolutions asking the board to reconsider its action.[89]

Oddly enough, even John Harper, the young club member from Bakersfield whose report had instigated the club's change of position, was upset at the board's action.[90] Harper felt that the board "woke up when . . . it was too late."[91] He wrote a characteristically lengthy and articulate two-page letter to the board terming its action "a colossal error" that was "not only tardy but futile."[92] He also wrote to President Will Siri, explaining that it was "generally accepted here" that the Sierra Club's opposition was just "so many words backed by no concerted effort."[93]

Siri's response was patient; he felt that Harper simply did not understand how the Sierra Club operated. The process of changing a club position took time and was bound to be difficult, as divergent opinions could not be reconciled overnight. As to a Mineral King campaign, the club had no well-oiled administrative machinery to start up. Instead, "[o]n nearly every conservation issue we undertake, the club's effectiveness depends on the determination, skill and resourcefulness of a few dedicated individuals." Mineral King, said Siri, "is fortunate because it has in you a brilliant and persuasive advocate."[94]

Harper's unexpected reaction also led both David Brower and Ansel Adams to write lengthy replies to Harper explaining their evolving positions. Brower's letter was heartfelt; he did not think that Harper "would want the Sierra Club to be wrong simply because you think it is too late to be right."[95] Adams told Harper that "when it is apparent that previously-held policies become *support* of damaging projects I feel, in all conscience, that we must change to meet new threats to the integrity of the wild places of our land."[96]

The lectures to the young Sierra Club member had their intended effect. Harper wrote to the club's Conservation Director, Mike McCloskey, saying that the battle "looms not as hopeless as I had earlier thought."[97]

As the Sierra Club's president, though, Siri fully understood that, in opposing the ski development, the club was starting an uphill battle at a late date with little prospect for success and with internal dissent. McCloskey became alarmed about the outpouring of dissent by local chapters over the change in position. He worried that if the objections surfaced in the media, "[T]he Club's voice will be divided and it will be confusing to the public."[98]

The board's September 1965 meeting had reconsideration of the new Mineral King position on its agenda. Nine days before the meeting, club member Robert Marshall, from Southern California, dispassionately laid out the case against Sierra Club opposition to the new ski development. His "strongest objection" to the board's decision was that "it cannot be achieved without a major national campaign, and . . . no such campaign is contemplated." There was virtually no outside pressure in opposition, and little legal basis to appeal existed. Since the Sierra Club had agreed to skiing in the valley in 1949, the only change was that "we have become more sophisticated about the characteristics and needs for natural values." Furthermore, the new Mineral King policy "will definitely impair the defense" of San Gorgonio, and the charge that the club is "unreasonable and uncompromising" will seem credible.[99]

However, the surge of protest within the club began to recede. One contributing factor was a report that board member Fred Eissler had written and distributed in July 1965 after he and his family spent much of a nine-day trip in Mineral King. He raved about the beauty of the valley and the surrounding country, calling it "one of the finest wilderness type areas we have ever seen." He was emphatic: "All the evidence indicates that a ski development would completely destroy the uniqueness of Mineral King and a large area adjoining it."[100]

Eissler's report resonated. Personal knowledge of Mineral King remained a scant commodity among Sierra Club decision-makers, and the report's descriptions helped fill the informational gap. When the board of directors met in September 1965 to reconsider its decision, the meeting turned out to be anticlimactic. Board members remembered well the difficult, emotional meeting in May over Mineral King and had no appetite for another such wrenching session. Only one director indicated that he would change his vote.[101]

The board, however, made one additional alteration in the club's position that would have significant long-term consequences. It recommended that the Mineral King game refuge should become a part of Sequoia National Park, which surrounded the valley on three sides.[102] As the club's press release distributed two days later explained, Mineral King "is logically a part of Sequoia National Park and is too important to be spoiled with massive development."[103]

Meanwhile, the organizations of Walt Disney and Bob Brandt were busily preparing responses to the Forest Service's prospectus. Competition between the two arose, and both settled on huge project proposals that far exceeded the Forest Service's expectations.

3 : Dueling Applications

While the Sierra Club agonized over Mineral King, the Forest Service's February 1965 prospectus provoked a flurry of media attention and a frenzy of activity among individuals interested in building the resort. The *Fresno Bee* newspaper immediately designated Robert Brandt as a leading contender, declaring that he is "heading the currently interested group of developers, the forest service [*sic*] people say."[1]

Brandt recognized early on that politics would play a role in the Forest Service's decision on an award of this magnitude. The final choice potentially could be made in Washington, DC, by the chief of the Forest Service or even by his superior, Secretary of Agriculture Orville Freeman. Brandt designed a political strategy focused at those levels.

In April, Brandt wrote to Eugene Wyman, a prominent Los Angeles attorney with political connections whose wife, Rosalind, had been the youngest person ever elected to the Los Angeles City Council. Brandt listed all the actions he had taken—including meeting with Slim Davis "at least half a dozen times" and with the Sierra Club—and asked for Wyman's suggestions about how to proceed.[2] In turn, Wyman wrote a "Dear Orville" letter to Freeman on Democratic National Committee stationery about "our very good friends," Robert Brandt and Janet Leigh. Wyman told Freeman that whatever help Brandt could get "will be deeply appreciated."[3] While Freeman's written responses to both Wyman and Brandt were noncommittal,[4] Brandt had succeeded in identifying himself to Freeman as a person with important connections in the Democratic party.

Because of the work already completed by his consultant, American Resort Consultants, Brandt was well positioned to respond to the Forest Service's prospectus. He soon hired an architect, Harry Gesner, to prepare architectural drawings for his proposal. Gesner was Brandt's friend; they rode off-road vehicles and skied together.[5] Gesner had gained some fame in 1957 as the architect of the so-called wave house in Malibu, California, which reportedly influenced the design of the world-renowned Sydney Opera House.[6]

During World War II Gesner had been stationed with ski troops in Colorado,[7] so he also worked on the layout for the ski runs of the Brandt proposal. On one occasion while working in Mineral King, Gesner was nearly swept away in an avalanche. He was rescued using a basket hung under a helicopter.[8]

The issuance of the prospectus surprised the Disney forces, with Walt Disney characterizing its timing as "unpropitious."[9] Bob Hicks, who had been purchasing land in Mineral King for Disney, contacted the Forest Service to get a copy of the prospectus so that he could then send it on to the Disney organization.[10] But he need not have bothered. The day before the prospectus was released to the public, Slim Davis, the assistant regional forester overseeing the project, had written directly to Walt Disney. Davis reminded Disney that he had met with Disney and his staff in 1960 and discussed Mineral King. Davis enclosed two copies of the prospectus "in the expectation that your interest in the area and its potential continues to prevail."[11]

Hicks recognized that Brandt had a head start.[12] However, the Disney organization's personnel were extremely capable and hurried to catch up. Hicks quickly met for five hours with Forest Service personnel, who agreed that the requirements listed in the prospectus were only minimums and a submitted bid could exceed them. The agency wanted to maximize income and would select the highest bid unless another cause for rejection appeared.[13] From then on, Disney envisioned a large project for Mineral King.

By early April, Hicks and Disney consultant Buzz Price had sketched out a work program for an application due in less than four months.[14] Hicks was then charged with preparing the application. Hicks told Walt Disney, through Disney's aid Royal Clark, that he had met with Slim Davis of the Forest Service, who had declared that political backing for an all-weather road would be an important factor in who was chosen. Hicks also reported that Bob Brandt "has impressed the Forest Service with his seriousness in preparing for the Application."[15]

The Disney team was soon moving at full steam. Willy Schaeffler, the ski expert, would design the ski lifts and tramways.[16] Price and Hicks hired the Pasadena firm of Ladd and Kelsey as the architects for the project. This firm designed many iconic buildings in Los Angeles; among them was the chapel featured at the end of the movie *The Graduate*, made two years later, in which an agonized Dustin Hoffman pounds the glass in the chapel's loft attempting to disrupt the wedding of his costar, Katharine Ross.[17] Price and Hicks instructed Thornton Ladd to design the initial phase of a large project, one that ultimately might accommodate 20,000 skiers per day and have 10,000 beds available.[18]

Meanwhile, the National Park Service touched base with the Forest Service about the development. The superintendent of Sequoia National Park confirmed that "we are not opposed to the proposal in principle." However, he warned that the Park Service would not pay for the road and "would be very definitely concerned that the road construction is not destructive" to the roadside groves of sequoia trees "and to other natural beauty in the Park."[19]

The Sierra Club now had a new policy opposing development of Mineral King but no plan for implementing it. The task of creating a strategy fell to thirty-one-year-old Mike McCloskey. Raised largely in Oregon, McCloskey had attended Harvard University and then served two years in the army. He worked for over three years as a field organizer for the club in the Northwest, gaining a comprehensive knowledge of environmental issues in that region and extensively interacting with Sierra Club members.[20] He had then joined the San Francisco headquarters of the Sierra Club.

McCloskey possessed two qualities that would shape his work on Mineral King. First, he loved politics and understood its workings. In his early twenties, McCloskey had run for the state legislature in Oregon, losing by 2,500 votes out of 25,000 votes cast. He had learned how to seek endorsements, how to craft political messages, and in his words, "how politicians think and react," and he had gained insights that would help him to become effective in influencing them.[21]

Second, McCloskey had attended law school at the University of Oregon. The experience taught McCloskey that he did not want to actively practice law, but it also ingrained in him a lawyerly approach to attacking problems. He understood the importance of administrative processes and the use of procedural platforms, such as public hearings, as vehicles to promote positions. And, as a lawyer, he foresaw the role that litigation might play in an environmental dispute.

David Brower was McCloskey's superior, but Brower ended up spending little time on Mineral King. In part, this situation was likely due to Brower's having coauthored the 1948 Sierra Club report that had all but endorsed the use of Mineral King as a ski area.[22] Brower was also increasingly consumed with defending himself on internal issues about his management. McCloskey would lead the Mineral King opposition.

Sierra Club President Will Siri took on the uncomfortable task of formally notifying the Forest Service of the Sierra Club's change in position on Mineral King. He wrote to Charles Connaughton, the regional forester in charge of the California national forests. Siri framed the change as "long in gestation," while admitting that "it would have been much more timely to have conveyed this viewpoint to you four months ago and perhaps even two years ago." Though the club was "anxious to promote skiing and do[es] not object to properly located developments," it "cannot condone the sacrifice of fragile wilderness areas." The Sierra Club, he told Connaughton, also feared that construction of a road through Sequoia National Park "would require the removal of many large sequoia trees and mutilation of canyon walls."[23] Siri requested a public hearing on the ski proposal, and the club issued a press release reiterating that request.[24]

The Siri letter and press release were the Sierra Club's first efforts to articulate publicly its rationale for opposing the Mineral King ski area. Over the next couple of years, the club's reasons for opposing the ski proposal would evolve. The initial thrust of that opposition, however, centered on procedural fairness: shouldn't the Forest Service at least *hear* the opposition case before committing itself to a ski facility in this beautiful area?

The Forest Service refused a hearing. Regional Forester Connaughton's reply to Siri neatly combined the idea that the Forest Service had already decided its policy on Mineral King with the assertion that a hearing *had* been held:

> As some members of your board know, the recreation development of Mineral King has been foremost in Forest Service planning since before 1949, when the first development prospectus was issued. . . . On March 13, 1963, Congressman Hagen conducted a public hearing in Visalia to determine what could be done to expedite development. We have the record of this hearing and it discloses no opposition.[25]

The agency later also argued that it had sufficiently communicated with the public through talks by its employees on the project.[26]

Connaughton's letter referred to the 1953—not 1963, as the letter mistakenly stated—hearing sponsored by the Tulare Chamber of Commerce. While not a formal government hearing, and while the public was not expressly invited, that hearing had allowed anyone to talk who wished. But it had occurred twelve years before, did not address the present prospectus, and was principally designed to promote a ski resort rather than examine the impacts of such a resort. Nonetheless, for the ensuing seven years, the Forest Service would rely on that earlier convocation as a sufficient "public hearing."

McCloskey knew nothing about this 1953 gathering, and it took him another month to track down information about it. After he did, on August 7, 1965, he appealed Connaughton's denial of a hearing to the chief of the Forest Service, Edward Cliff. The lengthy letter of appeal laid out six reasons why, in the club's view, a hearing was needed. After correcting Connaughton's erroneous date for the 1953 hearing, McCloskey dismissed that event as one "organized by the

Tulare County Chamber of Commerce to promote development." And he attacked Connaughton's citing of "continuous" Forest Service planning for Mineral King.[27]

Logically organized and strongly reasoned, McCloskey's letter lacked one essential component: legal authority requiring the Forest Service to hold a hearing. Absent that authority, McCloskey could only weakly plead that "it is coming to be Forest Service policy to hold hearings on important land use questions . . ."[28]

The big question hovering over the proposed ski facility was how to obtain an upgraded, all-weather access road to Mineral King. Both Walt Disney and Bob Brandt recognized the road's critical importance. Moreover, both understood that only the government could build the road; a private development at Mineral King could not afford the massive capital investment needed. Both set out to solve the problem through different approaches.

Brandt thought he saw a potential solution at the federal level. In 1964, the U.S. Department of Commerce was tasked with carrying out a study of scenic roads and parkways.[29] Completed in late 1965, the study contemplated construction of a national and state system of scenic roads and parkways costing between four and eight million dollars.[30] Brandt and Janet Leigh met in Washington with the study's director and raised the possibility of a "scenic road" to Mineral King. As Brandt put it, he wanted to "see if the Mineral King Road would fit into the Scenic Road and Parkway Study."[31] However, while clever, Brandt's idea was a long shot. Federal funds for the highway were not then available,[32] and substantial federal funding for scenic roads never appeared.

In any event, Brandt was playing catch-up on the road; Disney had begun working on the problem well before the prospectus was released. Deciding to begin in California rather than Washington,[33] Disney identified a key player in state government who could help: California Senate President Pro Tem Hugh Burns. A burly, friendly man, Burns wielded considerable power in the California legislature and had sponsored major highway bills. He hailed from Fresno, a city in the San Joaquin Valley located only a couple of hours away from Mineral King.

Harrison Price and Lloyd Wright, a lawyer and Disney confidant, had traveled to Fresno and conferred with Burns about "Mr. Disney's interest" in Mineral King.[34] The Disney personnel had located the right person. The first step in getting the Mineral King road built was to formally list the road as a state highway, so if the Division of Highways formally found the existing road deficient, Burns promised to introduce legislation in 1965 to list the road as a state highway.[35] By August 1, 1965, just before responses to the Forest Service prospectus were due, the Burns legislation reached the desk of Governor Edmund G. "Pat" Brown for signature. Only then did McCloskey find out about the bill from a Sierra Club board member[36] and hurriedly write the governor urging a veto.[37] The action was futile.

The helpful Senator Burns also agreed to undertake the next step in the process. Highways on the state list competed for construction funds from a limited pot of money, and Burns would urge the California Highway Commission to prioritize building the road.

Thus, the considerable influence of Walt Disney had moved the Mineral King road several steps closer to realization.

By summer 1965, with applications responding to the Forest Service prospectus due at the end of August, tension built among parties interested in Mineral King. As John Harper reported, "[r]umors by the bushel are circulating, mostly unfounded."[38] Accurate information was at a premium.

In mid-August the Disney forces launched a public relations campaign. A press release announced that Walt Disney Productions would apply to the Forest Service to build a ski resort at Mineral King and that the company's board of directors had approved this step.[39] Slim Davis of the Forest Service thought that Walt Disney had issued the press release "to quell the numerous rumors that were flying" about Disney intentions,[40] but those rumors would be put to rest in less than two weeks when the bids were due. Instead, the press release was likely strategic: the company sought to begin associating the Disney name, with its positive connotations, with Mineral King, knowing that a favorable public perception of his application would affect the Forest Service's view of it.

As anticipated, some newspapers responded to the Disney press release. The *New York Times* published a short article headlined, "Sierra Nevada Resort Is Planned by Disney,"[41] while the *Los Angeles Times* printed a brief article about Disney's project that erroneously located it in Sequoia National Park rather than in Sequoia National Forest.[42] By the time Bob Brandt announced, over ten days later, that he was submitting a bid, Walt Disney had publicly framed the competition on terms favorable to him. The *Los Angeles Times* published an article about the Brandt application, but its headline read, "Disney's Mineral King Proposal Challenged."[43]

The day on which bids were due, August 31, 1965, promised to be a memorable one in the history of Porterville, California, the small town in the San Joaquin Valley where the headquarters of Sequoia National Forest was located. The opening of the Mineral King bids would be a signal event for the city. At the Forest Service offices, excitement "crackled in the air."[44] The office was soon "crawling with Madison Avenue types."[45]

The Disney organization carefully orchestrated the presentation of its bid. The main attraction would be Walt Disney himself, who would fly up from his Burbank headquarters in the company's jet. He would be introduced to Forest Service officials and personally submit the bid. Disney would support the application with exhibits that would remain covered until the bid was turned over.[46] They included artists' renderings of Disney's proposed ski area and Mineral King Village.

Bob Brandt planned an even more grandiose unveiling of his proposal. The Forest Service had informed him that no oral presentations would be allowed.[47] However, it would permit a very long trailer containing exhibits, and that is what Brandt prepared. Bob Hicks, in charge of the Disney presentation, later complained that Disney had wanted to bring a trailer but was told that it could not, while Brandt had prepared the trailer first and then convinced the Forest Service to allow it.[48]

Press coverage was extensive, and Walt Disney effected a telegenic entrance. He was photographed exiting the plane and being met by Ray Buckman, a longtime local resident known as the "mayor" of Mineral King, and by children waving flags.[49] A ten-person entourage accompanied him, including Bob Hicks, Buzz Price, and Willy Schaeffler.[50] Disney "gave everyone an opportunity to shake his hand or discuss the proposal."[51]

Disney had themed his application around the idea of a Swiss "contemporary Alpine" village, a choice reflecting his admiration of Zermatt, Switzerland. He told the press that the Disney company "will stay close to God in our development and try to complement the work He has done in this magnificent place."[52]

Bob Brandt, however, also knew something about Hollywood entrances. His fifty-five-foot trailer contained a dozen three-dimensional contour maps and models.[53] Brandt's motif incorporated a Viking architectural theme described by one local newspaper, in perhaps an excess of enthusiasm, as "'extraterrestrial' in concept, yet totally functional."[54] The presentation included a model of a fifteen-foot bronze "Nordic" statue to be sited at the entrance to his planned village on the valley floor. Brandt's proposal also featured a restaurant, with a circular glass wall, that was to be located atop White Chief Peak.

Applicants' materials were set up in a large room where they could take questions. Brandt's wife, the actress Janet Leigh, was born in the San Joaquin Valley town of Merced and accompanied him to Porterville. Wearing faded blue jeans and sneakers, she radiated movie-star quality. She and Brandt showed visitors through the trailer and answered questions.

The Forest Service received six applications in total.[55] Los Angeles architect Ragnar Kvale and his brother Kjell submitted one. Ragnar had been a ski instructor at Sun Valley where he taught movie mogul Darryl Zanuck, who then signed him as an actor. Ragnar later turned to architecture and designed the original Sahara Hotel in Las Vegas.[56] His brother Kjell was one of the largest distributors of imported cars in the United States, operating a hundred dealerships around 1970.[57] Their application proposed a man-made lake in the Mineral King Valley.

The Forest Service was ecstatic. Slim Davis boasted that the Forest Service had "never had a response like this"[58] and that the proposed development had "the largest single income potential in the history of the service."[59] Three applications each proposed to spend over thirty million dollars, shocking the agency officials. "Even in their wildest dreams" they had not expected the proposals to exceed ten million dollars.[60] John Harper reported Forest Supervisor Lawrence Whitfield's admission that he and his staff were "flabbergasted" by how the proposals exceeded the specifications in the Forest Service's prospectus.[61]

The Forest Service promised applicants a decision within thirty days.

Disney and Brandt received the lion's share of the press coverage, and it soon became apparent that one of them would win the prize. The two applications[62] had one important feature in common: they proposed very large ski facilities. Both promised to attract large numbers of people to the Mineral King Valley. For example, the Disney proposal envisioned that use of the valley in the year 2000 would total between 1.2 and 1.5 million visitor days.[63]

The Disney submission outlined the following features:

- Visitors would park before the entrance to Mineral King in an area accommodating 2,500 vehicles, and they would be transported into the valley by "a new conveyance system aesthetically compatible with the alpine setting."
- The village would be sited at the lower end of the valley in an area where cabins were now located. It would include a 200-room hotel, a three-story hotel with 400 rooms, and 200 dormitory rooms. By 1976, there would be 2,000 guest rooms with 7,200 beds at low, medium, and higher prices, plus other accommodations for employees.
- A cafeteria, a medium-priced restaurant, and a higher-priced res-

taurant would be featured, as well as a mall-like promenade. The development would have a village conference center and a 100-seat restaurant at Aspen Flat. Restaurants would crown two peaks.

- The village would include a chapel, an ice-skating rink, convenience and specialty shops, a theater, a general store, and a post office. There would be a heliport.
- A series of fourteen ski lifts would transport skiers out of the valley. Six lifts would ascend from the Mineral King Village, while seven more would be located in the upper Mineral King area at Aspen Flats. Lift capacity would total 3,000 skiers per hour.
- The ultimate development at Mineral King would include lifts to all major snow basins in the surrounding mountains, with lift capacities exceeding 10,000 persons per hour.[64]

The Disney proposal emphasized the company's experience in managing crowds and its familiarity with other ski facilities, such as Sugar Bowl.

The proposal, however, also spent much time on Disney's ability to preserve Mineral King, as well as on his history as a conservationist and advocate for wildlife, particularly through his films. A brochure prepared for the proposal declared that "the objectives of conservationists and those of Walt Disney Productions entertainment and recreation have coincided for many years." Walt Disney, the proposal emphasized, recognized "*[a]n obligation* to preserve the natural beauty and unique alpine environment of Mineral King."[65] The Disney press release reiterated the point, declaring that "Disney stressed that his master-plan is based on the need to preserve Mineral King's natural beauty."[66]

The submission of Robert Brandt's Mineral King Recreational Development Company outlined a project of comparable scope:

- Parking facilities would accommodate over 2,000 cars. The parking area would be close to the lifts and eventually would be double-decked.
- The village center would include a 180-bed lodge, with overall housing available for 1,600 people in dormitories, a motel, apartment

buildings, and chalets. The apartment units would be privately purchased but available for rental.

- The lodge area and village center would include clothing stores, a beauty shop, a barber shop, a gift shop, a general store for hardware and sporting goods, a sauna, a theater, a bowling alley, and a chapel. Two swimming pools and an ice-skating rink would be built.
- The initial lift system out of the valley—four lifts, a tramway, and a gondola—would serve 6,200 skiers daily.
- "Second order" and "third order" lifts were also listed. The second-order lifts were defined as feasible at the present time, and they would approximately double the daily capacity of the initial lifts. The third-order lifts required study over a longer period.[67]

Brandt's application reflected his extensive investigation of the valley before the Forest Service issued its prospectus. It was more detailed than the Disney proposal and intended to convey the impression that Brandt could quickly convert his plans into reality. Additionally, Brandt understood that Disney had vast experience in managing an entertainment enterprise, while he had none, so he attempted to counteract this Disney advantage by gathering a board of directors with nationally known names to advise him.[68]

One other feature distinguished the Brandt application: its treatment of the danger of avalanches in the Mineral King Valley. Brandt emphasized the avalanche study that he had commissioned and the necessity of accounting for avalanches. Citing this factor, Brandt located his central village in a different place than Disney, outside the main valley.[69] The Disney application recognized the risk from avalanches but did not dwell on it in depth.[70]

The Forest Service quickly began to consider the applications. The prospectus promised that the service would apply four criteria to choose the winner: (1) the suitability of the proposed development in meeting the public need; (2) the bid fee based upon a percentage of receipts, with a 2 percent minimum; (3) verification that the applicant's financial resources were sufficient to meet the requirements of the prospectus; and (4) proof of the applicant's experience, character, and ability to provide the necessary public services in an efficient and satisfactory manner.[71] While the second and third criteria might be objectively measured, the first and fourth criteria were subjective, giving the Forest Service substantial discretion in making its choice.

Three days after the applications were submitted, Slim Davis wrote to Richard Costley, his superior in the Forest Service's Washington Office, that "[w]e believe the award will go" to either Disney or Brandt.[72] Bob Hicks visited the Forest Service office in Porterville one week later, on September 8. He reported to Walt Disney his "impression that the decision on the award for the permit at Mineral King had already been made," because the staff members who had been evaluating applications were away on other business.[73]

That quick decision never came. Instead, the competition turned into a nerve-wracking four months for both Walt Disney and Bob Brandt.

As events unfolded in Porterville, the Forest Service in Washington, DC, rejected the Sierra Club's appeal of Regional Forester Charles Connaughton's refusal to hold a public hearing on the proposed ski development. It saw no need for "another public hearing," as the decision to issue a prospectus "was based on exhaustive studies and planning." Studies of the area "have been on a continuing basis," and the recreation area management plan was "essentially completed" before the prospectus had been issued. Last, the valley's designation as a game refuge did not prevent the secretary of agriculture from allowing other uses in it.[74]

McCloskey plodded on, appealing the denial to Secretary of Agriculture Orville Freeman. He pressed the point further, meeting with Assistant Secretary of Agriculture John Baker in Washington to urge a hearing.[75] The Forest Service remained unconvinced.

To the extent it existed, the opposition to the development of Mineral King looked "almost hopeless."[76] William Bergren, whose family had camped at Mineral King for years, had written numerous letters to public officials protesting the development. He concluded that, "[t]o be quite realistic, only a miracle of some sort could do much good now."[77]

The Forest Service placed much of its authority for decision-making at the local forest level, subject to oversight by the regional forester and, ultimately, the chief forester in Washington, DC.[78] In the case of Sequoia National Forest, Forest Supervisor Lawrence Whitfield reported to Regional Forester Charles Connaughton in San Francisco. Working under Connaughton as an assistant regional forester was Slim Davis.

On an important matter like Mineral King, Davis and Connaughton recognized that they would have to pass the final decision by the top Forest Service administrators in Washington, DC. These were the chief of the Forest Service, Edward Cliff, and, working under him, Richard Costley, who was in charge of recreation. The chief, in turn, reported to Orville Freeman, the secretary of agriculture.

Born and raised in Minnesota, Freeman had worked his way through the University of Minnesota as a janitor while also playing quarterback on the football team. At the university he became close friends with Hubert Humphrey, who would become vice-president of the United States in 1965. During World War II, Freeman served in the Marine Corps and suffered a jaw wound from a Japanese sniper bullet. After receiving a law degree in 1946, Freeman was elected governor of Minnesota in 1954 and later reelected twice.

During the 1960 presidential election, he supported Humphrey but then pledged his allegiance to the candidate who won, John Kennedy. Freeman was a Lutheran deacon, but when Kennedy's Roman Catholicism became an issue during the election, Freeman declared on television that religious bigotry had no place in Minnesota politics. After Freeman was defeated for a fourth term as governor in 1960, Kennedy appointed him secretary of agriculture, where at forty-two he was the youngest ever to hold that position. His work as secretary emphasized making food available to alleviate hunger by establishing the food stamp and school breakfast programs.[79]

Connaughton and Davis assumed that they would run Connaughton's decision on the Mineral King bids through the office of the chief of the Forest Service, mostly for informational purposes. That assumption proved erroneous. Shortly after the Porterville office received the bids, Orville Freeman informed Chief Cliff that Freeman "would like to be in on this before a decision is made."[80]

While the secretary's insistence on participating flummoxed at least some Forest Service personnel in California,[81] in Washington the step seemed logical. The deputy chief of the Forest Service, Art Greeley, wrote that Mineral King "is a 'hot' case in California; Governor Brown is interested in it."[82] Politics demanded that higher Washington officials decide the matter. Hoping to keep some control over the ultimate decision, Slim Davis suggested that Forest Service personnel could discuss their recommendations with the Washington, DC, decision-makers.[83]

In the meantime, Forest Service officials in California tried to address several financial issues that had arisen from the bids. One involved Bob Brandt's funding. Brandt had informed the Forest Service that the Mary Carter Paint Company, a paint manufacturer diversifying into land development, could supply financing of $10 million and, "depending on demand," up to $40 million,[84] so Davis briefly looked into that company.[85] A related issue involved difficulties in comparing monetary returns to the Forest Service from the Disney and Brandt proposals.

Another concern was avalanches. Davis met with Willy Schaeffler, Disney's ski expert, to have him "clarify how adequate avalanche control would be achieved." Davis noted that in the Disney written brochure, a "commitment for thorough future studies and control is made, but no details are given." Schaeffler told him that Disney would use "massive earth-and-rock diverters" designed to turn slides into each other. In controlling slides by explosives, "the use of artillery, if available, would be favored." Otherwise, "explosives would be placed by hand, dropped from lifts or helicopter, or fired by air cannon."[86]

Davis "gained the impression that Walt Disney Productions' proposal fully recognizes the importance of thoroughly studying the Mineral King avalanche hazard situation." But his use of the word "impression" for an important safety issue was oddly vague after Davis had just attended a meeting on that subject.[87]

Davis also raised the issue of avalanches with Brandt and drew a furious reaction. The Brandt avalanche consultant, Edward R. LaChapelle of the University of Washington, was a renowned expert in this area and had written the Forest Service's first handbook on avalanches.[88] Brandt's team interpreted Davis's inquiry as suggesting that their findings on avalanches required further study. Philip Lundstrom, Brandt's chief consultant, indignantly objected to "[t]his downgrading of our work." And, in a statement aimed directly at Disney, he declared that other contenders probably erred by "put[ting] main buildings in the path of the largest avalanche in the area." Any applicant who did that, charged Lundstrom, "has disqualified himself as 'experienced' or 'able.'"[89]

Davis quickly retreated, disclaiming "any intention to downgrade the avalanche findings contained in the thorough, well-prepared proposal" of Brandt's company. He observed that the proposal itself recognized the need for further study. Then, however, he defended the avalanche work of "other proponents"—such as Disney—by noting that the location of structures might change during the initial three-year permit period.[90] Plainly, the applicants' investigations into avalanches was in dispute, and Slim Davis seemed defensive about the Disney work on this problem.

The questions over finances and avalanches, however, were a sideshow at this point. Within days, the Regional Office reached a recommendation, and the head administrators of the Forest Service in Washington quickly concurred. On September 30, 1965, Ed Cliff, the chief of the Forest Service, wrote Secretary of Agriculture Orville Freeman that "[u]pon full analysis, we believe the Disney proposal is clearly the better of the two."[91]

Cliff cited two "swaying considerations." First, the Disney proposal "plans a larger investment and, consequently, will serve more people." Second, Disney would bring in "nearly four times as much receipts" in the forecasted years.[92] In the eyes of the Forest Service, bigger was better, both in numbers of people and monetary return—a fact that the perceptive Bob Hicks had recognized while drafting Disney's proposal.[93]

After learning that Secretary Freeman had reserved a role for himself in the final decision, Brandt and Disney stepped up activity to solicit political support for their bids. The political divide was apparent: Walt Disney was a Republican, while Bob Brandt and his wife, Janet Leigh, were Democrats. The California governor, Pat Brown, and the president, Lyndon Johnson, also were Democrats, placing Disney at a political disadvantage. Indeed, while the Johnson administration had awarded Walt Disney the Presidential Medal of Freedom in 1964, a well-known story (whose details vary) had Disney wearing a pin for Johnson's opponent, Barry Goldwater, to the awards ceremony.[94] Moreover, as Bob Hicks noted in early August, "We have been told by several different people in the state not to underestimate Brandt in . . . the right political connections."[95] So the Disney personnel set about overcoming that political deficit.

Hicks, a "local boy," pitched the Disney plan to politicians and businesspersons in Tulare County. He became a familiar sight at meetings of service clubs and chambers of commerce.[96] Hicks also contacted other officials, among them State Senator Hugh Burns, the Democrat helping Disney with the road, and he planned to contact Harlan Hagen, the local congressman and also a Democrat.[97] In Washington, George Murphy had just assumed office as a California senator. He was a longtime friend of Walt Disney, who had appeared in a full-page advertisement for Murphy just before the election.[98] Murphy strongly supported the Disney proposal and tried to call Orville Freeman.[99] But Murphy was a Republican.

Brandt went in a different direction. He did throw a large, impromptu cocktail party at a motel in Visalia in late October.[100] He urged attendees to write Orville Freeman asking him "to award the project on the basis of merit alone, disregarding political considerations or the familiar name."[101] But Brandt focused most of his attention on California Governor Pat Brown, employing the extensive political connections of his wife, Janet Leigh.[102] Brown had earlier appointed Leigh to a position on the State Recreation Commission, and she was featured in a widely publicized 1961 photo with Brown, actor Gary Cooper, and actress Cyd Charisse. Leigh also was well known to President Lyndon Johnson, who in 1964 had named her to the National Advisory Council for the Peace Corps.[103]

Brandt argued that the California Forest Service officials had treated him unfairly in recommending Disney, and he merely sought a "level playing field" for the final decision. Bob Hicks was worried about Governor Brown's influence. Ronald Reagan would run against Brown the following year for governor of California, and Walt Disney was a Reagan supporter.[104] If Disney publicly supported Reagan, Hicks reasoned, Brown might respond by supporting Brandt.

By mid-October, with no word from Orville Freeman's office about a decision, political rumors reached a frenzy. An October 21 newspaper article reported "rumors say that Robert Brandt . . . has the edge over Walt Disney" and spoke of "unconfirmed reports that the Kennedy family is interested in investing in the development proposed by Brandt."[105] Another rumor spread that Disney's bid had been disqualified. Bob Hicks privately charged Congressman Harlan Hagen with being "obviously in Brandt's corner" and reported Hagen as saying "the only applicant playing politics is the Disney organization."[106] A final rumor projected a Walt Disney win because he had promised President Lyndon Johnson that he would build a new Disneyland in Johnson's home state of Texas.

As for the Forest Service, it was a disciplined agency, and the rank and file normally would accept decisions of those higher in the organization. But this situation seemed different. Slim Davis told Willy Schaeffler, Disney's ski consultant, that if Secretary Freeman reversed the region's recommendation of Disney, "there would be quite a major uproar and a tremendous impact on the career people in the Forest Service."[107] The tension within the agency was palpable.

Irvine Sprague, Pat Brown's representative in Washington, DC, had been pressing Freeman's office to hold some kind of hearing on the

Mineral King proposals.[108] However, the Forest Service opposed the idea. Tom Hughes, Freeman's aide, brought the issue to a head by proposing a three-person committee made up of himself, Assistant Secretary of Agriculture John Baker, and Ed Cliff or Art Greeley from the Forest Service. The committee would hold a hearing and then make a recommendation to Freeman.[109] Orville Freeman accepted the idea but limited the hearing to the Disney and Brandt proposals.[110] Two days later, the other applicants were informed that their applications had been denied.[111]

Assistant Secretary Baker telegrammed invitations to Brandt and Roy Disney, who both quickly accepted. Bob Hicks consulted by telephone with Slim Davis who, abandoning any pretense of impartiality, counseled Hicks on the various issues that he thought were likely to arise at the hearing, which Davis would attend. He "emphasized it would make a big difference to have Walt [Disney] in person" at the hearing.[112] Disney was Davis's choice, and he apparently reasoned that, having recommended Disney internally, he could support that recommendation by helping Hicks. Hicks also met with Forest Service personnel in Porterville, spending three-and-a-half hours—including an hour and a half after the office closed—"review[ing] in depth the Department of Agriculture press release calling for a presentation in Washington."[113] Service personnel were prepping their preferred candidate for battle.

On November 5, 1965, the hearing began in Washington, DC, before Tom Hughes, John Baker, and Ed Cliff. The Walt Disney proposal was heard first, and the Disney contingent included Walt Disney, executives Donn Tatum and Card Walker, ski expert Willy Schaeffler, economic consultant Buzz Price, and the project's manager, Bob Hicks. Assistant Secretary Baker gave a brief opening statement that introduced the three-person committee and other Forest Service personnel present, including Slim Davis, who are "most familiar with Mineral King and the proposals to develop it."[114]

Walt Disney explained the background of his interest in Mineral King, including his financing of the Sugar Bowl resort and work on the 1960 Winter Olympics. He emphasized his appreciation of nature and answered questions on, among other subjects, the use of cars at Mineral King, and his efforts to secure state funding for the new highway. Buzz Price explained the projections for usage of Mineral King.[115]

As head of a large organization, Walt Disney himself had relatively little knowledge of the specific details underlying his company's proposal, so he, Bob Hicks, and Price worked out a system of signals. If Disney could not answer a question, he would press Hicks's thigh for him to take over. In turn, if Hicks did not know the answer, he would do the same to Price.[116]

Bob Brandt's turn came several days later. At the two-and-one-half-hour hearing, he continued to exhibit showmanship by employing "a large layout of scale models of ski lifts, lodges and other facilities."[117] Slim Davis later reported in detail to Hicks about the Brandt presentation. According to Davis, Brandt had with him Phillip Lundstrom, his resort consultant; two officials from the Mary Carter Paint Company, a potential investor in his project; Henry Diamond, a member of Brandt's advisory team and the legal adviser to Laurance Rockefeller, the American financier and conservationist; and Ed LaChapelle, the avalanche expert.[118]

Davis said that the committee frequently interrupted Brandt when he tried to present new material. Brandt knew that he entered the hearing in second place, given the recommendation of the Forest Service in California. Accordingly, he would have tried to bring in new material—such as information on his financing—where he could. Brandt argued that his proposal had studied avalanches in detail and had sited facilities based on that study, while the Disney proposal was weaker on avalanches. According to Davis, however, the committee twice cut off Brandt's attempt to show that the Disney plan presented "an extreme avalanche hazard."[119]

On November 10, Slim Davis sent Deputy Chief Art Greeley an analysis of two issues: the avalanche hazard at Mineral King and the dispersal of persons to the ski slopes from the parking areas proposed by Brandt. He confirmed the Disney avalanche projections and criticized two aspects of Brandt's proposal, including its financing.[120]

Davis's analysis strongly slanted in favor of Disney. Tom Hughes reported to Secretary Freeman that the Brandt people "put heavy emphasis on danger of avalanches in the areas where Disney would build his village." The Forest Service, he observed, "tends to discount this danger and the facts will have to be carefully checked."[121]

The parties anxiously awaited a final decision. Then events on the Disney side took a bizarre turn. The financial size of Brandt's proposal had surprised the Disney people, and Hicks began to suspect that the financing offered by the Mary Carter Paint Company might be criminally tainted.[122] Disney hired a private investigator in Florida, an ex-FBI agent, to look into that company.

On November 30, Price and Hicks sent the investigator's preliminary report to Walt Disney. They informed Disney that "[i]ndications are that the Mary Carter Paint Company is a front for the flow of underworld money into legitimate businesses" and suggested the investigator could obtain sufficient documentation "to begin publicizing these connections."[123] The investigator's five-and-a-half-page report devoted about three pages to the Mary Carter issue and connected Teamster President James Hoffa to it, but the report was vague about the sources for its findings. It cited individuals such as "a source who is familiar with the Las Vegas, Nevada, gambling interests," "an informant," and "a confidential source of information."[124] In the end, the Disney side did not pursue the matter.

Events then came to a head. On December 1, Art Greeley wrote to the three-person hearing committee, informing them that the submissions of Brandt and Disney on snow safety and road financing "give no basis to choose one over the other."[125] That conclusion effectively doomed Brandt's case by rejecting the disparity in avalanche control claimed by Brandt. That same day, Greeley also sent the committee a detailed analysis of the two bids by the Washington office and the regional forester in San Francisco.

The analysis overwhelmingly favored Disney. The Disney proposal would provide "appreciably more capacity to serve people in every activity than would the less clearly presented combination of Brandt's proposals." Disney's net worth was four times that of the Brandt group, so Disney was in an "appreciably stronger position financially." And Disney "has already demonstrated that it can do an outstanding job in projects quite comparable to the one he proposes at Mineral King."[126]

The Disney people, however, waited in a state of high anxiety. Roy Disney, Walt's brother and overseer of the company's finances, had attended the Washington hearing. On December 6 he wrote Orville Freeman inquiring about "when a decision might be forthcoming."[127] To the Disney organization, delay signaled that a decision in their favor was wavering because of politics.

In fact, political forces *were* in play. On December 9, Secretary of Agriculture Freeman sent his regular weekly report to President Johnson on important issues in the Department of Agriculture. Mineral King made the list. Freeman told Johnson that there were two excellent proposals and that interest had focused nationally on the decision. He then summarized what he saw as the political situation:

> Initially, Disney sought to stir up political support by approaching Congressmen all over the nation. His actions were probably dictated by the fact that he is a prominent Republican who now supports Reagan for Governor of California. Brandt, on the other hand, has been an active working Democrat. The Governor and a number of Californians have talked to me about this case. A number of Members of Congress in both parties are vitally interested. It will command wide public attention.[128]

He told Johnson that he had established a special review committee "[b]ecause Mr. Brandt thought the Forest Service was partial to Walt Disney Productions."[129]

Freeman then promised that his special committee would make a recommendation soon, which he would review personally. He concluded:

> The decision will be made based upon which development will be best for the citizens of California and the nation and will bring the greater return to the Federal Government. If the proposals are

equally balanced, I will rule for [Brandt's] Mineral King Development Corporation.[130]

By this point, however, the post-hearing analysis of the proposals by the Forest Service meant that they were not "equally balanced." Undoubtedly tipped that Disney was closing in on the approval, Brandt frantically dispatched a flurry of telegrams to Democratic contacts addressing avalanche safety in increasingly desperate language. One, to Congressman Harlan Hagen, cited a new comparative safety analysis and claimed that Brandt "has proved beyond any reasonable doubt" that Walt Disney Productions "has made gross errors in evaluating the public safety hazard."[131] Finally, Brandt wrote directly to President Johnson, charging that the Forest Service has been "grossly unjust to our group in judging, compiling, and analyzing data" about safety at Mineral King.[132]

The efforts failed. The key was Tom Hughes, the most politically attuned of Freeman's three-person committee and the one least connected to the Forest Service. Hughes explained his conclusions to Paul Popple, an assistant to President Johnson: "There is no question in my mind that Disney had a far superior proposal. . . . I think we went to extraordinary lengths to make sure Brandt had every opportunity to present his case."[133] After meeting together, on December 15, the three members of the hearing committee—Baker, Hughes, and Cliff—signed the draft report prepared by Art Greeley.[134]

Kept apprised by Hughes,[135] Freeman agreed with them and telegrammed Roy Disney that same day announcing the award of the permit. A telegram transmitting the bad news went out to Bob Brandt, followed the next day by a letter of explanation containing excerpts from the review committee's analysis.[136]

Brandt was crushed; he sincerely believed that his proposal was superior. But he faced difficult obstacles.

First, in 1965 the name Walt Disney was magical. His creation of Disneyland, a television show, a long string of movies, and nature documentaries had forged for him a unique place in American life and consciousness. People felt personally connected to him and wanted to be associated with him. As early as 1960, Slim Davis had enthused after his first meeting with Walt Disney:

> [We] were both impressed with Mr. Disney's sincerity and realistic approach. He has succeeded in almost everything he has ever undertaken, and has surrounded himself with the most qualified men available for all his enterprises. Since we have had an overdose of experience with permittees who operate on a shoestring, I hope it will be possible to further stimulate his interest in the Mineral King Valley.[137]

Second, Disney proposed a large project backed by solid financing. Brandt, in contrast, had to cobble together his financing from a number of sources. His financing was never going to appear as safe as that of Disney.

Third, the Disney proposal promised greater financial return to the Forest Service than did Brandt's. Disney had submitted a proposal for an extremely large ski area, and this size would generate more fees for the agency. The size also aligned best with the Forest Service's conception of its organizational mission as the securing of the greatest good for the largest number of people over a long period of time.

Finally, Disney presented less risk than Brandt. Disney had a track record of creating entertainment complexes. Brandt could cite no record of similar accomplishments.

Consequently, the Forest Service *wanted* Disney. A development like this one would make or break the careers of key Forest Service personnel involved, and Disney was the safer choice. This attitude, however, also resulted in differing treatment of Disney and Brandt, just as Brandt charged in his post-award letter to the president. The nebulous decision-making criteria set forth in the prospectus gave the Forest Service enormous discretion in making a choice. The criteria also meant that the proposals submitted were likely to vary in their content, thus making it difficult to compare them.

Then there was the question of avalanches. Brandt's avalanche report was detailed and prepared by an unquestioned expert, perhaps *the* national expert. The conclusion that a village should not be sited where Disney proposed raised an important issue, and Disney had paid less attention to the subject of avalanches.

Recognizing this key difference, Slim Davis and the Forest Service officials devised a way around the problem. Avalanches could be studied more carefully in the next three years before the final permit was issued, and the Forest Service would insist Disney do so. Indeed, conducting such a study now became one purpose for the three-year interim period before the final permit.[138] By taking this position, they could feel comfortable that Disney would ultimately choose a safe location for the facilities, and they could downplay the issue's significance at the present stage of decision-making.

By the time the bids reached Orville Freeman's desk for decision, the Forest Service's recommendation had the considerable weight of all the key agency personnel behind it, including Chief Ed Cliff and Deputy Chief Greeley. As Cliff had told Freeman, he "did not know how we could justify not making the award to the Disney group."[139]

Bob Brandt had done well to skillfully marshal political forces in such a way that he received a hearing in Washington. But he could not move the Forest Service's bureaucratic apparatus far enough to win the prize.

Bob Brandt left the Mineral King stage. Walt Disney was elated, writing Orville Freeman that everyone at the studio was extremely happy about the award. He emphasized, "Above all, we plan to preserve the natural beauty of the area."[140] To Disney, the battle had ended.

Actually, it had just begun.

4: A Cabinet Brawl

The Forest Service awarded Walt Disney Productions a three-year permit to plan its Mineral King development. The prospectus, however, warned that "[i]mprovement of the 25-mile access road from State Highway 198 . . . to such a standard that winter visitors can drive their own cars to Mineral King must also be programmed" during that period. The applicant must "solve the winter access problem" and "make appropriate arrangements" for access. A long-term permit would issue when the "first contract is let for a significant portion of the road."[1] While words in the prospectus like "programmed" and "appropriate" could be interpreted flexibly, Bob Hicks and Walt Disney Productions knew that a development of the size promised in their proposal hinged on an upgraded access road.

In September 1965, as the Disney and Brandt proposals vied for approval in Washington, Hicks had met again with State Senator Hugh Burns, who asked to borrow the Disney proposal so he could "[j]azz up the highway boys on getting the road built."[2] Once more, Burns was as good as his word. By November, the California Highway Department started to plan an all-weather road to Mineral King.[3]

However, funding the planned road remained a problem. Although estimates varied, the road would be very expensive, perhaps over $25 million. The Forest Service's prospectus emphasized that the service would not fund it, and the National Park Service likewise would not pay for the stretch within Sequoia National Park. As for the County of Tulare, it loudly cheered Disney's development but immediately demurred when the question of the road's funding arose.

After Disney won the competition in December 1965, Bob Hicks turned his attention to securing that funding. First, though, he wanted to resolve a personal issue: what would his role be in the planning effort for Mineral King?

The development of the various Disney enterprises was at a pivotal point, and a lengthy article in the May 1966 issue of *Fortune* magazine examined the situation. The article featured a large picture of Walt Disney drinking tea with Julie Andrews, the star of the recent and very successful Disney picture *Mary Poppins*. Disney planned to spend $35 million at Mineral King and up to a whopping $500 million building the Disney World facility in Florida. The company was transforming from a predominantly motion picture company to a broader entertainment and recreation enterprise. The ski development at Mineral King was an important component of this planned evolution.[4]

Although Bob Hicks had headed the Disney response to the Mineral King prospectus, the Disney company did not employ him. He worked as an independent contractor for Buzz Price's company. When Disney won the rights to Mineral King, Hicks decided that he wanted to regularize his work relationship with Disney.

After going through several intermediaries, Hicks was squeezed in for five minutes with Walt Disney. He told Disney that he would like to be the project manager of the Mineral King development. Disney did not respond directly. Instead, he said "Well, we have to go to Europe, I have got to study all the resorts there so we can do the best that was ever done." The five minutes soon expired, and Hicks left.

Disney never directly said "yes" to Hicks, but he soon found himself on the payroll of Walt Disney Productions.[5] The able Hicks would remain at the center of Disney's Mineral King efforts for the next thirteen years.

The Forest Service also moved quickly to appoint a liaison who would oversee the Disney planning effort. The employee selected was Pete Wyckoff. He had worked in the Division of Recreation Management in San Francisco under Slim Davis and had an extensive background in recreation and winter sports.[6] He had skied throughout the western United States and in Europe, was a member of the National Ski Patrol, and had attended classes on how to control avalanches. Like Hicks, Wyckoff would work on Mineral King during the entire period of controversy over it.

The conditions Disney faced relating to the road were specific and demanding. Within three years, a contract would have to be awarded for improving the road to public winter access standards, and it would have to cover "a significant portion" of the road. In addition, the prospectus required funds to be "programmed" for completion of the road within five years of the award of the initial contract.[7]

Hicks talked to Sandy Quinn, an assistant to U.S. Senator George Murphy, about the road problem. Murphy was a noted Hollywood actor before entering politics, and Ronald Reagan would later credit him with his own entry into politics. Reagan laughingly told Murphy that if Murphy could be elected, then so could he. Murphy was also an old friend of Walt Disney and often cited Disney's campaign advice to him: "Talk to enough people and you'll win."[8] Murphy had done so, defeating an incumbent Democrat, and he became an energetic supporter of Disney's Mineral King development.

The Disney personnel also decided to approach Democratic Governor Pat Brown, who had supported Bob Brandt.[9] They found Brown ready to overlook Disney's past fight with Brandt and quite receptive. Facing a tough reelection battle against Ronald Reagan, Brown saw the ski area as providing an economic benefit for California that he could tout. Buzz Price's company had estimated that benefit at an eye-popping one billion dollars in investments, payrolls, and sales within fifteen years.[10] So Brown agreed to help Disney with the road. Disney also would reach out to other elected state and local officials, and Sandy Quinn inquired into any possible federal monetary assistance for the road.[11]

This multipronged political outreach brought immediate results.[12] By early March 1966 the California director of Public Works contradicted statements by two lower highway officials and agreed to recommend that the state finance the new highway, although it would be four to five years before a real program was developed.[13] The new road appeared on the agenda of the California Highway Commission's April meeting, with Walt Disney Productions hosting the commission's dinner on the meeting's first night.[14]

A principal reason why the Mineral King highway was close to leaping to the top of the freeway planning list[15] was the promise of a grant by the United States Department of Commerce under the federal Public Works and Economic Development Act. Congressman Harlan Hagen claimed credit for the idea of pursuing the grant, and by mid-February Disney had contacted Governor Pat Brown about it.[16] Brown moved immediately, working through his influential Washington contact, Irv Sprague, who could virtually ensure favorable action by the Johnson administration. The grant would cover part of the highway's planning costs.

In the interim, however, the National Park Service was becoming restive about the section of the road that would cross Sequoia National Park.

The California Highway Commission's decision to plan the Mineral King highway inevitably drew the attention of the Park Service in California and its Washington overseers, the director of the National Park Service and the secretary of the interior. The Park Service instinctively questioned the necessity for a road through a national park whose purpose was serving lands outside that park.

The Park Service also had another concern. The existing road to Mineral King affected two groves of sequoia trees within Sequoia National Park, passing through the Atwell Grove and near the East Fork Grove. One widely seen picture of the existing road showed a mammoth sequoia tree intruding into the road. Sequoia National Park had been created to protect sequoia trees; thus, the Park Service would carefully examine the effect of any proposed road on those two groves.

Early reaction to the road was negative from the Park Service and the Department of the Interior in Washington, DC, particularly that of Stanley Cain, the assistant secretary of the interior for Fish and

Wildlife and Parks. Cain wrote Secretary of the Interior Stewart Udall that "[t]he little I have heard about the USFS-Disney development up to now would not lead me to approve a road easement." Cain explained that "I do not like giving an easement for a road . . . which . . . is not any part of our development plans for park purposes."[17] Cain's reaction was also uninformed. At this point Cain was unaware that a road through the park to Mineral King already existed.[18]

The Park Service's point person on the ground was Frank Kowski, the superintendent of Sequoia National Park and a well-respected, thirty-year veteran of the Park Service. Kowski determined that the best course of action was to cooperate with the state and seek ways of minimizing the new road's impacts on the park.[19] After several meetings, he thought he had resolved the road alignment problems.

But Washington intervened in the person of George Hartzog, the director of the National Park Service. Hartzog had a telephone conversation about the road with Kowski, who left the call disturbed and quickly protested to his immediate supervisor, Regional Director Ed Hummel. Kowski read Hartzog's position as "adamant in his objection to a new road" and thought that Hertzog had totally misread the political situation.[20]

Kowski, however, did not set policy for the Park Service. In Washington, Assistant Secretary Stanley Cain argued that the Department of the Interior should not allow the cutting of a single redwood tree for the road. He reasoned that such a position was demanded since the department "is taking strenuous measures to acquire redwoods elsewhere," a reference to the ongoing efforts to enlarge Redwood National Park. He urged adoption of a principle: "[P]arks are not for the purpose of auto travel to somewhere else."[21]

In September, state highway planners asked for Park Service concurrence with a proposed a set of standards for the upgraded road.[22] The service resisted. After some debate, Ed Hummel wrote back saying that before approving the road, the Park Service had "to know what the ecological effect such a road would have on park values and assurance that all alternative solutions for transportation had been explored."[23]

At this point, it was apparent that the Park Service would not easily approve the part of the new road that went through Sequoia National Park.

During this mid-1966 period Disney paid little attention to the Park Service, assuming its concerns would be resolved. Disney's efforts focused on the road's funding. The approach was two-pronged.

First, Disney widely promoted its Mineral King development plans, seeking to generate the political pressure needed to solve the road situation.[24] In June the press was invited to a two-day briefing at the Disney studios in Burbank, California. Attendees saw filming at the studios and visited the newest Disneyland attraction, the "It's a Small World" ride, which one visiting journalist termed "a charming 13-minute boat ride." Most importantly, they met personally with Walt Disney.[25]

Disney also produced a brochure, entitled *Walt Disney's Plans for Mineral King*, that was circulated broadly and read closely by the Sierra Club, among others. The cover featured a photograph of Walt Disney displaying a model of the ski runs at Mineral King. The brochure promised "an experience with the outdoors with those who love nature—or who want to learn to love it."[26] It projected that the Mineral King development could easily accommodate up to 20,000 skiers at one time.

At the same time, the brochure emphasized Walt Disney's goal of protecting the beauty of Mineral King. A paragraph signed by Walt Disney concluded:

> Our plan for the area is being guided by one other very important consideration: Mineral King's great natural beauty must be preserved at all costs.
>
> When I first saw Mineral King, I thought it was one of the most beautiful places in the world, and we will keep it that way. With its development, we will prove once again that man and nature can work together for the benefit of both.[27]

Finally, the brochure included "A promise from Walt Disney" about future growth that opponents would frequently cite in arguing against the Mineral King development. It declared in part: "All of us promise that our efforts now and in the future will be dedicated to making Mineral King grow to meet the ever-increasing public need. I guess you might say that it won't ever be finished."[28]

Walt Disney confidently guaranteed much. He believed that he could meld nature with large-scale recreation without harming the Mineral King environment, and he described a large development that could expand in the future.

Disney also continued to build political support for the road. In a close race for reelection with political newcomer Ronald Reagan, California Governor Pat Brown agreed to meet Walt Disney in Mineral King and announce the road funding plans. In September 1966, with the temperature in Mineral King hovering around 20 degrees, Disney jetted in and then drove to the valley. He joined a large group of people, including Regional Forester Charles Connaughton, State Highway Engineer J. C. Womack, and a host of Disney executives and consultants.[29] A Park Service attendee described Disney as engaged and active, but later in the day he retreated to one of the small buildings in the valley to warm himself. He looked ashen and did not feel well.[30]

At an 11:30 program in front of the press,[31] Governor Brown announced that California and the federal government would build a $25 million highway "to transport two and a half million tourists annually to Mineral King." The first $3 million would come through a federal Economic Development Administration grant, and Brown would ask the California Legislature to request an additional $9 million loan from that agency. While the governor did not explain where the remaining road money would come from, he praised the economic benefits of the Disney development. "I hope," concluded the governor's press release, "that ten years from today I can stand here with Walt Disney again and look around at the wonderland that will have been created."[32]

The press extensively covered the gathering. Many readers saw an engaging but somewhat incongruous photo in their newspapers. Walt Disney and Pat Brown stood in front of a sign for the trail leading out of the Mineral King Valley up to Eagle Lake, with rocks and trees in the background. Both pointed up to some natural feature of the area. Disney was comfortably dressed in baggy pants, a jacket, and an outdoors hat. In contrast, Brown sported a dark blue blazer, grey pants, and a tie.

The point, though, was made. Disney and Brown had joined in the road project, and the road would be built.[33]

While Disney pushed forward, the Sierra Club spent much of 1966 on other environmental battles. Particularly occupying the club's time were proposals to expand Redwood National Park to save old-growth sequoia trees that lumber companies were rapidly cutting. The club, however, began to focus on the road to Mineral King.

In January, Mike McCloskey promised that "we are going to wage a rear guard campaign to try to deny use of public funds in the construction of the road."[34] But the club's efforts to acquire information both about the federal grant and the action by the California Highway Commission always trailed the quickly moving events. The club sought to appear before the Highway Commission to oppose funding of planning studies for the Mineral King highway, but it was apparently unable to discover when the commission would consider the issue. Likewise, when McCloskey wrote to the Economic Development Administration seeking information about the potential federal grant, the agency replied that it had not received an application "filed by Mr. Walt Disney."[35] Of course, it was the state, not Disney, that would apply. When McCloskey inquired again later in the year, the agency responded by sending him the press release announcing its decision to award the grant.[36]

Nor was the Forest Service any more cooperative. When McCloskey asked when the agency expected to receive the Disney development plan in detail, the Forest Service was vague. After explaining that the Forest Service permit did not set maximum limits on the size of the development, which "was a surprise" to McCloskey, it then raised doubts about whether the Sierra Club "would be able to look at Disney's development proposal."[37] The club did form a Mineral King Task Force with twenty-four people,[38] but it operated sporadically. Moreover, dissent within the club over Mineral King still surfaced here and there, with members interested in skiing protesting the club's opposition to the ski facility.[39]

The Sierra Club also faced a more fundamental problem in forming an effective opposition to the Disney project: exactly *why* did the club now oppose the development in Mineral King? A well-articulated statement of opposition grounded in environmental principles was needed to persuade anyone, particularly given Walt Disney's promise that he would protect Mineral King.

The club would gradually develop a comprehensive opposition over the next two years. Now, however, John Harper, who had initially raised the Mineral King issue within the Sierra Club, stepped in again to begin formulating that opposition.

In a "Dear Friends of Mineral King" letter that Harper signed in his individual capacity, he attacked the rationale for the road's financing. Public roads, declared Harper, should be financed with public funds "so long as the benefit therefrom is returned to taxpaying citizens." Here, argued Harper, the "benefit is Mr. Disney's, almost exclusively," and the Disney enterprise should "not be launched with a $25 million gift from the citizenry." "Are you," he concluded, "willing to pay Disney's way to Mineral King?"[40] While not even a formal Sierra Club document, Harper's letter was the first attack directly against Disney in a war that would gradually put the company's public image at risk.

A second emerging opposition theme was that Mineral King's exclusion from Sequoia National Park stemmed from a historical mistake. The area logically belonged in the park; a look at a map, showing the valley's location between two large parts of the park, visually supported that case. The only reason it was not in the park had been the potential for mineral development that was never realized.

Later in the year, a third theme would begin to surface: the Disney development was simply too big for the valley. Joe Fontaine was a member of the Sierra Club from Bakersfield who would become a central player in the controversy. He wrote a letter to a newspaper in early December stating that Disney's project could generate up to four million visitor days by 1976, a number that exceeded present visits to Yosemite National Park. Disney's proposal did include vehicle parking outside the Mineral King Valley itself, with some sort of people-mover bringing visitors in to the resort. Nevertheless, Fontaine reasoned, these millions of people cannot "use a valley each year that is less than a mile wide and only two miles long" and "leave anything worth going to see" there.[41]

The Sierra Club also continued its long-running efforts to secure a public hearing to air its opposition. Finally, it identified a platform to publicly make its case against the Mineral King development.

After many years of consideration, in 1964 Congress had passed the Wilderness Act. The law's premise was that certain public lands possessed outstanding qualities untrammeled by development and should be permanently protected as wilderness. The act fundamentally changed federal land use policy, which traditionally had been oriented toward using the public lands. The act also established a process for designating lands already within national park boundaries as wilderness areas. After holding public hearings, the National Park Service would recommend to Congress which parklands should receive permanent wilderness status. The lands in Sequoia National Park were scheduled for examination in late 1966.

The Park Service released for public comment its recommendation that Congress should designate as wilderness more than 85 percent of Sequoia and Kings Canyon National Parks.[42] Because the law defined wilderness as a roadless area, the existing Mineral King road within Sequoia National Park could not be included as wilderness. Accordingly, the designation process had to address lands in that park immediately adjacent to the road. The Park Service proposed to start the wilderness area one mile out from both sides of the existing road.

The Sierra Club saw the upcoming hearing on the wilderness proposals for Sequoia National Park as its long-sought opportunity for publicly opposing the Mineral King development. The club could do so through its recommendations on setting the wilderness boundary around the road. As it had for other national parks, the club would argue that the boundary should be placed at the two edges of the existing road—a line that would defeat efforts to widen the road into Mineral King or add new segments.

In one sense, this strategy hijacked the hearing. Its subject was wilderness, not the Disney proposal for Mineral King, and the Park Service, not the Forest Service, was holding the hearing.[43] But with the Forest Service still refusing any hearing on Mineral King, the club felt no compunction about seizing this opportunity. It orchestrated presentations so that press reporting on the hearing would focus on the Mineral King resort.

The Wilderness Society, a key supporter of the Wilderness Act, began the attack ten days before the hearing. The society opposed commercial development at Mineral King, claiming that it would "degrade the values of adjoining Wilderness Areas." The Wilderness Society argued against setting the wilderness boundaries away from the road's edges. It also objected to using lands located inside Sequoia National Park as sites for counterweights for ski lifts.[44] These were weights that would be placed close to the top of the ski lifts ascending from the Mineral King Valley to prevent the lift lines from sagging.

In a statement released the same day, the Sierra Club joined the attack. It seconded the Wilderness Society's position on wilderness boundaries: they should extend from the edge of existing roads and developments "so that the buffer between developed areas and wilderness heartland is protected from encroaching development." The club applied that principle to Sequoia National Park, arguing that the wilderness areas should extend from the edges of the existing Mineral King road.[45]

On November 21, 1966, the Park Service opened the hearing on its wilderness recommendations for Sequoia National Park, and attendees filled all 125 seats at the Chamber of Commerce building in Fresno, California. The first group to speak was the Washington, DC–based National Parks Association. The association argued that Mineral King's location presented "special circumstances" such that "extreme caution must be exercised to prevent the establishment of a gaudy mountain carnival since the effect on the wilderness areas proposed would be material." It reasoned that wilderness must start at the road's edge; otherwise, "new incursions will result in a steadily retreating wilderness." The National Parks Association bluntly addressed the Mineral King development: the Park Service should "vigorously resist[] the reconstruction of [the Mineral King road] to high volume, all weather standards."[46]

Mike McCloskey appeared for the Sierra Club, reiterating the club's position about the location of wilderness boundaries and roads. McCloskey conceded that some modest improvements for recreational development of the Mineral King Valley "might be reasonable." But in the next instant he directly attacked the Disney development: "[T]he Park Service should not aid and abet the destruction of this valley with a mountain Disneyland."[47] Thus emerged an image—a Disneyland in the mountains—that would irritate the Disney company for years.

Finally, the Wilderness Society appeared through the testimony of George Marshall, also a board member of the Sierra Club. After reiterating the road-boundary argument, Marshall veered off into a new, legal direction. He suggested that it would violate the National Park Service Act to permit construction of a high-standard road across a portion of a national park solely to afford access to a non–national park development.[48]

The wilderness hearing in Fresno was far from one-sided. The Disney personnel knew that the Sierra Club would use the hearing to attack the Disney ski proposal, and they worked hard to craft a rebuttal. Bob Hicks was tied up for three weeks working on the wilderness issue,[49] and he had plotted strategy at a meeting with Chief Forester Ed Cliff, Slim Davis, and other Forest Service officials.[50] When Donn Tatum, who would later become the president of Walt Disney Productions, took the podium, he launched a well-prepared and strategically tailored offensive at the Sierra Club's position.[51]

Tatum immediately attacked the club's weakest point, the lateness of its opposition to the project. No organized groups, said Tatum, had "ever advised Walt Disney Productions of their opposition to this project" during much of Disney's preparatory work.[52] He then broadened the argument, terming the club's opposition "not responsive to the needs of the general public," thus trying to label the opposition as both unfair and selfish. There could be no "Disneyland," he stressed. The very argument about a Disneyland, he contended, indicates either unfamiliarity with Disney's proposed development or disparagement of the Forest Service's "outstanding record in the conservation and administration of public lands."[53]

Finally, Tatum played the key card: Walt Disney. "Perhaps more than any other American," said Tatum, Disney "has dedicated himself to informing and educating the public about the beauty and fascination of nature and the need for conservation of our natural resources." He finished by quoting Walt Disney's promise that he would maintain the natural beauty of Mineral King.[54]

Other individuals testified for and against the Mineral King proposal. After two years, a public hearing on a tangential wilderness issue had brought the debate about Mineral King into the open.

In the aftermath of the Fresno hearing, some assessment of the overall status of the dispute over Mineral King became possible. The strength of the forces favoring the development was overwhelming.

The Disney materials submitted at the hearing highlighted the array of politicians who backed the development.[55] In addition to Governor Pat Brown, Governor-elect Ronald Reagan and Lieutenant Governor-elect Robert Finch had endorsed the project, as had the mayor of Los Angeles, Sam Yorty. The state's two Republican senators, Tom Kuchel and George Murphy, were on board. The Democratic Congressman for the Mineral King area, Harlan Hagen, had been defeated in an upset by a Republican, Bob Mathias. However, Mathias—born and raised in the San Joaquin Valley but famous as a two-time winner of the Olympic decathlon before he was twenty-two years of age—had announced his support for the project. No major politician opposed the development.

Support for the Disney project appeared in important newspapers after the hearings. In a sharply worded editorial entitled "Obstruction at Mineral King," the *Los Angeles Times* bluntly rejected the Sierra Club position. Mineral King, said the paper, "represents a wasted natural resource," and "an enlightened U.S. Forest Service . . . decided last year that the isolated valley should be made available to more than a handful of hikers." While the Sierra Club "deserves praise for its many worthwhile conservation efforts," it should not be permitted "to deny this much-needed recreational opportunity for many millions merely to satisfy a few thousand wilderness purists."[56]

Even *Sports Illustrated* weighed in, giving the Sierra Club a lesson in how direct attacks on Walt Disney might fare. "Although some of Disney's productions do not happen to suit our tastes, it is unreasonable to characterize him as a wanton defiler of nature." While "we are among the most fervent supporters of the Sierra Club," here its "rhetoric is not wholly justified by the facts."[57]

The prognosis for the club's opposition appeared grim. John Harper was near panic. He reported to Mike McCloskey that "we are catching it hot and heavy down here" over the Mineral King road issue. Harper feared that "an overwhelming uprising of the public" in favor of the road could result in "unprecedented public support for what heretofore have been considered appalling but unpopular threats to the Sierra Nevada."[58] McCloskey, however, had much more experience than Harper in public battles like this one, and he took a longer view. From his perspective, the hearing had brought several benefits.

First, the Sierra Club no longer stood alone in opposing the Disney development. In an era of few national environmental organizations, two prominent ones—the National Parks Association and the Wilderness Society—had joined the club in opposing large-scale development in the Mineral King Valley. With their actions, the opposition took on added weight.[59]

Second, the press covered the hearing as a dispute between Disney and the Sierra Club and its allies. Each side received coverage, and that commensurate treatment legitimized the Sierra Club position.[60]

The publicity also brought a broadening of public knowledge about Mineral King itself. A principal difficulty faced by the Sierra Club was the public's unfamiliarity with the valley and its beauty. Now, Mineral King was becoming better known. Ironically, because Walt Disney stressed that he would preserve the magnificence of the valley, the fact of its beauty would not be contested in the dispute.

A fourth benefit that the hearing brought to the Sierra Club was the framing of the issue as more than local in nature. Since 1953, a drumbeat of support for a ski area had issued from local officials and business interests situated near Mineral King. Now, the statewide press coverage of the wilderness hearing implied that others throughout California had a stake in Mineral King's future.[61] Of course, many of those "others" might be skiers, and thus favor the development. But broadening the interests concerned with the dispute benefited the Sierra Club. Moreover, if the club could extend those interests to reach nationally, people in other parts of the country might agree with the club.

Finally, the hearing indirectly aided the Sierra Club's position that Mineral King belonged in Sequoia National Park. The wilderness hearing was *about* Sequoia National Park, and the club's testimony linked Mineral King to the park.

Objectively, however, little at the hearing could give the Sierra Club any comfort that its recommendations on the wilderness proposal would prevail. The club was asking the Park Service to adopt a wilderness boundary at the roadside, a location that would doom the new road to Mineral King and in effect veto the Forest Service's ski project. The Park Service interacted with the Forest Service on issues throughout the country and knew that adopting the Sierra Club position on wilderness locations would severely damage the agencies' relationship.

So, while the hearing helped the Sierra Club in several ways, it did not immediately advance the club toward its goal of stopping the project. Coming out of the hearing in late 1966, the momentum strongly remained with Disney.

Then, on December 15, 1966, just over three weeks after the end of the Fresno wilderness hearing, Walt Disney died at age sixty-five.[62]

Walt Disney's unexpected death struck at the core of the Disney organization, for he was involved in every aspect of its major activities. In particular, the company's aspirations for the ski resort at Mineral

King had originated in his own skiing experiences. Mineral King was *Walt Disney*'s project.

Roy Disney, his brother and the person who became head of the company, immediately announced that the company's work would continue. He recognized that "[t]here is no way to replace Walt Disney" but promised that "[a]ll of the plans for the future that Walt had begun will continue to move ahead."[63] By January 11, a company representative had assured those attending a dinner of a local chamber of commerce that the Mineral King project would go forward. Walt Disney "gave the world his promise" about Mineral King, and "we intend to carry it out."[64]

Nonetheless, Disney's death would significantly affect the Mineral King project. For one, while his image would remain closely associated with Mineral King, he could no longer lend his actual presence at crucial points, as he had in appearing at the Washington, DC, hearing convened by Secretary of Agriculture Freeman, or with Governor Brown in the valley. Equally important, the Disney organization would feel compelled to pursue the Mineral King project because it had been Walt Disney's idea. That compulsion would persist even when the circumstances around the development radically changed.

Just as Secretary of Agriculture Orville Freeman had final approval of a ski development in Mineral King, another member of the Johnson administration, Secretary of the Interior Stewart Udall, had ultimate authority over a road through Sequoia National Park. A native of Arizona, Udall came from a long line of public servants.[65] His father was chief justice on the Arizona Supreme Court and his grandfather was a member of the Arizona territorial legislature. After he attended the University of Arizona between 1938 and 1940, Udall had spent two years performing Mormon missionary work in Pennsylvania and New York and then joined the Air Force. He served as a gunner on a B24 bomber, flying fifty missions over Western Europe.

Following the war, Udall returned to the University of Arizona, where he played on the first Arizona basketball team to be invited to the National Invitational Tournament. Upon graduation with undergraduate and law degrees, Udall practiced law until he was elected as a congressman in 1954. Six years later, he persuaded Arizona Democrats to support John F. Kennedy for the 1960 Democratic Party nomination for president, and after the election Kennedy appointed him secretary of the interior. Udall had wide interests. It was Udall's idea to have the poet Robert Frost recite a poem at Kennedy's inauguration, and Udall invited Pulitzer Prize–winning author Wallace Stegner to be the department's writer in residence. As secretary of the interior, he traveled to Africa and climbed Mount Kilimanjaro.

During his first years as secretary, Udall was heavily involved in national controversies over natural resources, ranging from the passage of the Wilderness Act of 1964 to proposals involving dams in the western United States.[66] Udall was concerned about the environment. In 1963 he published a book entitled *The Quiet Crisis*. A landmark for its time, particularly coming from a public official, the book stressed the preservation of scenic landscapes. Udall's book was one of the first steps in what would develop into the environmental movement in the United States. And the proposed road through Sequoia National Park directly implicated a specific Udall concern: the impact of automobiles on the natural environment.

On January 6, 1967, Udall responded to a personal letter from Otis Chandler, the publisher of the *Los Angeles Times* and a strong proponent of the Disney project. Udall characterized the development plan for Mineral King as a "good one." However, he continued, "Director Hartzog and the Park Service feel very strongly that the proposed major access highway through a choice section of Sequoia National Park is ill-conceived," and "[q]uite frankly, at the moment I share this opinion." His objections centered on the role that the automobile would play in the development: "The experience of the postwar years tells us that the combustion automobile with its fumes, noises, and accompanying clutter is a paramount blighting influence within National Parks."[67]

Consequently, he told Chandler, the best way to make Mineral King into the "finest outdoor recreation area in the West" was to exclude automobiles and provide access by a modern electric railway system. "Walt Disney himself loved railroads," Udall argued, and "we do not consider that our insistence on a railway solution will make this project uneconomical."[68]

Udall was serious about pursuing alternative transportation. In January, he received a feasibility study for a monorail to Mineral King from George Hartzog, the head of the National Park Service. Hartzog had concluded that "it appears that a monorail is a feasible form of transportation . . . which would be far less damaging not only to the redwood groves but to the mountain slopes above and below the road." While the monorail was estimated to cost $73.7 million, Hartzog calculated that the proposed road improvements to Mineral King would cost up to $50 million. When damage to the area by the road was factored in, concluded Hartzog, the road would cost more than the monorail.[69]

Udall followed up by contacting the federal Economic Development Administration, which had approved the grant to California for planning the Mineral King highway. He convinced the agency that, if the plans included a means of access other than by road, the agency could consider a financing grant for it.[70]

On March 12, 1967, a *Los Angeles Times* article headlined "Udall Bids for Monorail Route to Mineral King." The "nature loving Interior secretary" was worried that, even if the new road avoided the sequoia trees, it "would leave irreparable long-term scars." Udall "operates from the premise that park developers . . . will be more honored 25 years from now for the roads they do not build than for the roads they do."[71]

The Disney company rejected this idea. The previous November, Sequoia National Park Superintendent Frank Kowski had requested that the Disney organization undertake a study of transportation alternatives, including a railway and a monorail. The company had reluctantly done so and delivered it to the Park Service on March 16, 1967. It examined three types of railroads; a monorail was not even considered because "earlier studies" by Disney had concluded that a monorail would cost more than other types of rail access.[72]

Accompanying the study was a letter from Donn Tatum of Walt

Disney Productions to Stewart Udall that sought to bury Udall's idea once and for all. It listed six reasons why an alternative monorail or rail transportation system into Mineral King would not work. Tatum also emphasized that the Forest Service's prospectus had required a road.[73] His message was clear: the Park Service was seeking irrelevant information and unnecessarily delaying the project.

The chief of the Forest Service, Ed Cliff, thought that the time had come for Udall to cease opposing the road. He convinced Orville Freeman to write directly to Udall,[74] and Freeman did so in personal terms. Freeman said that he had been involved in all the key decisions regarding the development and was personally invested in its success. The Forest Service had issued the Mineral King prospectus, said Freeman, only after "a firm agreement was reached between our two departments in connection with this matter." He ended with a plea to Udall: "Would you, then, join with me in informing the California authorities they can plan on a right-of-way through the Sequoia National Park?"[75] Donn Tatum at Disney also wrote to Udall, as did the head of the California Highway Commission, Gordon Luce.

Udall refused to budge. In Udall's absence, his associate bluntly told Luce: "[W]e do not believe that it is realistic to continue to assume that a two-lane highway system can cope with the projected volume of traffic" for the Mineral King development. Once Mineral King has reached a level of minimum development, "we feel there will be pressure to expand the means of access." Udall, the letter concluded, was "not in any position to make a decision concerning your request until we are able to evaluate a comprehensive and well-done report on the various alternatives."[76]

Udall's response to Tatum was more tactful but equally emphatic. He began by trying to soothe Tatum: "As you know, we ourselves feel that the Mineral King plan is a good one." But the Department of the Interior held it important "to stimulate the exploration and development of equally well devised, non-highway solutions for access to Mineral King." The Disney railroad study was not enough;

Udall wanted an evaluation of a monorail as well. Once he received a complete study, concluded Udall, "I will then want to discuss the alternatives with Secretary Orville Freeman."[77] As far as Freeman's letter was concerned, Udall delayed any reply.

Pressuring Udall for a favorable decision on a new road through Sequoia National Park had failed.

In the meantime, Disney still needed to convince the California Highway Commission that it should prioritize funding the Mineral King road over other highway improvements. The political calculations had become more complex. The new governor, Ronald Reagan, was publicly committed to budgetary tightening, but he had supported the Mineral King project during the election. The opposing political tensions surfaced in a March 1967 article in the *New York Times*—a piece that demonstrated how the Sierra Club's opposition had now succeeded in elevating discussion of the Mineral King project to the national level. The article noted that, while Reagan had endorsed the project during his campaign, he had been silent on the subject since then. The article quoted a "highly placed state official" who said "privately" that "I don't see why the Federal and state governments should subsidize the road."[78]

The California Highway Commission's April 1967 meeting brought the matter to a head, and Disney's political muscle again proved decisive. Expressions of support poured in from Orville Freeman, both of California's senators, the mayor of Los Angeles, Congressman Bob Mathias, and the local state senator and assemblyperson. After a contentious hearing, the commission voted five to two to allocate $20 million in state funds to the road over a five-year period. While original plans had called for the completion of the Mineral King road by 1971, a two-year delay would occur, but that outcome was acceptable to Disney.[79]

In a little over two years, then, Disney had convinced the State of California to build and largely fund the Mineral King road. The most significant remaining hurdle was obtaining Stewart Udall's approval for the segment of the road that would cross Sequoia National Park.

The design of the new road—in particular, whether a two-lane road would be sufficient—was tied to the capacity of Disney's Mineral King development. The Forest Service prospectus for Mineral King had set only small minimums for the size of the development. The Disney project would be vastly larger—but exactly how large? Any uncertainty about its ultimate size implicated a fundamental issue: whether the Forest Service knew what it was approving for Mineral King.

The size issue surfaced in February 1967. Pete Wyckoff, the Forest Service employee assigned to the project, had met at the Disney headquarters in Burbank with Bob Hicks and key Disney personnel planning the Mineral King development. Disney engineers had created a large-scale relief map that delineated the usable base area of the valley up to a 20 percent slope. In a memorandum, Wyckoff observed that Disney was "now considering high rise structures to provide for the large expected capacity at Mineral King without using any more land than necessary." What "concerned" Wyckoff was "their thinking toward ten story buildings." As Wyckoff understated, "such high structures would be rather stark against the mountainside." Disney planners also talked about extending structures into the upper part of the valley, which Wyckoff had thought was to be left relatively undisturbed, perhaps for a golf course.[80]

Wyckoff raised a related concern about the use projections for the Mineral King resort, which showed summer visits as high as 24,000 per day. Wyckoff was "not sure the area can stand that many people." He hoped "the Disney plans will be flexible enough to cut down on that much possible use should experience dictate."[81]

Finally, Wyckoff's memorandum raised the pricing for visitors, expressing hope that the Forest Service "will retain a firm control on the entertainment prices to the public at Mineral King." If not, Mineral King "could become a rich man's resort which is certainly not what we have in mind or what Disney has advertised as family entertainment."[82] Wykoff copied his memorandum to Bob Hicks, perhaps intending to convey a message.

The memo illustrated that the Forest Service had little control over the Disney planning. The Sierra Club had made the size of the development a major issue, coining the phrase "mass recreation" in the valley. If ten-story buildings became part of the project, they would empower the club's opposition. Equally important, at this stage the Forest Service had no strategy in place for limiting the size of the Mineral King development, seemingly a prerequisite for preserving the valley's natural environment. Ironically, while the Disney company was pondering ten-story buildings in the relatively small valley, it published the inaugural issue of the company's *Mineral King Newsletter*, a publication designed to promote the project. The issue announced the discovery of the three largest known foxtail pine trees in the world at a location just two miles north of the future Disney village.[83]

Wyckoff's memorandum disturbed the usually smooth interactions between Disney and the Forest Service. The Disney personnel were particularly upset about the suggestion of a "high priced rich man's resort rather than one for the family"[84] and about potential limitations on site capacity. After Hicks brought both of these concerns to Wyckoff's attention, Wyckoff retreated. He was "sorry my memorandum . . . caused a degree of concern" and emphasized that the memo contained only his "personal thoughts."[85]

However, Wyckoff remained uneasy about ultimate capacity. If Mineral King attracted 26,900 visitors on a summer weekend, and one-quarter of them hiked, that use would place 6,700 individuals on the trails, alongside the streams, around the lakes, or camping at the higher elevations. "We don't know," Wyckoff told Hicks, "if the soils and vegetation can withstand such heavy potential use."[86] Wyckoff ended by summarizing his concern to Hicks:

> What I am inferring, Bob, is that at some level Mineral King has a capacity limit. As you have indicated, the capacity may be dictated by the aesthetics or physical limitations of the site; or it may be the access facilities. But we should be considering a limit during the early planning stage.[87]

Wyckoff was worried that Disney's development might be too large.

After the California Highway Commission voted to fund the road, the Sierra Club sought to formalize its opposition by articulating its case against the development at Mineral King. In May 1967, the club released a document authored by Mike McCloskey and entitled "Why the Sierra Club Opposes Development of Mineral King."[88] The opposition, presented in partly exaggerated terms, now rested on five principal grounds.

First, the club argued that the project was simply too big. At 2.5 million visitors per year, the valley would host 800,000 more annual visitors than Yosemite National Park.[89] The statement even claimed that the density in Mineral King at peak use would exceed that of New York City.

The second ground aligned with the conservation theme raised by Stewart Udall: the overpresence of the automobile. The development "would bring too many cars into Mineral King Valley."[90] The number of cars, the club alleged, could require as much as 150 acres of parking, "or fully one-half of the valley floor." This charge, though, was highly questionable, as Disney's plans called for parking cars outside the valley itself and transporting visitors into it.

Third, the twenty-five-mile Mineral King road "would be choked." It might, charged the club, take as long as fifteen hours to drive in or out of the valley. Here, the club's position clashed with the conclusions of the California Department of Transportation, which found that the road would be adequate except for a couple of very high-volume days. But the charge raised the specter that the two-lane road would eventually expand into four lanes—the possibility that concerned the Park Service.[91]

Next, the club alleged that the project "was not planned with protection of Sequoia National Park in mind." It claimed that building the ski lifts for the project would require anchoring the supports for them within the adjacent Sequoia National Park.[92] This claim was more verifiable than the other charges—and more troublesome for the Disney proposal.

Finally, the Sierra Club attacked the road's cost, asserting that "[q]ualified experts warn" that it might be twice the now-estimated

$23 million. The club added that funds allocated to this project would come at the expense of other highway projects.[93]

During this period the National Parks Association, led by Anthony Wayne Smith, also stepped up its opposition. An editorial in the July 1967 issue of *National Parks* magazine and a Smith letter to Stewart Udall strongly objected to the project. The editorial said the project "conflicts with the national interest, and should be completely revised" by adding the land to Sequoia National Park.[94] Some of the charges made were inaccurate. Bestor Robinson, former president of the Sierra Club and now a supporter of the Mineral King project, fired off a letter to the magazine correcting, among other facts, the article's statement that Mineral King was "vital habitat" for the cougar and grizzly bear.[95]

Stewart Udall remained the last major administrative obstacle to the Disney development in Mineral King, and the Forest Service began to intensively lobby Udall's immediate subordinates. Ed Cliff, chief of the Forest Service, wrote a lengthy, almost passionate letter to Edward Crafts, head of the Bureau of Outdoor Recreation in the Department of the Interior.[96] Cliff knew him well; Crafts had worked for decades in the Forest Service before switching to Interior in 1962 to head the new recreation bureau.[97] According to Cliff, the Forest Service had "studied the area and its potential for more than two decades" and had approved the project after it "checked, and rechecked, every conceivable consideration." Cliff emphasized Orville Freeman's "commitments to both the desirability of developing Mineral King and the necessity of doing it in harmony with its unique environment."[98]

Crafts was convinced and forwarded Cliff's letter to Udall. Crafts stated that he had "looked into this very carefully" and recommended approval.[99] He followed up by traveling to California and flying over Mineral King. He reported that the local park superintendent, Frank Kowski, felt the road would be needed for emergency access even if a monorail or other alternative type of transport were provided.[100]

Stewart Udall was becoming increasingly isolated. Although the Park Service still balked, within the Department of the Interior hierarchy only Stanley Cain remained adamantly opposed to the road, suggesting again to Udall that the road "is logically the first step of a pair of such roads that would give traffic separation."[101] But Udall showed no signs of capitulating. His silence jeopardized his relationship with Orville Freeman, who had lent his personal imprimatur to the project and still awaited Udall's response to his most recent letter.[102]

What accounts for Udall's recalcitrance? At this time, he was engaged in intricate, difficult negotiations with Governor Ronald Reagan on expansion of Redwood National Park. There is some suggestion that Udall might have been holding the Mineral King approval hostage to gain leverage in those negotiations.[103] Most likely, however, his opposition stemmed from a deeply held belief that the proposed road represented a continuation of failed past practices that centered on the automobile.

Udall had elaborated on his vision in a June 1967 article for the *Los Angeles Times* magazine, entitled "The Face of Tomorrow." His general theme was "failure through fragmentation" in dealing with natural resources. Udall argued that "[w]e failed to view the whole picture, to search for ways in which to maintain balance between the works of man and the ways and wisdom of nature."[104] He sought to apply technology to avoid environmental destruction, and he viewed Mineral King as a "signal case" in point.

Udall framed the issue as he saw it:

> The question is whether to let private enterprise (Walt Disney Productions) drive a double roadway, some 100 feet wide, through the uniquely beautiful mountainsides leading to Mineral King or to provide instead some form of electric railway as access to the planned winter and summer resort.[105]

Udall then pictured Mineral King as he saw it could be:

> At stake are not only the groves of old-growth redwood and the superlative mountain scenery which would be inflicted with irrepara-

> ble long-term scars, but the very air of the resort valley itself. Picture the 15,500 acres of . . . the Mineral King site, developed as delightfully as the Disney people are demonstrably capable of doing; and imagine them seen through air as crystal clear as the air cupped in that valley today . . . the closest automobile held 25 miles in abeyance, at the other end of a clean, electric-powered transportation line. [N]owhere would the scene be dimmed by the dismal pall of the internal-combustion chamber.[106]

Udall got some important facts wrong, infuriating the Forest Service. Slim Davis immediately dispatched a memorandum to Forest Service Chief Ed Cliff noting "two major inaccuracies" in the article: the road would not be nearly 100 feet wide, and no redwoods would be destroyed.[107] Moreover, Disney's proposal promised to include an as-yet undesigned people-mover that would keep vehicles out of the Mineral King Valley itself.

On August 4, 1967, Udall finally replied to Orville Freeman's April 14 letter. "We are," said Udall, "troubled by the side effects of the Disney plan as well as by the plan for a new highway into this beautiful but fragile valley." Udall assured Freeman that "I have been deeply involved in the policy issues posed by the Mineral King development plan for nearly a year now," a riposte directed at Freeman's emphasis on his own personal involvement in the matter. Udall also argued that, contrary to Freeman's claim, neither the Park Service nor the Interior Department had firmly committed to the road through Sequoia National Park.[108]

Udall concluded optimistically that "there is every reason to believe that exciting new transportation alternatives are on the horizon" and that the funding by California "should not, by itself, sweep all other options aside." Indeed, Udall thought that if a railroad or monorail was viable, he and Freeman "might even break new ground" by insisting that the California legislature authorize it. Finally, in a postscript, Udall suggested that a special study committee might be useful.[109]

Disney quickly sent Freeman detailed "comments" rebutting the Udall letter,[110] but Udall held the high ground. He wanted an alternative to the road and was willing to hold the project hostage to achieve that goal. A major flaw in Udall's strategy, however, was that he had not initiated any process within the Interior Department that could produce a specific alternative to the road. He felt that the responsibility for finding that alternative lay with the Forest Service and Disney. So, the impasse continued.

Orville Freeman, however, was becoming very upset.

Freeman and the Disney personnel worried that, if Interior did not commit soon to the road, the California transportation money would disappear, so they brainstormed on how to force a decision from Udall. Disney mulled over setting a meeting with Freeman and requesting that Freeman bring Udall to the same meeting. It pondered using Senator Robert Kennedy of New York to "exert influence" over Udall.[111] Disney also worked the press. A September 29 article proclaimed that "Disney Halts Mineral King Development," with Bob Hicks blaming the delay on Udall's department.[112]

In the meantime, Freeman replied to Udall's letter of August 4, 1967, in strong language. He declared himself "very disappointed" by the letter and warned that failure to reach agreement on "improving a few miles of existing road must be a growing source of embarrassment to the Federal Government." He described himself as "frankly amazed" at Udall's claim that the Park Service had not firmly committed to the road, and he rejected a special study committee. Udall and his department, charged Freeman, "are clearly attempting to limit our activities and block National Forest development in ways that are not justified." Only in conclusion did he adopt a slightly milder tone, urging Udall's prompt endorsement of the road, an action which "will be sincerely appreciated by me as well as by countless thousands of Americans now and in the years to come.[113]

In late September, Roy Disney tried a direct approach, writing a five-page letter to Udall, ending with a request for an appointment "to discuss these matters at your earliest convenience."[114] When Udall did not respond, Roy Disney sent a telegram on October 11 saying he "would very much appreciate a reply to my letter."[115] He received back only a short letter from Stanley Cain citing "some major unresolved issues surrounding this proposal." Another part of the effort to pressure Udall was an October 1967 article by California Senator Thomas Kuchel in *Western Ski Time* magazine, pointedly entitled "Mineral King: The Opportunity Should Not Be Lost."[116] Kuchel met personally with Udall to lobby him.

The pressure finally caused a crack in Udall's wall of opposition. As Freeman aide John Baker reported the next day, while Udall "stood absolutely pat," he "intimated, but was not explicit that he would not mind being overruled by the Bureau of the Budget or the President." Udall seemed to be signaling a face-saving way in which he could drop his opposition.[117]

Philip "Sam" Hughes, the deputy director of the Bureau of the Budget in President Lyndon Johnson's administration, acted as a kind of one-person appeals board in resolving disputes within the administration. A career civil servant known for his skill at addressing bureaucratic tangles, Hughes was aware of the impasse over the road. A furious Orville Freeman had sent Hughes a draft of a letter that would have requested the President's Council on Recreation and Natural Beauty to decide the dispute. Hughes rejected this idea but suggested to Freeman that he could arrange a meeting between Udall and Freeman.[118]

The Sierra Club recognized that the dispute over the road was reaching a turning point. Mike McCloskey wrote to the club's Mineral King Task Force stating that Udall "is under heavy pressure from the promoters, the Forest Service, and skiers to give way." He urged the task force members to "do all you can to encourage letters to Udall."[119]

Then, the dispute between Udall and Freeman erupted into the press.

On December 3, 1967, the *New York Times* published an article headlined "2 Cabinet Aides Clash over Park" and subtitled "Freeman Development Plan Is Attacked by Udall."[120] The article outlined the dispute in detail and quoted from the "tart letters" that Freeman and Udall had exchanged. "The split is so wide," concluded the article, that some members of Congress think that President Johnson "might have to referee the dispute." A similar article appeared three days later in the *Los Angeles Times*.[121]

The articles brought the matter to a head. On December 7, Sam Hughes of the Bureau of the Budget summoned both Freeman and Udall to decide the matter.[122]

Udall may well have determined that, at this point, he had to cease direct opposition. In addition to the array of elected officials pressing him, Sam Hughes was not neutral on the matter. He had previously written to Congressman Wayne Aspinall, chair of the powerful Interior and Insular Affairs Committee, assuring him that Mineral King would go forward.[123] Finally, Udall rejected any direct appeal to President Johnson, as Udall felt some uncertainty about their relationship.[124]

At the meeting, Udall surrendered. He agreed that a road could be built through the park.

Freeman was exultant. He wrote in his journal that he had "won a victory over Brother Udall," with whom Freeman had "been furious . . . because he is simply grandstanding to a few Sierra Club types" and had been "arrogant and high-handed." Freeman reported that, at the meeting with Sam Hughes, Udall had "capitulated immediately under the condition that I make it clear that he had fought a hard fight and had been defeated at a higher echelon." Udall "was completely unabashed by this position, hardly contending that there was any merit in his action in the first place."[125] Freeman concluded:

> So I'll make an announcement that Mineral King goes forward between Christmas and New Year's alleging that great safeguards have been instituted to protect the area that the road goes through and any pollution from the development in the valley. I have a lot less regard for that man [Udall] the more I work with him. . . . It's remarkable over the years that we have gotten along as well as we have I guess and perhaps I shouldn't judge him too harshly but I really don't have much respect for him.[126]

Udall closely negotiated his terms of surrender. He edited Freeman's proposed press release to excise language suggesting that it was a joint approval and that Udall's principal concerns had been met.[127] He told Freeman that "it is vital from my point of view that the press release be recast so that it is essentially an Agriculture announcement." Udall insisted on other terms as well. Freeman could "run over" him providing "there was no dispute in the conditions insisted upon by the Park Service and the Federal Water Pollution Control Administration."[128]

Two days after Christmas, Freeman distributed a press release entitled "Road to Mineral King Area Approved." Its wording began awkwardly: the Mineral King plan "is ready to proceed."[129] The *Washington Post* reported that "President Johnson wanted the issue settled,"[130] and a *New York Times* article observed, near its end, that the Sierra Club was "exploring to see if we have any other recourse."[131] Roy Disney issued a public statement expressing pleasure at the approval,[132] and Orville Freeman wrote to him, "I wish you God's speed in bringing your brother's dream to a successful conclusion."[133]

When Martin Litton of the Sierra Club wrote to Stewart Udall expressing unhappiness about the approval (while also praising Udall's decision to veto a transmountain road through the Great Smoky Mountains National Park),[134] Udall was philosophic. He handwrote Litton back stating, "Wish I could win them all, but that's too much to hope. Why don't you people raise more hell with Freeman and the Forest Service?"[135]

Disney still had to complete its plan for development, but the Forest Service was certain to approve it. The Mineral King development seemed assured.

5: A Recreation and Conservation Plan

When Stewart Udall conceded that a road could be built through Sequoia National Park, Orville Freeman thought the battle was over. So did others. Udall, however, had reserved jurisdiction over the location and standards of that road. To the frustration of the Forest Service and the Disney executives, it would take another year to work through those questions.

Assistant Secretary of the Interior Stanley Cain, still an avowed opponent of the road, seized the initiative. On January 4, 1968, Cain sent a memo to Park Service Director George Hartzog stating that, while the service would have to issue a permit for the road, it still has "an important hold over several matters for which the Secretary has deep concern."[1] The Park Service should satisfy itself on the road's location, standards, and manner of construction, and on the lack of danger from silt. Cain also stressed Udall's concern over the "construction by Disney within the ski bowl area"—a subject outside Interior's jurisdiction. He followed up with Hartzog a week later, emphasizing "that the Secretary expects" Sequoia National Park "will suffer minimal damage" from the road.[2]

Cain's instructions to Hartzog indicate that while Udall deeply opposed the road, he generally disliked the Disney ski area in Mineral King as well. An interaction between Udall and Freeman confirms this conclusion. After Udall's "capitulation" on the road, the two met for lunch on March 1, 1968. Freeman observed in his diary that at lunch Udall "was miserable about Mineral King."[3] Almost two years later, after Udall left office, he expressly stated that he opposed the Mineral King development.[4]

Developing the Park Service's standards for the Mineral King road proved a lengthy process. The agency hired a consultant, John Clarkeson, to advise it on the issue.[5] Later, further studies were recommended to determine the Disney project's effect on water resources.[6] On several occasions Park Service officials missed deadlines to provide a draft of the permit's terms for the road.[7]

Another important issue involving the Park Service festered below the surface: the question of electric transmission lines. Disney was examining whether the Mineral King facility could produce its own power in the valley, an alternative that would avoid long overhead power lines. But that alternative posed problems, including transporting the fuel for the power plant to Mineral King.[8] So, most likely, the power would be transmitted through power lines from around Three Rivers, and these lines, too, would require Park Service approval.

Clarkeson released his report on the road for Interior at the end of July, and it proved to be exactly what the Forest Service feared.[9] He proposed an alternative routing for the upgraded road that adhered more closely to the existing road. The give-and-take over Clarkeson's report played out over the next months. Clarkeson produced a supplement to his report,[10] while the California highway engineers stood behind their location for the route.[11]

Meanwhile, opposition to the Disney project grew steadily and became increasingly national.

The *New York Times* reacted with editorial fury to Stewart Udall's agreement to approve the road. It castigated Orville Freeman for his "stubbornness [that] has cleared the way for a commercial project that will ruin one of the nation's truly majestic wilderness areas." Udall, charged the *Times*, "has now bowed to the pressures from Secretary Freeman and the Bureau of the Budget" and agreed "reluctantly and regrettably" to the road. The paper urged President Johnson to intervene and "prevent the impending destruction of a precious piece of the nation's wilderness heritage."[12]

Others wrote letters. For example, Alfred Knopf, head of the Knopf

Publishing Company which had published some Sierra Club books, wrote to President Johnson that "Walt Disney's good name would become very unpopular with future generations" if the Mineral King resort proceeded.[13] A Sierra Club staff member on the East Coast telegrammed McCloskey that there was "much more interest here in [the] East than I had anticipated" about Mineral King.[14]

Reacting to the volume of mail opposing the Mineral King development, Orville Freeman complained to John Baker, his assistant secretary, about being "a bit disappointed that the Disney people have proved as inept or as unwilling to state their case."[15] In response, Baker and Ed Cliff contacted Roy Disney and talked "very straight" to him about responding to the increasing public opposition to the Mineral King project. Disney, however, convinced Baker that there were good reasons for "taking it easy" and "not to stir up the *New York Times*."[16]

For Walt Disney Productions, however, the discussion with Baker and Cliff would evolve into a major strategic choice. It would have to decide whether to vigorously defend its Mineral King development in the public sphere, an option that presented the possibility of damage to the Disney image as the environmental debate intensified, or to adopt a lower profile with a less confrontational approach. The choice was difficult for a company that greatly prized its image yet was deeply committed to the project.

As for the Sierra Club, its opposition to Mineral King received a jolt of new energy from two graduate students at the University of California, Los Angeles. John Rettenmayer was a doctoral candidate in business who would later teach at the college level, and Albert Hill was seeking a master's degree in botany. In July, they led a "hike-in" and "camp-in" at Mineral King. As the *Fresno Bee* reported, Rettenmayer "complained there is a lack of detailed information about the project" and charged that the Forest Service was "mesmerized by the scope of the Disney proposal."[17] The hike-in, though, was not designed to be entirely one-sided; Forest Service personnel were invited to attend and present their position on developing Mineral King.[18]

Rettenmayer, Hill, and their colleagues brought a distinct flavor of late 1960s protest to the opposition. In March 1969 a small group of thirty environmentalists would picket the Disney Studios in Burbank.[19] Students were accused of removing survey stakes marking the location of the proposed Mineral King road.[20] Plans also were in the works to "lie in" in front of bulldozers if construction on the road began.[21]

Aided by Hill, Rettenmayer also wrote a "Summary of Mineral King Development" that they characterized as cataloging "what may happen to Mineral King." The paper was another step in the evolution of the arguments against the development. In addition to points raised previously, Rettenmayer and Hill stressed an issue that struck at the heart of the Forest Service's management of the project. They argued that not only had the Forest Service never set any limits on the maximum size of the development, the service "is only now conducting studies of the probable impact the development will have on the area." Those studies, the two activists charged, "should have preceded any decision to develop Mineral King and should have provided guidelines for the size of the project."[22] The allegation directly challenged the Forest Service's long-standing claim that it had undertaken exhaustive studies before issuing the prospectus.

The recommendations in the Clarkeson report for major changes in the plan for the road to Mineral King generated months of back-and-forth between the Park Service and the Forest Service. Frustrated, Orville Freeman wrote yet another "Dear Stew" letter to Stewart Udall seeking final action on the road permit.[23] Udall replied to Freeman that no permit would issue until the Forest and Park Services agreed on location and design standards. He also expressed concern that the "size of the planned Disney development" might generate a later request for a bigger road. But Udall also appended a handwritten note: "Orv, I'm pushing my people. We'll get it done if we both let them know we want [it]."[24]

Udall's statements committing to the road satisfied the California Highway Commission. It adopted a budget for 1969–70 that included

$1.8 million for grading on the Mineral King highway.[25] The state was ready to start work. One member of the commission suggested that the road be named the Walt Disney Highway.[26]

Finally, after a meeting in San Francisco on December 16, 1968—nearly one year after Udall's "capitulation" on the road issue—the Park and Forest Services reached a tentative agreement on road standards.[27] The Forest Service had at last won the battle for its road. Disney was due to submit its final plan to the Forest Service for the ski development within weeks.

Meanwhile, the controversy over Mineral King grew even more intense.

Jack Hope was a writer for *Natural History* magazine, a publication of the American Museum of Natural History, and had been researching an article on Mineral King. Hope was the first national journalist to undertake an in-depth look at the Mineral King controversy.

In November 1968 the magazine published Hope's lengthy article, accompanied by pictures that documented the valley's splendor.[28] The article's title, "The King Besieged," prefigured Hope's conclusions, which generally disfavored the ski development. Indeed, Hope later actively opposed the development, even suggesting to Mike McCloskey that he would be glad to organize picketing of the Department of Agriculture in Washington, DC.[29] The press release issued by *Natural History* about the piece was pointedly titled: "Long Live the King!"[30] The Forest Service and Disney disputed parts of the article, and Disney quickly sent in a brief response stating that the concept of the facilities discussed in the article "is substantially in error."[31]

The Hope article began by discussing the idea, often propounded by the Forest Service and Disney, that developing Mineral King would allow the public to drive straight into the Sierra Nevadas to experience the near-wilderness around them. But, thought Hope, this idea has "great naïvete" to it. Building roads to make wilderness more accessible to millions, despite the democratic overtones of the idea, is something like "carving up Michelangelo's statue of 'David,' so that each of us might own one splinter."[32]

Hope also examined the philosophical differences in the opposing positions of the Forest Service and the Sierra Club. Each faction, said Hope, "has come to regard itself as the champion of a cause called 'conservation.'" He attempted to separate the "apparently single beam of 'conservation'" into conflicting components. The Forest Service had long espoused the Gifford Pinchot view of conservation: "the greatest good of the greatest number for the longest time." The agency would cite statistics about the growing need for recreation in California, and, from the agency's point of view, those numbers would essentially decide that Mineral King's future was as a resort. Hope said the answer was not that simple: "Who can say, for instance, whether a ski resort, a semideveloped campsite, or a primitive landscape will be of the greatest benefit to people who have not yet been born?"[33]

Hope thus pinpointed the central difficulty in defining "conservation." That malleable concept did not supply anything approaching a precise benchmark for decision-making about Mineral King.[34]

As 1968 neared its end, the Disney team was finalizing its master plan for Mineral King, meeting several times with Forest Service personnel. Disney's 1965 bid promised that vehicles would be parked outside the valley; from there, individuals could access ski lifts and immediately take to the slopes, or use some form of transportation to the hotel accommodations and main lodge within the valley. After investigating various possibilities, Disney settled on a cog-railroad for that transportation.[35] In addition to the usual two rails, this type of railway has a third rail in the middle with cogs that are engaged by a cogwheel on the locomotive, thus enabling the train to go up steep inclines.

Finally, at this eleventh hour, the Disney team became concerned about the content of the permits that the Forest Service would issue. The service would grant a "term permit" for thirty years, but the law limited that grant to eighty acres. It also could issue annual permits that had no acreage limits but were subject to yearly renewal. Service permits for other large ski developments throughout the country had responded to these legal restraints by issuing the thirty-year term permit for acreage containing most buildings supporting the development—the lodge, hotel, and so on. The annual permit then covered the ski lifts and runs, gondolas, and service roads. In Disney's case, it would receive a thirty-year term permit for 60.7 acres and an annual permit for 256.1 acres.[36]

Until now, the Disney team had showed no concern over these permit limitations, particularly the need for annual renewals, even though it would invest $35 million dollars in the overall Mineral King ski area. Now, on the eve of submission of Disney's plan, the company's chief lawyer, Dick Morrow, wanted "some kind of assurance" that the company would have the "right of refusal" for a new permit at the end of the thirty years. He also sought a commitment that the annual permit would be renewed.[37] Morrow's concerns, which the Forest Service did not resolve, marked one of the few times that any questions had arisen regarding the legal underpinnings of the Mineral King development.

By the end of December 1968, the Mineral King planning process was set to conclude. The Forest Service looked forward to the Disney plan with great anticipation. As Richard Costley, the service's director of recreation, explained, "The [Disney] company has so much at stake that I am sure the Forest Service is going to be pleased over, and proud to be associated with, whatever the end product will be and how it will be operated."[38]

On January 8, 1969, Walt Disney Productions submitted to the Forest Service its *Master Plan Presentation of Walt Disney Productions' Mineral King Project*.[39] The plan listed two major aims: (1) to provide year-round recreational facilities for people of all ages, income levels, athletic abilities, and free-time interests; and (2) to preserve the scenic values and alpine environment of the Mineral King area.[40] It described a spectacular development.

The plan's most innovative feature was locating the parking outside the valley, thus excluding automobiles from the valley itself. The Mineral King Village would be situated in the valley about two-and-a-half miles from the parking structure. That structure was the answer to what the plan termed "[o]ne of the greatest design challenges . . . : 'What should be done with the guest automobile?'" The arrangement would keep all vehicles out of the valley and out of sight, "thus furthering the aim to protect the area's scenic values."[41] An electric cog-railway, "aesthetically compatible with its Sierra surroundings," would constitute the sole means of in-valley transportation.

Hicks termed the elimination of automobiles on the two-and-a-half-mile stretch from the reception area to the village as "the most significant, far-reaching aspect of our Master Plan." This parking location, said Hicks, "permits the planning of a unique village . . . and, most importantly, the development of all-year recreational facilities compatible with Mineral King's natural beauty." An architecture styled "American-Alpine" would be used, with building designs "a combination of traditional mountain forms and the natural character of the American Sierra."[42] In the first year, the capacity would be 1,505 guests, with that number rising thereafter. And 90 percent of the accommodations would be in the modest to low-price categories.

The ski facilities would be extensive. In year one, ten lifts would operate, with that number rising to twenty-two—a combination of chair lifts and gondolas—in the fifth year. By then the facilities would serve 4,000 overnight skiers plus an additional 4,500 day skiers on weekends and holidays. The ski areas in the first phase would traverse five snow bowls located adjacent to each other, while one ski run for intermediate skiers would extend for nearly three miles with a vertical drop from 11,100 feet to 7,400 feet.[43]

Multiple opportunities for non-ski play were included. Visitors could engage in sledding, ski-bobbing, riding inner tubes and snow pans, and snow sculpturing. Heated outdoor swimming pools would be available, as would indoor and outdoor skating rinks, a ski jump amphitheater, and trails for cross-country skiers.[44]

Disney also planned "an extensive summer recreational program" that included fishing, picnicking, hiking, camping, and horseback riding.[45] The plan estimated that 60 percent of visits to Mineral King would occur during the summer and off-season periods. Interestingly, though, the original attendance projections for the development were revised downward from 1.7 million visitors in the fifth year to 986,000.[46]

Disney's summary of the plan touted its conservation aspects. The goal was to provide "additional and badly needed recreational opportunities for the general public, while preserving and maintaining the natural beauty of the area." Walt Disney Productions "has dedicated itself to establishing at Mineral King new standards of excellence for conservation-oriented recreational development." The company would rely upon a voluntary Conservation Committee to help it set those standards. The committee was comprised of a variety of conservation luminaries, including Horace Albright, former director of the National Park Service; Bestor Robinson, former president of the Sierra Club; and Thomas Kimball, executive director of the National Wildlife Foundation.

Finally, Disney cited Buzz Price's estimate that economic benefits totaling $500 million would accrue to California during the first ten years of operation.[47]

In short, the plan outlined a large, comprehensive ski development operated with Disney efficiency and flair but also pledged to environmental sensitivity. The plan assumed compatibility between a high level of development and the environmental protection of the valley and the surrounding areas. Indeed, a Forest Service paper discussing the Master Plan promised even more, promoting the plan as "designed to actually enhance the beauty of the area."[48]

Slim Davis of the Forest Service remembered the delays that occurred in 1965 when Orville Freeman's office took control of the final decision between Walt Disney and Bob Brandt. He quickly moved to avoid a similar delay at this juncture. On January 9, 1969, the day after the Forest Service received the plan, Davis sent a memo to Richard Costley, the director of the Division of Recreation in Washington, DC, that assumed plan approval would occur at the California level of the Forest Service. He emphasized that "we are committed to two joint press conferences with Walt Disney Productions on January 27, and it is most important that no word of our acceptance of the plan be given out before then or that our authority to approve it be preempted."[49] While Davis went through the motions of asking some Forest Service experts for comments on the plan, from his standpoint the outcome was preordained.

Still, some slight discomfort arose within the agency. One review commented that the Forest Service must avoid the appearance of "trusting" Disney just because "[we] grew up with Mickey Mouse." It continued: "A clear statement showing the maze through which [Disney] development plans must pass and the control we can exercise should be helpful."[50] The suggestion was ignored.

Surprisingly, though, Costley recorded some concerns in a memo to file. He noted that "by necessity" the Office of the Chief of the Forest Service had been "caught in a severe time crunch" in its review of the plan. He cited "general disappointment with the lack of detail in the plan" but conceded no questions could be raised about it since the plan "included pretty much what the [Forest Service] Region had advised Disney should be in it." He emphasized to Slim Davis that the plan should allow changes to be made as new information became available and "that all details, as far as site and facility plans are concerned, are still subject to Forest Service approval." This emphasis, said Costley, was needed "to slay the dragon which might be raised by some that the plan is pretty much of a 'blank check.'"[51]

Other comments drifted in. However, on the thirteenth day after the plan's submission, Jim James, the supervisor of Sequoia National Forest, wrote to Card Walker, the executive vice-president of Disney Productions. James approved the Disney master plan.[52]

The Forest Service and Walt Disney Productions announced the approval on Monday, January 27, 1969, at press conferences in Los Angeles and San Francisco.[53] Orchestrated with the usual Disney efficiency, the conferences were accompanied by a flurry of press releases describing and extolling the plan.[54]

Disney's achievement was unquestionably impressive. It had designed a large, complex project in a recreational field new to the company, and it had excited the ski community with the prospect of a world-class facility. At the same time, it had persuaded the State of California to build the Mineral King road, thereby solving the access problem that had long stymied efforts to develop the valley. And it had Stewart Udall's word that the road could cross Sequoia National Park. Securing the road was, by itself, a remarkable feat of political engineering.

Finally, the Disney executives had honored the memory of Walt Disney. As Roy Disney put it in a public statement, the approval of the project "will permit the realization of one of Walt Disney's last and greatest dreams—the development of one of the world's most outstanding all-year recreational facilities."[55] According to an Australian magazine, Roy Disney declared that the start of work in the valley "will be the happiest moment of my life." The magazine also told its readers that "[p]lans are afoot to rename the valley in honour of Disney" at the opening of the village in 1973.[56]

The Forest Service's approval, however, did not end public controversy over Mineral King's future. Instead, the approval intensified the now-national debate on the issue. Citizens wrote their representatives in Washington, DC, pro and con. Immediate reactions from the press varied. Still adamantly opposed to the development, the *New York Times* charged that "[t]he only word to describe this hideous project is scandalous."[57] California papers almost universally took the opposite tack.[58]

Time magazine slightly equivocated. It observed that Mineral King was not wilderness and cited the statement of Disney officials that the horse-renting concession currently in the valley was polluting the Kaweah River. Then the article changed direction. It declared that "[n]o doubt the developers intend to mine Mineral King with the same antiseptic efficiency and imaginative salesmanship that they exercised on Disneyland itself," and adverted to critics who envisioned a possible "village of Snow White Synthetic or Plastic Alpine." The ending of the article, however, returned to a more favorable view of the project, citing "the need for well-planned recreational development."[59]

As for the principal protagonists in the drama, after more than three years of debate over the project, the competing arguments of the Forest Service and the Sierra Club had crystallized. Both released brochures soon after project approval that comprehensively laid out their respective positions.

In February 1969, the Forest Service published *Mineral King: A Planned Recreation Development*. The document covered a wide variety of topics but repeated certain themes. First was the necessity for the facility. The ski project "is needed to meet rapidly expanding public demands for this type of recreation." The public, the Forest Service stressed dramatically, "needs the development, almost desperately."[60]

A second theme was how the project would harmonize with nature. The development would be "skillfully blended into the alpine setting." Its principal planning guideline is "to protect the resource while developing it, and do it in complete harmony with the surroundings." The development "will not be a 'Disneyland!'" Walt Disney, reminded the Forest Service, promised as much when he explained that Disneyland provides entertainment, while Mineral King supplies outdoor recreation.[61]

The brochure stressed the expertise infused into the project. Disney undertook "an aggressive study and planning program," and completed numerous studies to the tune of over $500,000. And, added the Forest Service, Disney could be trusted for a practical reason: as a maker of motion pictures, "[i]ts success depends upon its public image." Disney was "not likely to put that image in jeopardy by risking a miscue at Mineral King."[62]

Fourth, the Forest Service would retain continuing jurisdiction over the project, an authority that had received little emphasis before. "[E]ach plan and even each supporting blueprint—area-by-area, site-by-site, facility-by-facility, and structure-by-structure—is subject to Forest Service approval (and/or veto)."[63] The agency had not abdicated its responsibilities to Disney.

The brochure then reiterated an argument that the Forest Service had consistently made: Mineral King was not a wilderness area. Many objectors to the development "jumped to the conclusion that the development of Mineral King, in effect, must be a violation of wilderness values." But it could not be, said the Forest Service, because the valley "could never meet Congressionally established wilderness standards."[64]

Sixth, the project made economic sense. Using capital letters for emphasis, the brochure boasted that within fifteen years "there will have been a total expenditure in investments, payrolls, retail sales, etc., of ONE BILLION DOLLARS."[65]

Lastly, the brochure attacked opponents of the development. Most who originally questioned the Forest Service plans, it said, already enjoyed the valley, principally those with summer homes. They were supported by others, presumably a reference to the Sierra Club, "who consistently oppose any further development of the mountain areas of the West."[66]

The Sierra Club contested these arguments in a brochure entitled *Mineral King at the Crossroads*. It began by reiterating a comparison consistently found in the Sierra Club's arguments about the development: Mineral King could become "another over-developed Yosemite." Moreover, the Disney development was designed to attract almost one million visitors per year—half that of Yosemite, which the club told readers was approximately eight times the size of Mineral King.[67]

The brochure stressed Mineral King's uniqueness and special characteristics. Not only is the two-mile long valley essentially unspoiled, it provides access to a number of alpine lakes on trails which "radiate in all directions." While some development in the valley now exists, "the remainder is wilderness where mule deer and other wildlife abound."[68] And, in a jab at the for-profit nature of the Disney resort, the club added that admission to Mineral King had been free until now.

The Sierra Club charged that the sheer numbers of visitors would cause damage. The tiny valley would be subjected to 5,000 to 10,000 people per day. Visitors would be housed in a five-story "hotel complex," a choice that prompted the Sierra Club to fashion a pointed comparison: while the hotel in Mineral King would have 1,030 rooms, the Disneyland Hotel had only 608 rooms—and the largest hotel in

Los Angeles, the Biltmore, had 1,500 rooms. The village "would dominate the view from every direction."[69]

Moreover, the destructive effects of the development had been insufficiently studied and "grossly underestimated." Indeed, charged the club, to its knowledge no study had assessed the effect of construction activities on Mineral King's habitat for wildlife, and the possible water quality impacts "present[ed] serious questions." And the damage could be even greater in the future: after all, Walt Disney himself had declared, "I guess you might say that it won't ever be finished."[70]

The Sierra Club brochure also attacked the Mineral King highway's crossing of Sequoia National Park. The club had procured a copy of the Clarkeson report on the highway's route and broadcast Clarkeson's criticisms of the road's features. The road would require removal of eight million cubic yards of soil, "with attendant scarring and erosion of the steep hillsides."[71]

All of this discussion led to the Sierra Club's conclusion: "massive commercialization of Mineral King is a monumental mistake." The Mineral King Valley, argued the club, belongs in Sequoia National Park.[72]

While the public debate continued, the governmental decision about Mineral King's future had been made. The Sierra Club had lost. But while the club pondered whether any further action remained available, the Mineral King Valley sent a deadly reminder of its majesty.

Walt Disney Productions had hired experts to record snow depth in Mineral King and assess the avalanche danger. During the 1968–69 winter, the third year of Disney's survey project, two Disney consultants spent the winter in Mineral King recording data. One was Dave Beck, accompanied by his wife Susan. The other, Walter Ballenger, lived in a cabin located about two hundred yards away from the one used by the Becks. Also staying that winter, in a cabin next to the Becks, were Randy Kletka and Gary Kirk, both in their early twenties, and both friends of Dave Beck.[73]

Snow fell relentlessly that winter. Twenty-three inches dropped over a fifty-six-hour period that included Christmas. Beck and Ballenger found evidence of eleven major avalanches in the ensuing days. Six more storms arrived in January, bringing more avalanches. By February 15, the snow stake on the floor of the Mineral King Valley read 128.5 inches.[74] The snow accumulation made any real surveying impossible.

The next week, Bob Hicks, Disney's project manager, consulted with the company's ski expert, Willy Schaeffler, and then told the surveyors to leave the valley for the time being.[75] In addition to the snow conditions, a CBS television crew from New York was scheduled to film in Mineral King on the upcoming Saturday for a program regarding the Sierra Club, and Hicks "absolutely did not want them [Beck and Ballenger] talking to the TV crew." The Becks left with Gary Kirk on Friday, February 21. But Ballenger decided to stay, as did Randy Kletka. In January Kletka had driven his car up the Mineral King road as far as he could, and it was now covered with snow.[76]

It snowed all weekend—at least twenty-five inches on Sunday. Wally Ballenger told Randy Kletka to move into the Becks' cabin. Conditions were so severe that they discussed calling for an evacuation.

On Monday night a tremendous avalanche thundered down the mountain and buried both the Ballenger and Beck cabins. Ballenger unsuccessfully tried to phone Kletka. After hours of digging his way out, Ballenger broke an air hole through the snow to the surface. The opening was twelve feet above the cabin's roof. When Ballenger looked around, he could see no familiar landmark. He could not locate the Beck cabin where Kletka was staying.[77]

On Wednesday, February 26, Dave Beck arrived by helicopter with Pete Wyckoff of the Forest Service. Beck finally located his cabin, and after other Forest Service personnel arrived, they dug a twenty-three-foot shaft down into it. They found Kletka's body. He had tried to dig himself out but had asphyxiated.[78]

The loss of such a young life was both tragic and unexpected. Beck, the avalanche expert, never thought an avalanche of this size was possible at that location.[79] The avalanche caused substantial damage. As one Forest Service official described, "It looks like a battlefield after the shells quit falling."[80]

For Disney and the Forest Service, whose plan depended on the safe insertion of large numbers of people into Mineral King, the situation posed the specter of a public relations disaster if the valley was perceived as unsafe. Jim James, the superintendent of Sequoia National Forest, quickly assured the public that the Mineral King Village planned by Disney would not have been affected, although more protection for the cog railway transporting visitors would be needed. He also said avalanche control crews would have prevented snow accumulations like this one.[81] The public relations situation worsened for Disney when one initial press report on the avalanche identified Kletka as a Disney employee,[82] which Bob Hicks denied.

Newspaper coverage of the avalanche at Mineral King, however, soon faded, and the story moved in a far different direction. On June 5, 1969, the Sierra Club filed suit in federal court challenging the Forest Service's approval of the Mineral King development and the Park Service's approval of the road.

THE NEW WORLD OF THE COURTS

6: Formulating a Lawsuit

The January 1969 decision of the Forest Service to approve the Disney plan came amid a remarkable surge in public concern over environmental degradation. This movement coincided with the growing opposition to the war in Vietnam and the rise of the so-called counterculture in the latter part of the decade. The year 1968 had proved tumultuous, with the media transfixed by protests against the Vietnam War at the Democratic Convention. It was "a political and societal maelstrom of unprecedented intensity."[1]

The next year, 1969, saw events like the Santa Barbara oil spill and the fire on the Cuyahoga River in Cleveland. The idea that industrial development was imperiling the country's environment lodged itself in the American consciousness.[2] By the early 1970s, some popular opinion polls found that more Americans were concerned about the environment than any other domestic problem.[3]

This developing environmental consciousness, along with an evolution in the Sierra Club's makeup, greatly affected the club's internal dynamics and bolstered its willingness to engage in the relatively new tactic of litigation.

The Sierra Club was an organization traditionally devoted to outdoor activities such as hiking, mountain climbing, backpacking—and skiing. In recent years, however, the club had changed. To begin with, membership had continued to skyrocket. In February 1969, it had 79,000 members;[4] a year later, membership would balloon to 113,000.[5]

The Sierra Club had always been California-centered. By the end of the 1960s, it had grown into a national entity. It now had a strong East Coast presence and also a small international footprint.[6]

The focus of the club's conservation efforts was changing. Its actions in the 1950s and most of the 1960s had centered on preserving parks and affecting decisions about public lands. By 1969, the organization's view of conservation increasingly included environmental quality issues. The Sierra Club had become concerned with air and water pollution, and it was now an advocacy organization with a strong political component. It also was "far more combative" with both industry and government than it had been in its early days.[7] Moreover, it was gradually expanding its professional staff to support these efforts.[8]

The new members joining the Sierra Club reflected this fundamental change in attitude. In the mid-1960s, three-quarters of the members joined for the outings program and only one-quarter for the "conservation program" that included opposition to the Mineral King ski area. By the early 1970s, the ratio had flipped; the new members were largely interested in the broadened conservation program, that is, in environmental protection.[9]

Responding to these changes, the Sierra Club board of directors had become more aggressive. New members comfortable with environmental activism were replacing older, more conciliatory board members. These new members included individuals from the East Coast, most notably Supreme Court Justice William O. Douglas for a short period. The changes meant that board meetings, always open to the public, became fractious, with the "new wave" clashing with the "old guard." Mike McCloskey worked in the middle of what he termed "open warfare."[10]

As the Forest Service moved to approve Disney's Mineral King plan in 1969 and the Sierra Club contemplated its next steps, another factor affected the club's response: the conflict between David Brower and the Sierra Club's board of directors. In early 1969, matters came to a head when Brower unilaterally published a page-and-a-half advertisement in the *New York Times*, captioned "Earth National Park," which sought to expand the club's reach in international environmental issues. Ed Wayburn, a physician and the board's president, was very upset. On January 28, Wayburn suspended Brower from spending Sierra Club money.[11] At the next board meeting on February 8, the board supported Wayburn by a seven-to-six vote.

The dispute then broadened. Two opposing slates of candidates ran for open board positions, one supporting Brower and the other opposing him. On April 16 the results were in: Brower's slate had lost. Brower left the Sierra Club on May 3 to form a new environmental organization, Friends of the Earth,[12] and a significant number of the Sierra Club staff who supported Brower followed him out the door.

After Brower's resignation, the board of directors appointed Mike McCloskey as interim executive director of the club. His position was precarious, as some board members wanted to hire an entirely new leadership team. One rumor had Stewart Udall interested in the position.[13]

One of the first issues facing McCloskey was the club's response to the Forest Service's approval of the Disney plan for Mineral King.

Mike McCloskey differed from David Brower in numerous respects. One of the most important was his dual background; he had trained as a lawyer and run for political office. This background led him to recognize the potential synergy between litigation and a political goal, in this case preserving Mineral King.[14] Youthful in appearance and mild-mannered, McCloskey was well-suited to weigh the competing considerations that argued for and against a lawsuit over Mineral King at a time when such lawsuits were rare.

To begin with, the Sierra Club occupied an awkward position. It had taken a strong stand on Mineral King, raising it as a national issue. The club had put its prestige on the line in reversing its earlier position approving a ski development in Mineral King, a reversal about which both the Forest Service and Disney regularly reminded the public. Skiers accused the club of having "double-crossed" them.[15] In their view, the club had suggested Mineral King as an alternative to a ski resort at San Gorgonio in Southern California;[16] then, after San Gorgonio was close to being protected, it reneged on what the skiers believed was its commitment to Mineral King. The charge stung. As Sierra Club president Ed Wayburn later admitted, "To some extent it was (I say advisedly was) a valid argument," a cost of the club's evolution.[17]

Over the past several years, the club's attention had primarily focused on large efforts that had been successful, such as the expansion of Redwood National Park. McCloskey recognized that the club had not "put heavy resources into the Mineral King battle" as it had in these other disputes.[18] So the question now was whether or not the club should invest in the only option left available: filing a lawsuit.

But what would a lawsuit accomplish? From the club's perspective, a lawsuit made sense only if it formed part of a larger, coordinated campaign to save Mineral King. But to be successful, that campaign would take a long time. In January 1969, Richard Nixon took office as president and brought with him two new political appointees: Walter Hickel as secretary of the interior in place of Stewart Udall, and Clifford Hardin as secretary of agriculture in place of Orville Freeman. In all likelihood, both Hickel and Hardin would strongly favor the Mineral King development. Hickel, a fascinating person who had gone to Alaska with 37 cents in his pocket and become a millionaire real estate developer, had been confirmed by the Senate only after a contentious hearing process. His statement at a press conference that he did not support "conservation for conservation's sake" had fueled the opposition.[19]

In short, the support needed for a political solution on Mineral King did not exist at this point, although the level of opposition to the ski resort reflected in the national media was a hopeful sign for the club. Still, a lawsuit could buy time to keep the issue alive when the granting of the last permits needed for the development, including the road through Sequoia National Park, appeared imminent. A lawsuit might delay the project and be "a dramatic way of keeping the pressure on."[20] It would also help establish the Sierra Club's *bona fides* in the rapidly changing world of environmental organizations. It would show that the club was dynamic and strong, even without David Brower.

A lawsuit, however, would significantly affect the club's now frayed relationship with the Forest Service, and perhaps even its relationship with the Park Service. At that time suits of this kind were rare, and defendants could easily take personal offense at them. But the club's relationship with the Forest Service had already deteriorated in recent years. In particular, the refusal of the Forest Service to even hold a hearing on Mineral King had exasperated the Sierra Club.

Moreover, the Forest Service was enamored with Walt Disney Productions as its permittee and had deferred to that company on the features of the Mineral King development. If the Forest Service had shown any inclination to compromise on the size of the ski area, the Sierra Club might have pursued an agreement. After all, the club's interest in skiing was long-standing, and its pronouncements on Mineral King sometimes stated that it did not oppose *all* development there.

But no inclination to compromise appeared; the two organizations were not communicating well. As McCloskey put it, at this point the Forest Service "did not know how to talk to us,"[21] and the Forest Service administrators undoubtedly felt the same way about the Sierra Club. They complained that the club misstated certain facts about the development,[22] and some of the complaints were accurate.

A lawsuit challenging approval of the road through Sequoia National Park would involve the National Park Service as a defendant. Here, though, the club's considerations were different. The Park Service had never shown enthusiasm for the road. While the Park Service would be a defendant in such a Sierra Club lawsuit, it was unlikely to be upset by a challenge to the road.

One other factor complicated the Sierra Club's decision about whether to litigate: the expense. Mike McCloskey knew that the club could not rely on volunteer lawyers from its ranks to undertake such litigation. If the club hired an outside lawyer and the case was appealed, as was probable, it would drain money from an organization already reeling from financial difficulties. The situation had worsened because of a 1966 decision by the Internal Revenue Service to revoke the Sierra Club's tax-exempt status on the ground that the club was engaging in lobbying.[23]

After weighing these considerations, McCloskey determined to recommend litigation. If the club was committed to saving Mineral King, it would show its resolve by a legal challenge. Moreover, the club was used to fighting battles, such as opposition to dams on the Colorado River, that had long odds of success. Finally, the Sierra Club leadership perhaps wanted to disprove David Brower's parting charge that the club would now "revert to its days as an organization of companions on the trail."[24] The Sierra Club was ready to enter the new world of environmental litigation.

Still, two hurdles remained. McCloskey needed to find a lawyer, and the lawyer had to confirm that a lawsuit had legal merit.

Environmental lawsuits were rare in 1969 but not unprecedented. After the Glen Canyon Dam was built on the Colorado River, the Sierra Club had sued in 1962 in a futile attempt to stop the filling of Lake Powell behind the dam. The club had feared that rising water could damage the picturesque Rainbow Bridge natural arch.[25] A federal court had dismissed the case.[26]

Three years later, however, a case on the East Coast dramatically illustrated the potential uses of litigation for environmental protection. The Consolidated Edison Company had proposed to build a "pump-storage" hydroelectric facility at Storm King Mountain on the Hudson River in New York. The proposal sparked a loud outcry from river users and those seeking to protect the mountain.[27] Opponents cobbled together a group of lawyers to oppose the facility's approval by the Federal Power Commission. One was David Sive of New York City, who also chaired the Sierra Club's Atlantic Chapter. Sive would become a member of the club's board of directors in 1968.

In late 1965, the United States Court of Appeals in New York City awarded a resounding victory to the opponents of the Storm King facility. The court first held that the opponents had "standing" to sue. Standing required that, to bring suit, a plaintiff must show it was injured in a way that courts would recognize. The court then found that the Federal Power Commission's decision-making was flawed in numerous ways. The commission had "ignored certain relevant factors and failed to make a thorough study of possible alternatives to the Storm King project."[28]

In San Francisco, interest in using legal tools to protect the environment had led to the formation of the Conservation Law Society, one of the first nonprofit groups in the nation organized to provide legal services solely on environmental issues. The society had close ties to the Sierra Club; Dick Leonard, a lawyer and club board member, had led its formation, and the society had offices in the same building as the club.[29] Through its general counsel and lone full-time employee, Robert Jasperson, the Conservation Law Society gave legal advice to the Sierra Club and other nonprofit groups.

McCloskey had sensed that the approval of Mineral King raised underlying legal issues, albeit ones that were inchoate at the time. The Sierra Club had formed a Legal Committee headed by Phil Berry, who would become president of the club later in 1969. A small part of the committee's work had involved Mineral King.[30]

McCloskey had also sought help from the Conservation Law Society. He asked it to research "causes of action"—the formal term for legal claims for relief—for potential use in a lawsuit against the federal government over Mineral King. McCloskey was not overly hopeful; in January 1968, he wrote John Harper that "We are looking into some of the remote possibilities of legal action, but they don't appear very promising at this time."[31] But Robert Jasperson was more positive. He personally toured Mineral King[32] and then, in April 1968, sent McCloskey a seven-page letter discussing potential legal issues.[33]

In 1969, as the final approval neared on the Mineral King project, Jasperson produced another memorandum on a potential lawsuit that he called "Sierra Club vs. Walt Disney at Mineral King."[34] A lawyer working part-time for the Conservation Law Society, Greg Archibald, wrote an initial draft of the lawsuit.

However, Jasperson's small legal shop did not possess the resources needed for intensive litigation,[35] so the Sierra Club's Legal Committee began to look for counsel. The search was unstructured; the committee members contacted people they knew to see if anyone might be interested. Don Harris, a member of the now three-person legal committee, was socially acquainted with a young lawyer named Lee Selna, and Harris reached out to him.

By the end of February, the search was over. The club agreed to hire Selna, a partner with a San Francisco firm that had offices across the street from the Sierra Club and that specialized in business litigation and transactions. As Selna said much later with a laugh, "In a well-organized selection process, I would never have been picked."[36]

Selna came from Oakland, California, and had grown up camping in the Sierra Nevadas. He was the first in his family to attend college, working his way through the University of California at Berkeley on a Navy scholarship. Selna spent three years as a Navy gunnery officer on an attack transport, where he lost part of his hearing. He then attended law school.[37]

Ironically, Selna's first position as a lawyer was with the Pacific Gas and Electric Company, a public utility in Northern California. He worked on the company's bid to site a nuclear power plant fifty miles north of San Francisco. The Sierra Club board of directors had opposed the plant, and one of the key opposition leaders was Phil Berry.[38] The utility dropped its plans for the plant in 1963.[39]

By early 1969 Selna was thirty-five years old, had been a lawyer for eight years, and had never handled a case in federal court. However, he was intrigued by the Mineral King case and unafraid of the challenge. He was calm, careful, and well-organized, and he projected a maturity beyond his years. As it turned out, he produced excellent legal work.

Once hired, Selna turned to the foundational question: Did the Sierra Club have a case?

Until now, the Sierra Club 's opposition to the Mineral King development had centered on arguments intended to sway public opinion: the project was too big, was insufficiently planned, would destroy the valley's beauty, and so on. In contrast, the legal analysis focused on the Forest Service's authority to approve the development and the

Park Service's authority to approve a road through Sequoia National Park. In other words, the question was whether or not Congress had authorized the two agencies to take their intended actions. As a result, any overlap between legal claims in a lawsuit and the political arguments against the project might well be small and coincidental. Mike McCloskey recognized as much, telling a magazine that "not all of the legal issues embody the major policy questions of greatest concern to conservationists."[40]

The federal statutes governing actions by the Forest and Park Services exhibited several distinct features. First, they were both aged and patchwork in nature. The general laws controlling both agencies had largely been enacted in the nineteenth and early twentieth centuries, and they did not map easily onto modern land use disputes. Congress had slightly rectified the situation for the Forest Service in 1964 with the passage of the Multiple Use and Sustained Yield Act, which codified the principle of "multiple use" so ingrained in the Forest Service's administrative fabric. However, the other old laws affecting actions by the Forest Service remained in force.

These laws displayed some idiosyncratic elements. In creating national parks administered by the Park Service or placing specific lands under the governance of the Forest Service, Congress often passed individual laws applying only to particular areas. Consequently, a lawyer looking for a legal hook in the Mineral King situation was, in a sense, on a hunt for buried treasure. A particular law applicable only to Sequoia National Forest or Sequoia National Park—and perhaps long overlooked—might be highly relevant.

Overall, though, the Sierra Club's legal analysis faced one formidable barrier: federal law generally invested public agencies, particularly the Forest Service, with large discretion in making decisions concerning public lands. The service's well-known slogan for the national forests, "Land of Many Uses," reflected this range of choices.[41] On those few occasions where individuals, usually business interests, had sued challenging agency decisions involving public lands, the courts had largely deferred to the agencies' expertise in making those decisions. For example, in one important 1915 case, President

William Howard Taft had withdrawn land from oil and gas development despite a lack of express statutory authority to do so. The Supreme Court upheld his decision.[42]

In short, a plaintiff faced an uphill battle challenging the discretion exercised by the Forest Service and the Park Service in making particular decisions. The choice to put a ski area in Mineral King, as opposed to preserving the valley for camping or other low-intensity uses, seemed a paradigmatic example of the type of discretionary decision that courts tended to uphold.

One countervailing factor was at work. Confident of its discretion in deciding land uses, the Forest Service had paid little attention to the specific laws governing its decisions. The service assumed that whatever choices it made fell within its broad discretion. In the case of Mineral King, this inattention prevailed even after the project had generated heated controversy; the Forest Service had rarely consulted its legal staff in the approval process. Only after the Sierra Club announced in 1969 that it intended to sue did Slim Davis seek legal advice on issues that might arise.[43]

The facts of the Mineral King dispute did point to a couple of legal issues that the Sierra Club would want to examine and that might avoid a direct and likely unsuccessful challenge to the agency's exercise of discretion. The first centered on the Mineral King road. It would cross Sequoia National Park, but its primary and perhaps only purpose was to serve a development on Forest Service lands that lay outside the park. Did the Park Service possess authority to approve a road through a national park for that purpose?

In 1916, Congress had passed the law that established the National Park Service, authorizing it to "regulate the use of" national parks. In doing so, the agency was to use "means and measures" that "conformed to the fundamental purpose" of those parks. Congress then defined that purpose: "to conserve the scenery and the natural and historic objects and the wildlife therein," and to use such means "as will leave them unimpaired for the enjoyment of future generations."[44] Even earlier, Congress had created Sequoia National Park via an 1890 law containing similar provisions. It mandated the secretary of the interior to make regulations for "preservation from injury of all timber, mineral deposits, natural curiosities or wonders within said park, and their retention in their natural condition."[45]

Did the pending approval of a road through Sequoia National Park conflict with these purposes? The Sierra Club might argue that, while a road could be authorized to access places within the park—that is, a road to help enjoy the park's "natural curiosities or wonders"[46]—the road to Mineral King did not serve that purpose. Still, this argument could prevail only if the new road brought no benefit, or perhaps only minimal benefit, to Sequoia National Park.

One could envision a counterargument that at least some benefit existed. For example, a Park Service employee had earlier opined that the new road might lead to greater use of the park. Another had suggested the opposite, that it would actually reduce park use, presumably because visitors might choose to see Mineral King rather than journey into the park. Either way, the road arguably would serve a park-related purpose.

Electric transmission lines through Sequoia National Park also would be needed to serve the Mineral King development. Could the Park Service approve transmission lines across the park—lines that would be highly visible—to carry electricity used outside the park? Here, buried in the set of archaic statutes governing Sequoia National Park, the Sierra Club lawyers found a surprising provision. Congress had passed a statute specifically addressing the authority to allow transmission lines through Sequoia National Park. The statute stated that the Park Service and the secretary of the interior could not grant a permit for "the transmission of power" within Sequoia National Park without specific authority of Congress.[47]

On its face, this statute posed a serious problem for the Forest Service's project. It presented one of the few legal issues previously considered by the service's lawyers, who had issued a confusing one-page opinion and suggested that the service inquire into how the Department of the Interior interpreted the statute.[48] Ultimately, the National Park Service lawyers had determined that a transmission line could be authorized, but their reasoning was murky.[49] The issue was real.

The effect of the ski development on the game refuge in the Mineral King Valley also presented an area of inquiry. When Congress created Sequoia National Park but excluded Mineral King, Congress had established a game refuge in the valley. Intuitively, one might think that constructing a large ski resort, with hordes of visitors per year, could not be consistent with the use of that same area as a game "refuge." The Forest Service, however, had never seriously analyzed the issue. In a memorandum, Forest Supervisor M. R. "Jim" James dismissed it on the entirely unconvincing ground that the use of sixty cabins in the area "has already accustomed the resident animals to living in close proximity to humans."[50]

However, Jasperson and Selna had to consider that, in designating the area as a game refuge, Congress had rejected placing Mineral King in Sequoia National Park. By doing so, it necessarily envisioned at least some nonpark uses of Mineral King, and the area had previously been used both for camping and as a site for cabins. The legal question would become: at what point do other uses of the valley become "too much" so that they are incompatible with the designation as a game refuge? A judge would likely find that factual line hard to draw. Litigating it would require considerable "expert testimony," that is, testimony from individuals with professional credentials and expertise about how the development would affect animals using the valley.

In burrowing through the old laws that governed Sequoia National Forest, Jasperson and his compatriots found yet another provision that could affect the future of Mineral King. A law called the Reorganization Act of 1939 might be interpreted to transfer jurisdiction over administration of the Sequoia National Game Refuge from the secretary of agriculture to the secretary of the interior.[51] If so, the secretary of the interior would have to approve the Disney development's impact on the game refuge. Here, though, a judge was likely to be skeptical. The secretary of the interior had never asserted jurisdiction over the game refuge, and the Forest Service certainly did not think that its authority over the refuge lands had been altered.[52]

Another aspect of the Disney permit raised a more central issue. The Forest Service possessed the authority to grant permits for lands, such as Mineral King, that it managed. It could grant a "term" permit allowing "hotels, resorts, and any other structures or facilities necessary or desirable for recreation, public convenience, or safety." The same law, however, also limited this authority. The Forest Service could allow such use and occupancy of lands "not exceeding eighty acres and for periods not exceeding thirty years."[53] It was this provision that concerned Disney's lawyer just before approval of the Disney plan.

The Forest Service was well aware of this acreage limitation on these "term" permits, for a large ski resort would occupy far more than eighty acres. In the past, the service had circumvented this limitation by granting both a term permit and what was known as an annual permit. This latter type of permit was yearly in duration but renewable each year. Thus, under the Forest Service's "dual permit" configuration for the Disney development at Mineral King, the main village complex would receive the thirty-year term permit, while the ski lifts and other facilities that spread out from the valley floor would get annual permits.

While Disney would have to be satisfied with this permit arrangement, its legality appeared quite different from the Sierra Club's perspective. Disney would be building one large, unified development at Mineral King. The village—the subject of the thirty-year term permit—made no sense without the ski facilities authorized by the yearly, revocable permits. Given this symbiotic relationship, the Sierra Club could charge that the annual revocable permits were a subterfuge designed to avoid the eighty-acre limitation imposed by Congress. The Forest Service, the club could claim, was in fact violating the explicit acreage limitation imposed by Congress on long-term permits. The club could couple that claim with a related argument: the annual permits were not in reality revocable, given the large Disney investment in the ski area.

In response, the Forest Service would argue that, as long as the area of the development over eighty acres was limited to yearly, revocable permits, it had complied with the letter of the law. That law imposed no limitation on how yearly permits might relate to the thirty-year term permits, and the interplay between the two types of permits fell within the Forest Service's discretion to manage the public lands. Additionally, a court could not presume that the Forest Service would always renew the yearly permits, a fact which the Sierra Club's argument had to assume.

Moreover, the agency would ferociously oppose this claim, for it had used the same dual permit mechanism to approve numerous other ski resorts on Forest Service lands. In effect, the Sierra Club would be arguing that all permits granted under this arrangement—including for resorts such as Vail, Colorado—had violated federal law. The Forest Service could be counted on to bring the consequences of this argument to a court's attention.

Finally, there was the question of whether federal law required the Forest Service or the Park Service to hold a public hearing prior to approving the development. Such a claim was attractive to the Sierra Club. A favorable ruling would not require the court to second-guess the land use decisions of the Forest Service or the Park Service, and thus would avoid challenging the agencies' exercise of discretion. The judge would simply hold that the law demanded a certain process before the agencies could act.

The Sierra Club lawyers, however, found little to support this argument. Stewart Udall had belatedly adopted informal procedures that would have required a hearing on the configuration of roads through national parks,[54] but Secretary Walter Hickel had revoked them.[55] The club would have to argue that Hickel's revocation was invalid, a difficult argument.

Hovering over the potential lawsuit, however, was a separate, critically important issue that could prevent a court from considering any Sierra Club claim. That issue was the question of the Sierra Club's legal standing to bring the case.

While federal courts in the United States were established to decide cases, they gradually recognized the need for some limits on their power, as an unelected branch of government, to adjudicate *all* disputes brought to them. The courts determined that they would not decide a case simply because a plaintiff wanted a legal issue resolved. Instead, to bring a case, a plaintiff would have to show a legally sufficient interest in the dispute, that is, that the plaintiff had "standing" to sue. The law at this time was vague on whether the doctrine of standing originated in the Constitution or was court-made. It presented, however, a real barrier to some plaintiffs.

Traditionally, economic injury from the defendant's disputed actions would afford the plaintiff standing to sue and have the court decide the dispute. However, difficulties with standing arose when a plaintiff challenged an action taken by a public agency on noneconomic grounds. This was the situation often posed by the emerging field of environmental law.

The courts in the past had emphasized that a plaintiff must show, as the Supreme Court put it in an early twentieth-century case, that he or she "has sustained or is immediately in danger of sustaining some direct injury." The injury must be individual and specific. It was not enough, warned the court, that the plaintiff "suffers in some indefinite way in common with people generally."[56] This limitation led lawyers to question whether the Sierra Club had standing to bring challenges like the one contemplated for Mineral King. Not only was the club's injury environmental, not economic, but that injury might be suffered "in common with people generally."

However, as environmental issues came to the forefront in the late 1960s, lawyers began exploring new arguments about standing law to avoid these constraints. After all, without standing in environmental cases, government agencies could violate the law with impunity, as no plaintiff could challenge them. In the litigation over Storm King Mountain in New York, in which environmental groups challenged the Federal Power Commission's approval of a storage facility that would provide electricity, the plaintiffs successfully put forth one such argument. In that case the commission had held a lengthy hearing before an administrative law judge before issuing a license for the plant. The Federal Power Act established these procedures, and the environmental plaintiffs had participated in the administrative hearing. When the plaintiffs sued, the commission attacked their standing.

In *Scenic Hudson Preservation Conference v. Federal Power Commission*, the court of appeals rejected that attack. A law like the Federal

Power Act, ruled the court, "may create new interests or rights and thus give standing to one who would otherwise be barred." It also emphasized that a plaintiff need not have a "personal economic interest" to sue.[57] After *Scenic Hudson*, other courts began to recognize the standing of plaintiffs to sue when they had participated in similar administrative proceedings.

This emerging line of authority, however, might not help the Sierra Club with Mineral King. Unlike in *Scenic Hudson*, the statutes governing the Forest Service did not establish administrative procedures allowing protesting parties to participate before the agency. Indeed, no law even required the Forest Service to hold a public hearing before approving the Mineral King proposal. Thus, the Sierra Club needed an alternative theory of standing.

One possibility was to argue that the courts should broaden their conception of injury to include a new kind of injury: damage to individuals' ability to use and enjoy Mineral King. Members of the Sierra Club could readily show such injury, as they used Mineral King for hiking and pack trips. Another, broader theory would emphasize the Sierra Club's history of long-standing interest in the government's stewardship of the Mineral King area and argue that this interest alone provided the club with a sufficient stake to support standing. This argument played to the club's strength, which was its long track record of concern over Sequoia National Park. It also avoided having to show particularized injury through past use of Mineral King. Lee Selna worried that, if a showing of past use was required, a court could view the club as suing for its own personal, selfish reasons, and thus be less inclined to recognize the club's standing.[58]

This same concern led to rejection of another, easier "fix" to the standing problem that Jasperson had suggested: include as plaintiffs individuals with cabins in Mineral King on lands leased from the Forest Service.[59] They could argue that the Disney proposal would economically harm them, as the Forest Service planned to take away their rights to use the land there.

Whatever argument the club chose, the federal government would vigorously challenge its legal standing. The Forest Service well understood the consequences if groups like the Sierra Club had standing to challenge service decisions. Given the rapidly growing interest in environmental issues, the Forest Service would find itself in front of judges defending challenges to many of its decisions. For an agency convinced of its expertise in making those decisions, that prospect was unacceptable.

Lee Selna would choose what theory to follow in arguing the Sierra Club's standing.[60] While a lawyer, Mike McCloskey had no background in litigation; he would largely defer to Selna's recommendations.[61] This decision, however, was just one of many in the mix. While some would later claim that the Sierra Club sued over Mineral King as a "test" case to establish standing in the courts, that claim was inaccurate.[62] The club was trying to stop the development, and establishing standing was just one of the hurdles it faced.

Selna also had to decide which defendants to name in the lawsuit and where to bring the case. Most of these choices, however, were not difficult. He would sue the secretary of agriculture, the Forest Service, and the superintendent of Sequoia National Forest, who had formally approved the Disney plan. Other defendants would be the secretary of the interior, the National Park Service, and the service's regional director, who were soon to approve the road through Sequoia National Park. That left only one important question: Should the Sierra Club sue Walt Disney Productions?

Disney seemed a logical defendant, for it was the company's development that would cause any actual environmental injury. The original draft of the Sierra Club "complaint," the legal document that would initiate the suit, handwritten by Greg Archibald in Jasperson's office, listed "Walt Disney at Mineral King" as the lead defendant.[63] However, naming Disney had two large downsides.

First, much of the public revered the name of Walt Disney. It might well seem quasi-sacrilegious to make Disney a defendant in a case like this one. As one Sierra Club member put it, "To sue Disney . . . would be like suing motherhood, the Flag, and the Boy Scouts all at once."[64] Moreover, as one of the associate lawyers working with Selna would later recollect, Disney really "didn't do anything wrong";[65] it had "merely acted in response to a bid from the Forest Service."[66]

Second, Walt Disney Productions was a large corporation with formidable resources. It would hire skilled legal talent to defend the case alongside the government lawyers representing the agency defendants. Suing Disney might well make the case harder to win and much more expensive. Indeed, recognizing the suit's potential cost, Selna's firm had agreed to charge the Sierra Club a significantly reduced rate for its work,[67] and the club had issued a call for donations to support the litigation.[68] No one, however, could anticipate the full cost, as the case would sail into uncharted legal waters.

So Selna decided to leave Disney out of the case. He reasoned that the case centered around use of public land, and thus the public agencies in charge of that land were appropriately held legally accountable. But Selna also respected the Disney resources. As he put it, "I was just as happy not to have to be fighting that . . . Goliath with my slingshot."[69] As Mike McCloskey explained to the *Wall Street Journal* about why Disney was left out, "We do think Disney is planning something inappropriate, but we think it's the government's responsibility to make it appropriate."[70] Of course, even if it was not named, Disney could choose to intervene in the case. But that would be Disney's choice, not the Sierra Club's.

Another question was where to file the suit. The options were the federal courts in Fresno, San Francisco, and Washington, DC. Litigating in the nation's capital presented formidable logistical issues, since both Selna's and the club's headquarters were in San Francisco. Fresno was located closest to Mineral King and to Porterville, where many of the relevant documents were housed in the Forest Service office. But judges in Fresno were considered more conservative than those in San Francisco, and the club feared they might be swayed by the economic benefits that the Disney project would bring to the San Joaquin Valley. Consequently, San Francisco was the easy choice for the lawsuit's venue.

While the Sierra Club formulated its case, public controversy over the Disney plan continued to boil. In April 1969, the dispute was the subject of a report on the CBS Evening News. The reporter recognized the valley's beauty, opening his report by declaring, "There isn't much wild country left quite as spectacular as this valley. . . ." During the report Mike McCloskey accused the Disney development of putting in features—"swimming pools and theatres, uh, bowling, whatever . . . that really don't serve any purpose but as amusement which can easily be put in Los Angeles or some other place far away from the mountains." In response, the Forest Service spokesman emphasized that "We have pledged ourselves not to do anything even remotely resembling Disneyland. There'll be no fantasies, no garish signs. The activities up here will be those that you find in other mountain areas. There'll be horseback riding, swimming, perhaps some things like square dancing in the evening . . . rather than discotheque type dancing."[71]

The chief of the Forest Service, Ed Cliff, found it necessary to justify the agency's actions on Mineral King to the new secretary of agriculture, Clifford Hardin, because the development "has attracted some national attention." Cliff assured Hardin of his personal conviction that "we will have a superlatively developed outdoor recreation opportunity."[72]

The growing controversy alarmed Disney. The company did not understand the nature of the heated opposition that it faced. At a UCLA forum, students had depicted Mickey Mouse as cutting down sequoia redwood trees. In May, Bob Hicks described the company as "puzzled" by the uproar and said it was "trying to counter this inaccurate publicity by getting factual information to the public."[73]

Donn Tatum, now president of Walt Disney Productions, appeared on local television in Los Angeles to rebut an editorial objecting to the use of state highway funds for the Mineral King road.[74] The com pany also released a public statement defending its development "[i]n view of the recent public discussion regarding this project," and it sent the statement to all its employees.[75] Disney found itself on the defensive, with Bob Hicks unhappily complaining that "I don't feel we have to apologize for Disneyland."[76] A San Joaquin Valley newspaper reported Hicks's lament that "his company's image is being tarnished by objections being raised against Mineral King."[77]

The company also worried about the impending lawsuit. At a Sierra Club press conference announcing the suit, Mike McCloskey disclosed that Roy Disney had contacted the club several weeks earlier, and Bob Hicks had come to the Sierra Club offices. When asked what Disney's purpose was, McCloskey chuckled: "They wondered whether we were going to sue them."[78]

The Forest Service felt the pressure. When the service's Pete Wyckoff wrote to Disney's Bob Hicks suggesting changes to certain lifts and other features of the plan, he expressed concern about locating skiing facilities directly across from the development's reception area. Wyckoff told Hicks that "we cannot afford to disfigure the landscape with heavy timber cutting and large cut and fill sections" immediately adjacent to the reception center, "where all visitors will get their first impression of Mineral King."[79]

Even Slim Davis, of all people, had a few second thoughts about the Forest Service approval. He admitted to the supervisor of Sequoia National Forest that "from a technical standpoint we are a little late with impact surveys for Mineral King." A survey, he said, "should have been completed prior to the prospectus, and from this we should have come to a decision as to whether the prospectus should be issued."[80]

But second thoughts did not matter. With the Park Service seemingly poised to issue the road permit to the State of California, the Sierra Club filed its lawsuit on June 6, 1969.[81] The suit received national attention in the press.[82]

7: A Shocking Injunction

After filing the lawsuit, Lee Selna awaited the answer to an important question: What judge would hear the case? It was initially assigned to Judge Alfonso Zirpoli, who was no stranger to controversy. A year later, President Nixon would castigate him as "the worst judge on the Federal bench" because of a decision he handed down broadening the rights of conscientious objectors to the Vietnam War.[1] But Zirpoli declined the Mineral King case without explanation, and it was transferred to a second judge, William Sweigert.

Although a Democrat, Bill Sweigert at a young age had become a protégé of Earl Warren, a Republican who was now the chief justice of the United States Supreme Court. When Warren had become California's attorney general, he appointed Sweigert as his assistant, and Sweigert followed Warren to Sacramento when Warren was elected governor. Warren later appointed Sweigert to two positions in the state trial courts and then convinced President Dwight D. Eisenhower to make him a United States district judge.

In 1959, Sweigert assumed the federal bench in San Francisco, a court whose docket was filled with well-publicized cases.[2] For example, at the time the Mineral King complaint was filed, Sweigert was handling a criminal prosecution brought by the government against August Owsley Stanley III. Widely known as "Bear," Owsley had gained fame for supplying psychedelic drugs to the Grateful Dead.[3]

Raised by progressive parents, Sweigert had written a memorandum that defended the New Deal and influenced Warren's thinking as governor. He argued that government must act "whenever the projects of the smart and the swift so selfishly develop in size or purpose as to endanger the welfare of the community as a whole."[4] As a judge, he was an independent thinker; he would later decide that plaintiffs could challenge the constitutionality of combat actions in Cambodia on the grounds that Congress had not passed a declaration of war. The decision caused a national furor and was overturned by an appellate court in 1972.[5] Two years later, he would throw out the National Football League's rule that severely restricted player free agency.[6]

From the Sierra Club perspective, Sweigert's assignment to the case appeared favorable. Sweigert would not instinctively side with the government.

Along with initiating the case, Selna filed a motion for a preliminary injunction that would bar the Forest Service from issuing any permit to Disney and the National Park Service from approving the road through Sequoia National Park. The motion was set for hearing on June 30, a little over three weeks later. The federal defendants had to move quickly to oppose the injunction.

The defense was assigned to Paul Locke in the San Francisco office of the United States Attorney, who handled land and natural resource matters. But some preliminary work had taken place earlier just before the Sierra Club announced it would sue. In February, Slim Davis had sent a memorandum to the Forest Service's regional attorney noting that "there appear to be three issues which the Sierra Club will wish to argue." They concerned the Park Service's authority to approve a powerline through Sequoia National Park serving the Disney development, the Forest Service's authority to combine term and annual revocable permits for that development, and the legality of building the development in the Sequoia National Game Refuge.[7]

Responding to the game refuge claim was relatively simple. The club's argument would have to be factual: the large development would so overwhelm the area that a game refuge could no longer practically exist. The Forest Service response would rely on two provisions. First, the statute creating the refuge stated that its purpose was "to protect from trespass the public lands . . . and the game animals which may be thereon."[8] The Disney development, the government would argue, would not violate the statute because Disney would not be a trespasser.

Another provision of that statute appeared even more helpful to the Forest Service. It stated that the lands in the game refuge "shall continue to be parts of the Sequoia National Forest and nothing . . . shall prevent the Secretary of Agriculture from permitting other uses of said lands," as long as they were consistent with the purposes for which the refuge had been established.[9] In establishing the game refuge, the Forest Service could argue, Congress had foreseen "other" uses—such as a large ski resort—that were consistent with the purpose of the game refuge. The Forest Service would ask the court to find a ski area consistent with a game refuge.

The Forest Service would invoke much the same idea in responding to the dual permit issue. The Mineral King development as a whole would greatly exceed the eighty-acre statutory limitation on thirty-year term permits. Davis estimated that the term permit would cover sixty-one acres including the village area and lifts, while the revocable annual permits would encompass an additional 256 acres. The latter would include the ski trails, parking areas, and service roads.

The Forest Service would be "accused of exceeding its authority if both a Term and Annual Permit are issued to one permittee to cover improvements related to one use."[10] The service would respond that it unquestionably possessed authority to issue revocable annual permits. The court, the service would argue, had no legal basis for deciding that the service would *always* renew those annual permits, and thus that the annual revocable permits were effectively term permits exceeding the eighty-acre maximum.

Furthermore, as the service's in-house lawyer emphasized, the power to issue revocable annual permits was couched in broad language. In the past, the secretary of war had issued these permits for construction of railroad tracks, the same type of long-term investment as a ski area, and those permits had been routinely renewed.

Congress was aware of this use of revocable annual permits and, the argument would go, had impliedly acquiesced in that use by never interfering with it.[11]

Finally, the United States attorney general had issued an opinion in 1928 addressing the fact that annual permits were authorizing "substantial improvements" unlikely to be revoked. The opinion concluded that it was simply "a matter of departmental policy" whether to issue such a permit.[12] The attorney general's opinion would not bind the court, but the long-standing nature of the practice might cause the court to pause before invalidating the dual permit system.

As to the road through Sequoia National Park, the question would be whether or not it served a park "purpose." The Park Service informed its lawyers that the proposed permit—still not actually issued—had two helpful provisions. It called for the construction of overlooks for viewing scenery in the park, and it required suitable access and connections to existing roads within the park. Indeed, the road could even "provide the potential for new access to a section of the park that was previously inaccessible."[13]

These provisions might supply the park purpose needed to approve a road through Sequoia National Park. Moreover, the Park Service had approved similar roads through other national parks; thus, like the dual permit system, the park purpose issue was freighted with historical precedents.[14] Still, these two benefits to Sequoia National Park were plainly tangential to the road's principal purpose.

The strongest Sierra Club claim was the assertion that federal law flatly prohibited the approval of a power transmission line through Sequoia National Park. Here, the federal defendants would have to argue that the court must interpret the law more narrowly than the language on its face would suggest. The statute's purpose, they would argue, was only to prohibit transmission lines from hydroelectric facilities, not to prohibit *all* transmission lines.[15]

The other issues that the Sierra Club might raise seemed weaker. While the club claimed a right to hearings on the Mineral King project and on the road, it could point to no statute or agency rule requiring them. Finally, the government saw no merit in the claim that the Department of the Interior, not the Department of Agriculture, had jurisdiction over the game refuge. An earlier internal governmental memorandum had explained that the transfer of power over the refuge to Interior related only to minor functions, not to management of the game refuge.[16]

The Sierra Club's lawsuit was the most publicized environmental case since the 1965 litigation over Storm King, but it was not the only such case. Challenges were gradually popping up nationwide. Federal officials worried that judicial decisions would constrain their discretion in deciding land uses or, at a minimum, litigation would subject projects to lengthy delays.

Accordingly, whether the Sierra Club possessed standing to sue greatly concerned the government defendants. They would vigorously argue that groups like the club did not have the requisite legal injury to bring these types of suits. Establishing a narrow standing rule would stifle what federal managers viewed as a dangerous threat to their administration of the public lands.

As for Disney, it had to decide on its response to the lawsuit. The decision had two aspects. On a legal level, did the company want to intervene in the case to protect its interests? More generally, how would it respond publicly to the Sierra Club's action, which attacked the Disney project? Disney was an entertainment company that now found itself appearing in the press at the center of an acrimonious dispute. It had never faced public controversy of this nature, much less charges that its actions were antienvironmental.

After the lawsuit was filed, Disney had its lawyers research the legal issues posed by the Sierra Club's complaint.[17] Disney was unafraid to litigate. However, broader considerations were at work.

For one, Roy Disney had never felt completely comfortable with the Mineral King project. As was often the case with internal Disney deliberations, he had played devil's advocate and questioned the project. However, one comment by Roy stuck in the mind of Bob Hicks: "We're in the movie industry and the amusement park business. We're not in the ski business." Hicks perceived Roy Disney as having opposed the project.[18] After his brother Walt passed away,

Roy "was very nervous about the project because he was getting increasing mail and comments criticizing Disney for the project, and he didn't like that."[19]

Also affecting the choice was the fact that the opposing litigant was the Sierra Club. Like it or not, the club retained its status as an admired conservation group with a lineage stretching back to John Muir. If Disney had a positive image, so did the Sierra Club. Indeed, a *Newsweek* article on the lawsuit framed the dispute as a question of "Mom v. Apple Pie" and suggested that such a tussle was "plainly anybody's ball game."[20] If it intervened in the case, Disney and the Sierra Club would be firing legal allegations directly at each other. This type of interplay did not appeal to the company.

Nor did the federal government urge Disney to enter the lawsuit. Attorneys with the Justice Department in Washington, DC, discussed the issue, and a draft document suggested that "it would be advisable to have Walt Disney Productions, Inc., in the case as a defendant." This draft even raised the possibility that the government could ask the court to order Disney into the case involuntarily. But the idea quickly died.[21]

In the end, Disney opted not to intervene in the litigation. Best not to play that game, concluded the Disney management, even if it meant ceding all direct control over the case. It wanted distance from the fight.

Even with this choice, however, Disney still had to fashion a public response to the lawsuit. It increasingly faced charges of planning a "Disneyland" in the mountains, an allegation that was not literally accurate but that sounded plausible given the size of the development and Disney's reputation as an entertainment company.

Opponents were including Disney cartoon characters in their attacks. The Sierra Club's Mineral King Task Force advertised its second annual "hike-in" with a drawing of Mickey Mouse looming above Mineral King with an ax,[22] while a newspaper commentator remarked that "[t]here is something about the idea of Mickey Mouse in the Sierras that does not appeal to me."[23] A *Los Angeles Times* article told the public: "The name calling has been vicious and pickets have appeared outside the [Disney] Burbank studio during a stockholders' meeting and have threatened to lie in front of bulldozers at Mineral King."[24] A Bakersfield, California, newspaper—an ardent supporter of the project—jumped in to defend Disney: "[W]e will not accept the 'exploiter concept' currently being placed on Walt Disney Enterprises as seeking to exploit California's precious natural resources."[25] Another newspaper decried the idea of the company being "placed in the spot of a villain."[26]

For a company fixated on its public image and justifiably proud of Walt Disney's efforts to document nature in his thirteen "True-Life Adventures," the onslaught was both puzzling and deeply offensive. In late August, Ansel Adams wrote Phil Berry, the president of the Sierra Club, recounting a conversation with a friend "who is close to the Disney family and group." The friend had told Adams, "The Disney people are completely bewildered by the attack on the Mineral King project. They consider themselves top conservationists."[27]

At this point, the company rejected abandoning the project and thus ending the controversy. But it did consider an effort to compromise that might help its image. In a lengthy internal memorandum, Bob Hicks floated the idea that the company should move the parking structure further away from Mineral King Valley in the hope that it "might appease some of the critics."[28] However, the idea initially encountered some internal resistance.[29] While Hicks persevered,[30] raising the matter with the state highway engineers and the Forest Service, in the end he put it aside for the moment.

On June 30, 1969, Judge Sweigert held oral argument on the Sierra Club's motion for a preliminary injunction. The motion sought a court order that would prohibit the Forest Service and the Park Service from issuing permits for the Mineral King development and for the road until a trial could take place on the club's case. The judge had before him briefs from both parties.

Lee Selna argued first for two hours and, in response to Sweigert's request, gave a "detailed explanation of the club charges." The judge noted that the federal agencies involved are "running these things," a comment that seemed to suggest he might defer to them.[31] At the end of the day, Sweigert adjourned the case until 2 p.m. the following afternoon, when he heard from Paul Locke on behalf of the government defendants.

The parties' arguments centered on the legal requirements for a preliminary injunction. The Sierra Club had to show a "likelihood of prevailing on the merits of its case," in other words, that it was more likely than not that the club would win the case at trial. The club also had to show that "irreparable injury" would occur in the period before its case would come to trial: that the defendant's actions would cause harm that could not be fixed later.

On the "likelihood" issue, Lee Selna tried to bolster his challenge to the dual permit system. He stressed the combined $60 million investment of Disney and the state in the road and ski development.[32] He argued that, given this large amount, the yearly permits will "automatically be renewed."[33] He was asking the court to look at what would realistically occur with such a large investment. A Forest Service refusal to renew was extremely unlikely.

Paul Locke had made an important tactical choice in formulating the government's opposition argument. He decided to emphasize that no irreparable injury was likely to occur in the near future, and thus that the court had no reason to intervene now with an injunction. He argued that no construction for the road was planned before July 1, 1970—a year later. So in the government's view, an injunction would only delay planning and escalate construction costs.[34] Locke also contested Selna's charge that the development would be inconsistent with the game refuge, insisting that it "cannot be taken for granted" that persons using the resort will be detrimental to game in the area.[35] In sum, he argued that the Sierra Club had failed to show "an imminent and strong threat of irreparable harm to the forest or to the park."[36]

Selna countered by saying that "[w]e have information that the [road] permit would be issued at any time."[37] Once the National Park Service approved the road, Disney would "automatically" get a permit[38] because, under the conditions of the 1965 award to Disney, the last step needed before issuing the ski development permit was the road approval. As he put it, after the road permit was granted, "everything else will flow automatically."[39] To him, the irreparable injury was imminent.

At the end of the second day, Judge Sweigert took the case "under submission," announcing that it would be several weeks before he ruled. He allowed the Sierra Club to file a brief on why it had standing to sue.[40]

Paul Locke's decision to emphasize the lack of irreparable injury had one immediate effect. Fearing that granting any permits before the judge ruled might supply the injury that Locke had argued was missing, a Justice Department lawyer in Washington, DC, Thomas McKevitt, requested that the Department of the Interior issue no permits for the road before the judge ruled.[41] At least in this interim period, the Sierra Club's suit had effectively blocked the road permit. The club, though, knew nothing of this consequence, since it was not publicly announced.

On July 24, 1969, Judge Sweigert issued his Memorandum of Decision. He had written it without aid from his law clerks, an indication that he viewed the case as important.[42] He granted the preliminary injunction to stop the Mineral King development until a trial was held.

Sweigert began by briefly summarizing the development at Mineral King, terming it a "private hotel-resort, winter-summer complex."[43] He then launched into a discussion of the legal issues presented by the Sierra Club, starting with the Forest Service's use of the dual permit system. Sweigert termed it "the device" of using two kinds of permits, a choice of words that prefigured his thinking.

He found that the statutory language authorizing permits decisively favored the Sierra Club's position. While the statute allowed a thirty-year term permit "not exceeding 80 acres,"[44] it also set forth specific uses for that acreage, including hotels and resorts. The statute's legislative history, he thought, indicated that Congress intended the eighty-acre limit to include all structures and facilities related to the use; for example, the acreage was to provide "'elbow room' for ski lifts and other related service facilities." Given this purpose, the question was "whether this dual permit device is intended to circumvent the clear eighty acre limitation . . . and thereby accomplish what would be in effect a violation of the section."[45]

Sweigert found it "questionable" that the annual permits were actually revocable "at will."[46] Then he moved to the heart of the matter and largely accepted Lee Selna's argument that the dual permit system circumvented the eighty-acre limitation. The uses granted by the two permits "admittedly relate to a single, unified project and are obviously interlocked and interrelated." He continued:

> It is inconceivable that [the Department of] Agriculture would, or could under the terms of the "revocable" permit and the circumstances of its issuance, suddenly and "at will" require the Developer to remove ski lifts, towers, refuse and sewage disposal, parking areas and roads covered by that permit and thus effectively destroy the 35 million dollar investment made by the Developer under his 30 year-80 acre term permit.[47]

Thus, he concluded, the dual permits "may involve" a legal violation. A contrary conclusion would have to assume that, in enacting the acreage limitation, Congress "contemplated that it be circumvented, even nullified, by the device of coupling two different kinds of permits for a single, unified, private hotel-resort development." Certainly, reasoned Sweigert, Congress "could not have been so naïve as to think that 'revocable' permits, issued under such circumstances, would *really* be revocable."[48]

Next came the legality of a permit for the road through Sequoia National Park. Sweigert recognized that the National Park Service had explicit statutory authority to build roads in the national parks and that "the wide discretion of Interior in that respect should not ordinarily be interfered with." However, he found that the highway was not designed and intended as an adjunct to the park; rather, it was a "connecting link" to convey patrons into Mineral King. Here, Sweigert's conclusion was more tentative: "the question arises" whether the highway is within Interior's power.[49]

The transmission line through the park was next.[50] The statute here was specific and applied only to Sequoia National Park: no permit for transmission lines "shall be granted or made without specific authority of Congress."[51] The secretary of the interior interpreted this statute as applying only to the development of hydroelectric dams, but the statute on its face was not so limited. Thus, Sweigert concluded, there "arises the further question" of the secretary's authority to permit the transmission line.[52]

Finally, the opinion addressed the lack of public hearings. He dismissed the 1953 "hearing" organized by the Chamber of Commerce, and his reasoning was short and to the point: there was no record of any hearing called by the Forest Service or Interior. Sweigert also found a "further question" about the validity of Interior's revocation of Stewart Udall's eleventh-hour rule that had required a hearing on roads through a park.[53]

In sum, Sweigert reached no definitive conclusions about the Sierra Club's legal claims. But he found them serious, and his discussion of the dual permit "device" all but decided that it was illegal.

The federal defendants' objection to the Sierra Club's standing was quickly batted down.[54] Paragraph 3 of the complaint alleged that the club "by its activities and conduct has exhibited a special interest in the conservation and the sound maintenance of the national parks, game refuges and forests of the country, regularly serving as a responsible representative of persons similarly interested." The club's interests, continued the paragraph, "would be vitally affected by the acts hereinafter described and would be aggrieved by those acts."[55] These allegations were sufficient to support standing, thought Sweigert.

Lastly, the opinion turned to whether or not there was sufficient injury to justify an injunction. Here, Sweigert focused on the effect of the Department of the Interior's grant of a permit for the road. The defendants had stressed that, even if the Park Service granted the permit, the State of California would not even take bids until May 1970, and no construction would begin until July—a year later. In reasoning less convincing than the rest of the opinion, Sweigert found that the state "will be in a position to control the time within which highway construction contracts will be let," and the Sierra

Club "should not be left to 'watchful waiting' upon the State."[56] Therefore, he found sufficient irreparable injury.

Other aspects of the opinion were noteworthy. First, Judge Sweigert addressed how much deference the judge would give to the government's discretion. He expressly recognized that the scope of judicial review over decisions by federal agencies on public lands "is a particularly narrow one."[57] An emphasis on that theme could easily lead a court to interpret generously the discretion that Congress had conferred on the Departments of Agriculture and Interior, and thus uphold their actions. Instead, the opinion had focused on the actual language of the statutes and the congressional intent underlying those statutes.

Second, he dismissed the Forest Service's suggestion that accepting the Sierra Club's challenge to the dual permit system would jeopardize other ski resorts, finding that argument "beside the point."[58] It was not clear, though, *why* it was beside the point. Third, the opinion never mentioned the possibility that a large resort development could violate the valley's status as a game refuge, likely because the Sierra Club had downplayed that issue in its argument.

Last, Judge Sweigert took note of the national debate over the need for environmental protection. He emphasized that the court "is not concerned with the controversy between so-called progressives and so-called conservationists." Instead, the question was whether or not action by administrative agencies "even when taken in the name of progress, conforms to the letter and intent of the law as laid down by Congress."[59]

While Selna had prevailed on the injunction issue, the battle was not yet over. A preliminary injunction would only provide interim relief before trial. If a preliminary injunction was granted to a plaintiff but the defendant ultimately prevailed at a later trial, the injunction's operation during the intervening period before trial could financially harm that defendant. Accordingly, a trial court could order a plaintiff to file a bond that would cover a defendant's potential losses while the preliminary injunction was in effect. In a Colorado case, the Sierra Club had recently been required to file such a bond in the amount of $7,500.

The Sierra Club wanted to avoid a bond for two reasons. First, the club was having difficulties paying for its litigation expenses. The legal bills were already much higher than anticipated, and given the projected costs of the road and the Disney development, the government could request a large bond.

Second, the use of bonds in environmental lawsuits was a new legal issue. Environmental groups bringing cases could be expected to argue that the bond requirement, which made sense in commercial litigation between private parties, should be waived or greatly lessened where the plaintiffs alleged that public agencies had violated environmental laws. In these cases, injunctions could prevent irreparable environmental damage. That damage should not be allowed to occur, the argument would go, just because the environmental group trying to prevent the injury could not afford a bond.

As he often did on less formal matters, on July 31 Judge Sweigert received the parties in his chambers rather than in the courtroom.[60] The purpose was to finalize the terms of the injunction that the court would grant, and during the meeting, the government asked the court to impose a $75,000 bond.[61]

The court denied the bond. Judge Sweigert explained that the injunction at this point was not likely to produce costs or damages to the defendants, and it would not prevent investigation, planning, surveying, and designing of the Mineral King development and road as long as the terrain and physical features were not affected.[62] He also said that he might reconsider his decision on the bond at a later time. As Lee Selna informed Mike McCloskey, Sweigert wanted the issues "presented by the case resolved as quickly as possible."[63]

The judge then signed the preliminary injunction. It barred the Forest Service personnel from "granting any permits, right-of-way or approvals with respect to the Mineral King development plan of Walt Disney Productions, Inc." Likewise, the secretary of the interior, Walter Hickel, and the secretary of agriculture, Clifford Hardin, were prohibited from granting any permits for the highway. The order stated that "for the present, no bond is required," but the court was "specifically reserving the right" to require that a bond be furnished.[64]

Sweigert's action ended the first round of the litigation. The Sierra Club had swept the board.

Figure 1. The Mineral King Valley. Photograph by Chris Jordan-Bloch, Earthjustice.

Figure 2. Robert Hicks. Courtesy of Mineral King Preservation Society, Robert Hicks Papers.

Figure 3. Wilfrid "Slim" Davis. Courtesy of U.S. Forest Service.

Figure 4. Suggestion of possible ski lifts in Forest Service prospectus for Mineral King.

Figure 5. John Harper. Courtesy of Susan Dearing.

Figure 6. Robert Brandt and Janet Leigh presenting Brandt's proposal for Mineral King to Sequoia National Forest Supervisor Lawrence Whitfield. *Merced Sun-Star*.

Figure 7. Pete Wyckoff. Courtesy of U.S. Forest Service.

Figure 8. Map from newspaper article showing the relationship between Mineral King and Sequoia National Park. *Christian Science Monitor.*

Figure 9. California Governor Pat Brown and Walt Disney meeting in Mineral King on September 19, 1966. Courtesy of the Los Angeles Public Library.

Figure 10. Stewart Udall (center) and Orville Freeman (right) with Senator Henry Jackson at press conference on North Cascades National Park. Courtesy of Special Collections, University of Arizona Libraries.

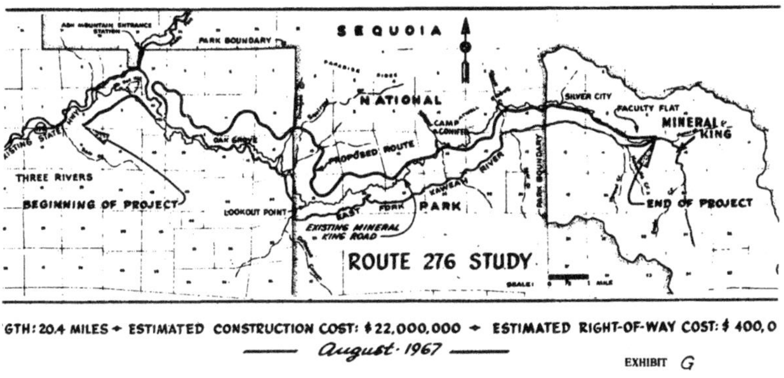

Figure 11. Map of the California Division of Highways showing proposed Mineral King road.

Figure 12a. *Mineral King at the Crossroads.* Brochure distributed by the Sierra Club in 1969. Thanks to the Sierra Club's William E. Colby Memorial Library for use of its historical archives.

Figure 12b. *Mineral King: A Planned Recreation Development*. Brochure distributed by the Forest Service in 1969.

Figure 13. Lee Selna. Courtesy of Leland R. Selna Jr.

Figure 14. Michael McCloskey at press conference announcing the Sierra Club's lawsuit over the Mineral King development. Photograph by Susan Landor Keegin.

Figure 15. Erwin Griswold, solicitor general, before the Supreme Court building. Getty Images.

8: The Shutout

The district court's injunction reshaped the controversy over the Mineral King development. Before that time, neither the Forest Service nor Walt Disney Productions had seriously entertained the possibility of losing the case. The Forest Service was shocked to find its authority questioned and was particularly distressed about the decision's potential to interfere with permits long in effect for other ski resorts in national forests.

Disney's concerns were narrower but equally troublesome for the company. Mineral King had become a national issue, and the company faced the prospect that critics would cite Judge Sweigert's decision to brand the company as an environmental lawbreaker. While its choice to stay out of the suit afforded the company some distance from the proceedings, its name remained closely associated with Mineral King. The decision placed the Disney image at risk. This circumstance was far from what the company had anticipated in 1965 when it submitted its application to the Forest Service.

In its initial public statement on the decision, Walt Disney Productions plaintively declared that "[i]f there is some real legal issue as to whether the Federal agencies acted properly in offering Mineral King for development by private enterprise, we believe this should be settled as quickly as possible." The company "continue[s] to believe enthusiastically" in the project's potential.[1] However, the Disney company soon sharpened its public response.

On July 30, it issued a statement from Card Walker, the executive vice-president of Walt Disney Productions.[2] It started by recapping the injunction and emphasizing that Disney "is not a party to the dispute between the Sierra Club and these federal agencies." Just as the company had not wanted to confront the club by intervening in the case, it continued trying to separate itself from the lawsuit.

Walker then got to the point. The legal issues raised by the project's opponents, insisted Walker, "do not, in any way, relate to the reputation of Walt Disney Productions as a world leader in the field of family recreation and entertainment, and as a recognized leader in the field of conservation." Nor were these opponents challenging the company's ability "to create and operate a recreational facility, which will be a credit to the state of California." Finally, Disney cited its "utmost good faith" in carrying out its preparation for the project. The Disney master plan "has been developed with the complete knowledge and approval of the Forest Service."[3]

The implication was plain: if a legal problem existed, it originated with the Forest Service. Disney was a bystander, not an instigator of a legal violation.

In short, Disney found itself in the uncomfortable position of being at the center of an environmental controversy and lawsuit it wanted nothing to do with. The statement closed with the same hope Disney had expressed just days after Judge Sweigert's ruling: "[W]e believe this should be settled as quickly as possible."[4]

Disney's strategy for responding to the controversy soon began to evolve. On July 26, Bob Hicks told a meeting of the California League of Cities that the Sierra Club intended to "wait us out" in the hopes of derailing the project. Disney, he continued, "has no intention" of giving up. He urged a grassroots campaign to secure legislation from Congress that would moot the lawsuit by authorizing the project.[5] Five days later, he reiterated the point: "It is now a political issue and the ultimate solution, if there is to be one at all, must be resolved by the politicians."[6]

Ironically, Disney now found itself agreeing with the Sierra Club about how Mineral King's future should be decided. Mike McCloskey had long sought to turn Mineral King into a political issue. The club's position continued to be that Congress should pass legislation, but of a different kind than that urged by Disney: it should incorporate Mineral King into Sequoia National Park, and thus prevent the development.[7]

Walker's public statement accurately portrayed Disney's initial actions on the project. The company had responded to the Forest Service's prospectus and played by the rules in designing its project. The part of the project directly attributable to Disney, however, was its massive size. The company had greatly exceeded the minimum size set by the Forest Service prospectus, and it never seriously considered a smaller project. The Mineral King development, Bob Hicks had told a panel at a California State Chamber of Commerce meeting in 1967, "promises to be the most complex ski facility to plan of any in this country—primarily because of its tremendous size and number of varied and separated ski areas."[8]

But times had changed, and what in 1965 seemed like a golden opportunity for Disney had turned into a serious and uncomfortable challenge. The company was along for the ride with the Forest Service, and that ride had gotten rough. As much as Disney now publicly sought to distance itself from the service, the Mineral King project locked them together.

By later in the fall, however, the company had regrouped from the shock of the injunction, and it launched a counterstrike aimed at members of the public who might wonder if Disney was developing an environmentally damaging project. Disney announced formation of an Independent Advisory Council of conservationists who would advise the company "on the project as it develops" and assist in planning to make Mineral King an "educational showcase." The group would also consult on a series of motion pictures with conservation subjects, and the first two would be on "vanishing species" and "the understanding and wise management of our total environment."[9]

The members of the council who had agreed to advise Disney were impressive. They included Horace Albright, former director of the National Park Service; Thomas Kimball, executive director of the National Wildlife Foundation; and Eivind Scoyen, former superintendent of Sequoia and Kings Canyon National Parks. But the most startling participant was Bestor Robinson, a former president of the Sierra Club.[10]

Moreover, the members of the new Disney council were serious about supporting the project. For example, Horace Albright had previously written a lengthy letter, published in the *New York Times*, that responded to a *Times* editorial opposing the Mineral King project. Disney now took the opportunity to rerelease Albright's letter to the press. The release noted that Albright "has been familiar with the Mineral King area . . . for 54 years."[11]

The new group overlapped substantially with the voluntary Conservation Advisory Committee that Disney had announced when it submitted its master plan for Mineral King the previous January.[12] But the announcement of the earlier group had passed almost unnoticed. The Disney strategists had decided to reboot the advisory group after the Sierra Club's victory in court.

The group's formation was a public relations coup for Disney. Having Bestor Robinson, a past Sierra Club president, on the council strongly suggested that the environmental community did not fully support the club's opposition to the project. As one Sierra Club member wrote to Mike McCloskey, "[Y]ou have got to hand it to them: it was a pretty smooth ploy" and "would seem to indicate that Disney is not about to give up." The member thought that, because of the group, "many people will be favorably inclined toward the Disney development."[13]

Disney would not easily abandon its Mineral King project.

As news of Judge Sweigert's opinion spread, another affected interest group snapped to attention: the skiing community. The loss of the dreamed-of ski resort at Mineral King, just when it seemed ready to go, would be a serious blow. However, a much bigger concern had arisen: the possibility that the Forest Service had violated federal law by using the dual-permit system to avoid the eighty-acre limitation on long-term permits. The agency had employed that system on many ski resorts, and skiers now awoke to the possibility that the permits allowing those developments might be defective.

Ski publications rallied the troops. The September 1969 issue of *Skiing* magazine carried an editor's column warning that "the Mineral King controversy pales before the fight we're all going to be in if Judge Sweigert's ruling is carried to its logical conclusion." The ruling, it warned, "cast doubt on the legal validity of 84 existing ski resorts that use Federal lands." Skiers "may suddenly find ourselves without a slope to ski on." The column ended with a plea borrowed from the French Revolution: "*Aux armes*, fellow skiers. Act before it's too late."[14] An article in another magazine, *Western Ski Time*, worried about "[h]ow many ski areas will fall" if the Sierra Club was correct on the dual permit issue. In the worst case, it warned, "every existing permit could be automatically invalidated!"[15]

Skiing magazine published perhaps the most insightful article about how the permit issue might play out. Entitled "Defend Your Right to Ski," it began with a call to action in capital letters: "DON'T PANIC, SKIERS, BUT BE PREPARED TO MAN THE BARRICADES!" It then identified the dual permit issue as "an accidental and extremely dangerous outgrowth of the bruising fight the Sierra Club has been waging against the development of Mineral King." This observation was correct. The Sierra Club's purpose was not to stop all ski resorts; it had simply latched onto a legal argument against Mineral King that might prove to have collateral consequences. The article quoted Ed Cliff, the chief of the Forest Service: "If the injunction becomes permanent, it could have a great bearing . . . on many other developments."[16]

The article continued that, while the Sierra Club claimed it is "not interested in carrying on a vendetta against skiing, skiers, and ski areas," Sierra Club allies would oppose new ski developments. It also cited a statement by a representative of the "Winter Sports Committee of the Sierra Club," at a ski association convention, that the club was "interested in the overall success" of the Disney development. To Mike McCloskey's dismay, a member of the club apparently had made that statement, despite the club's policy opposing the development. The statement added punch to the claim that the Sierra Club was "double-dealing" and was untrustworthy.

In the end, though, the article pointed out that, at least to some extent, skiers and members of the Sierra Club shared common interests. "Skiers are also conservationists," it noted, and "the last thing they want to do is to slug it out with other conservationists." But they would do so if necessary.[17]

The alarm spreading through the ski community was justified. The Sierra Club had shown no interest in challenging existing ski permits, but the legal issue posed by the dual permits in the Mineral King litigation could apply to other ski developments where permits were renewed annually. Moreover, even if the club ultimately lost this case, the same issue could be raised in other lawsuits challenging proposed ski developments.

The County of Tulare, which had strongly supported the Mineral King project at the political level, now also sought involvement in the case. At the recommendation of Disney personnel, the county hired E. Lewis Reid, a San Francisco lawyer. Reid had previously worked in Washington as minority counsel for the Senate Interior and Insular Affairs Committee and had become familiar with the Mineral King issue through briefings from Disney representatives. After Reid moved to San Francisco, Disney had hired him as a legal consultant on Mineral King, and so his representation of the county was logical.[18]

In short, the Sierra Club's initial success had stirred up a hornet's nest of opposition.

Judge Sweigert's decision elated the Sierra Club. In its view, the decision both validated the club's opposition to the Mineral King project and raised the political stakes. At best, if higher courts upheld the decision, the project would be stopped in its tracks for a considerable period of time, perhaps even until Congress intervened with new legislation. As an article in *American Forests* magazine recognized, to the club the injunction seemed a "portent of things to come in the fight between public agencies and conservationists."[19] The case showed that environmental interests could use the courtroom as a forum in which to air complaints about actions of the Forest Service, such as its denial of requests for public hearings.

The club also felt confident that it could overcome objections to its standing to sue in environmental litigation. Twelve days before the Mineral King ruling, a New York federal court had affirmed the club's standing in a challenge to a proposed highway.[20] The August 1969 edition of the *Sierra Club Bulletin* proclaimed that "the way is now clear for court review of any legally questionable transportation project which requires federal action or financing."[21]

The Sierra Club still faced the nagging problem of paying its legal bills. The lawsuit had cost far more than Mike McCloskey originally projected, a surprise that reflected the club's lack of experience in environmental litigation. The club owed a considerable amount to Lee Selna's firm. The September issue of the *Sierra Club Bulletin* contained a plea to members for financial help.[22]

Lee Selna was well aware of those monetary shortages as the club tried to right its financial ship after David Brower left the organization. Still, he had a lawsuit to prosecute, so in a letter to McCloskey he outlined his proposed next steps in the litigation and their attendant costs as the case proceeded to trial.[23] However, Fred Fisher, the chair of the club's Legal Committee, balked at Selna's proposal. The club's financial problems, he thought, "appear to be not just serious but critical." He did not think the club could "afford the luxury" of following Selna's suggestion that he begin factual development of the case.[24]

By November, however, the situation had slightly improved. Helped by a new grant from an anonymous lawyer who had donated a significant amount earlier, the club had paid its legal debt down to $6,000. The financial distress was also lessened by the club's rapid increase in membership and its accompanying influx of dues. But future funding for the litigation remained in question, and the club had just started to grapple with supporting the burgeoning number of requests to institute other cases, as word of the Mineral King injunction spread.[25]

Meanwhile, an acrimonious debate broke out between the government and Disney over how to respond to the Sweigert decision.

After the court granted the preliminary injunction, the government defendants had to choose a course of action. In discussing that choice, the issue of standing stood out as crucial. As the environmental movement continued to grow nationally in 1969, lawsuits began to be filed against government defendants, and they often challenged decisions that, like that of Mineral King, concerned uses of federal lands. The lawsuits questioned the Forest Service's long-held assumptions about its authority, and they posed the specter of judicial decisions that would interfere with the service's discretion in unprecedented ways. This concern animated the government's thinking about what steps to take next.

Paul Locke, the government attorney in San Francisco handling the case, debated the options with Department of Justice attorneys in Washington, DC.[26] One possibility was asking Judge Sweigert to reconsider his ruling, but the group recognized the very low probability of success in such a request. More pragmatically, the government could appeal the injunction to the United States Court of Appeals, where the government could strongly challenge the standing to sue of environmental groups like the Sierra Club. If the government chose that action, the question was whether or not the government should, in addition to standing, also raise the substantive issues that challenged the legality of the Forest and Park Services' decisions.

The other strategic alternative was to forgo any appeal but seek an early trial of the case, a course of action Locke recommended. Judge Sweigert had indicated to the parties that a quick trial was probable, but when the trial would take place was uncertain. For one thing, the Sierra Club might press strongly for discovery, a process that would involve depositions and answering questions known as "interrogatories," and that would probably delay the trial.

The Department of Justice follows a well-established process, involving the Office of the Solicitor General, for deciding whether or not to appeal adverse decisions by district courts. Appointed by the president, the solicitor general oversees all government cases in the Supreme Court. But the solicitor general, at that time Erwin Griswold, also has to approve all appeals from district courts to courts of appeals, a requirement intended to ensure uniformity among the appeals taken by the government in cases throughout the United

States. And in this instance, the United States Court of Appeals for the Ninth Circuit, in San Francisco, would hear the appeal.

The Solicitor's Office sought the views of the Forest Service and the Department of the Interior, and their legal departments weighed in with recommendations.[27] Their common theme was concern over the threat that cases like Mineral King posed to the discretion exercised by these agencies in making decisions.

The Department of the Interior's response urged that the government only appeal the question of standing, not the substantive issues in the case. Any trial, it reasoned, should come only after a decision on the appeal of the standing issue. Interior thought that the district court's opinion expanded standing "far beyond" that allowed by previous Supreme Court cases. It warned that such broad standing "could subject this Department to substantially more instances of litigation than at present and could delay many of [its] programs."[28]

The Office of the General Counsel in the Department of Agriculture submitted a twenty-page, single-spaced memorandum arguing that Judge Sweigert had wrongly decided the injunction. But the memo concluded that, "irrespective of whether the administrative determinations regarding Mineral King are lawful or appropriate," the Sierra Club lacked standing, and an appeal should be taken on that issue. It warned of potential apocalyptic administrative consequences: "The precedent effect of this case . . . could seriously disrupt the orderly administration of the National Forests . . . and the management of all the public lands, if not the administrative function of the entire Executive branch of the Federal Government."[29]

On September 11, 1969, Shiro Kashiwa, head of the Lands and Natural Resources Division of the Department of Justice, which represented the government defendants in the case, sent a memo to Griswold attaching a summary of the various departmental recommendations. Kashiwa characterized the standing issue in dramatic terms: "(1) whether the Sierra Club, or similar organization, is to be permitted to impede or delay federal authorities relating to public projects . . . and (2) whether federal activities . . . are to be overseen in detail by the courts." He noted that four similar cases were pending in the federal courts of appeal. However, the lengthier background summary recommended appeal of the entire preliminary injunction, including the substantive Mineral King issues. It informed the solicitor general that "[t]ime is very important, since the Disney interests may withdraw from the project if much more time elapses."[30]

Finalizing a recommendation to the solicitor general fell to Peter Strauss, a young lawyer in that office. Strauss's five-page memorandum was more neutral in tone than the recommendations from the Departments of Interior and Agriculture, whose actions were being challenged. Strauss recommended an appeal of only the standing issue, not the other substantive issues raised by the Sierra Club.

His memorandum cut to the core of what the Sierra Club was proposing in seeking standing. The conservation interest that the club sought to protect in challenging the Mineral King project was not "ascribable to a small or finite class; it is an interest of the public as a whole." The question was whether or not the Sierra Club could seek relief enjoining violations of statutes aimed to protect the public. The Supreme Court, concluded Strauss, had not yet affirmed such broad standing.[31]

Strauss would limit the appeal only to standing for several reasons. Notably, at least with respect to the question of approving an electric transmission line across Sequoia National Park, he thought that "it appears the Secretary [of the Interior] may indeed have been wrong."[32] He also foresaw an increased chance for success on the substantive issues if the government had a chance to develop a record of past uses of the dual permit system. It could only fully develop that record at trial.

Five days later, on September 24, Erwin Griswold agreed with Strauss. He handwrote in that the appeal was limited "as to standing" only.[33]

Walt Disney Productions reacted explosively to this decision. It saw the recommendation to appeal only the standing issue, and not the substantive issues raised by the Sierra Club, as betraying Disney's goal of having the case decided as quickly as possible.

The company's ire erupted in a letter from Donn Tatum, now president of Walt Disney Productions, to Clifford Hardin, the secretary of agriculture. Tatum got immediately to the point. The company had concluded that the development at Mineral King "will be postponed indefinitely, and perhaps permanently, unless the attitude and actions of the various Federal governmental departments now directing its course are completely changed."[34] Tatum complained that Disney had accepted the government's invitation to bid based on the "clear cut representation" that the Forest Service possessed legal authority to approve the project. Accordingly, it was imperative that all the legal questions be resolved quickly. Without such a resolution, the company could not spend further money.

Tatum then attacked the Forest Service's recommendation that the appeal be limited to standing:

> [It] is not possible to describe adequately the amazement and dismay with which we received the news that the Department of Justice, with the concurrence of the Secretary of Agriculture, has decided not to press for the speediest possible clearing up of these legal questions; but, instead, has determined to test through appeal procedures the right of the Sierra Club [i.e., its standing] to file the law suit which has brought this project to a complete stop.[35]

Tatum charged that secret motivations might well underlie the Forest Service's recommendation:

> [It] is so obviously contrary to the best interests of the viability of the Mineral King project that many people who know the facts can only conclude that the decision has been made to abandon the development of Mineral King, and that this course offers the best guise under which to accomplish that objective.[36]

Tatum then veered off in a strange direction. The Sierra Club, he wrote, "is an outstanding conservation organization of long standing," and "[w]e see no reason why the Government should seek to preclude it from raising, in the proper way, serious questions affecting the administering of the public lands." With respect to Mineral

King, the standing question "is a secondary and irrelevant issue." If the government believes that it must raise the issue, "it should be litigated along with the main issues; not concentrated upon while the crucial matters remain dormant and unresolved."[37]

Tatum closed his letter with a threat. If the government's decisions on Mineral King were upheld, Disney "stand[s] ready to complete the project." If not, Walt Disney Productions "will expect to be reimbursed by the Government for all costs incurred in fulfillment of our obligations under the initial prospectus and three-year planning permit."[38]

Disney understood why the government proposed to limit the appeal to standing. As litigation over federal agency decisions blossomed across the country, the question of the plaintiff's standing became critically important to the government. However, an appeal only on standing seemed to disregard the effect that this choice would have on Disney's proposal for Mineral King, and Disney's strong letter sought to change that dynamic. Tatum went over the heads of the government's lawyers and demanded that the secretary of agriculture intervene.

In suggesting that an appeal only on standing was obviously wrong, Tatum stood on debatable ground. Good arguments existed for that choice. If the government appealed the standing issue alone, it would streamline the appeal and focus the court's attention. And if it won, the case would be over. The decision whether to appeal, and what to appeal, was not open and shut, as Tatum portrayed it.

Then there was Tatum's charge that appealing only standing might indicate the government's desire to abandon the Mineral King development. The idea was preposterous. The Forest Service had not even remotely suggested such an intent, as Tatum certainly knew. Tatum's purpose in raising the unfounded charge was plainly to rattle the Forest Service and convey the high level of Disney dissatisfaction.

Finally, the letter opined that the Sierra Club *should* have standing in cases like this one. This suggestion, too, could simply have been part of Disney's strategy to get the attention of the Forest Service. But Tatum followed it with an encomium recognizing the club as an outstanding conservation organization. This part of the letter is truly puzzling because—"outstanding" organization or not—it *was* the Sierra Club that was blocking Disney's Mineral King project.

The statement about the Sierra Club reflected the strange position Walt Disney Productions now occupied. The company was committed to the Mineral King project; it was a Walt Disney priority. Times had changed, however, and the environmental movement was sweeping the United States. A main theme in that movement, a deep concern about the functioning of natural systems, strongly connected with Disney's history.

Walt Disney's nature documentaries—including such well-known films as *Seal Island* and *The Living Desert*—were truly groundbreaking. Some would later criticize them for a tendency to imbue animals with anthropomorphic tendencies and for "staging" events,[39] a charge that Disney did not completely deny.[40] However, the documentaries brought to millions a basic understanding and appreciation for wildlife that otherwise was far outside the realm of their experience. Largely because of these films, in 1955 the Sierra Club had awarded its honorary lifetime membership to Walt Disney.[41]

The Disney company was rightfully proud of its achievements in the wildlife films. The attitude in Tatum's letter toward the Sierra Club may have stemmed, at least partly, from a feeling that the two organizations had common interests that were being lost in the dispute over Mineral King. Perhaps that suggestion reads too much into Tatum's statements about the club, but given that the Sierra Club's litigation was challenging a Disney project, the statements were surprising.

The letter from Donn Tatum hit the Forest Service like a thunderbolt. The last thing it wanted was for Disney to withdraw its project. A. W. Greeley, the associate chief of the agency, responded to Tatum that he "feel[s] quite certain [Chief Cliff] will want to talk to you as soon as he has personally had an opportunity to entirely reconsider with our Counsel the points made in your letter."[42] The Forest Service wanted to quickly quell any Disney mutiny.

The Disney complaint also attracted the immediate attention of

Shiro Kashiwa, the head of the Land and Natural Resources Division at the Department of Justice. He sent a memo to Erwin Griswold protesting the decision to appeal only the standing issue and requesting a conference. Kashiwa was blunt and hyperbolic. An appeal only on standing "is so dangerous to ultimate success in the case and would so prejudice our position in this and other pending cases that no appeal at all would be better."[43] While the logic of that charge was questionable, Griswold quickly capitulated, undoubtedly seeing no reason to waste his political capital on this question. On September 30, he replied to Kashiwa that a conference was unnecessary and that he had authorized an appeal on all issues.[44]

Tatum's letter had achieved some change. While the appeal would go forward, it would include the substantive legal issues raised by the Sierra Club that underlay Judge Sweigert's injunction. Tatum thought that a quick trial was the best course to get the whole case resolved, but this change would help if the government lost the standing issue. The court of appeals might then still proceed to reverse the preliminary injunction on the substantive grounds, and perhaps even end the case in Disney's favor.

Secretary Hardin sent a formal reply to Donn Tatum on November 13. The district court's decision, he told Tatum, "is as shattering to our hopes as it is to yours," but the Department of Agriculture is "firm in its determination to develop Mineral King." The department wanted to move aggressively "as soon as the temporary stumbling blocks can be removed." Hardin, however, also noted that the case presented issues—specifically, standing and the legality of the dual permit system—"of importance to the government beyond the immediate situation" of Mineral King. An appeal of the injunction, concluded the Department of Justice lawyers, "is the one most likely to result in the earliest resolution of the issues in this case."[45]

Tatum had no choice but to acquiesce in the government's decision. Still, his reply to Hardin made clear that Walt Disney Productions remained unhappy. He chided Hardin that if Judge Sweigert's "invitation for an early trial on the merits had been accepted, it is possible that the case could have been in trial right now." For good measure, Tatum noted pointedly that, although the court had entered the preliminary injunction on August 4, the government still had not yet filed its opening brief on appeal.[46]

As it turned out, the government filed its brief that very day, December 1, 1969.

As the end of 1969 neared, the national surge of interest in environmental issues swelled. The newsworthiness of the high-level dispute over Mineral King between two such well-respected institutions, Disney and the Sierra Club, drew the press to the case.

Newspaper editorials on the subject showed some signs of differing attitudes toward the Mineral King development. The California newspapers, whose readers were the most likely to ski at Mineral King and reap its economic benefits, solidly supported the development.[47] Otis Chandler, the publisher of the *Los Angeles Times*, continued to advocate for the project, and Marilyn "Missy" Chandler, his wife, wrote directly to Secretary of Agriculture Clifford Hardin complaining about the delay in construction.[48]

NBC aired a story decidedly favorable to the development on its weekend news produced out of Los Angeles. "Because the Disney name is well-known," said the television reporter, "the Sierra Club has used the corporation as a fall guy, depicting Mickey Mouse as the spoiler of the wilderness."[49] Finally, newspapers in the San Joaquin Valley condemned the lawsuit, with one decrying "the fetish the Sierra Club has of keeping the common people out of the mountains."[50]

In the east, the *New York Times* continued to vigorously oppose the project, no doubt influenced by John Oakes, a member of its editorial board and an active member of the Sierra Club. The headline on its latest editorial underscored its position: "The Scandal of Mineral King." It charged the previous secretaries of agriculture and the interior with compiling "an abysmal record" regarding the fate of Mineral King and declared that the new secretaries in the Nixon administration "have an opportunity to right this wrong." They "can still quash the Disney plan." The question was "Who Watches the Watchmen?" according to the *Times*, and the Sierra Club "is performing a public service in standing up to this threat."[51]

The *Christian Science Monitor* joined in. It feared that "daily ant-swarms of people emanating from the proposed 3,000-car underground garage cannot help but disastrously change the remote and peaceful character of the valley." Then, in a sentence that validated Disney's fear about harm to its image, the *Monitor* asked, "[W]here the developer goes, can the honky-tonk be far behind?"[52] Papers in places like St. Louis and Kansas City also editorialized against the project.[53]

Overall, most newspapers supported the project. But an editorial opposition had developed, arising largely in the East and Midwest.

Several lengthier articles sought to place the dispute into a broader context. They began to identify the clash of underlying values held by the interested parties and how those values influenced their views about Mineral King's future. One lengthy piece in the *New York Times Magazine* ultimately sided with preserving the valley, but its analysis traced part of the conflict as originating in a battle over terminology. "Both sides," said the article, "claim to be conservationists," so the author suggested reframing the conflict as "recreationists v. protectionists."[54]

Another key underlying issue discussed in the article was the relationship of nature to human development and technology. Crediting the Disney team as "talented people" who "know what they are doing," the article reported that a Disney official was confident about avoiding avalanches: "We can make [the snow] move when *we* want, not when *it* wants."[55] Similarly, Disney had proposed to avoid floods in Mineral King by channelizing Monarch Creek, and Slim Davis of the Forest Service was quoted as "chuckling" while approving this type of "tampering with nature": "Let's say we'll complete nature's job sooner." Mike McCloskey's rejoinder was sharp: "That's typical of the Forest Service." It believes "Nature doesn't know what it is doing. *We* know better."[56]

The initial drafting of the government's appeal was delegated to a lawyer in the appeals section of the Justice Department's Land and

Natural Resources Division in Washington, DC. Jacques "Jack" Gelin, age thirty-five, had worked in the Justice Department for two years after spending the previous ten years practicing in New York City. Gelin would go on to handle over 250 appeals for the government over his career.[57] His supervisor was Billingsley "Bill" Hill, an experienced appellate lawyer in his fifties. Both were very able lawyers.

The brief that the government filed on December 1, 1969, took a far different approach than the strategy it had quickly put together for Judge Sweigert's court.[58] There, the government had challenged the need for injunctive relief by arguing that no irreparable injury—a prerequisite for such relief—was threatened at that point. Now, on appeal, the government attacked the heart of the Sierra Club's substantive case and challenged the club's standing. It sought a knockout blow to end the case.

At its outset, the brief informed the court that the case "is of great importance to the Departments." It "squarely presents" the issue of whether management of the public lands "shall remain, as intended by Congress, in the executive departments, or whether the federal courts, at the behest of . . . private litigants who may be dissatisfied with management decisions, will become immersed in the management of the public lands or agencies."[59]

The unifying theme woven through the brief was the vast discretion that the law afforded agencies, such as the Forest Service and the Park Service, to manage the public lands. It cited a large number of past judicial decisions. For the most part, those decisions did not address the issues presented in Mineral King, but they demonstrated that, over the years, the courts had consistently deferred to the choices made by the federal land agencies. The brief argued that management decisions regarding public lands differed from other types of federal decisions in that they "are accorded a much greater degree of deference."[60] The brief sought to inculcate within the court a feeling that a ruling for the Sierra Club would be seen as an outlier.

Also included with this deluge of cases was information regarding past permits issued by the Forest Service using its dual permit system. That practice had resulted in facilities worth over $1 billion in value, and the secretary of agriculture had previously disclosed the dual permit practice to a congressional committee. Thus, the brief argued, Congress had received notice of this practice and had impliedly ratified it by not passing legislation to change it. The brief defended the dual permit practice as "eminently sensible" and then boldly asserted that "[t]o forbid it is patently ridiculous."[61]

As promised, the brief also attacked the Sierra Club's standing to bring the case. It invoked the principle, from a 1928 Supreme Court decision, that a person seeking judicial review "must have a direct personal interest in the administrative act" challenged.[62] This direct personal interest, the government continued, differs from an injury suffered by the public generally, which would not support an individual's standing. It argued that the Sierra Club fell squarely within the latter category. The district court's "extreme position," which the brief labeled the "general interest theory" of standing, would eviscerate the long-standing rule requiring a "legally protected interest."[63]

In short, the government's brief amounted to a full-throated defense of the traditional limitations on standing and rejected any adjustment of that status quo to account for environmental harms. It positioned the Sierra Club as a disruptive plaintiff that sought to place decisions regarding the management of the public lands in the hands of the courts. The brief imparted a message: the court should avoid the chaos that would ensue from a flood of cases if the Sierra Club position was adopted.

This overall approach de-emphasized the specific statutory provisions on which the Sierra Club based its case. For example, the club's argument that the dual permit system was illegal derived largely from the plain statutory language in question. In establishing different types of permits and limiting term permits to eighty acres, the Sierra Club asserted, Congress had meant what it said. In contrast, the government's brief dismissed those differences as "peripheral matters" and "incidental features" of the agencies' basic authority.[64]

Sending another signal to the court about the case's importance, the government filed a motion to accelerate oral argument of the appeal. The motion alleged that Walt Disney Productions, Inc., had spent $750,000 on the project and that delay would cause considerable economic loss in Tulare County.[65]

Ten days later, the court of appeals granted that motion and ordered the Sierra Club to file its brief a few weeks later, with the government's reply brief due two weeks thereafter. The order placed Lee Selna in a time crunch, since the court had permitted two ski groups and the County of Tulare to file *amicus curiae*—"friend of the court"—briefs.[66] This was a type of brief filed by interests that were not formal parties to the case but that held views they wished to bring to the court's attention. An *amicus* brief cannot raise new issues but might give the court a broader understanding of the case by indicating who was likely to be affected by a decision in the case, or by supplying legal, political, or social scientific information.

In this case, the Sierra Club had unsuccessfully opposed the filing of both briefs, and it would have to reply to them and to the government's brief. Finally, the court set the case for a very early oral argument on February 9.

The future seemed to darken for the Sierra Club.

On January 19, 1970, the Sierra Club filed its opposition brief. While the government's opening brief had tried to de-emphasize the claims of statutory violation by enveloping them in an overall cloak of broad agency discretion, the Sierra Club took the opposite tack. It focused closely on the specific claims—for example, that the government was acting illegally in issuing permits for the resort development, that explicit statutory language prohibited the routing of transmission lines through Sequoia National Park, and that the Park Service lacked authority to approve a road serving nonpark land.

The government's discretion, argued the club, did not extend to violating federal law, and the law's provisions violated here were particular and binding, not elastic as the government would have it. For example, the statute governing transmission lines said that "no permit, license, lease, or authorization for . . . transmission lines . . . or for the development, transmission, or utilization of power . . . shall be granted" in Sequoia National Park "without specific authority of Congress." That unambiguous language, declared the club, left no room for the Forest Service to inject discretion into its meaning.[67]

On standing to sue, the Sierra Club sought to ride the wave of recent cases that had recognized broadened environmental standing, terming them a "major metamorphosis" in this area of law. The club dismissed as outdated the traditional line of cases that would have disallowed the club's standing. As the brief put it, the government defendants "have cited many cases on the standing issue, but have failed to analyze those cases in the light of law's recent development and the policy considerations which have shaped the decisions." It painted the government as having violated the law and now trying to position itself as "beyond the reach of justice" by denying standing to objectors.[68]

The briefs of the government and the ski associations had also raised the specter that, if the Sierra Club succeeded in invalidating the dual permits for Mineral King, that ruling would jeopardize the legal status of numerous ski resorts throughout the country. The ski groups' brief dramatically charged that the district court's decision on the Forest Service's permit authority "threatens the continued existence of some eighty-four established ski areas throughout the United States which presently operate under such permits."[69] It attached an appendix listing all those ski areas and their permitted acreages.[70] The government and its allies effectively conveyed to the court the idea that invalidating the dual permit mechanism could have significant consequences.

Recognizing that this argument might trouble a court, the club tried its best to turn the history to its advantage. Whatever harm the grant of the other ski permits caused, said the club, was long in the past "and there is no point in challenging their illegality at this late stage." However, these past actions show why "it was absolutely essential that destruction be enjoined . . . in this case" *before* it could occur.[71]

The government's reply brief, filed just three days before the oral argument, reiterated the themes in the opening brief. It began: "Stripped of its allegations of bureaucratic tyranny, Sierra Club's lawsuit seeks to enlist the powers of the federal courts to overturn a policy decision regarding the management of federal land."[72]

Such challenges, warned the federal defendants, did not belong in the courts.

In short, the parties' briefs framed the case as a clash between traditional, settled doctrines of standing and agency discretion, and new legal approaches that could address the growing concern over environmental degradation.

As the date of the oral argument approached, the government made a last-minute decision about who would argue its case. While Jack Gelin had principally written the brief, both the Department of Justice and its client, the Forest Service, were sensitive to some criticisms about its work defending the case in the court below. Days before the oral argument, the head of the Land and Natural Resources Division decided that Walter Kiechel, second in command of the division, would argue the case.

Three judges would hear the appeal. Circuit Judge Frederick Hamley had served on the appellate bench for fourteen years after being appointed by President Dwight Eisenhower in 1956. Hailing from Seattle, Hamley had a background in Washington state politics.[73] The other two judges had been appointed in 1969 by the newly elected President Richard Nixon and thus had sat on the appellate bench for less than a year. Judge John Kilkenny, sixty-nine years old, had been a past president of the Oregon Bar Association and was an amateur historian who had written a book about Irish settlements in eastern Oregon.[74] The third judge, Ozell Trask, was sixty-one and had practiced in Phoenix, Arizona, where he had worked on important water law issues.[75]

The oral argument was lively, with the judges questioning both sides. They expressed interest in whether, if the Sierra Club lacked standing, any other individual or group would be able to challenge such actions by federal agencies. By the end of the argument, however, the judges seemed skeptical of the Sierra Club's positions.[76] Selna's takeaway from the argument was that he had lost.[77]

While the advancing of the oral argument seemed to promise a quick decision, six months passed without any ruling. Meanwhile, the Sierra Club again pondered how to pay the bill for its attorney's fees. As of March 17, 1970, the amount owed had ballooned to almost $23,000.[78] Disney continued its low level of activity on the project. It also had to endure a small number of pickets protesting at its annual stockholders' meeting, with some carrying signs modifying the well-known antiwar slogan "Make Love, Not War" to read "Make Love, Not Resorts." The stockholders remained firmly in favor of the Mineral King development.[79]

Then, on September 16, 1970, the court of appeals issued its opinion. The government won a total victory. The court denied the Sierra Club standing and flatly rejected all its substantive claims.

9: Standing Front and Center

The court of appeals' opinion was written by Judge Trask, one of the new Nixon appointees.[1] The opinion first summarized the background of the dispute. Included was a long quote from the Forest Service's announcement approving the Disney plan that emphasized its twin goals of providing a needed public service and assuring a development "without substantial impairment or permanent undesirable ecological impact." The opinion then turned to the Sierra Club's standing.

After citing the traditional requirement that a plaintiff must show that governmental conduct invades or will invade a legally protected interest, the court noted that more recently a "profusion of cases . . . have developed new precedents on the law of standing." The Sierra Club asserts a "special interest in the conservation and sound maintenance of the national parks and forests and particularly lands on the slopes of the Sierra Nevada mountains." But, said the court, the federal defendants share that same special interest. Moreover, the ski associations have many members who favor the agencies' actions. "[W]ithout a showing of more direct interest," the court concluded, the club's concerns could not support its standing to challenge the government's actions.[2]

The court found unconvincing key recent decisions relied on by the Sierra Club. In those cases, the opinion explained, particular factors afforded the requisite standing to the plaintiffs. In the Storm King case, for example, the Federal Power Act awarded standing by its own terms. In a second case involving the renewal of a television station license, a statute authorized listeners to claim the renewal was not in the public interest. The direct effects of a proposed highway on plaintiffs in a third case provided sufficient injury to support their standing to sue.[3] No such factors existed here.

The key, thought the court, was the prerequisite that a plaintiff allege that it was "aggrieved" or "adversely affected" by the agencies' actions.[4] A Supreme Court case handed down earlier in 1970 had recognized that the aggrievement or effect need not be economic; it might be aesthetic, conservational, or recreational.[5] The court of appeals conceded as much. But the Sierra Club simply had not alleged that it was aggrieved or had been adversely affected, "other than the fact that the actions are personally displeasing or distasteful to them."[6]

The opinion's conclusion on standing validated the government's strategy of emphasizing that issue on the appeal. Without standing, the Sierra Club's case was over.

Then, however, the outcome took an even worse turn for the club. The court proceeded to consider the substantive claims that had formed the basis for the preliminary injunction issued by Judge Sweigert. The court's reason for taking this unnecessary step was unclear. In any event, a major victory for the government then blossomed into a spectacular win. The court found that none of the Sierra Club's substantive claims had the slightest merit.

The court first made short shrift of the dual permit issue. The district court had been concerned about the combination of the term and annual revocable permits, but that did not matter to the court of appeals. The court cited a total of at least eighty-four recreational developments on national forest lands in which the Forest Service had employed the combination of permits. That total, thought the court, "is convincing proof of their legality." The use of dual permits seemed reasonable. And, the court added, the planning reports of the Forest Service are "[e]vidence of great concern for the ecology of the area and the preservation and conservation of natural beauty and environmental features."[7]

The road came next. The court zeroed in on the weakness of the

Sierra Club's position on the issue: no statute or case directly limited the Park Service's ability to approve such a road. The secretary of the interior had "wide discretion . . . in managing national parks to construct and improve roads and trails." Once again, the record "shows a great deal of concern in its planning for preservation of aesthetic and ecological values." Moreover, the court found "no logic" in a distinction that would sustain the legality of a "twisting, substandard, inadequate road" through the park but outlaw "an improved all weather two lane highway" going to the same place.[8]

The rest of the Sierra Club's case quickly collapsed. While the statute seemed to preclude power lines within Sequoia National Park, the court accepted the government's contention that it applied only to lines from hydroelectric plants. As for the lack of public hearings, the court found that one had occurred in 1953—the hearing organized and promoted by the Chamber of Commerce. There was also the 1967 hearing held by the California Division of Highways regarding the road. Thus, the matter of public hearings "cannot be considered a substantial factor in this proceeding."[9] Finally, as to the game refuge, the court quoted the law establishing the refuge and found "no substance" to the Sierra Club's argument that the project would interfere with the refuge.

Overall, the court's opinion reflected the emphasis in the government briefs on the wide discretion possessed by the federal land management agencies. The court did not read the statutes as setting specific limits on that authority, but more as establishing a framework for the agencies' actions. Viewed in that light, the Sierra Club's arguments gained no traction.

Only one part of the decision might help the club to pursue its sole course of further action: convincing the United States Supreme Court to hear the case. Judge Hamley had split from his colleagues on the issue of standing. In a concurring opinion—not dissenting, because he agreed with the other two judges that the Sierra Club should lose on the substantive issues—Judge Hamley pointed out that the Supreme Court had now held that a legal wrong might be aesthetic, conservational, or recreational. He thought the Sierra Club had standing to challenge that type of wrong.[10]

The club, he explained, represented thousands of members "who have a deep interest in aesthetic, conservational and recreational values of a kind intended to be safeguarded by the statutes in question." If an agency disregarded those statutes, and "the result is that the described values are being undermined or disregarded," this action constituted a legal wrong to the members. The Sierra Club, the organization chosen by these members, had standing to challenge that wrong.[11]

Judge Hamley's views on standing did not affect the outcome of the case. Overall, the opinion amounted to a disaster for the Sierra Club's growing legal efforts generally and, in particular, for its challenge to the development in Mineral King.

Ever conscious that the litigation over Mineral King was part of a larger political effort where public perception was critical, Mike McCloskey tried to downplay the result to the press. In the immediate aftermath, he characterized it as "a temporary setback—no more than that. We feel it will be reversed by the Supreme Court."[12] Other public appraisals by Sierra Club officials were more frank. Phil Berry, the Sierra Club president from 1969 to 1971, was "quite shocked" by the decision.[13] He termed it "extremely unfortunate," complained that "[w]e think the judges are dead wrong on the law," and promised an appeal.[14] Other conservationists were likewise dismayed.[15]

Having participated at the court of appeals level, the ski associations were ecstatic. Their overriding concern was defending the Forest Service's practice of granting term and annual permits that together exceeded eighty acres. The Ninth Circuit opinion validated that practice. A December 1970 edition of a ski magazine proclaimed, somewhat oddly, that the court's ruling "has to be viewed as the biggest defeat preservationists in southern California have suffered" since the earliest days of motion pictures in Hollywood.[16]

For Disney, the opinion seemed to validate its decision to persist with the Mineral King project despite the adverse publicity. The company could use the opinion to neutralize the attacks made against it. Donn Tatum, the company's president, released a statement promising that "we stand ready to move ahead whenever the necessary permits are issued." Stressing as always that Disney was not a party to the litigation, it called upon the Sierra Club to "accept the opinion of the court in good faith" and "work constructively with the Disney organization and the representatives from all levels of government" on the Mineral King project.[17]

But the plea was in vain; the Sierra Club was in no mood to concede defeat at this point. Nonetheless, the club was far from achieving its goal of incorporating the valley into Sequoia National Park. Indeed, the political support for the development seemed more steadfast than ever, with Senator George Murphy reporting earlier in the year that he had met with President Richard Nixon, who gave a "full endorsement" to the Mineral King project.[18] In a statement reflecting the unsettled political times that featured sometimes violent protests over the Vietnam War, Murphy praised skiers because "I don't know any bomb-throwers who are involved in skiing."[19]

While protecting Mineral King had come to symbolize what the Sierra Club now stood for, one consequence of the litigation was that the question of preserving the valley had now become intertwined with the larger question of legal standing. From the club's standpoint, a particularly troubling aspect of the new standing decision was that, while not effective nationwide, it would bind all federal courts in the western United States, including Alaska—areas of paramount concern to the club.[20]

Furthermore, the ruling ran counter to what appeared to be a well-defined movement in the federal courts affording groups like the Sierra Club standing to sue. In July 1969, the Sierra Club's Legal Committee, now coordinating with forty lawyers nationwide, had reported that "[f]or all practical purposes we think we have achieved standing to sue in federal courts where any aggrieved party can contest government action."[21] An October 1970 article in the *New York Times* had reported that the "trend of recent Federal court decisions has been to accord full hearings to citizen groups protesting federally sanctioned developments such as highways and power plants."[22] Suddenly, however, the openness of the courts to environmental suits appeared questionable, as the Mineral King decision "jolted and puzzled."[23] Moreover, by this time the Sierra Club had instituted a wide variety of lawsuits challenging various governmental approvals.[24] Unless the standing question was resolved, many of these suits might end up on the judicial trash heap.

Because of these consequences, the Sierra Club's board of directors quickly determined to appeal the decision to the United States Supreme Court.

With the Ninth Circuit's decision came the loss of the injunction entered by Judge Sweigert that had barred both development at Mineral King and approval of the road. An issue of pressing concern to Lee Selna was the possibility that work would soon begin on the project. Accordingly, the Sierra Club sought an order from the Ninth Circuit "staying" (i.e., delaying) the dissolution of Judge Sweigert's preliminary injunction until the club could seek review in the Supreme Court. Although its opinion decisively rejected all the Sierra Club's arguments, the Ninth Circuit quickly granted the stay. This fast action surprised the Forest Service lawyers, who had been pondering whether to oppose the request or to ask the court to require a bond.[25]

In the end, though, the Sierra Club may not have needed the stay order. The National Park Service, now educated on how the lengthy legal battle could unfold in various "ups and downs," opted for prudence. The Park Service director for California concluded that the service "should not take any action . . . that might jeopardize the situation" and decided that he would not yet sign the permit for the road.[26] The litigation remained too unsettled.

The Sierra Club turned to convincing the Supreme Court to review the case. The odds of success in this endeavor, however, were very low. In 1971, the court would only agree to hear 5.8 percent of the requests for review filed with it, whose formal name was a "petition for a writ of certiorari."[27] Most likely, the court would issue a simple order denying the Sierra Club's petition, and that would end the case.

However, Lee Selna did hold a few helpful cards. First, the burgeoning field of environmental litigation was drawing national attention, and the court might be attracted to an important case in that new field.[28] More important, the Sierra Club's petition could cite what is known as a "conflict" among the lower courts of appeals. This is a situation where different geographic branches or "circuits" of the lower federal appellate courts had reached opposite conclusions when addressing the same legal issue.

Here, while the Ninth Circuit rejected the Sierra Club's standing in the Mineral King case, the Second Circuit Court of Appeals in New York had reached the opposite conclusion earlier that year in its decision regarding an expressway along the Hudson River.[29] In the Mineral King opinion, the court had recognized the Hudson River decision, saying "we respectfully disagree" with it.[30]

The Sierra Club's petition to the Supreme Court hit hard on the conflict between the two decisions:

> The cases are indistinguishable. In each, the Sierra Club was a plaintiff. In each, it alleged that a government official (undoubtedly invested with broad authority and discretion in many areas) had overstepped the bounds of his authority in a particular area. . . . In each, the objective of the lawsuit was to prevent unauthorized and unlawful destruction of an important scenic and recreational resource. In each, the Sierra Club had a number of members in the general area of the proposed construction. . . .[31]

The Sierra Club also argued that the Mineral King decision conflicted with other court of appeals decisions on standing, although the conflicts in those cases were not as overt.

Additionally, the club sought to interest the court in the case as an exemplar of the concern over environmental degradation that had become a national issue. It preached, somewhat awkwardly, that "[w]e learn that America the Beautiful can be America the Ugly unless positive steps are taken to preserve it."[32]

The Ninth Circuit's opinion, however, had denied the Sierra Club standing and had decided against the club on the substantive merits of the case. Overturning the standing part of the decision would leave the rest of the lower court's opinion intact. To save Mineral King, the club needed the Supreme Court also to hear the five other substantive issues that the court of appeals had rejected, such as the dual permit issue. Raising all these issues could make the case appear overly complicated; the court might decide to await a later, simpler case on standing. This possibility concerned Selna, but he had no choice.[33] So the petition argued these issues as well.[34]

After the briefs were filed, the Sierra Club could only wait. The case was now officially known as *Sierra Club v. Morton*, as President Richard Nixon had fired Secretary of Interior Walter Hickel for writing a letter, which quickly became public, chastising Nixon for "embracing a philosophy which appears to lack appropriate concern for a great mass of Americans—our young people."[35] Nixon replaced him with Rogers C. B. Morton of Maryland. Then, on February 22, 1971, the Supreme Court agreed to hear the case. The legal opposition to the development of Mineral King might yet rise from the dead.

The case had now transformed in importance. As one newspaper recognized, "This question of right to sue pushed the issue beyond the development of Mineral King, by raising a threat to one of the conservationists' prime weapons, the court battle."[36] Facing more delay, the disappointed Disney management responded with its usual reminder that "Walt Disney Productions, of course, is not a party to this litigation" and hoped for a quick resolution. Meanwhile, it said, the company would concentrate its efforts elsewhere.[37]

One other important piece of new information surfaced at this time. A February 1971 news article reported statements from California transportation officials that the cost of the Mineral King road had now risen from $25 million to $38 million in only three years through "inflation." Moreover, the officials predicted, the cost could rise to $42 million by the time construction began.[38] The state highway engineer for the area cited special environmental considerations that would go into the road's construction as "one reason" for the increase.[39] A critic of the road offered another explanation: the original estimate for building the road had been unrealistically low.[40] Whatever the reason, the huge cost increase guaranteed more controversy over the appropriateness of spending such a large sum on a road leading to a private development.

Meanwhile, a dispute broke out between the Sierra Club and its environmental group allies about how to present the standing issue to the Supreme Court.

A decision that a party lacks standing to sue has important ramifications. It means that the underlying legal dispute will not be heard in the case, or perhaps ever. But as of 1972, the law of standing was comprised of a highly uncertain set of legal principles.

At its core, the doctrine of standing ensures that courts will only decide cases brought by individuals with a sufficient stake in a dispute to vigorously litigate it. The single constitutional provision widely understood to relate to standing is the requirement, found in Article III of the United States Constitution, that federal courts can only adjudicate "cases" and "controversies."[41] However, the relation of this provision to standing was not clear, and the cases filled in meaning by emphasizing one factor: the nature of the harm suffered by plaintiffs.

Traditionally, the harm that would support a plaintiff's standing to sue was economic injury. In the 1960s, however, litigants sought to bring new types of cases before the courts, such as alleged violations of the "one person–one vote" principle. Cases like these did not arise in a context in which a plaintiff alleged economic injury. Instead, these new plaintiffs were attempting to enforce "public law," legal provisions that benefited the public as a whole, rather than trying to remedy a private, individual economic injury. The environmental movement typified this type of plaintiff who sought to enforce laws such as those governing Mineral King against public officials like those in the Forest Service.[42] The scope of standing that the courts would recognize, said a leading legal treatise at the time, would determine whether courts would exercise "judicial control over public officers" in the manner sought by these cases.[43]

When the Sierra Club case reached the Supreme Court, the government had consistently argued that a plaintiff lacked standing to enforce such laws. It contended that laws like those governing the Forest Service benefited the public generally; thus, a plaintiff alleging a violation of them did not suffer any injury different from that of other members of the public. Accordingly, the government concluded, such plaintiffs lacked the specific injury needed for standing to sue.

Then, in a 1970 case, *Association of Data Processing Service Organizations, Inc. v. Camp*, an opinion by Justice William O. Douglas seemed to recognize broadened standing. The case involved a lawsuit that sought to overturn a banking regulation. The court began its discussion of standing by declaring that "The first question is whether the plaintiff alleges that the challenged action has caused him injury in fact, economic or otherwise."

In this case, said the court, the plaintiff had standing because the injury claimed was future loss of profits. But the court then explained that an injury to a noneconomic interest also could supply standing. That interest, at times, "may reflect 'aesthetic, conservational, and recreational' as well as economic values." The court concluded, "We mention these noneconomic values to emphasize that standing may stem from them as well as from the economic injury on which petitioners rely here."[44]

The court thus seemed to recognize that noneconomic injury—such as environmental injury—could supply standing. What it had not yet determined was the type of proof needed to show injury of an environmental nature, and whether a group, such as the Sierra Club, could be among or represent the injured.

This 1970 decision had not yet arrived when, a year earlier, Lee Selna drafted the Sierra Club's complaint challenging the federal agencies' decisions on Mineral King. As he considered standing at that point, one important fact seemed to stand out: the Sierra Club's unique history. Not only was it the best-known conservation group in the United States, its principal focus during the previous one hundred years had been to preserve the Sierra Nevadas, of which Mineral King and Sequoia National Park formed a part. The club's connection with these two areas was strong,[45] and this history of involvement, concluded Selna, should validate the Sierra Club's standing to sue over Mineral King. Approval of the development there would injure the Sierra Club's long-standing interest in the area.

Selna knew that standing cases often featured individuals, rather than organizations, who could show that a defendant's action had harmed them. He was aware that individual members of the Sierra Club had used Mineral King each year, often leading backcountry trips out of the valley, and that the Disney development would affect their use of the area. He thought, however, that it seemed almost "stupid" to drag these individual members in as plaintiffs when the club's interactions with the area had historically been so much more comprehensive.

Reflecting Selna's reasoning, the core allegation of the Sierra Club's complaint in the district court focused on the club's "special interest" and how the government's action on Mineral King would affect that interest:

> For many years the Sierra Club by its activities and conduct has exhibited a special interest in the conservation and the sound maintenance of the national parks, game refuges and forests of the country, regularly serving as a responsible representative of persons similarly interested. One of the principal purposes of the Sierra Club is to protect and conserve the national resources of the Sierra Nevada Mountains. Its interests would be vitally affected by the acts hereinafter described and would be aggrieved by those acts of the defendants.[46]

Now, as Selna contemplated his brief before the Supreme Court, he knew of the court's recent statement in the *Association of Data Processing* case that injury to environmental interests could support standing. But Selna had to decide what type of injury to those interests he would argue, and he decided to retain the approach taken in the courts below. The Sierra Club brief argued that the club was one of the "oldest, the largest and most respected conservation organizations in America," and it had a "special interest" in the Mineral

King area. The Disney development would damage this interest and thereby provide the needed "injury in fact" to establish standing. The Sierra Club's opening brief declared:

> It is sufficient that the Sierra Club has alleged its interest in the preservation of conservational, recreational and aesthetic values of Mineral King and Sequoia Park and that it has alleged that construction plans approved by the Secretaries of Agriculture and Interior threaten those interests.[47]

The brief thus centered on injury to the club's organizational interests. It did not argue that Sierra Club chapters or members used Mineral King for hiking and recreation, and that the huge Disney development would affect this use.

This choice of injury turned out to be controversial.

The environmental movement had grown substantially since the case had been filed in 1969, and, like the Sierra Club, new environmental organizations had begun to litigate. The question of standing at issue in the Mineral King case was vitally important to them.[48]

One person who well understood the importance of standing was James Moorman, one of the few attorneys who could then claim a history as an "environmental lawyer." Moorman had spent three years in the section of the Department of Justice that later would defend the Mineral King case. He was active in the nascent national network of environmental lawyers.

In 1969, Moorman joined the newly formed Center for Law and Social Policy in Washington, DC. The center was one of the first law firms that dedicated its practice to specialized litigation in the emerging areas of consumer rights, health law, and environmental law. At the center, Moorman litigated a challenge to the trans-Alaska oil pipeline that had received widespread attention. He worked there with Bruce Terris, another lawyer of increasing national prominence. Terris had previously worked for five years in the Office of the Solicitor General, the same office now handling the Mineral King case for the government before the Supreme Court. Terris had argued sixteen cases before that court.[49]

Responding to requests from environmental organizations, the Center for Law and Social Policy agreed to file a "friend of the court" brief in the Mineral King case in the Supreme Court. It would represent the Wilderness Society, the Izaak Walton League, and Friends of the Earth, the organization formed by David Brower after he left the Sierra Club. Terris took the lead in writing the brief.

Focused on the standing issue, Terris and Moorman reached a significant conclusion: the Supreme Court would likely reject the Sierra Club's arguments that injury to the club's interests was sufficient to show standing. The club, they believed, had to show more than "intellectual interest" in the area.[50] In their view, the Sierra Club's brief ignored two arguments to the court on the standing issue that would be more convincing. Both centered on actual use of Mineral King.

First, the club was comprised of numerous local chapters, and some had visited and used the Mineral King area for organized activities. Second, individual members of the Sierra Club used Mineral King each year. They hiked out of the Mineral King Valley, camped there, and for decades led pack trains out of the valley. The Disney development would markedly affect these uses of Mineral King, a distinctly particularized impact on the chapters and individual members.

The environmental groups' "friend of the court" brief argued this alternative "use" ground for standing. A problem with the argument, however, was that the court record compiled before Judge Sweigert contained no evidence of actual use of the area by Sierra Club chapters or its members. That evidence had been unnecessary under the Sierra Club's interest theory. The brief conceded the deficit of evidence on use, admitting that the factual argument about the Sierra Club members' use of Mineral King "is not supported by evidence of record" in the case. Thus, it said, the court should order the case sent back to the trial court for evidence to be presented on this contention.[51]

Terris and Moorman were convinced that the Sierra Club's interest theory would not prevail, and with his extensive Supreme Court experience, Terris's opinion in particular could not easily be dismissed. Moorman, also quite strong in his belief, took those concerns directly to the Sierra Club Legal Committee. He suggested that, given the case's importance, they should take over representation of the case in the Supreme Court, thereby permitting the experienced Terris to orally argue the case and to press the direct use theory.

Lee Selna strongly resisted this change.[52] Not only did he believe his interest approach would result in a broader rule of standing, he thought that requiring use of Mineral King by individuals was essentially silly. He found it self-evident that an organization like the Sierra Club, with its long and intimate familiarity with Mineral King, had the requisite interest to support standing. He also worried that a rule requiring "use" would need proof of such use in individual cases that might be difficult to produce.[53]

A debate ensued about control over the case. Don Harris, the cochair of the Sierra Club's Legal Committee, consulted with one of his attorney partners, Gary Torre, who had previously been a law clerk to Justice William O. Douglas. Harris reported to Moorman that Torre "feels strongly from his Supreme Court experience that the Court would rather hear arguments from the counsel who had been charged with the case throughout its development rather than from a Supreme Court practitioner in Washington." Harris concluded that "[w]e have confidence in Lee Selna, and for various reasons . . . are unwilling to consider a change in counsel or in briefing method at this point in time."[54]

So Selna's theory of the standing issue remained intact, and he would argue the case before the Supreme Court.

Drafting the government's response brief fell to Terry Bray, an assistant to the solicitor general, with the aid of Jack Gelin, the lawyer who had principally written the government's brief in the court of appeals.[55] The Forest Service now increasingly faced lawsuits challenging its exercise of discretion. From the service's viewpoint, the goal of the brief was to persuade the court to adopt a standing rule that would prevent these challenges.

The government's overall attitude toward such issues, however, had slowly evolved as the environmental movement grew across the country. Congress had responded in a bipartisan manner by enacting important new air pollution legislation and the National Environmental Policy Act, which required preparation of a new document, the "environmental impact statement." A considerable amount of proposed environmental legislation was pending in Congress, and President Richard M. Nixon had established the Environmental Protection Agency by executive order the previous December. Finally, Congress had created the Council on Environmental Quality to coordinate environmental protection efforts within the Executive Branch.[56] As the council's first head, Nixon appointed Russell Train, who had a background in water policy and wildlife conservation. Train would later become the administrator of the Environmental Protection Agency.

A lawyer by training, Train recognized the importance of the standing issue now in front of the Supreme Court. He was also in contact with leaders in the environmental movement. They urged a bold departure from past positions on the standing issue: the government should "confess error" and agree that the Ninth Circuit's decision on standing was incorrect.

A "confession of error" would be extraordinary, but Train was convinced that it should happen. On May 25, 1971, he wrote to the solicitor general, Erwin Griswold, suggesting that the United States confess error in *Sierra Club v. Morton*. Griswold replied to Train that he would consult with the affected divisions of the Department of Justice and then would "write you further."[57]

In response, the head of the Appellate Section of the Department of Justice's Civil Division, the section which defended a vast array of actions against the United States, expressed an interesting view of the case. He thought it "seems unlikely" that the Supreme Court would find that the Sierra Club lacked standing. But he opposed confessing error because that step should only be taken where the government could make "no presentable argument," and this case did not fall into that category. Moreover, he found it "clearly in the Government's interest to make every effort" to oppose standing because, if the Sierra Club's position were adopted, it would "result in a proliferation of suits—many vexatious—by all kinds of groups purporting to possess some kind of 'interest' in the matter in controversy."[58]

The Land and Natural Resources Division, which represented the Forest Service and the National Park Service, predictably resisted throwing its clients overboard with a confession of error. The head of the division termed such a step "unthinkable." The case, he said, "involve[es] substantial issues relating to the appropriateness of the invocation of judicial power."[59]

That was more than enough to convince Griswold. He wrote Train back, repeating the principal points raised by the Justice Department's divisions and concluding that the law was far from clear. Thus, it was in the interests of all concerned that the Supreme Court decide the issue. Then, he promised care in presenting the government's views to the court: "Needless to say, we will endeavor to present it [the question of standing] in a full and fair way."[60]

As it turned out, the government's brief did not adopt the "hard line" approach to standing that the Forest Service undoubtedly would have preferred.[61] Its position was more nuanced.

The government's opposition brief did begin by attacking the heart of the Sierra Club's standing theory, the idea that its long-standing "interest" sufficed to give it standing. The government would have none of it. After first characterizing the statutes at issue in the case as protecting "the public at large," it outlined the core ground for its rejection of the Sierra Club position:

> A claim of interest to assure that these public officers live up to their responsibility—and that is all petitioner has claimed here—is not enough, by itself, to entitle either a single member of the public or an organization like petitioner to seek judicial review of these officers' conduct of their public responsibilities.[62]

The Sierra Club "does not claim that it has suffered a distinctive or discriminating harm, which would differentiate it from the public at large."[63] Departing from this requirement of harm, said the government, would entirely undermine the "injury in fact" requirement for standing.

Surprisingly, however, at various places the government's brief suggested ways in which it agreed that the Sierra Club might have established standing in the case. It admitted that the club "might have claimed a more traditional basis for standing" but had not done so, opting for "an undifferentiated 'public interest' in assuring that park and forest administrators obey governing statutes." Several pages later a footnote clarified this "more traditional basis." The government cited parts of the *amicus* brief by Jim Moorman and Bruce Terris, which argued for the Sierra Club's standing as (1) a local organization interested in protecting Sequoia National Game Refuge, Forest, and Park, or (2) an organization which used the areas and represented the interests of its members who used them.[64] And, the government conceded, if an individual citizen could establish standing under these principles, "we see no reason why organizations such as the Sierra Club could not claim standing as representative of that interest."[65]

Another part of the government's brief emphasized the argument about standing that the Sierra Club had not made. "It is apparent" from the briefs of the friends of the court, said the government, that "there may exist numerous, rather concrete relationships between the Sierra Club, its members, and one or another of the particular federal lands at issue here, which could support a claim of injury in fact." But the club "has chosen to rely . . . only on its national interests in conservation and maintenance of public reserves and a general interest in the Sierra Nevada Mountains." The government concluded that the club's effort "appears to be to require the Court to decide a rather broad and sweeping question, when a narrower issue might suffice to resolve this aspect of the dispute."[66] The club had not opted for the common litigation strategy of seeking a narrow win but had instead sought a broader rule.

Finally, the government tried to distinguish the Mineral King situation from cases like the Storm King dispute.[67] Those cases, said the government, involved statutes where Congress had particularly defined parties as "aggrieved" in acts such as the Federal Power Act, thereby endowing them with standing to litigate. The federal land statutes involved here contained no similar empowerment.

In all, the government adopted a moderate position on standing. It had not taken the kind of categorical position broadly opposing standing that the Forest Service would have preferred. That position could be found in the *amicus* brief of the County of Tulare, which accused the Sierra Club of seeking "to abolish the requirement of standing" and "to interpose years of delay" implementing administrative decisions "at the instance of any 'public interest' group."[68]

Since the inception of the litigation, Lee Selna had firmly believed that requiring actual use of Mineral King to establish standing made no sense. He reiterated that viewpoint in the club's brief replying to the government's opposition. A litigant "need not, and therefore should not, resort to artifice by alleging injury to an inconsequential but unique material interest when injury to the litigant's aesthetic, conservational or recreational interest is the real reason for the lawsuit." While the Sierra Club had sponsored pack trips originating in Mineral King, that activity "is of such little importance to the Club that it would not incur all of the disadvantages of litigation in an attempt to protect it."[69] The adversity required of a party to establish standing did not arise here from an interference with pack trips, but from the club's interest in Mineral King and Sequoia National Park which the Disney plan threatened.

Finally, the Sierra Club reply brief charged that, in suggesting that use of Mineral King might support standing, the government had an ulterior motive. The Sierra Club had won a preliminary injunction in the district court, and one legal consideration in the granting of such injunctions is the effect on the "public interest." By championing "use" as the test for standing, Selna reasoned, the government sought to establish a decisive advantage in opposing claims for injunctions. Under its position, the government won either way—it was a "heads I win, tails you lose" proposition. "[E]ither the courthouse door is barred for lack of assertion of a private, unique injury or a preliminary injunction is denied on the ground that the litigant has advanced private injury which does not warrant an injunction adverse to a competing public interest." The Sierra Club's lawyers "shaped their case to avoid this trap."[70]

In the end, though, Selna seemed to hedge his bets just slightly. His brief told the court: "While not emphasized in the record, there is no dispute that the Club represents the interest of its members who actually physically use and enjoy Mineral King and Sequoia National Park in their present state."[71] An accompanying footnote added that this "use and enjoyment is graphically detailed" in a letter, included in the case record, in which Mike McCloskey had requested the Forest Service to hold a hearing on the proposal to develop Mineral King.

By early fall 1971 the briefing was completed and the case advanced toward oral argument before the Supreme Court. Meanwhile, the national controversy over Mineral King had grown even more heated and would continue after the case was argued.

Disney remained uncomfortable with its position at the center of a national environmental controversy and continued efforts to separate itself from the litigation. But the separation proved impossible. During summer 1971, a task force established by famed consumer advocate Ralph Nader announced opposition to the Disney project. Its report charged that the project was too large and ecologically destructive, and it criticized the maneuverings that had placed the Mineral King road in the state highway system.[72]

In November 1971, the attacks on Disney reached a new height when *Ramparts* magazine published a lengthy article entitled "Disney's War Against the Wilderness." The cover of the issue featured a caricature of Walt Disney wearing Mickey Mouse ears and digging up the ground with a spade while animals watched. The article spoke of Disney's "attempted rape" of Mineral King. Not since John Muir's fight to prevent the dam in Yosemite Park's Hetch Hetchy Valley, the article breathlessly proclaimed, "has there been a conservation battle of such watershed proportions." The article concluded that "[i]t is the end to all our childhood fantasies": Mickey Mouse and

Smokey the Bear, the Forest Service's widely known cartoon mascot, "conspiring to tear up the wilderness."[73]

The *Ramparts* article could be dismissed as the anticorporate rant of a left-wing magazine. And the article's emphasis on "wilderness" was not technically accurate, as Mineral King did not legally qualify for wilderness status. But it grabbed some of the public's attention and argued against the project in evocative images.

Then, in early 1972, another lengthy article entitled "Mickey Mouse in the Mountains" appeared in the venerable *Harper's Magazine*. Although far less one-sided than the *Ramparts* piece, the article was skeptical of the Disney proposal. Its subtitle read: "The Folks That Brought You Disneyland Yearn to Turn California's Mineral King Valley into a Mammoth Ski Resort." It picked up on the Sierra Club theme that the development was not properly planned and questioned how a development this big could not affect animal life in the valley's game refuge.[74]

Within Disney's ranks, Bob Hicks continued to press his proposal to extend the Mineral King rail system and terminate the Mineral King highway so it would not need to enter Sequoia National Park. In August 1971, he circulated internally a lengthy memorandum discussing the finances of extending the train and noting that the members of Disney's Conservation Advisory Committee viewed the change favorably.[75] He followed up with another long memo in December concluding that the railway extension would be feasible, although it would "require top level approval by the Forest Service."[76] The politically savvy Hicks was readying a final push for the project if the litigation ended favorably for Disney. His proposed alternative could serve as a concession by Disney to further protect the environment and enhance its public image.

As for the Sierra Club, Mike McCloskey's view of the litigation as part of a broader political campaign drove him, once again, to articulate in writing the reasons why the club opposed development of Mineral King. With coauthor Albert Hill, he published a 1971 brochure entitled *Mineral King: Mass Recreation Versus Park Protection in the Sierra*.[77] The piece repeated many now-familiar Sierra Club arguments, such as objections to the project's size and to the lack of public hearings. But it also emphasized two other important themes.

One was that the Forest Service had "barged ahead" with the project using "single-minded mission-oriented thinking" without answering "basic ecological questions." This argument attacked a core, longstanding Forest Service defense of the project: that it had been carefully planned. The service emphasized that the project would meet environmental standards, but the brochure argued that no such standards could be specified without prior ecological studies. Moreover, no one even knew the project's ultimate size, because the Forest Service had imposed no ceilings on that size. Indeed, the brochure alleged, "the whole idea of ceilings on size is foreign to the Service." In short, the Sierra Club skewered the Forest Service's approach to the development as an object lesson in "how not to plan a public resource."[78]

A second argument by McCloskey and Hill challenged the Forest Service's fundamental assumption, oft-repeated by Disney, that a large ski resort could be built compatibly with the natural environment in Mineral King. The club described the "underlying premise" as "you can vastly increase visitation and still maintain a reasonably natural condition by skillful design and cosmetics." The Sierra Club rejected that premise: "It is specious to assert you can build a hotel and entertainment complex, a so-called 'self-contained village,' as large as in our major cities and still preserve a sense of naturalness and the integrity of a fragile ecology and its beauty."[79]

One other organizational development at the Sierra Club during 1971 would prove significant over the long term: the club began creating its own legal staff. The cost of the Mineral King litigation had led the club to recognize that using in-house lawyers would be much less expensive. So, Don Harris and Fred Fisher secured a grant from the Ford Foundation to establish what would be called the Sierra Club Legal Defense Fund.

The fund quickly decided upon an executive director. Jim Moorman took the job and began work in August.[80] By the end of 1971, the defense fund would report involvement in over seventy cases and administrative matters nationwide, ranging from supervising volunteer lawyers to active litigation.[81]

As for the Forest Service, it could only wait. However, the service began to display sensitivity to the allegations, pounded home by the Sierra Club, about the project's unknown ultimate size and lack of planning. It started signaling that, if necessary, it would intervene to limit the project's size. On November 19, 1971, Chief of the Forest Service Ed Cliff wrote California Congressman Don Clausen that "[t]he ultimate development in Mineral King will be governed by the carrying capacity of the valley and the surrounding terrain." He noted that "[c]ontrol on capacity can be taken if necessary."[82] At the same time, the service continued to confidently assert that the Disney project would be compatible with the Mineral King environment.

The Supreme Court scheduled the case for oral argument on October 18, 1971. But in September, two unexpected developments upended the court's personnel. On September 17, 1971, Justice Hugo Black announced his retirement from the court after thirty-four years of service. He died eight days later.[83] Six days after Justice Black's resignation, Justice John Harlan also resigned. He too passed away by the end of the year.[84]

The resignations produced speculation about how the shortage of justices would affect the court's work. The *Fresno Bee* incorrectly reported that the court had postponed the hearing in the Mineral King case until it had its full complement of nine members.[85] However, the court decided not to await the new appointments, perhaps fearing lengthy confirmation battles in the Senate. It recalendared the oral argument in *Sierra Club v. Morton* for Wednesday, November 16, 1971. The Sierra Club, aware of the importance of the standing issue but also needing the court to reach the substantive legal issues on the Mineral King project, requested extra time for oral argument. The court quickly denied the request.[86]

Traveling alone, Lee Selna journeyed from San Francisco to Washington, DC, to argue the case. In contrast, the solicitor general, Erwin Griswold, faced a trip of less than two miles from his office to the Supreme Court.

10: Opening the Courthouse Door

When the Supreme Court convened on November 16, 1971, seven justices took the bench: Chief Justice Warren Burger and Justices William O. Douglas, William J. Brennan, Byron White, Potter Stewart, Thurgood Marshall, and Harry Blackmun.[1] Predicting the outcome was impossible. The law of standing was in flux, and the court was addressing it in the new context of an environmental case.

Lee Selna and other lawyers supporting the Sierra Club were confident that at least one justice, William O. Douglas, would favor broad standing in environmental cases. Douglas had a long history of publicly supporting environmental protection;[2] he was "a one-man lobby shop for the environment."[3] His work included numerous letters on environmental issues and the publication in 1965 of his book *A Wilderness Bill of Rights*.[4] Given this history, Douglas was almost certainly sympathetic to the Sierra Club's position.[5]

Selna did not know, however, that Douglas was seriously considering removing himself from the case. The problem stemmed from Douglas's relationship with the Sierra Club, which included a brief stint on the club's board of directors. Concerned about a potential conflict of interest in this case, Douglas had instructed a law clerk to prepare a chronological summary of his official contacts with the club.[6] They were numerous.

Douglas was a life-long conservationist widely known to be interested in public land decisions. His outspokenness had led the Sierra Club's board of directors in 1959 to vote Douglas a "life membership" as a tribute. Two years later, Douglas had agreed to election to the club's board of directors. Douglas attended a board meeting in 1962 but did not enjoy it. He resigned by the end of the year, ostensibly because the Sierra Club was "now engaging in litigation."[7]

The resignation, however, did not completely sever Douglas's connection to the club. He retained his life membership, and in 1969 he approved use of his name to support David Brower's slate of candidates to the board of directors during the highly contested Sierra Club election that year. Douglas did not resign his life membership in the club until 1970.[8]

When the court called *Sierra Club v. Morton* at 11 a.m., he had not decided if he would remain on the case.

The court of appeals' opinion in the Mineral King case forced the structure of the oral argument prepared by Lee Selna. On a national level, standing was the issue that would most affect future environmental litigation. Moreover, if the Sierra Club lacked standing to sue, its challenge to Mineral King was over. At the same time, the court of appeals had ruled against the Sierra Club on all of its substantive challenges to the approval of the Disney development. If the Supreme Court sustained the club's standing but failed to address those other issues—or, worse, ruled against the club on those issues—the challenge to Mineral King would almost certainly die. So Selna's oral argument had to include those other issues.

Selna brought a prop with him to the court that sat on an easel: a map of the Mineral King area. The map showed the old road into Mineral King and the planned new road, and it distinguished the Forest Service land from the land in the nearly surrounding Sequoia National Park. The prop immediately came into play. After Selna began his argument by summarizing the background of the case and mentioning the game refuge in Mineral King, Chief Justice Burger interrupted, wanting to know what designation on the map corresponded to that area.

When Selna identified the game refuge, the chief justice asked if that area was part of Sequoia National Park. The chief justice's failure to comprehend one of the central geographical distinctions of the case was not entirely unexpected; busy with administrative duties as chief justice, he often took the bench with incomplete knowledge of the cases.[9] But his questions did not make for an auspicious start for the Sierra Club.

Nonetheless, the prop served to get all the justices on the "same page" as Selna proceeded. And he found the follow-up question from the chief justice more hopeful: "[W]hen you say that it [the new road to Mineral King] serves no park purpose, do you mean that . . . its only purpose is to serve the white area which is not part of the park?"[10] Selna quickly agreed; his geography presentation had yielded some fruit.

The argument turned to the heart of the standing issue. Trying to emphasize the club's long-standing interest in Mineral King, the linchpin of its standing theory, Selna stressed that the Sierra Club had helped draw the boundary lines that led to the formation of the game refuge in 1926. However, when he cited use of Mineral King by some club members as an "incident of the club's interest in the area," Justice Blackmun seized on this statement to ask, "Does the record show that?" Blackmun thus signaled his apparent interest in whether or not the record contained evidence of actual use of Mineral King by Sierra Club members.

Selna pointed to testimony in the record about such use in 1920 and a statement by the then-director of the National Park Service: "They [the Sierra Club members] go in there nearly every year . . . and know every nook and corner of it." Blackmun was not satisfied: "But there isn't any direct testimony by the members of the club anywhere in the record, is there?" Selna had to concede there was not. Then, suggesting the weakness of Selna's historical evidence, Blackmun commented that the statement "goes back to the days of John Muir, doesn't it?" Selna could only agree.[11]

The court let Selna argue for a period of time without interruption, and he touched on the need for the court to reach the substantive issues. Justice Potter Stewart then initiated an important exchange exploring the limits of the club's standing theory. Stewart hypothesized the existence of a fan club—"Friends of Walt Disney

Productions"—and wondered if it could enter the case on the side of the government. Selna responded that the court would have to evaluate the club's standing "on a case-by-case basis." Stewart then pressed him: "[O]n what criteria?" Anticipating this key question, Selna explained:

> A variety of criteria might be appropriate. As: has the organization been in existence, and has it taken a stand over an extended period of time that's consistent with its stand? Has it done anything which gives it special expertise in the area that it tries to argue about? Does it have an educational program? Does it write on the subject? Do its members use the area? Is it adequately staffed, so that it can present a case in a way that a court can understand it?[12]

But Stewart foresaw a practical problem, wondering whether "all of these things would have to be tried out and litigated and decided before one could decide whether or not this organization was a proper party." Selna thought the criteria "rather quickly and rather easily could be determined by the court."[13]

Stewart then pursued the issue, inventing yet another hypothetical group, the "Friends of Bigger Highways," which favored the new Mineral King highway. Could it have standing? Selna thought it "conceivable" that the group could.

The exchange initiated by Stewart probed the logical extent of the Sierra Club's interest theory, and his hypotheticals suggested concern both about the theory's reach and the types of proof it required. Fortunately for Selna, Chief Justice Burger jumped in to throw him what looked like a lifeline. Two years previously, Burger had authored a case decided by the court of appeals for the District of Columbia, *Office of Communication of United Church of Christ v. F.C.C.*,[14] in which consumers had been granted standing to challenge a decision by the Federal Communications Commission on a television license. Now, Burger asked "wasn't there a suggestion" in that decision "that the principal test of such an organization is whether it's truly representative of the interests that it seeks to assert."

Burger was perhaps signaling that he was favorably inclined toward broader standing based on interests.[15] However, he then turned to the limits of the club's theory, asking Selna: "Then it wouldn't make any difference whether it was organized last year or 70 years ago, would it, really?" Selna answered that the organization's age might tend to show "whether it's truly representative."[16]

Potter Stewart, however, was not through dissecting the interest theory. He again bore in, wanting to know if "an old man who for seventy years has had a very genuine interest" in a subject could bring the lawsuit. Justice Blackmun raised the possibility of John Muir as a plaintiff. Selna answered affirmatively.

Justice Blackmun, however, also seemed to have concerns similar to Stewart's about the limits of Selna's theory. First, he posited that something other than a broad and general interest would be needed for standing. For example, could the Sierra Club challenge a nuclear plant to be located on the Mississippi River? Selna hedged a bit. He didn't know if the club had a chapter there or expertise in that field. But any group "would have to have competence in the area in which it sought to represent the public interest."[17]

Selna moved on, attacking the Ninth Circuit's statement, in discussing standing, that the Sierra Club had not asserted damage to any of its property or threats to its status. These types of injuries, Selna thought, are not redressable in this case because they are outside the purpose of a conservation statute. That is why the court should adopt the club's standing theory, urged Selna, because conservation groups "may be the only people who will step forward to challenge the illegality."[18]

Selna then tried to pivot from standing to the substantive issues raised by the Mineral King approval, but Blackmun cut him off. He directed Selna back to standing with a question that followed nicely from Selna's point that the club might be the only type of entity that could challenge illegal action. Blackmun asked, "If an organization like the Sierra Club is not qualified to bring litigation of this kind, who would be [able] [t]o protect overreaching by the Government in an area of this kind where, I take it, private plots of land are not anywhere near the Mineral King development?"[19]

The thrust of the question favored the club, since it highlighted a potential consequence of upholding the government's position. But Selna faced a problem responding. There *were* some privately held lots in Mineral King, and some cabin owners held leases on public land and would be economically affected by the proposed development. Selna tried to explain this situation and then agree with the broader point—the potential lack of available plaintiffs with standing. The discussion, however, trailed off into details about those private holdings. The opportunity for Selna to hammer home his point drifted away.

Selna spent the remainder of his opening argument trying to address the substantive issues. He touched on the argument that the highway had no purpose associated with Sequoia National Park, and he argued the dual permit claim as well. Here again, though, Justice Blackmun intervened with a question that touched a Sierra Club nerve: "And yet it [the dual permit mechanism] has been used rather widely, has it not?" Selna sought to factually distinguish the earlier permits for ski areas; here, in contrast to those situations, the uses on the revocable permit lands are "absolutely indispensable."[20]

It sounded weak. So Selna retreated to a stronger point. Congress had deliberately established a limit of eighty acres, and the secretary of agriculture at the time had essentially said this acreage would be sufficient. In doing so, the secretary thus "represent[ed] that if he could grant permits for up to eighty-acres," the practice of combining permits would be discontinued. Then, no doubt concerned by the specter that his position would invalidate all of the eighty-four previous ski permits, Selna argued that the dual permits had not been a consistent administrative practice of the Forest Service. And the court, he proposed, could make its decision applicable only in the future so that it would not affect existing permits.[21]

Finally, after briefly arguing that the Disney development would severely impact the game refuge, Lee Selna sat down.

Erwin Griswold, the solicitor general, then took the podium. The contrast with Selna was pronounced. The sixty-seven-year-old Griswold traveled in the highest echelon of the legal profession. Before being appointed solicitor general, Griswold had forged a distinguished academic career highlighted by service as dean of the Harvard Law School for over twenty years. There, at a small dinner given annually for new women students, a famous story had him asking the women, including Ruth Bader Ginsburg, to justify their presence at the school when their spots could have gone to men. He later informed Ginsburg that he was seeking information that could help him persuade dubious faculty members present at the dinners about the merits of admitting women.[22]

The legendary Griswold knew the justices on the court and was their intellectual equal. He had argued cases in front of the court twenty-nine times before he became solicitor general, and dozens since then. He was brilliant, and his oral argument in this case was surprising.

Griswold opened by trying to establish a theme about "the setting in this case": that the Mineral King Valley was not pristine. He stated: "Mineral King is not a wilderness area, and has not been for nearly a hundred years."[23] He listed the existing development in the area, which included cabins, sixty summer homes, two small resorts, a pack station and public campgrounds. The point was to downplay the environmental consequences of the development.

Griswold then moved into the standing issue, labeling the case "in a very real sense . . . the ultimate case on standing." As his argument on standing later unfolded, it contained little of the nuance found in the government's written brief. Instead, he immediately went for the jugular: "If the petitioner here has standing then I believe it's fair to conclude that any one who asserts an interest in a controversy has standing."[24]

Justice Douglas interrupted Griswold to lead him down a side path. He asked about a new Michigan law that afforded citizens standing to sue in that state's courts and about bills pending in Congress that would grant citizens standing. Griswold acknowledged the bills but hedged about their legality. He was "not sure" that Congress had the power through legislation to create the constitutionally required standing.[25]

But Griswold had embarked on a mission and returned to the consequences of the Sierra Club's position on standing. He pointed out that the club alleged no ownership interest or interference with its activities, or even a special interest in Mineral King. The complaint just alleged a "special interest in the conservation and sound maintenance of the national parks, game refuges and forests of the country." But that interest, Griswold declared, "would include New Hampshire and Maine as well as California."[26] He painted a picture of widespread geographic standing if the court accepted the Sierra Club argument.

Justice White tried to rein him in with a question: "[W]ould they need only to amend the allegation, to say that . . . their members continually run pack trips into Mineral King?" The government's brief had seemed to concede that such actions could demonstrate standing, and Griswold grudgingly responded that it "would help, but they have not done it."

Then Griswold did something curious, calling the court's attention to the *amicus* briefs filed by the County of Tulare and the Far West Ski Association. Both briefs, he said, "it seems to me, are in some respects rather better than the brief which we have filed."[27] This was a remarkable statement by the government's chief lawyer about the brief produced by the office that he directed. His statement indirectly endorsed the arguments in those two "friend of the court" briefs that sought to sharply curtail standing. The government's brief had not gone that far.

Griswold's overall point was that the Sierra Club had chosen to rest on its interest theory of standing and had not argued use of Mineral King as the basis for injury. Now, said Griswold, it must accept the consequences of that choice. He drove home what he saw as those consequences through a series of hypothetical questions:

> If it is the fact that it [the Sierra Club] is a group that gives it standing, how big a group must it be? Three members or five or fifty? Or fifty thousand?
>
> What reason is there for picking any number? If any group has

> standing because it has an intellectual or emotional interest, does it not inevitably follow that any individual who asserts an interest likewise has standing to raise these legal questions?
>
> If the Sierra Club has standing, as Mr. Justice Blackmun suggested, would not John Muir have standing?
>
> If the Sierra Club has standing, why does it not follow that . . . my estimable former student Ralph Nader [would] likewise have standing to raise in court any questions of law which appeal to them as being in the public interest?[28]

The chief justice cut off the soliloquy, asking if the solicitor would accept the holding on standing found in the television licensing case Burger had authored, which found that listeners had standing to challenge the renewal of a television license. Here, Griswold conceded a bit, allowing that he "can accept" the holding "perhaps because I happen to like the outcome." The Mineral King case, he explained, was different because no administrative proceeding had taken place before the Forest Service's issuance of the permit. In the television case, the parties had appeared before the Federal Communications Commission and made arguments. But the television case was "very close to the line."[29]

He then returned to the parade of horribles that he envisioned flowing from the Sierra Club's position, and the court listened without interrupting him. Lawsuits, he said, could be brought against government officers and served anywhere in the United States. Theoretically, "we could have a thousand suits brought by interested individuals and organizations . . . with resulting vast confusion."[30]

The Constitution, concluded Griswold, did not intend courts to operate in this fashion. If standing was broadened, the country might have a system of government where "every legal question arising in the core of government would be decided by the courts." For emphasis, he reiterated his overall theme: "If there is standing in this case, I find it very difficult to think of any legal issue arising in Government which will not have to await one or more decisions of the Court" before the government administrator could act.[31] He concluded that Congress, not the courts, should provide any needed check on agencies such as the Forest Service.

At this point, the chief justice adjourned the argument for lunch.

When the argument resumed, Griswold had only seven minutes of time remaining. Instead of addressing the substantive legal issues of the Mineral King appeal, such as the acreage limitation on permits, he returned to his theme that the Sierra Club's position on standing could lead to disastrous results. Would courts not be better off, he contended, "if they do not undertake to decide all the legal questions that anyone—anyone—wants to present to them?[32]

Unlike the written brief produced by his office, which Griswold apparently disliked, his oral argument launched a wholesale assault on the Sierra Club's position. He claimed that if accepted, the club's position would cause widespread, adverse consequences to the executive and judicial branches of government. In the process, he avoided referring to the specifics of standing in environmental cases. Rather, he portrayed the issue broadly in terms of standing to adjudicate controversial "social and economic controversies," framing the issue in a way that he must have felt would concern the court.

When Griswold finally turned to the substantive issues of the Mineral King controversy in the last minutes of his argument, he tried a new approach. The court, he said, could deal with the substantive merits by concluding that "the legal situation is such that no showing of facts would warrant" an injunction. In other words, the court could avoid an extensive, issue-by-issue analysis of the substantive issues by concluding that, viewed as a whole, they would not support the district court's order enjoining the Mineral King project until trial.[33]

Justice White did not understand, asking whether Griswold was saying that the court should not decide the substantive issues. The following colloquy ensued:

JUSTICE BYRON R. WHITE: We don't have, finally, to decide them?

MR. GRISWOLD: You don't have, finally, to decide them. But my position is that it can be readily found that they are not serious enough so as to warrant the granting of a permanent injunction.[34]

Here, Griswold invited the court along a narrow, inconsistent path. He would have the court avoid addressing the specific allegations of illegality raised by the Sierra Club while, at the same time, overturning an injunction on the basis that those same allegations were insubstantial.

He then quickly skipped through the substantive issues. He emphasized the past use of both term and revocable permits on eighty-four occasions over many years. Then, taking a few liberties with the record, he justified the "park purpose" of the new Mineral King highway on the ground that the road "will enable people to see areas in the park which would not otherwise be available to them." He also informed the court that he was "advised" that the road would improve access to fight forest fires in Sequoia National Park—a previously unexpressed justification for the road that Park Service employees had come up with just before the argument.[35]

Finally, he reached the question of the electric power line through the park. Here, he admitted that when the statute was "read alone, it becomes very difficult to deal with," since it seemed to prohibit electric transmission lines through Sequoia National Park. He urged the court to narrowly limit that prohibition to include only power originating from hydroelectric facilities.[36]

Just before Griswold's time expired, Justice Blackmun posed a question revealing his mastery of the factual background. His notes on the case showed that he thought the substantive claims were serious. The question he asked dealt with an issue that had recurred throughout the Mineral King dispute: would the road be big enough to service all the projected visitors to the valley? After observing that it was a two-lane road "with little turn places or passing places," Blackmun commented: "It strikes me as though this is likely insufficient for the number of daily guests and trucking requirements for the Disney Center."

Griswold answered that if additional capacity proved necessary, the proposed permit required supplying it through "mechanical means" rather by than enlarging the road. He advanced the very unlikely idea that the mechanical means "would be helicopters or maybe some other kind of airplane."[37] So, his otherwise powerful argument ended by drifting into fiction.

Lee Selna had used almost all his allotted time in his opening argument, but Chief Justice Burger allowed him a few extra minutes because Griswold had run over. Selna tried to rebut Griswold's repeated suggestion that the Sierra Club sought all-encompassing standing: "[It] should be clear from our argument that we do not urge that the doors of courts be opened wide to anyone."[38] Under the club's interest theory, the court could test an organization's or an individual's qualifications to serve as a plaintiff.

Then he turned to the club's actual use of Mineral King. Yes, he affirmed, the club has run pack trips in Mineral King, and this fact was not alleged in the complaint. But Selna held to his position: any interference with the pack trips by the Disney development "would not have been of sufficient importance to this Club to undertake the litigation." Selna refused, as a backup, to grasp the alternative "use" theory urged by the Wilderness Society brief. Finally, he said that the club's theory would not inundate the courts with litigation. The "practicalities and the realities" of carrying out this type of litigation would limit such suits.[39]

Soon thereafter, the argument ended.

Two days later, the court convened in private to discuss the case. Both Justices Blackmun and Douglas took notes describing the deliberations, and those notes afford insights into the thinking of the seven justices.

The chief justice spoke first. He saw the issue as "how much judicial surveillance" there should be on executive actions. Burger exhibited caution and wanted the case decided "very narrowly."[40] He raised the same issue that was heavily discussed during the oral argument: If the Sierra Club had standing under its theory, what was the stopping point? Burger seemed to indicate that he might support a limited holding granting standing.[41]

Justice Douglas initially passed on expressing any opinion. He later explained to the justices that he "may end up not participating" because of his ten-year association with the Sierra Club. He informed them that he had resigned from the club a year previously and that he had stopped the work that he had been pursuing with environmentalists to preserve the Chesapeake and Ohio Canal.[42]

Justice William Brennan thought the case "did not require [the] Sierra Club to present the issue as broadly as it did" in its complaint. He thought that evidence of use by club members could be brought in under the allegations in paragraph 3 of the club's complaint. He later commented that he would not decide the case broadly but would overturn the court of appeals' ruling and send the case back to the trial court.[43]

Both Justices Potter Stewart and Byron White seriously doubted the Sierra Club's position. Under Judge Sweigert's ruling, thought White, "everyone in the US is now a private Attorney General."[44] The Sierra Club, he warned, "can't sue to enjoin an unaesthetic building in New York City." For his part, Stewart informed the justices that he "can't agree with the District Court" and "agrees with the Court of Appeal." Otherwise, he thought, there would be "no end to it."[45]

During the oral argument, Harry Blackmun had shown the most knowledge of the facts of the case, and he turned out to be deeply concerned about the environment. He understood the underlying issues in the case. His predecision memorandum set forth his "reaction" to the case: the court of appeals "should be reversed, and the temporary injunction reinstated."[46] Douglas read Blackmun as "about where WJB [Brennan] is" and "may be reaching for a position he emotionally desires."[47]

That left Thurgood Marshall. The Sierra Club had reason to think Marshall would incline toward expanded standing. Eight months earlier, Marshall had authored an opinion, *Citizens to Preserve Overton Park, Inc. v. Volpe*, in which citizen organizations sought to enjoin a freeway through a park in downtown Memphis, Tennessee. The Sierra Club had been one of the plaintiffs in that case, although not the lead plaintiff, and the case had not been decided on standing grounds. Nonetheless, the first part of Marshall's opinion read, "The growing public concern about the quality of our natural environment" had prompted Congressional legislation "designed to curb the accelerating destruction of our country's natural beauty."[48]

Moreover, before his appointment to the Supreme Court, Marshall had worked for the Legal Defense Fund of the National Association for the Advancement of Colored People. That organization's standing had been recognized in cases where Marshall was lead counsel.[49] The Sierra Club thought he would understand the need for standing in environmental cases.[50] His law clerk's memo on the case endorsed the Sierra Club's position, arguing in part that "[r]elaxed standing rules invariably protect minority interests who rely on the judiciary to vindicate their interests."[51]

During the conference, however, Douglas's notes showed Marshall as saying only that he would affirm the decision that the Sierra Club lacked standing.[52] The standing issue never seemed to engage him.

In short, the court was slightly uncertain but inclined toward affirming the decision of the court of appeals. Except perhaps for Blackmun and Douglas, if he stayed in the case, no justice showed interest in addressing the substantive issues of the Mineral King dispute. Their attention centered on whether or not the Sierra Club possessed standing to raise those issues.

Stewart, White, and Marshall appeared poised to deny the club standing, with two of them supporting the court of appeals' reasoning. Burger thought the club's interest theory seemed too expansive—he couldn't see the "stopping point." Brennan and Blackmun were sympathetic to the club, but neither expressed any real agreement with the club's interest theory. Brennan, in particular, was focused on whether or not the Sierra Club's complaint would support a finding of standing based on the actual use of Mineral King. And Douglas, who could be expected to affirm the club's standing, might drop out of the case.

Given the doubt about the Sierra Club's position, the chief justice assigned Potter Stewart to draft an opinion.

Stewart circulated his first draft to his colleagues in mid-February 1972. It began by recognizing the Mineral King Valley as "an area of great natural beauty nestled in the Sierra Nevada Mountains." Its inaccessibility and lack of development "have limited the number of visitors each year, and at the same time have preserved the valley's quality as a quasi-wilderness area largely uncluttered by the products of civilization." Stewart then described the actions of the Forest Service, "[p]rodded by a rapidly increasing demand for ski facilities," that resulted in the acceptance of the Disney proposal. Finally, Stewart summarized the litigation's history.[53]

Stewart then turned to standing, which he declared was traditionally defined as "[w]hether a party has a sufficient stake in an otherwise justiciable controversy to obtain judicial resolution of that controversy." He noted that where Congress had provided by statute for judicial review, "the inquiry as to standing must begin with a determination of whether the statute in question authorizes review at the behest of the plaintiff."[54] Here, the statute that the Sierra Club relied upon was section 10 of the Administrative Procedure Act, which authorized judicial review if a person could show that they were "suffering legal wrong because of agency action, or adversely affected or aggrieved by agency action."[55]

The question was what Congress meant by requiring a plaintiff to be "adversely affected or aggrieved." At this point, Stewart segued into the court's recent opinion in *Association of Data Processing*. In that case, the court had decided that plaintiffs possessed standing where they alleged that an administrative action had caused "injury in fact" and the injury was to an interest "arguably within the zone of interests" protected by banking statutes allegedly violated there.[56]

Stewart's draft opinion had now fully situated the standing issue. None of the court's previous cases had addressed an issue that "has arisen with increasing frequency" in recent years: "what must be alleged by persons who claim injury of a noneconomic nature to interests that are widely shared."[57] This was the heart of the standing question before the court: how far did standing extend to plaintiffs who were members of a large group holding environmental interests and whose injury was to those noneconomic interests?

The question of standing for such widely shared interests, Stewart said, was not present in the Memphis freeway case. The court there had found that members of the organizations had standing because they charged that the freeway would impair their use of park land. Stewart's discussion of the Memphis decision signaled where he was headed: in establishing standing, a plaintiff's use of the area of land at issue was important. The Sierra Club, of course, had declined to rely on such use.

Stewart confirmed that the *type* of environmental injury alleged by the Sierra Club could support standing. The club had pled that the change in uses caused by the development at Mineral King, and the attendant change in the aesthetics and ecology of the area, constituted injury. Stewart agreed that these concerns over "aesthetic and environmental well-being" were sufficient grounds upon which to seek legal protection.

However, Stewart's draft then rejected the Sierra Club's claim that it had alleged sufficient facts to claim such an injury. The "injury in fact" needed for standing, he explained, requires "more than an injury to a cognizable interest," such as an interest in the environment. It requires "that the party seeking review be himself among the injured." Here, the Sierra Club had "failed to allege that it or its members will be affected in any of their activities or pastimes by the Disney development."[58] He continued: "Nowhere in the pleadings or affidavits did the Club state that its members use Mineral King for any purpose, much less that they use it in any way that will be significantly affected by the proposed actions of the respondents."

A footnote elaborated this critical point. It recognized that the *amicus curiae* brief filed by the Wilderness Society asserted such use by club members, but the pleadings omitted those allegations.

Moreover, the Sierra Club's reply brief "specifically declines to rely on those individualized interests as a basis for standing."[59]

The Sierra Club's mistake, Stewart explained, was in regarding allegations of individualized injury as superfluous because the lawsuit was a "public action." The club had theorized that in such actions, the club's long-standing concern and expertise in the area gave it standing as a representative of the public. The gist of the error, instructed Stewart, was this: the court had broadened the *categories* of injury to include environmental damage, but it had not abandoned "the requirement that the party seeking review must himself have suffered an injury."

Stewart's draft opinion recognized that if an organization has members who are among the injured, it could represent those members in a lawsuit.[60] Stewart then went on to address a critical link. If a plaintiff had suffered this type of "individual injury," it could more broadly raise public interest issues in an environmental case. So, a means existed to raise the types of issues brought by the club in the Mineral King litigation.

The Sierra Club had claimed that the government was laying a trap by pressing for a narrow concept of standing based on individual injury as a means of preventing an injunction that would uphold the broader public interest.[61] The trap perceived by the Sierra Club, said Stewart, was illusory. Once standing was established, a party can assert the interests of the general public in seeking an injunction.

Finally, Stewart addressed the lack of a "stopping point" under the Sierra Club's interest theory, a weakness that had concerned several justices. Under that theory's logic, reasoned Stewart, "it is difficult to perceive why any individual citizen with the same bona fide special interest would not also be entitled" to initiate litigation.[62]

In sum, Stewart's draft expanded the type of injury needed for standing in a way that was largely favorable to those plaintiffs seeking judicial review on environmental grounds. It recognized environmental harm as a type of injury. However, it refused to abandon the traditional requirement that a plaintiff must suffer some sort of specific injury. In doing so, the draft slammed the door on the

Sierra Club's challenge to the Mineral King approvals. The club had gambled on a wider interest theory of standing and lost.

After the court's post-oral argument conference, William O. Douglas immediately began writing a dissent. He was the fastest writer on the court; Justice White described him as a "paper factory." Douglas may have concluded by this early point that he would not recuse himself because of his past relationship with the Sierra Club. In any event, by the time he released a draft of his dissenting opinion to the other justices on February 14, the same day Stewart circulated his majority opinion, he would not turn back.

Douglas's dissent would have almost no influence on the practical aspects of the law of standing as they further developed.[63] It would, however, become famous for its literate passion about the environment, its instruction on the perils facing wilderness lands, and its novel ideas on standing. Douglas was not primarily trying to convince his fellow justices to accept his position on standing; rather, he was reaching out to educate a broader public audience on environmental issues.

His first draft outlined his basic views and then, through seven more drafts still not circulated to the court, he added lengthy footnotes supporting those views. The footnotes cited a wide range of nonlegal authority. He then continued to fine-tune the dissent through more drafts.

The Douglas dissent as first sent to his colleagues proposed a new, innovative way of looking at standing. A natural resource at risk of being destroyed would itself have standing to litigate its future. Douglas explained that the "critical question" of standing:

> would be simplified and also put neatly in focus if we fashioned a federal rule that allowed environmental issues to be litigated . . . in the name of the inanimate object about to be despoiled, defaced, or invaded by roads and bulldozers and where injury is the subject of public outrage. Contemporary public concern for protecting nature's ecological equilibrium should lead to the conferral of standing upon

> environmental objects to sue for their own preservation. This suit would therefore more properly be labeled as *Mineral King v. Morton*.[64]

He would cite as the origin of this idea a recent article written by a young law professor, Christopher Stone.[65]

Douglas argued for this concept of standing by utilizing his knowledge of natural systems and his personal experience in the outdoors. He pointed out that other inanimate objects—ships and corporations, for example—are parties in litigation. Why not a river as a party? A river, he postulated, "is the living symbol of all the life it sustains or nourishes—fish, aquatic insects, water ouzels, otter, fisher, deer, elk, and all other animals, including man" who depend upon or enjoy it. Accordingly, people "who have a meaningful relation to that body of water—whether it be a fisherman, a canoeist, a zoologist, or a logger—must be able to speak for the values which the river represents and which are threatened with destruction."[66]

He then applied these principles to Mineral King. Those who "hike it, fish it, hunt it, camp in it, frequent it or visit it merely to sit in solitude or wonderment" legitimately speak for Mineral King. In a long footnote, he delved into the adverse environmental effects that he saw the Disney project causing to the valley. He then concluded: "Those who have that intimate relation with the inanimate object about to be injured, polluted, or otherwise despoiled are its legitimate spokesmen."[67] Douglas's theory would grant standing to the Sierra Club because of the club's relationship to Mineral King.

The Douglas dissent also explicated a second theme: the need for judicial review of government decisions concerning public natural resources. He appended to his dissent part of the transcript of the oral argument made by Solicitor General Erwin Griswold in which Griswold expressed the fear that expanded standing would lead to "government by the judiciary." Having laid out the Griswold view verbatim, Douglas flatly rejected it. Inanimate objects need spokespersons, he argued, because the pressures on public agencies to allow development of them "are enormous." He accused those agencies of being "under the control of powerful interests who manipulate them."[68]

Douglas cited the Forest Service as a chief offender. The agency, he charged, "was notorious for its alignment with lumber companies, although its mandate from Congress directs it to consider the various aspects of multiple use in its supervision of the national forests."[69] Douglas supported his argument with citations in footnotes that ranged from law review articles to newspaper excerpts to congressional materials.

He concluded by summarizing his rejection of Griswold's position about the effect of broader standing on the judiciary:

> The voice of the inanimate object, therefore, should not be stilled. That does not mean that the judiciary takes over the managerial functions from the federal agency. It merely means that before these priceless bits of Americana (such as a valley, an alpine meadow, a river, or a lake) are forever lost or so transformed . . . the voice of existing beneficiaries of these environmental wonders should be heard.[70]

If an inanimate object has standing, "there will be assurances that all of the forms of life which it represents will stand before the Court. . . . [T]hose people who have so frequented the place as to know its values and wonders will be able to speak for the entire ecological community."[71]

In sum, Douglas eloquently argued why the law must allow ecological views to be heard. He offered a new concept to accomplish that goal: granting standing to the inanimate objects being threatened. Interestingly, many of the examples he cited of individuals who could represent inanimate objects also would have standing under the majority's "use" rubric. However, under Douglas's conception of standing, they would represent the resource, not themselves.

After Stewart circulated his draft opinion to the court's other members, Thurgood Marshall responded almost immediately that he would join in the opinion. In a case full of surprises, Marshall's adverseness to the Sierra Club's standing would remain a mystery.[72] When the opinion issued, court watchers would be surprised.[73]

William Brennan also responded to the Stewart first draft. In a "Dear Potter" note to Stewart with copies to the other justices, he informed him that "[i]n due course I shall prepare a dissent."[74]

Chief Justice Burger then joined Stewart's opinion. Now, with Marshall and Burger agreeing with him, Stewart needed the agreement of only one more justice to form a majority.

On March 30, Justice Brennan circulated a dissent that tried to divert the court from deciding the standing issue. Brennan suggested that the writ of certiorari, the formal order issued by the court to hear the case, should be "dismissed as improvidently granted."[75] In other words, he sent out an eleventh-hour plea that the court should not decide the case but instead should dismiss it.

From the record and the assertions of the *amicus curiae* brief filed by the Wilderness Society, Brennan began, it seems that the Sierra Club and its members in fact use Mineral King. The club had not pleaded this use in its lawsuit, but that omission was because the district court found the club's "interest" allegations sufficient and did not require further allegations or evidence of use. The difficulty with accepting the excuse offered by Brennan, of course, was that the Sierra Club's brief in the Supreme Court had disavowed any reliance on standing based on use of Mineral King. But, Brennan went on, elsewhere the club did say that it "represents the interest of its members who actually physically use and enjoy" Mineral King. In this situation, concluded Brennan, the court should not decide the case on a basis that "could easily be avoided."[76]

Brennan's suggestion that the case be dismissed drew no support and was unconvincing. Brennan assumed that the Sierra Club would still have the opportunity to amend its lawsuit to show use after the Supreme Court decided the case, but this assumption was questionable. The club had steadfastly relied on the interest theory that the Supreme Court was about to reject and disavowed the use theory that Stewart's draft opinion adopted. Under those circumstances, the government would strongly argue that the club had waived any right to amend. An even larger problem, however, was that this argument supplied no reason for the court to avoid deciding the standing issue now.

A second version of Brennan's draft dissent, released one day later, argued that the court should decide the standing issue "only in a case that squarely presents it."[77] But this case did just that.

Brennan's attempt to sidetrack the issue attracted no support. He moved on.

On April 1, Byron White informed Potter Stewart that he joined in Stewart's opinion.[78] White seemed annoyed by how the dispute over standing had arisen. He queried bluntly, "Why didn't the Sierra Club have one goddamn member walk through the park and then there would have been standing to sue."[79] With White's assent, Stewart's opinion now had the four votes needed to form a majority of the seven justices and become the opinion of the court denying standing to the Sierra Club.

On April 7, Harry Blackmun circulated a dissent. While his dissenting opinion in *Sierra Club v. Morton* would be eclipsed by the remarkable dissent that Justice Douglas would file, it stands as a "cry from the heart" from a justice on the high court for only two years and still finding his voice there.[80]

Blackmun had studied the case carefully. The predecision memo that he dictated, part of his usual practice before oral argument,[81] began by stating that it was "a good environmental case with some specific facts and not mere speculation."[82] He entered the oral argument with a list of questions and concerns about the case. The oral argument had not changed his mind.

Blackmun's draft dissent began by describing Justice Stewart's opinion as a "practical one espousing and adhering to traditional notions of standing as somewhat modernized" by recent cases. But the Mineral King case, continued Blackmun, "is not ordinary, run-of-the mill litigation."[83] He continued:

> The case poses . . . significant aspects of a wide, growing and disturbing problem, that is, the Nation's and the world's deteriorating environment with its resulting ecological disturbances. Must our law be so rigid and our procedural concepts so inflexible that we render ourselves helpless when the existing methods and the traditional concepts do not quite fit and do not prove to be entirely adequate for new issues?[84]

According to Blackmun, the majority decision would result in the Disney development hastily proceeding to completion, and Mineral King would become defaced, at least in part, and cease to be "uncluttered by the products of civilization."[85]

Blackmun would adopt one of two alternative approaches to decide the appeal. The first would be to recognize the Sierra Club's standing "on condition that the Sierra Club forthwith amend its complaint to meet the specifications the Court describes for standing." This path would keep the merits of the case alive, and those merits "are substantial and deserve resolution." For example, he saw the dual permit device as potentially "a means of avoiding the 80-acre . . . limitation imposed by Congress" and raised the issue of the consistency of the "enormous development" with the game refuge.[86]

The second option offered by Blackmun was an "imaginative expansion" of the traditional concept of standing to "enable an organization such as the Sierra Club, possessed, as it is, of pertinent, bona fide and well-recognized attributes and purposes in the area of environment, to litigate environmental issues." The expansion, he thought, "need not be very extensive" and "would be no cause for alarm." No one need fear that "Pandora's box will be opened," as the courts can exercise appropriate restraints, as they have in the past.[87]

The Blackmun dissent then delved into some of the case's facts. It focused on the traffic that would use the new road, which would average one vehicle every six seconds, not including service vehicles. "Is this," asked Blackmun, "the way we perpetuate the wilderness and its beauty, solitude and quiet?"[88]

Finally, he pointed out what he viewed as an ironic result of the majority holding, which grounded standing in use of Mineral King. Those users would be fishers, campers, guides, or people with general outdoor prowess—people who, thought Blackmun, would be employed by visitors coming to the valley to ski. These users were unlikely to oppose the "Disney-governmental project" but would instead view it "as one that should benefit [them] economically."[89] Blackmun thus saw use-based standing as producing a counterintuitive result.

Douglas joined Blackmun's dissent. The alignment with Douglas felt strange to Blackmun, who thought that Douglas did not respect his intellectual abilities. Blackmun also worried that his dissent was too emotional. After his dissent was released to the public, he received a note of congratulations from a law professor whom he knew. Blackmun replied that he thought Douglas's dissent "truly an eloquent one" but not appropriate for him to join. He continued, "I am concerned about ecological problems, and I fear that my concern may have been much too apparent."[90]

As for Brennan's separate and final dissenting opinion, he agreed with Blackmun's second "imaginative" approach to expand standing. He also would go further and decide the club's substantive claims that the Forest Service and the Park Service had violated various laws in approving the project and the road. He concurred with Justice Blackmun that the merits of these claims "are substantial."[91]

The die was cast. Potter Stewart's opinion had garnered the needed four votes for a majority. The Sierra Club had staked its case on the interest theory of standing, disavowing the use theory, and it lost that bet.

However, just as the justices' positions were seemingly locked in, Potter Stewart decided to make one final change to his majority opinion. Stewart's opinion did not exhibit hostility to the Sierra Club's underlying substantive claims in the case; his concern was about ensuring meaningful limits on standing. Moreover, he had seen Blackmun's dissenting opinion, issued just days before, which had suggested a remand so the Sierra Club could amend its complaint.

And Stewart also had read Brennan's first dissenting opinion, which insisted that the Sierra Club could amend its complaint if the court dismissed the case.

At the last minute, Stewart decided to clarify the effect of his opinion on the Sierra Club's case. He handwrote a new, last sentence into footnote 8 of his draft opinion.[92] This footnote explained that the *amicus curiae* brief of the Wilderness Society had asserted that the Sierra Club members had used the Mineral King area, but that the club had declined to rely on this individualized use. Stewart's revised footnote 8, with its newly added last sentence, now read in pertinent part:

> [T]he Wilderness Society and others . . . asserted that the Sierra Club has conducted regular camping trips into the Mineral King area, and that various members of the Club have used and continue to use the area for recreational purposes. These allegations were not contained in the pleadings, nor were they brought to the attention of the Court of Appeals. Moreover, the Sierra Club in its reply brief specifically declines to rely on its individualized interest, as a basis for standing. . . . Our decision does not, of course, bar the Sierra Club from seeking in the District Court to amend its complaint by a motion under Rule 15, Federal Rules of Civil Procedure.[93]

For good measure, Stewart added another small change to the last paragraph of the opinion: "[W]e intimate no view on the merits of the complaint," that is, on the substantive allegations that the federal agencies had violated the law in approving the project.[94]

The opinion now made clear that the Sierra Club could try to keep the case alive on remand before Judge Sweigert by seeking to amend its complaint. One week later, on April 19, the court released its opinion in *Sierra Club v. Morton* to the public.

The Sierra Club's challenge to the Mineral King decision remained alive. However, it still faced significant, perhaps insurmountable obstacles.

THE FATE OF MINERAL KING

11: Cracks in the Wall of Support

Returning to San Francisco from the oral argument, Lee Selna had been "optimistic about the court's decision," and his optimistic view spread through the club.[1] A *Washington Post* article on the argument reported that Chief Justice Burger and Justice Harry Blackmun had appeared to favor the club's position.[2] The issuance of the decision came as a hard blow.

In its public reaction, though, the club sought to project a positive attitude. The most categorical statement came from Jim Moorman, now the executive director of the Sierra Club Legal Defense Fund, which would take over the case from Lee Selna. Moorman promised: "There isn't going to be any ski resort in Mineral King."[3] The Sierra Club's press release adopted the same attitude, declaring that the Sierra Club "interprets today's Supreme Court decision on the Mineral King case as a technical setback, but by no means the end of the line in the case."[4] The club had used a similar phrase—"temporary setback"—to describe the court of appeals' devastating decision two years before.

Despite the party line, hints of the club's great disappointment surfaced in the press. In the same Fresno newspaper that contained Moorman's statement, McCloskey admitted "We've been most shocked and dismayed by the rejection of our appeal." He continued that "at this hour it's not entirely clear what this [decision] means for environmental litigation."[5] The Sierra Club's president termed the decision a "grievous blow to democracy."[6]

Sequoia National Forest Supervisor Jim James asserted that the decision "cleared a major roadblock toward developing year-around recreation at Mineral King."[7] The Forest Service announced that it would "promptly review all elements of the plan with Walt Disney specialists." It would determine whether there was "agreement on any changes in the plan" and "pick up the development program" at the point where it had stopped three years before when the litigation began.[8] As it turned out, these unidentified "changes" would soon make headlines.

Card Walker, the president of Walt Disney Productions and one of the company's two leaders following the death of Roy Disney in December of the previous year, sang the same tune as the Forest Service. The court's decision, he declared, would allow the Forest Service to proceed with its plans for the development of Mineral King.[9]

The press had some difficulty deciphering the effect of the court's opinion. The headlines mostly reported the opinion as a loss for the Sierra Club, with some implying that the case was over. The *Los Angeles Times* titled one of its articles "Sierra Club Loses High Court Bid to Block Ski Resort,"[10] and the *San Francisco Examiner* headlined "Sierra Club Loses on Mineral King."[11] The *Washington Post* caption would perplex the average reader: "Ecologists Lose Suit But Win."[12]

Beneath the headlines, though, the coverage generally recognized that the opinion had left some room for further litigation over Mineral King. The *Los Angeles Times* thought that the decision "did everything but invite" the club to amend its complaint and again attempt to block the development.[13] More cautiously, the *New York Times* declared that "the new ruling . . . may not prevent conservation groups from filing suits in environmental cases."[14]

The dissent by Justice Douglas, with its sweepingly poetic references to various distinctive places, environmental features, and ecology, soon caught the attention of the press. Two major newspapers, the *Washington Post* and *Los Angeles Times*, reprinted excerpts from the dissent on their editorial pages.[15] Justice Douglas had aimed his dissent at an audience much wider than just attorneys and judges, so he undoubtedly approved.

Lost in the immediate flood of press coverage, however, was the fact that the decision had not disturbed the court of appeals' rulings against the Sierra Club on the substantive challenges to the Mineral King development. Even if the club successfully amended its complaint to establish standing, those rulings constituted a formidable barrier to ultimate success in the case. While the Sierra Club's press release claimed that the decision "has opened several avenues of legal recourse by which the club can win the battle,"[16] that claim was exaggerated. Even if the club could amend its complaint to establish standing, the outlook for winning the overall "battle" appeared grim.

Moreover, the effort to stimulate Congress into enacting legislation that would place Mineral King in Sequoia National Park remained stalled. Four nearly identical bills had been introduced proposing that course of action, but all four had been assigned to the graveyard of the House Committee on Interior and Insular Affairs.[17] They were going nowhere.

The Supreme Court's opinion on the issue of standing was, of course, vitally important to other environmental groups now filing lawsuits to challenge projects. The court had linked the injury needed for standing to use of an area, and the Sierra Club seemed well positioned to meet that requirement with Mineral King. But it was uncertain whether or not other environmental groups could show the requisite injury in various situations.

A *Wall Street Journal* article analyzing the *Sierra Club v. Morton* decision pinpointed this critical concern. Quoting an unidentified "court watcher," it stated that the Sierra Club may be able to prove the requisite injury, but "other groups may not be in a position to allege such injury."[18] Even the Sierra Club's press release, otherwise hopeful about the future of the Mineral King litigation, quoted Sierra Club President Raymond J. Sherwin to the effect that the decision "has left the entire issue of standing of public interest groups quite indefinite."[19] A publication of Friends of the Earth, the organization formed by David Brower, thought the decision "may hurt other groups more than it does the Sierra Club."[20]

As it turned out, the new groups were growing rapidly and generally had members whose use of particular areas and resources was affected by government action. They thus would usually be able to meet the test for standing established by *Sierra Club v. Morton*.

Meanwhile, the parties in the Mineral King litigation pondered their next moves before Judge Sweigert. However, the legal and political world of the Mineral King project had changed substantially since 1969, when the case had started. New forces would soon exert control over the project's future.

Most importantly, Congress had passed the National Environmental Policy Act of 1969. This law, known as NEPA, required federal agencies to prepare an environmental impact statement, or EIS for short, on "major Federal actions significantly affecting the quality of the human environment."[21] The EIS was to examine the environmental impact of a proposed action, any adverse environmental effects that could not be avoided if the project was implemented, and alternatives to the proposed action. The federal courts had increasingly enjoined projects until public agencies like the Forest Service met their obligations under NEPA.

The Forest Service would have to prepare an environmental impact statement for the Mineral King project—a "major federal action" that would affect the environment—before giving any final approvals. Recognizing as much, Slim Davis, still in charge of the project for the Forest Service, had tried to seize the initiative before the Supreme Court issued its opinion. In January 1972, he had forwarded a draft of an impact statement on Mineral King to the Forest Service's director of education in Washington, DC.

The cover letter accompanying the draft revealed Davis's annoyance at complying with NEPA. He argued that "[w]e are dealing here with a decision made long before" the enactment of NEPA, a decision "fully supported by the Government" up to the Supreme Court. He contended that, because the Forest Service had already contracted with Disney, the procedures of NEPA did not apply to the Mineral King project. His region of the Forest Service did not intend to send copies of the draft impact statement out for review or to hold public meetings. He was sending the draft statement to Washington simply to "anticipat[e] possible future challenges" after the Supreme Court ruled.[22]

The draft EIS prepared under Davis's direction defended the decision to develop Mineral King; it contained little analysis of the project's environmental impacts. For example, after listing fifteen categories of facilities that Disney would build at Mineral King, the draft deferred analyzing their impacts. It noted that "Mineral King has been termed 'unique,' but its really unique quality is the excellence of its winter sports potential."[23]

Four months later, the Washington office of the Forest Service replied to Davis, essentially rejecting his draft. It instructed that the EIS must scrupulously follow the Forest Service's NEPA guidelines, as "[i]t is going to be reviewed by a great many highly qualified and respected people and we want to be in the clear." Consequently, "[m]uch more needs to be included in the statement."[24]

Davis's attempt to shortcut NEPA failed. The Sierra Club's litigation had sensitized the Forest Service to the need for fully complying with federal laws regarding Mineral King. The Park Service also recognized that it must prepare an EIS for its decision on the road. Eventually, the obvious efficiencies led the two agencies to contemplate preparing a single document.[25]

The impact statement would affect the future of the Mineral King development in three important ways. First, it would take some time to prepare the document. Second, the EIS would be subject to judicial review, so the agency could not cut corners in the manner suggested by Slim Davis. Third, for the first time, the environmental effects of the Mineral King development would be subject to comprehensive analysis.

Meanwhile, Disney dropped a bombshell.

After the Supreme Court's decision, the Disney executives sought to generate new momentum for the project that would ensure the goodwill of the public, and, at the same time, blunt environmental attacks on it. The company decided to implement Bob Hicks's proposal to build a railroad to Mineral King. By doing so, it sought to smother the continuing criticism of the new road.

Disney carefully orchestrated the announcement using the methods that, in the past, had ensured favorable publicity for its project. A press conference would be held in the chambers of the Tulare County Board of Supervisors on May 3, 1972. It flew up journalists from Los Angeles on the Disney airplane.

Card Walker, the company's president, announced the major change in the project, which would obviate the need for a road through Sequoia National Park:

> [T]he Disney plan now includes an electrically-powered, cog-assisted railroad to take visitors into the Mineral King valley from a point in Sequoia National Forest just east of its common boundary with Sequoia National Park. We propose the extension of this transportation system westward across Sequoia National Park to a termination point in the Oak Grove area, which is below and outside the boundary of the National Park.[26]

The railroad would be publicly owned but operated by Disney under a thirty-year contract. By eliminating the part of the road through the park, it would save the State of California $30 million. The railroad would generally travel on the right-of-way that Tulare County owned for the existing road. Because of this change, the Mineral King development would no longer need to locate above-ground electric transmission lines through the park; the lines could be buried under the railroad right-of-way.[27]

Walker touted other benefits of these changes to the Disney plan. The change would eliminate the need for a parking structure near the valley, since visitors would now park before they boarded the railroad. Use of the railroad would distance the picturesque valley from the facilities needed to receive persons being transported there to ski.[28]

Finally, the new plan would reduce the number of visitors to the valley. Walker claimed that the original Forest Service prospectus had required applicants like Disney to plan facilities sufficient to serve the largest number of visitors that the public road to Mineral King could carry. Now, said Walker, Disney could scale down the recreational facilities, such as restaurants and ski lifts, because the new railroad would reduce the number of visitors. He "expect[ed] that visitation will average 4,000 per day."[29]

Walker stressed that Disney had formulated these revisions "under the guidance" of its Conservation Advisory Committee. Disney believed, and "the Forest Service concur[s]," that the changes "will substantially improve both the aesthetic concept and operational control of this project."[30]

In short, Disney proposed changes that it hoped would be game-altering and would regain momentum for the project. It sought to eliminate the problems that arose from building a new road through Sequoia National Park and avoid the need for securing funds for the road from the State of California. It projected a smaller Mineral King development, a change responsive to the Sierra Club's criticism that the project was "too big." And it sought to establish the project as a model for transportation into areas such as national parks. As Walker's statement put it, Disney hoped that the vehicle restrictions "will provide a prototype demonstrating that the public will accept access to our National Parks and Forests by means other than the automobile."[31]

As it turned out, this hope would not be fulfilled. Questions about the new proposal arose immediately.

To begin with, while Disney intended its new plan to create a sense of originality and environmental sensitivity for the project, its announcement mixed these themes with a negative message: complaints about how the company had been treated. Card Walker began his press conference defensively, declaring that, "to avoid misunderstanding or interpretation," he would read the Disney news release, "although I would prefer to ad-lib our proposal."[32] After announcing the new railroad and its benefits, Walker then returned to the claim of mistreatment:

> [W]e can no longer allow the good name and world-wide reputation of the Walt Disney organization to be attacked due to circumstances over which we have had no control. No longer will we allow our plans for this project to be misrepresented, as they often have been in the past.[33]

Disney was understandably unhappy with the attacks on its project, some of which had been extreme. At a time when it was seeking a new start, however, Walker's vague threats about what the company would "no longer allow" sounded off-message.

He noted that Disney had ceased all financial investment in the project three years earlier and "withdrew from active advocacy of the project at that time." But it was now advocating for the project again, declaring that it had "presented a plan today which fulfills the public need." Disney stressed, as it had for three years, that it was not a party to the litigation.[34] These points, however, seemed disjointed, not the type of smooth, forward-looking rollout that Disney had implemented in the past for its project.

Disney followed the announcement with full-page advertisements in the major California newspapers.[35] These ads, too, were defensive. Instead of emphasizing the extended railroad that it was proposing—a unique and important change in the Mineral King project—the ads defended Disney.

They featured a large picture of Walt Disney in Mineral King, an image that captured the development's key asset. The ski area was the idea of Walt Disney, still one of the most trusted persons in America six years after his death. The text of the advertisement, however, was a statement signed by Card Walker that began: "For the past six years, there have been so many distortions, so much misinformation, so many lawsuits and press releases that no one seems to remember what Walt Disney *really* had in mind at Mineral King." It continued that Walker did remember, because he had been there with Walt Disney. And, complained Walker, "I'm tired of hearing and reading the distortions, the misinformation, the lawsuits and all the press releases vilifying the concepts" of the plan.[36]

Only then, after objecting to accusations that it planned "Disneyland in the mountains" or "an amusement center," did the ad focus on the new railroad, declaring that "we have found *even better ways* to accomplish what Walt Disney set out to do." It ended with a plea to the public: "[T]he time has come to take a stand."[37]

Walker had brought Horace Albright, past director of the National Park Service and a member of the Disney Conservation Advisory Committee, to speak at the press conference announcing the railroad. Albright said the area needed protection but the Forest Service and Disney were now headed in the right direction.[38] That statement, however, raised an obvious question: If the project was "now headed in the right direction," in what direction had it been headed before?

The attacks on the project had thrown Disney off its game.

Other contradictions soon appeared. The full-page newspaper advertisement stated that Disney's plan to eliminate the highway across Sequoia National Park "has been approved by the U.S. Forest Service."[39] However, while the Forest Service in the past had proceeded in lockstep with Disney, its posture had changed. When Doug Leisz, the regional forester, took the podium at the press conference, he did declare that his department concurred in the new conceptual plan. But Leisz then pointed out that many details of the new proposal were lacking and intensive study would be needed.[40]

Indeed, Bob Hicks himself had recognized internally that a railroad like this would require the Forest Service to "abandon . . . its basic requirements" that an all-weather, public road must reach the first ski lifts. Slim Davis had conceded the new proposal had some merit but warned Hicks that the change "would require top level approval" by the Forest Service.[41] No such approval had yet occurred. Moreover, Leisz stated at the press conference that the cost of the rail transportation to users "would definitely be a factor in approval of this new plan."[42] Charges that Mineral King would only serve the higher income brackets had forced the Forest Service to emphasize that it retained authority over the new proposal.

The written statement of Leisz, also released at the press conference, reinforced the new theme of continuing government control.

It opened by "reaffirm[ing] . . . that the final decision responsibility for the development and character of Mineral King is with the government." For example, the railroad would allow access to the valley and ensure that the use of Mineral King would not be "limited to a few of the wealthy alone."[43] He also told the audience that the Forest Service was fully committed to controlling maximum numbers in Mineral King Valley.[44]

The Forest Service also announced that it would prepare a full environmental impact statement before approving any modifications to the approved master plan. And, in what the Sierra Club must have seen as an astonishing turnaround in the service's attitude toward public participation in Mineral King decisions, Leisz declared that the EIS procedure "will provide for full public involvement."[45]

While the proposal for the railroad was exciting, critical details were missing. There was initial confusion about basic issues. For example, a question arose about whether or not building the railroad would mean that the project no longer required a permit from the Park Service. The regional director of the Park Service at first thought that the new transportation method "would not affect Sequoia National Park" and thus remove the need for a permit.[46] Less than two weeks later, the Park Service corrected itself, since the railroad—like the previously proposed road—would transect the park.[47]

Another important gap involved financing the railroad. Disney foresaw public financing through a bond or other similar mechanism, with railroad users paying it back over a thirty-year period. This method, though, placed responsibility for securing the financing in the hands of the County of Tulare, which in the past had adamantly refused to participate in funding the road.

At the press conference, Card Walker suggested that the burden lay on Tulare County to provide sources of financing. In a rare sign of disorganization among the Disney managers, Bob Hicks immediately clarified that statement: "We would conceive of it as a joint venture between the county and perhaps the state or federal government."[48] But the clarification only highlighted the complexity involved in implementing the financing. Herding public officials at multiple levels of government toward a unified financing plan would be difficult and likely time-consuming.

Unsure of exactly what Disney was proposing for financing, the county asked Disney for clarification. Three weeks later, Donn Tatum, now the chairman of the board of Walt Disney Productions, explained in more detail. Disney proposed that revenues from the train's operation would pay for the nonprofit railroad, with fares set to cover the costs of operation and maintenance as well as principal and interest. The capital would come from revenue bonds issued to private investors "by the governmental agency or agencies which would own the train." Disney would operate the train but not guarantee revenue adequate to service the debt.[49]

Tatum's letter could not have allayed the County of Tulare's concerns about potential liability if the revenues from the train's operation proved inadequate to pay for the bonds. Moreover, the allocation of responsibility in the Disney proposal was awkward. Disney would supply the designs for and operate the railroad, but would bear no responsibility for its construction and financing. The public agencies responsible for these tasks remained uncertain.

Finally, another lurking issue would arise later. If the railroad traveled through the park and required a permit from the National Park Service, that permit would have to be annual and thus revocable. Because the new railroad required debt financing, the question would be whether bonds could be sold to finance a railroad situated partially on federal land and subject to a revocable permit. Much later, Disney would conclude that the bonds could not be sold.[50]

Overall, the rollout of the changes gave the distinct impression that Disney had not fully formulated the plans it was announcing. And looming over the whole announcement was an inconsistency. Disney had previously insisted that a railroad was infeasible.[51] For example, when Disney was pressing Stewart Udall in 1967 to approve the road, Roy Disney had written Udall that mechanized transportation to Mineral King "would not be economically feasible and would not best serve the general public. No other method of access can compare with a road in terms of economy, feasibility, and availability to the widest range of income levels."[52] Now, however, Disney was championing a railroad. What had changed?

Reacting to this uncertainty, the California press did not greet the announcement with the unalloyed enthusiasm and endorsement that Disney had always received in Mineral King matters. At the press conference, Card Walker almost immediately faced a skeptical question: "If [the] original proposal protected this area why does the [news] release state a scale[d]-down plan?" Walker's response sounded weak. The original proposal "has been misinterpreted by the press" as a $35 million project, but this was the "ultimate" project, not the "basic" project.[53]

The announcement did attract support from local newspapers in the San Joaquin Valley serving areas that would benefit economically from the Mineral King development. But the reaction of the *Los Angeles Times*, which had long and vigorously lobbied for the project, was restrained and partly critical. The newspaper's May 7, 1972, editorial, "New Developments on Mineral King," praised the new railroad, which made the Mineral King development "an even more attractive proposition" and "could become a model for systems to keep cars out of parks." It continued to see the project as "a correct application of the policy of balanced use of the national forests."[54]

But the editorial also found "a rather large feasibility gap" arising from the fact that Disney "wants nothing to do with financing, operating or, if necessary, subsidizing the railroad." The editorial then turned to the Forest Service, previously viewed by the paper as a model public agency facing unwarranted resistance from the Sierra Club. Now, said the *Times*, although the service had endorsed the general idea of a railroad, "[t]his flexibility does not prevent misgivings about the competence of the Forest Service as judged by past performance." The Forest Service, it charged, had blocked earlier consideration of rail access. In short, the agency had lost credibility.

The editorial returned to the finance issue. Here, the paper's turnaround from its prior attitude was startling: "In Mineral King, where a single entrepreneur will be benefitted, it would be especially inappropriate for the government to pay for the access." It then backed off, but only a bit. It reasoned that a government railway subsidy would be acceptable in some situations, and "[s]tudies may at least indicate where the Disney organization can remain aloof from the finances of a railroad to serve Mineral King."[55]

The *Times* editorial brought a reaction from Disney: Card Walker felt compelled to write a letter to the editor. First, he said, the editorial incorrectly stated that Disney would have nothing to do with operating the railroad; instead, Disney would contract to operate it on a nonprofit basis, thereby assuring the lowest possible cost. Second, Walker took issue with the statement that Disney was suggesting the government pay for the access or proposing a government subsidy. Rather, it was proposing that private investors buy bonds to finance the project. Finally, he addressed whether or not building the railroad would require the County of Tulare to transfer the right-of-way to the existing road to Walt Disney Productions, a private corporation. Disney, said Walker, did "not believe it would be in the public interest" for that transfer to take place, as would be necessary if Disney were to own the railroad system.[56]

One other article illustrates how the solid backing of the development in the press had weakened. The leading newspaper in the San Joaquin Valley, the *Fresno Bee*, had long boosted the project. Now in a lengthy article, Ron Taylor, the reporter who principally covered the project, noted that the new plans "sounded impressive, but details were conspicuously lacking." In particular, questions remained unanswered about who would issue the bonds for the railroad and who would build it. The article recognized the difficulties of siting ski areas, reporting that environmental protection requirements were squeezing the finances of small ski resorts in the Lake Tahoe area. But it found that the Forest Service had given "[l]ittle or no forethought . . . to the environmental impact of the highway through the groves of Sequoia trees in the park, as the Sierra Club noted." And in a major turnaround, it criticized the Forest Service's overall planning for the project: "From a public point of view, the Forest Service planned the $35 million Disney Mineral King project after the fact. In 1965 it had set minimum development standards but had done nothing to establish what the maximum use could or should be."[57]

The aftermath of what the *Fresno Bee* article termed the "dramatic announcement" of the railroad unsettled Disney's management. Key elements of the proposal remained to be worked out, and sources of traditional support for the project had waivered. But the announcement did force the Sierra Club to face, for a final time, the question of whether it totally opposed a ski development in Mineral King.

One goal of Disney's new proposal was to blunt a number of the criticisms that the Sierra Club had leveled against the project. It accomplished that goal.

The new railroad proposal seemed to eliminate the need for a new road into Mineral King, the source of much of the club's opposition. It called for burying the electric transmission lines along the railroad's right-of-way. Disney also committed to an "automobile-free" Mineral King Valley and limited the number of users in the valley, reducing the park's winter capacity from 14,000 to 8,000, thereby also lowering the number of ski lifts that would initially be constructed. Finally, the Forest Service stressed its authority to impose maximum limits on the number of users of Mineral King, and that it would seek public input before approving the new plan.

In short, the Disney proposal and the Forest Service's statements responded to many of the Sierra Club's criticisms of the project, particularly the oft-repeated charge that the project was "too big." The changes forced the club to reevaluate its position.

Always attuned to the formation of public opinion—much like Disney in this respect—Mike McCloskey immediately responded to the announcement of Disney's change in plans. A press release was headlined "Sierra Club Will Still Oppose Mineral King Development." The changes, said McCloskey, indicate that Disney "apparently recognizes that its previous plans were overblown." The project, he continued, "is still huge, and we have seen no guarantee that it won't grow even larger."[58] However, the Sierra Club board of directors would meet that very weekend to consider the question of continued opposition.

The board held an extended discussion of the matter. The fundamental question soon surfaced: "[W]hether the Club's previous policy on Mineral King opposed any ski development whatsoever or only a development on the grandiose scale of the Walt Disney Productions proposal."[59]

While McCloskey's public posture was one of continued opposition, he recognized that it was not a settled issue. He told the board that it faced a "clear policy question" of "whether or not to categorically oppose any development" in the valley. The club's past policy, he said, had "left open the possibility of eventual Club approval of a 'small' ski development." Indeed, at the press conference announcing the lawsuit in 1969, McCloskey had stated that the club was not "dogmatically against any further construction" in the valley.[60] However, Phil Berry, a member of the board and the former president, disagreed that any "void" existed in the club's policy; the club's position was that the Mineral King Valley belonged in Sequoia National Park.[61]

In the end, the Mineral King lawsuit drove the board's decision. Jim Moorman, now litigating the case, told the board that any approval by the club of a ski development in Mineral King would contradict the substantive allegations of the suit. Those allegations—including the challenge to the legality of the dual permit system and the impact on the game refuge—argued that a ski development in Mineral King like that proposed by Disney was illegal.

Moorman also stressed that "'modest developments' have a tendency to grow over the years." Disney was likely to seek expansion of Mineral King in the future, and opposition then would not be nearly as effective as "initial total opposition." Moorman urged the board to reject any policy that would "undermine the integrity of the laws which the Club has been raising in support of the lawsuit."[62]

In the end, the board adopted a motion that "reaffirm[ed] its opposition to any ski development in Mineral King, and to access facilities [i.e., road, rail etc.] to any such development, not consistent with present uses." It confirmed the board's policy that Mineral King should be incorporated into Sequoia National Park.[63]

The Sierra Club had transformed the dispute over Mineral King into a legal battle by suing, and some consequences of that action had now surfaced. The lawsuit was closely linked to an overall political program designed to attain certain conservation goals. But the lawsuit also affected the options available to the board in responding to the new Disney proposal, if the board wanted to remain consistent with its legal arguments in the case.

In announcing the changes to the project, Disney's newspaper advertisements had ended by posing a question about Mineral King's future: "Who really speaks for Mineral King?" The Sierra Club staff responded with its own question: "Is there anybody who really believes that if Mineral King could answer, it would say: "Walt Disney Productions, Inc."?[64]

The Sierra Club thus decided to continue litigating. However, while the club put on a confident public face, there appeared to be little left of its case. The problem arose from the court of appeals' opinion that preceded the decision by the Supreme Court. While the opinion had found that the Sierra Club lacked standing, the Supreme Court had established a different test for standing that the club should be able to meet. However, as discussed above, the court of appeals had also decisively rejected the substantive challenges that the club had raised against the Forest and Park Services, such as the challenge to the dual permit system. The club would need to find some way to argue that, despite the court of appeals' rulings, it could continue to raise those challenges.

First, though, it had to demonstrate in the district court the injury needed for standing. The club researched its past activities that involved Mineral King and members' use of the valley. It compiled a long list of past use. The club then proposed to amend its suit and add nine individuals as plaintiffs, including Martin Litton, Albert

Hill, and Larry Moss, its Southern California staff representative. The club sought to allege that:

> The Sierra Club has conducted outings over the years on a regular basis in the Sierra Nevada. . . . Sierra Club has conducted, and continues to conduct, substantial activities in and around the Mineral King area. In addition, several of the Club's chapters have conducted and continue to conduct outings in and around Mineral King on a regular basis. In addition, many of the Club's members individually or in informal groups undertake hikes and other trail outings in and around the Mineral King valley and engage in various outdoor recreational activities in and around the valley such as picnicking, hiking, climbing, photography, camping, and family outings.[65]

Notably, the amendments also alleged one new illegality: that the Forest Service had violated the National Environmental Policy Act by failing to prepare an environmental impact statement on its Mineral King project.[66]

Chances were good that the court would allow the Sierra Club to amend its complaint and allege its standing. The government opposed the motion to amend, arguing that the club could have made these types of standing allegations much earlier, and thus was fatally late with the request to amend.[67] The Sierra Club easily swatted away this argument. Justice Stewart's last-minute footnote in the Supreme Court's opinion had declared that the Sierra Club could attempt to amend its complaint, and the club was simply accepting that invitation.[68]

Judge Sweigert agreed, finding that "the allegations fall well within what we interpret to be the meaning of the Supreme Court opinion on this subject of standing requirements." Then, however, Sweigert proceeded to observe that the club might have difficulty overcoming the court of appeals' earlier decision that had rejected the substantive allegations of the Sierra Club's complaint:

> It should be noted . . . that while the Supreme Court thus apparently envisioned these curative amendments with respect to the thresh-

> old, procedural issue of standing, it omitted to resolve or even mention the Ninth Circuit Court of Appeals further ruling on the merits to the effect that, even assuming standing, plaintiff had failed to establish ground for preliminary injunction against the defendant federal agencies.
>
> It is not necessary, however, upon mere motion to amend, to consider whether for this reason further proceedings in this case may be an exercise in futility.[69]

In other words, even if the Sierra Club could prove its standing, Judge Sweigert was not convinced that anything remained of the Sierra Club's substantive case.

Taking its cue from Sweigert's cautionary language, the government quickly filed a motion to dismiss the entire case. Its argument was straightforward: the earlier decision by the court of appeals had established the law by rejecting all the Sierra Club's theories, a legal principle known as the "law of the case." The Supreme Court's opinion had not disturbed that part of the court of appeals' ruling. Thus, the government reasoned, the litigation could not go forward, as the Sierra Club could not win.

As for the new claim of failure to prepare an environmental impact statement, the government persuasively argued that it was premature. The Forest Service had committed to preparing an impact statement before making any final decision to approve the now reconstituted Disney project. Accordingly, the argument went, the Sierra Club could not allege a violation before the Forest Service and Park Service had even acted. This argument was powerful, abetted by the legal doctrine that a plaintiff could not sue until a case was "ripe." Under that doctrine, the government had to make a concrete decision before a plaintiff could sue.

Jim Moorman, now heading the club's legal team, recognized the strength of the government's motion to dismiss. He told his client that the government had "taken encouragement" from Judge Sweigert's remarks suggesting that the future of the case was doubtful. Moorman thought the Sierra Club would win the motion, "but the government may get some of our legal theories stricken."[70]

Moorman crafted a twofold response to the government's motion to dismiss. First, as to the substantive claims, he argued that the court of appeals had merely decided that the Sierra Club had made an insufficient showing to warrant a preliminary injunction. Thus, the court had not directly ruled on the substance of the claims, so the appellate court's statements about them did not bind Judge Sweigert.[71] The distinction was a narrow one. While perhaps technically accurate about the scope of the court of appeals holding, that court had addressed and clearly rejected the Sierra Club's core legal claims.

Second, given the announcement of the cog railroad, Moorman admitted that "it would appear that there will be no power line or new road on National Park land." This change of circumstances would render legally outdated the club's claims about these two parts of the proposed development. But he urged the district court to wait for the government to confirm these facts.[72]

Moorman also found it difficult to argue that the Sierra Club's claim regarding the environmental impact statement was not premature. He responded that the government had *already* decided to approve the Mineral King development before preparing the environmental statement, and thus was proceeding illegally.[73] The government, however, had issued no permits to Disney, so the "approval" did not yet formally exist. Faced with this set of facts, many courts would dismiss the case, knowing that the Sierra Club could return to court later if the government issued a final approval for the project after preparing the EIS.

The parties engaged in a lengthy oral argument before Judge Sweigert, now approaching seventy-two years of age and less vigorous than before.[74] On September 12, 1972, he filed his opinion. Perhaps annoyed by the court of appeals' dismissive reversal of his decision to grant the injunction, Judge Sweigert allowed the Sierra Club's case to continue. He accepted the Sierra Club's technical argument that the earlier court of appeals' opinion did not mandate dismissal because the court had only reversed the preliminary injunction. Ruling on the showing needed for that type of injunction, he reasoned, was different than making a final, determinative decision on the issues.

Thus, “notwithstanding the Court of Appeals’ ‘handwriting on the wall,’ plaintiffs still have the right to proceed on the merits.”[75]

Sweigert likewise declined to dismiss the environmental impact statement claim. He cited plaintiff’s complaint that the government had not complied with the National Environmental Policy Act and found this bare allegation sufficient to avoid dismissal.[76]

Relieved, Moorman told his clients that “the situation has been stabilized following the Supreme Court’s decision” and the Sierra Club lawyers would soon begin fleshing out the case.[77] The litigation, though, would play a very different role from this point on.

When the Sierra Club first filed suit, it sought to avoid what appeared to be the imminent construction of the Disney project and the expanded road through Sequoia National Park. Now, neither action would occur soon, as the government was sorting out the changes to the project, particularly the railroad, and preparing an environmental impact statement. However, when the case did come to trial, it still appeared that the Ninth Circuit’s earlier ruling would prevent obtaining relief on most of the club’s allegations. As a Sierra Club lawyer would later put it, “[w]e escaped somewhat narrowly” from having the case dismissed.[78] As for the impact statement, its legality could not be determined until it was written.

But continuing to prosecute the suit would serve two other purposes for the Sierra Club. First, it would signal that the club was firmly resolved to oppose the Disney development. Second, the club could now engage in the legal “discovery” process in the litigation, which allowed it to take depositions and seek documents from the government defendants and from Disney. Those steps would increase pressure on the government as it proceeded to consider the amended Disney proposal.

The aftermath of the Supreme Court’s decision brought yet another pivotal development, one that shined the spotlight on California Governor Ronald Reagan. The funding of the Mineral King road had been secured by transferring funds from other highway projects in burgeoning Southern California. However, Disney’s surprise announcement that it now favored a railroad rendered much of the new road unnecessary, and opponents of the Mineral King development pounced.

A principal opponent, California Assemblyman Edwin Z'Berg, pushed legislation to remove from the California Highway System the part of the road that the railroad would now cover, a move that would prevent the state from building this segment. On May 18, 1972, a bill to this effect passed out of an assembly committee despite opposition from the California Department of Public Works and the Forest Service. Significantly, Walt Disney Productions did not appear to oppose the bill.[79] Less than two weeks later, the bill—dubbed "this little turkey" by the assemblyman who represented the project area—passed out of the California Assembly.[80] The bill then narrowly passed the State Senate, putting the bill, and the road's future, in the hands of Governor Reagan.

Reagan and his advisers were conflicted. Reagan had strongly supported the Disney development, a position linked to his personal, "old Hollywood" ties with the late Walt Disney and with the project's fervent supporter, George Murphy. At the same time, however, Reagan the politician consistently preached fiscal conservatism, and the prospect of saving the money from the road attracted him. His secretary for resources, Ike Livermore, now became the central figure in Reagan's decision on the bill.

Livermore had been trying, with some success, to forge a more environmentally favorable set of positions for Reagan. For example, after taking the outdoor-loving Reagan on a backpacking trip, Livermore had convinced him to oppose the building of a controversial new road across the Sierra Nevadas. He also knew Mineral King "like the back of my hand," having owned and operated a packing service there when he was younger.[81]

Despite his own long-standing ties to the Sierra Club, Livermore did not oppose all development in Mineral King, but he concluded that the road was no longer necessary. He called Donn Tatum at Walt Disney Productions to make sure that Disney had abandoned the road, and he followed up with a letter. Livermore confirmed Disney's position that, if studies later indicated the proposed railroad was not feasible "for one reason or another," Disney "is not interested in reopening full scale automobile access on a volume basis to Mineral King." Therefore, concluded Livermore, Disney "will not pursue the objective of a state highway" to the Mineral King Valley.[82]

Livermore's assistant, Ford B. Ford, spoke to George Hartzog, the director of the National Park Service, who told Ford that he would be "delighted" if the road went away. The road, of course, had long vexed the Park Service, and Hartzog informed Ford that he thought such a decision "would redound to the glory of the Governor."[83] However, the Forest Service was a quite different matter. When Slim Davis heard that the governor might agree to the removal of the road, he placed an "anguished" call of protest to Livermore, who was a good friend and a person with whom Davis had skied.[84]

A battle then ensued inside the Reagan cabinet, as the Business and Transportation Agency wanted to retain the road as a backup for the Disney project. Much to Ike Livermore's annoyance, that agency's head, Frank Walton, composed a song about Mineral King that he sang to the governor at a going-away dinner for another Reagan aide. Caught by surprise, Livermore responded by singing an old Sierra Club song.[85] In the end, after an "intense and thorough discussion" among the governor's cabinet-level appointees and with the governor,[86] a majority of the cabinet recommended signing the bill to remove the road from the state system. Reagan did so.

Thus, the long controversy over the upgraded road ended. Reagan sent out a press release explaining that he remained "firmly in support of the development of Mineral King" and that the development "will not be hampered by lack of access by a high speed road."[87] The United States Ski Association felt differently. "By deleting this road," its press release warned, "development of Mineral King is set back for an indeterminable period of time, and perhaps forever."[88]

Events would soon show whether Ronald Reagan or the ski association possessed the better crystal ball.

12: A Park-Barrel Bill

As the dust settled after Disney's announcement proposing a railroad, fundamental changes in the regulatory controls over the ski proposal followed. Power had shifted. Before the litigation, the Forest Service had deferred to Disney on all major choices about the proposal, exercising only loose oversight over it. Now, responding to criticism of its lax control, the Forest Service assumed a much greater supervisory role. Two issues quickly rose to the top: the logistics of preparing an environmental impact statement, and the details of Disney's new railroad proposal.

The Forest Service felt the pressure of preparing the EIS, and problems soon arose. More precise Disney plans for the ski area were needed to analyze the project's environmental impacts.[1] Disney's public posture, however, was that it had offered its proposal for the railroad, and the next step was for the public agencies to approve it. The company was in no mood to expend additional resources to assist in the EIS process.

A related issue was that the EIS was legally required to discuss alternatives to the project that could reduce its environmental impacts. The analysis of smaller alternative plans, however, touched a nerve with Disney, as the project had to be sufficiently large to justify its capital investment. Bob Hicks noted the problem in an internal memorandum, observing that the impact statement would discuss the alternative of building a small lodge that would use vehicles traveling over snow for transport, with a possible upgrade to buses over the existing road. Disney, he had told Pete Wyckoff, "probably would not be interested in even considering such an operation." His memo then warned that the company would not want to state this publicly, as "it would invite additional opposition to us by those who would see an opportunity to start at a low level at Mineral King with expansion in response to the demand."[2]

The preparation of the environmental impact statement would be a complex undertaking, and the Forest Service set a completion date of July 1974. Many in the agency, however, thought that the deadline was wildly optimistic.[3] Their assessment proved correct.

The proposed railroad likewise raised difficult issues of implementation. An initial question was whether or not the National Park Service even possessed the legal authority to allow a railroad across a national park. The Forest Service thought that the "first step" should be the Park Service's approval of the right-of-way as well as obtaining "answers to the questions surrounding the access."[4] Ironically, this position placed the Forest Service in the same awkward posture that it had occupied between 1967 and 1969 concerning the road: waiting for a Park Service decision.

Final resolution of the question dragged on. In December of 1972, the secretary of agriculture, Earl Butz, wrote to the secretary of the interior, Rogers C. B. Morton, stating that Butz would have a "suitable agreement" drawn up between the agencies if the authority existed.[5] Nathaniel Reed, an assistant secretary under Morton, replied two months later. The Department of the Interior's head lawyer had advised that "the same legal concept" for the highway would apply to a railroad, thus indicating that the Park Service had authority to approve a railroad.[6]

But Reed went on to point out that the validity of such a permit remained an issue in the Sierra Club's litigation. Accordingly, Interior would be "reluctant to issue such a permit" without the express agreement of the Department of Justice. Otherwise, "unilateral action by this Department could have a significant effect on the pending litigation."[7] The Sierra Club's lawsuit thus continued to affect the government's actions. Six months later, Reed cautioned that the

Nixon administration had not even given wholehearted support to any road corridor crossing the park and that "[t]he Secretary has made this point very clear to me on a number of occasions."[8]

The approval of a railroad through Sequoia National Park would not come quickly, as the Forest Service had hoped. For its part, Disney by July 1973 was "advised" that the Department of the Interior would not approve a right-of-way for a railroad crossing Sequoia National Park. By this point, Disney thought that the Forest Service was going to recommend access to Mineral King by bus.[9]

Aside from the right-of-way, an even bigger practical issue loomed: would a cog railway actually work? The Forest Service needed to answer this question—it would no longer just accept Disney's word—but it did not possess the technical expertise to do so. The agency hired an outside consultant, Alan Voorhees and Associates, to analyze both the cog railway and other transportation alternatives.

Voorhees completed a draft report in January 1973, and Slim Davis of the Forest Service sent it to Disney for comments. The reaction was volatile. The costs that Voorhees estimated for the cog railway were much higher than the numbers that Disney had calculated. Although Disney had previously objected to "basic errors" in the Vorhees cost computations, those numbers had not changed.

The usually restrained Bob Hicks angrily wrote to Slim Davis. After detailing various points at which Disney contested the report's numbers, Hicks charged that the report was "in effect, biased against the cog railway, and has been since its inception." He saw the report as potentially causing the entire project to fail:

> When this report becomes public information, we feel that it will provide ammunition with which the opposition may further attack, in court, the accuracy and adequacy of the final environmental study. Further, from an economic point of view, it will make it totally impossible for the Board of Supervisors of Tulare County to justify the sale of revenue bonds to finance a cog railway where the initial capital investment is so unnecessarily high.[10]

Hicks threatened that "when your report is made public, we will have no choice but to state that we do not support its findings, and to point out its specific inaccuracies."[11]

Slim Davis responded to Hicks by vaguely promising that the Forest Service would have the consultant further revise the report before finalizing it and would "continue to keep in close touch with you."[12] The dispute illustrates how the relationship between Disney and the Forest Service had changed. Where the Forest Service and Disney had proceeded in tandem before, with the Forest Service generally deferring to Disney's conclusions, the agency had now assumed a much more active regulatory role.

The final Voorhees report, released by the Forest Service in June 1973,[13] did not greatly alter the conclusions of its earlier draft. It recommended four alternatives: an all-weather highway, a bus scheme, a cog-assisted railroad, and an aerial tram system. Now in full bureaucratic mode, the Forest Service responded by preparing an internal staff paper to consider "additional combinations of alternatives within the framework used in the Voorhees report."[14] The analytic process had mushroomed.

Disney had calmed down by this point and responded pragmatically to the paper. It still favored the cog railway, but it stated that improvements to the existing road which permitted driving speeds of 35 to 40 miles per hour also would support adequate visitor capacity at Mineral King. It rejected a busway and dismissed an aerial tramway because the public "would be reluctant to travel for such a long distance in a vehicle suspended in the air."[15]

Muddled at this point, the transportation picture soon blurred even more. The County of Tulare had concluded that, to issue bonds for building a railroad, it would need new authority from the California Legislature. As the *Los Angeles Times* wrote in an October 1973 article headlined "Planned Mineral King Project Appears Doomed," the legislature "could be less receptive to the project than it was in the mid 1960s."[16] Finally, the Park Service, after reading the Voorhees report, had begun internally to question whether the county even owned the right-of-way to the roadbed.[17]

In short, after a year of study, the transportation system to Mineral King remained up in the air. And Disney, which had sought to advance its project by proposing the cog railway, had lost control over the transportation issue.

Amid this confusion, and in an offhand way, the possibility arose of reaching some sort of settlement among the parties contesting Mineral King's future. Jim James, the supervisor of Sequoia National Forest, was set to retire at the end of May 1973. Before doing so, he put aside a career's worth of bureaucratic restraint and decided to vent his long-gestating frustration with the Sierra Club. "In order to save the taxpayer a few dollars, and my management team countless hours of wasted effort," he addressed a series of questions to the Sierra Club president about the club's position on additional sites on public land for skiing. Most important, James wanted to know if the club would support new downhill ski areas at two alternative sites, Slate Mountain and Sherman Peak, both located in Sequoia National Forest, and asked "[e]xactly what standards must be met in such a proposed development?"[18] James sent copies of his letter to numerous interested organizations, including ski associations and local Sierra Club chapters.

The Sierra Club might have been expected to dismiss the letter. Still, Mike McCloskey understood that the club's chances of a total win on Mineral King remained small, so he treated the letter seriously. McCloskey and three key Sierra Club people agreed to meet with James at his office in Porterville—much to the surprise of James. James told those attending the meeting that he "really just expected [the Sierra Club] to write him a letter telling him to 'go to hell.'"[19]

McCloskey expressed some interest in a potential deal. If a Mineral King ski area was put aside, he said, the club would devote "major resources" to examining the two sites mentioned by James, Slate Mountain and Sherman Peak.[20] James rejected the linkage, arguing that "Slate Mountain or Sherman Peak development should not be contingent on Mineral King." The underlying trade-off, however, held some promise. The Sierra Club would protect Mineral King, while the Forest Service would secure a ski development that the club would support. The ski associations would undoubtedly prefer Mineral King, but they might decide that certainty over a new development was better than doubts about Mineral King. Disney, of course, would lose. However, the company might not be completely unhappy about an excuse to exit the long-running battle and move on to concentrate on other ventures.[21]

In 1974 Disney had begun to examine the possibility of building a ski resort at Independence Lake in California. Located in the Sierra Nevadas above Lake Tahoe, it was not nearly as spectacular as Mineral King. But it was a man-made lake and thus did not present the environmental problems associated with Mineral King. Although the Sierra Club would pledge to work on it with Disney to some degree,[22] Disney's effort to develop at Independence Lake later proved unsuccessful, blowing up in a tangle of recriminatory statements.[23]

In the end, nothing came of the meeting. The brief opening for a settlement that arose from Jim James's venting was lost, and the war of attrition continued.

Preparation of the environmental impact statement continued into 1974. Pete Wyckoff grappled with assembling it, aware that the statement would have to pass judicial scrutiny. One Forest Service employee thought that Wyckoff tended to "see a Sierra Club lawyer . . . behind every criticism."[24]

The Forest Service was now committed to extensive public involvement in the preparation of the EIS. At the end of May 1974, it circulated a preliminary draft of the document to interested parties, including Disney and the Sierra Club.[25] The circulation of this draft drew several important responses.

First, because of the cog railway, the project now began to appear more like a destination resort, whereas its earlier version had emphasized day use. Patrons who took the railroad were more likely to stay overnight than if they drove in for the day.[26]

Second, the Sierra Club commented that the draft statement did not adequately define the Mineral King development because "no specific locations of buildings or facilities are shown or described, either in writing or on maps."[27] The previous year, as part of the lawsuit, the Sierra Club had requested copies of Disney's plans showing specific locations for each proposed building. Disney's lawyer had responded that "the exact placement of each structure" within the village "was never fixed and was intended to remain flexible until further development progressed."[28] A year later, nothing had changed; Disney would not spend the money needed to produce plans with specific locations. The Sierra Club protested that the impact statement could not accurately depict the environmental effects of the project without those locations.

Disney's response to the preliminary draft impact statement expressed alarm. It declared that certain elements of the project discussed in the draft would "place in jeopardy the ability of Walt Disney Productions as the permittee to successfully attain the goals of this project." Disney warned that the proposal's suggested limits on the project's size would adversely affect its financial feasibility. The Forest Service, it said, should no longer assume that Disney would invest $35 million during the first five-year period—the figure long cited as Disney's initial investment. The Disney response ended gloomily: "[W]e find ourselves in conflict with many of the economic projections and findings of this report, a fact which we have conveyed to the Forest Service at every opportunity during the past 18 months."[29]

By late 1974, an objective appraisal of the Mineral King project by Disney could only conclude that the project's completion now hinged on several uncertain contingencies. Jim Stewart, a principal deputy to Card Walker at the company, had taken on increased responsibility at Disney for the Mineral King project. As the Forest Service neared the formal release of its draft environmental impact statement in October 1974, it sent a prepublication copy to Disney. Stewart used the occasion to draft a memo, circulated internally at Disney, that took a hard look at the difficulties now faced by the project. The picture was grim.[30]

The long-running problem of transportation to the Mineral King Valley lay at the center of these difficulties. The Forest Service, said

Stewart, continued to use the figures for the railroad from the Voorhees study, an estimate that "makes Disney appear to be advocating a massively expensive access concept beyond the means of the average visitor." The Voorhees estimate "gives opponents of the project a supposedly authoritative source to quote when attacking the project, and creates a tremendous public relations problem for Disney."[31]

But that was hardly the only obstacle. Stewart reported "general agreement" that the Department of the Interior had no legal authority to grant a right-of-way for a railroad through Sequoia National Park, so Congressional legislation was needed. That legislation, said Stewart, does not seem likely "in the foreseeable future." Likewise, Tulare County did not have the authority to issue revenue bonds for transportation systems, so California legislation would be needed as well. Finally, Stewart thought it likely that Disney would be asked to guarantee the bonds for the cog railway,[32] a financial commitment it adamantly opposed.

As an alternative to the railroad, the Forest Service's draft EIS set forth the possibility of a visitor driving to Oak Grove, transferring to a bus that would travel to Silver City, and then taking a cog railway from there. Stewart concluded, no doubt correctly, that this combination of transportation methods "does not meet the Disney organization's objective of providing convenient and inexpensive access for both the day and overnight visitor." This type of access also raised the long-running issues of the grant of a right-of-way through the park and the ability to widen or realign the existing road. Finally, there was the question of who would pay for the train from Silver City. Stewart thought he knew the answer: "They apparently assume that Disney will finance and operate the train."[33]

Stewart's memorandum identified other difficulties. Stewart cited a warning from Disney's in-house lawyer that the impact statement might be legally inadequate because of the lack of specific plans. This situation "would place the Disney organization in an untenable position." Disney "would never spend the money to do such detailed planning without the assurance that the project would ultimately go forward."[34]

Stewart also was concerned about the dual permit issue, the legal authority of the Forest Service to combine the term permit with a revocable annual permit. A major new court decision involving the trans-Alaska pipeline had raised issues as to whether or not the annual permit granted by the government in that case was, in reality, not revocable. That same question, of course, had been raised in the Mineral King case: were the annual permits for a large portion of the ski development really revocable?[35] As for the litigation itself, Stewart bluntly concluded: "Recognizing the fact that Walt Disney Productions will never be able to achieve all of its original goals for Mineral King, why should we endure the negative publicity which will result from a lengthy trial?[36]

Stewart stopped short of recommending that the company drop the Mineral King project, suggesting only that Disney announce "we are certain that we could never support a number of the alternative means of access" discussed in the draft impact statement. But while a few of Stewart's conclusions in the memorandum were debatable, such as whether the Department of the Interior had concluded it could not approve a railroad through Sequoia National Park, the problems were real. And the company possessed little ability to resolve them.

Nonetheless, Disney's top management, led by Card Walker, decided the company would press on. Walker was very loyal to the memory of Walt Disney. For him, Walt Disney's dream still overrode the formidable array of adverse facts.

Meanwhile, the Forest Service plodded on, sending the draft environmental impact statement out for public comment in January 1975. The proposed development described in the document remained large; it would handle 2.8 million visitors a year, with a daily peak of 10,000 people and lodging for 6,000. It would feature eighteen ski lifts and ten restaurants.[37] A Forest Service spokesperson assured the public that this level of development "represents the governmental planners' estimates of what can be built suitably in Mineral King."[38] A cog railroad would transport visitors from Oak Grove to the proposed Mineral King village.

A flood of about 2,150 letters commented on the draft EIS.[39] Significant commenters, including the State of California, complained that the document was deficient because of "the lack of specificity of the proposed development plans."[40] The Department of the Interior agreed, and—ominously for the Forest Service—wanted the impact statement to evaluate the alternative of incorporating Mineral King into Sequoia National Park.[41] Even supporters of the development suggested changes to the draft statement. The County of Tulare wanted it to analyze an alternative resort open only during winter months, an idea completely unacceptable to Disney.[42]

Disney, too, was unhappy with the draft EIS. It commented that the cog railway described in the proposal "is not likely to prove feasible" because of uncertainty about the right-of-way and the requirement that a permit be revocable, "thereby undoubtedly prohibiting any private financing." Disney also noted that the EIS did not include "[p]erhaps the most feasible means" of access to Mineral King: improving the existing road to a 35 miles per hour standard.[43]

In short, little consensus existed over the features of the final development, and many questioned the Forest Service's environmental analysis.

To move the project forward at this point, the Forest Service had to establish some certainty about the transportation to Mineral King. Recognizing as much, in May 1975 it convened a meeting of the involved Forest Service personnel, and a revised proposal emerged. The railroad—so recently the innovative savior of the project—was unceremoniously dropped. Now, the project would provide all-weather access by reconstructing the existing road through Sequoia National Park as far as Silver City.

Large-scale facilities would be built at Silver City, with lodging for 1,500 people and support facilities for 4,000 daily skiers. Downhill skiing facilities would be developed below Silver City, even further away from Mineral King. Later, "access improvements" might permit expanding those recreation facilities into Mineral King.[44] In other words, the Forest Service proposed drastically reconfiguring the project to center it at Silver City rather than in Mineral King.

The service scheduled a meeting with Disney at which it "hope[d] to gain the permittee's [Disney's] support for the proposed revisions, and agreement from [Disney] to allocate time and dollars to complete certain agreed upon jobs."[45] Unsurprisingly, Disney rejected the Silver City proposal, which was nothing like the resort that Walt Disney had envisioned. More discussions ensued. By the end of 1975, the Forest Service seemed to settle on another modified proposal centered on a realigned, two-lane road that would generally follow the existing Mineral King road to the Faculty Flats area, located at the entrance to the valley. At that point, an electric bus would transport passengers into the valley, and the development there would serve 8,000 skiers and 6,000 summer visitors.[46]

By this point, Disney was completely flummoxed. Jim Stewart expressed the company's frustrations in a December 10, 1975, conversation with an unlikely listener: the Sierra Club's Mike McCloskey. According to Stewart, the new plan was only conceptual, and Disney "doesn't know what kind of planning assumptions" would go into the final environmental impact statement, now scheduled for release in two months. Stewart told McCloskey that he was "very dubious about whether Disney will ever come to terms with the Forest Service at Mineral King." Nonetheless, McCloskey reported, the top management at Disney was "still committed to 'hanging in there' . . . [a]s long as the possibility exists that a project might eventually be developed at Mineral King by Disney that is 'up to their standards.'"[47]

On February 26, 1976, the Forest Service announced that it had revised the proposal for Mineral King and completed the Final Environmental Impact Statement. The service had settled on a two-lane road to Faculty Flats near the entrance to the Mineral King Valley. An electric bus would transport visitors from there to the Mineral King Village. A parking structure for 1,000 autos would be built at Faculty Flats.

The service proposed a year-round complex at Mineral King capable of handling 8,000 people during the winter and 6,000 people during the summer. It emphasized that these capacities represented a 20 percent reduction from the earlier proposed winter capacity, and a 40 percent reduction in the summer from the size proposed in the draft EIS. There would be eighteen ski lifts and lodging for guests at the Mineral King Village in the valley, at Faculty Flats, just inside the entrance to the valley, and at Silver City.[48]

Having completed the EIS, the Forest Service was now legally positioned to formally approve the Mineral King development in 1976. Bob Hicks indicated that Disney was still willing to go ahead with the resort despite the reduction in its size and the reduced road standard.[49] The Sierra Club condemned the revised project as "too heavy handed," asserting that the resort would "seriously damage" Sequoia National Park and "severely compromise" the game refuge.[50]

But the Forest Service now faced a new serious problem. Political support for the project was collapsing.

The delay had brought fundamental changes in the once widespread political enthusiasm for the project. While Senator George Murphy had worked tirelessly supporting it, his political career lasted only a single term. He lost the 1970 election to thirty-six-year-old Democrat John V. Tunney. The new senator was the son of former heavyweight boxing champion Gene Tunney and Polly Lauder, an heiress to the Carnegie Steel fortune and a supporter of both the National Audubon Society and the Wildlife Federation.[51] Tunney was interested in environmental issues[52] and not naturally inclined to support the Mineral King project.

The other senator from California, Democrat Alan Cranston, had taken office in 1968. Cranston favored placing Mineral King in Sequoia National Park with possible provision for scaled-down recreational ski facilities.[53]

Another key supporter of the project, Governor Ronald Reagan, had been succeeded in 1975 by Democrat Edmund G. ("Jerry") Brown

Jr., the son of former Governor Pat Brown. The new Brown administration began reevaluating the Mineral King project. In September 1976, Brown's secretary for resources, Claire Dedrick, sent a letter to Regional Forester Doug Leisz that cited "differences of opinion" between the state and the U.S. Forest Service regarding the Mineral King development. She requested the California attorney general to "seek involvement" in the Sierra Club's Mineral King litigation.[54]

The biggest political loss, however, was the defeat of the local congressman, Bob Mathias. A Republican, Mathias had pressured federal officials to act and vigorously promoted the development. Mathias, however, had been swept out of office in the landslide 1974 Congressional election after the Watergate scandal. His replacement, John Krebs, was a Democrat from Fresno.

Krebs had a fascinating background. Born in Berlin, Germany, in 1926, his family moved to Tel Aviv in 1930. During World War II Krebs was a member of the Jewish military organization, the Haganah. He then worked as a diamond cutter in Tel Aviv until 1946, when he emigrated to the United States and attended college. After a stint in the United States Army, he attended law school and ended up practicing law in Fresno, where his interest in politics eventually led to his election to the county board of supervisors. In 1974 Krebs defeated Bob Mathias in a reapportioned congressional district.

The local newspapers and supporters of the Mineral King development pressed Krebs to clarify his position on that subject. Krebs delayed for a long time, saying that he wanted to study the issue, review pertinent documents, and hear from his constituents. Finally, on March 15, 1976, Krebs distributed a press release stating that the development proposed in the Final EIS "would not be in the best interests" of his district. "[T]he environmental toll," he concluded, "which would be exacted as a result of the proposed development would far outweigh the short-term economic benefits it might bring to the County of Tulare."[55] Krebs announced that he would introduce legislation to incorporate the Mineral King Valley into Sequoia National Park.[56]

Krebs's announcement signaled that the major political support for the development of Mineral King had crumbled. His position on Mineral King prompted harsh attacks from local officials who understood its threat to the Disney development. The chair of the Tulare County Board of Supervisors said that if Krebs introduced his proposed legislation to put Mineral King in the park, "you can start wearing the black arm bands" because "Mineral King has had it."[57] Krebs would lose his seat in Congress after the November 1978 election, at least in part because of his position on Mineral King.

The increased resistance to the Forest Service's Mineral King project now extended beyond elected politicians. The National Park Service had never fully supported an expanded road or railroad to Mineral King that would traverse Sequoia National Park. Now the service went much further.

In August 1975, the Park Service for the first time had recommended that Congress defer action on bills concerning Mineral King until the service could study adding the valley to the park. On March 1, 1976, the Park Service sent its completed report on the subject to, among others, Nathaniel Reed, the assistant secretary of Fish, Wildlife, and Parks in the Department of the Interior under President Gerald Ford.[58] The fifty-four page study found that developing a ski resort at Mineral King "within what is essentially an enclave of a national park would inevitably have a serious adverse impact on the park."[59] Based on the study, the National Park Service concluded: "We believe the best way to assure that adverse development does not occur in the Mineral King Valley is to add it to the park."[60]

The Forest Service recognized that, given the project's dependence on transportation that crossed the park, the Park Service's position would stop the Mineral King development in its tracks. As its in-house lawyer admitted in discussing the matter with Jim Moorman of the Sierra Club Legal Defense Fund, "if Interior will not give the go-ahead in some form to the corridor, the project is dead."[61] Even though it had completed the EIS, the Forest Service further delayed any final approval of the project.

That approval would remain in administrative limbo through

all of 1977 and into 1978. But another startling twist soon occurred: Judge Sweigert dismissed the Sierra Club's lawsuit.

The judge had semiretired, assuming the position of a "senior" judge in late 1973, but he had retained the Mineral King case. His dismissal order was entirely unexpected and shocked the lawyers in the case. Judge Sweigert was "weeding his garden" of cases and concluded that the Sierra Club had "fail[ed] to prosecute" the litigation, that is, that the club had taken insufficient steps to move the case forward to trial.[62]

The court's order was ironic. When the Sierra Club had sought to amend its complaint in 1972 to allege standing after the Supreme Court decision, the government had argued that final approval of the project would not occur until the EIS was complete, so the club's legal challenge was premature. The government's argument was then rejected by Judge Sweigert. However, as the EIS process dragged on, Judge Sweigert decided that the lawsuit had stagnated for too long without being brought to trial and dismissed it.

From the Sierra Club's standpoint, the crucial legal question was the type of dismissal ordered. If it was "dismissal with prejudice," then the club would likely be barred from bringing a new suit after the Forest Service finally approved the project. The Sierra Club's lawyers scrambled to address the judge's unexpected order. They filed a notice appealing that order to the Ninth Circuit Court of Appeals. At the same time, they filed a motion with Judge Sweigert asking him to rescind the dismissal, arguing that the government's delay in deciding on the final project was the primary reason the case had not yet come to trial. In the meantime, the judge's order became public, with the various stakeholders pointing to it in their efforts to shape public opinion.[63]

In the end, the Justice Department—now controlled by the new, more environmentally friendly administration of President Jimmy Carter—agreed not to argue that the case had been dismissed with prejudice. The Sierra Club thus might refile later.

Mike McCloskey's reaction to the unexpected situation was somewhat counterintuitive: he thought that now might be a good time to have the case dismissed. It appeared as if Congress might begin to act on legislation to put Mineral King into Sequoia National Park. McCloskey thought that if the lawsuit was no longer on the books, it could not be used as a "red herring" to deter legislative action.[64]

Judge Sweigert accepted the parties' agreement and signed an order dismissing the case "without prejudice."[65] The order ended the monumental legal battle, begun in 1969, that had resulted in a groundbreaking Supreme Court case on standing. While the Mineral King case sputtered to a close and would never be refiled, it had changed the course of legal history and of Mineral King's fate.

Then, yet another unexpected development occurred. A new assistant secretary in the Department of Agriculture, Rupert Cutler, was mounting an effort to fashion a compromise that would be acceptable to both Disney and the Sierra Club.

Cutler was well versed in the Mineral King dispute. His dissertation for a doctorate at Michigan State University had included an analysis of the earlier part of the Mineral King controversy. As the new assistant secretary of agriculture for Conservation, Research, and Education, he thought a compromise was possible even at this late date, but only if the scale of the development would not damage Mineral King and the surrounding environment. Throughout 1977 he met informally with Disney personnel, Department of the Interior officials, and "some congressional people."[66]

Rumors of a possible compromise surfaced in the press. A September article in the *Los Angeles Times* deemed the proposal for a Mineral King ski area "resurrected," quoting Cutler as saying, "We're looking for the answers, but it ain't easy."[67] The parties involved were unsure of what was happening. Ed Pell, a Sierra Club staff member, spoke to Jim Stewart of Disney, with Pell reporting that Disney "had no idea of what was going to happen next—it's up to the government." At Cutler's request, Disney had spent three months reassessing the design and cost of the project.[68]

Cutler settled on a modified project of 6,000 people per day in the winter, with transportation to Mineral King by bus from Silver City. The Forest Service would share the $15 million cost of rehabilitating the road so skiers could get to Silver City. In late November 1977, however, it became clear that the Department of the Interior did not agree with Cutler's proposal. Instead, Robert L. Herbst, the assistant secretary for Fish, Wildlife and Parks, indicated publicly that, while no final decision had been made, the Department of the Interior might accept the Park Service's position and support the Krebs bill to transfer jurisdiction over the valley to the Park Service.[69] Moreover, when Cutler finally released his plan in January 1978, Disney responded coolly that the scaled down plan "may be too limited for it to be economically feasible." Krebs dismissed it as "represent[ing] no major change from earlier plans."[70]

It was too late. Cutler could not assemble the pieces of a compromise acceptable to the interested parties. The stage was now set for the final act of the drama over Mineral King. For the first time, attention about the future of Mineral King shifted to Congress.

Bills to insert the Mineral King Valley into Sequoia National Park had been introduced since 1967 but had never even been afforded a committee hearing. Support for the legislation, however, had gradually accumulated over time. By 1973, seventeen members of Congress from California, and a like number from other states, had sponsored such legislation.[71]

By 1977, the support had grown even larger. Most important, the local congressman for the area, John Krebs, had introduced his bill, H.R. 1771, to incorporate Mineral King into Sequoia National Park. In that same year, Senator Alan Cranston had introduced a similar bill in the Senate. Cranston had just been elected majority whip in the Senate and exercised considerable influence over that body, while important changes in committee heads in both the House and

Senate had taken place. Momentum was growing to hold a hearing on the bill.

The interested parties jockeyed for political leverage throughout most of 1977. Then, in October of that year, events began to accelerate.

Congressman Phil Burton of San Francisco had first introduced a bill to make Mineral King part of Sequoia National Park ten years earlier and remained committed to that goal. Burton represented a middle-class congressional district in San Francisco and was one of the least likely persons to ever hike in Mineral King. He was overweight, a rumpled urban dweller, a chain smoker of unfiltered cigarettes, and a person far more at home drinking vodka with political cronies than trekking in the mountains. Burton once told a legislative aide that the closest he got to being outdoors was heading fifty yards into the forest to relieve himself.[72] He also said that, for him, "A wilderness experience [was] to see a tree in a god-damned pot."[73]

However, Burton cared about national parks because they were open to all classes of society. As one of his aides put it, Burton was committed to environmental preservation because "it was something for the people, the right thing to do,"[74] and he spearheaded the legislation that greatly expanded Redwood National Park. Burton was also one of the earliest opponents of the Disney development. A liberal, he saw the development at Mineral King as a government giveaway to private interests.

Burton was a master of legislative tactics and an energetic, forceful personality; the terms "crude," "intimidator," and "bullying" often came up in describing him.[75] Moreover, he was a major force among the Democrats in Congress. In 1976, most political observers tabbed him as the front-runner in the contest for a new majority leader of the House of Representatives. After leading on the first ballot, Burton lost the election by one vote—148 to 147—to Congressman Jim Wright of Texas.[76]

Burton moved on. He shifted his focus to a different goal: increasing the national park system. He used his position as chair of the

Subcommittee on Parks of the House Interior and Insular Affairs Committee as a base of operations. There, he worked closely with Morris Udall, the chair of the full committee and brother of Stewart Udall, who as secretary of the interior had played such a prominent role opposing approval of the road to Mineral King. In October 1977, Burton scheduled a hearing before his subcommittee on bills to place Mineral King into Sequoia National Park.

A colorful parade of witnesses marched in to testify before Burton's subcommittee. Nancy Ingalsbee, a single mother of three teenagers representing Southern California skiers, presented a petition on "340 feet of rumpled paper"[77] with individual messages written by skiers. She posed a question and then answered it herself: "What do we want? Only that which is rightfully ours. A fair share of our [public] lands."[78] Mary Ann Eriksen of the Sierra Club countered by arguing that approving a higher-capacity road into Mineral King "would be to dismember Sequoia National Park.[79]

The Carpenters' Union appeared, emphasizing both the number of jobs that the Disney development would produce and the increase in local property taxes.[80] Jerome Waldie, a former congressman representing the environmental group Friends of the Earth, condemned the Forest Service's new plan: "[S]caled-down is not good enough. Scaled-out is the only thing that will do."[81] The United States Ski Association pointed to the growing national demand for skiing on national forest lands, which it projected to increase 37 percent from 1970 to 1990.[82] Dave Beck, the ski expert who had measured snow in Mineral King for Disney during the winter of the 1969 avalanche there, submitted a letter stating that the area belonged in the park.[83] Slim Davis, now retired from the Forest Service, appeared on behalf of the United States Ski Association.[84]

Congressman Krebs also testified. He argued that Mineral King "is functionally part of Sequoia National Park."[85] He continued that intensive recreational use "would cause irreparable damage to the aesthetic values" of the valley.[86] Senator Cranston submitted a written statement in support of the Krebs bill. He declared that he was "not opposed to the development of Mineral King," but the National Park Service was the "best agency to administer" it.[87]

Finally, Jim Stewart testified for Disney and faced a now-boiling political caldron. As was the company's norm, he emphasized that Disney had "responded . . . in good faith" to the Forest Service's invitation. While "[i]t has never been our intention to become involved in a dispute over the use of public lands . . . we continue to support the Forest Service in its belief that Mineral King can meet an important recreational need."[88] Later, he raised a new theme: a violation of Disney's constitutional rights. He argued, "[O]ur company has invested more than $1.5 million in planning, design, [and] environmental studies in that area, and this legislation would constitute a taking of our rights at Mineral King without due process, and without any compensation."[89]

The headline of the next day's *San Francisco Chronicle* accurately captured the flavor of the hearing: "Sharp Debate over Mineral King's Fate."[90] The legislation to place the valley in Sequoia National Park was now cosponsored by sixty-three members of Congress, including twenty-one from California. One important political office, however, had shifted back to the prodevelopment side. S. I. Hayakawa, a Republican, had defeated John Tunney in the 1976 California race for the United States Senate, and he favored developing Mineral King. Hayakawa, a witty man with a penchant for wearing multicolored tam-o'-shanters, had gained notoriety as the president of San Francisco State University. He was particularly famous for an incident in 1968 when, less than a week after being appointed interim president, he jumped onto a sound truck at a student protest and ripped the wires from a loudspeaker.[91]

Burton scheduled another hearing on Mineral King legislation for late January 1978, a step that precipitated important developments. The administration of President Jimmy Carter needed to choose between the positions of the Park Service and the Forest Service, and a replay ensued of the 1969 process used to resolve the differences between Stewart Udall and Orville Freeman. The Office of Management and Budget had to decide between the National Park Service, which wanted to support legislation putting the Mineral King Valley into Sequoia National Park, and the Forest Service, which was promoting Rupert Cutler's effort to craft a compromise.[92]

The Carter administration decided to support the incorporation of Mineral King into Sequoia National Park.[93] A disappointed Cutler confirmed the decision in testimony before Burton's subcommittee. He noted "a fact of life which emerged" from his review: "[A] level of development which would be economically viable would have various impacts on Mineral King Valley."[94]

The director of the National Park Service also testified before Burton's subcommittee. He stated that, if Mineral King became part of Sequoia National Park, the service would create a plan for the valley.[95] But the outcome was clear: no large downhill ski resort would be built. The Forest Service press release on the new Carter administration position said as much, recognizing that inclusion of the land in the park "would all but foreclose the construction of any skiing facilities."[96]

Disney reacted bitterly. Card Walker wrote to President Jimmy Carter, terming it "extremely unfortunate that a very small but highly organized and influential minority of preservationists could impose upon Congress and your administration its narrow view of public land management."[97] Disney also began efforts to obtain reimbursement for its costs in planning the Mineral King development.

Less than three weeks after the Carter administration's announcement, the State of California chimed in. Governor Jerry Brown wrote to John Krebs stating that "I support the addition of Mineral King to Sequoia National Park" and that it "will make an admirable addition to the National Park System."[98]

Political support for the Disney project—near universal at its peak in 1969—had now largely dissipated.

Phil Burton possessed the political vision and vote-counting skills needed to pass complex legislation, and he saw opportunity in creating additions to the national parks. The House Public Works Committee for years had passed omnibus bills containing numerous public works projects located in different congressional districts, and Burton decided to appropriate that concept. He conceived of an omnibus parks bill that would attract political support by creating or adding to parks located throughout the country. His concept would eventually be termed a "park-barrel" bill in honor of the "pork-barrel" legislation that traditionally emerged out of the Public Works Committee.

In May 1978, Burton introduced the first version of his omnibus bill. At 157 pages in length, the bill included a hundred projects at a price tag of $1.8 billion. The ultimate scope of the bill and its cost were unprecedented. The park additions were located in more than two hundred congressional districts in forty-four states. The bill ended up including areas such as the Boundary Waters Canoe Area in Minnesota, the Pine Barrens National Reserve in New Jersey, and the Golden Gate National Recreation Area near San Francisco. It would add segments to eight wild and scenic rivers, create dozens of historic and cultural sites—and incorporate Mineral King into Sequoia National Park.[99]

After days of debate, the bill passed the House of Representatives in July 1978 by a 341 to 61 vote.[100] However, the bill faced a highly uncertain future in the Senate, largely because so little time remained before year-end adjournment. And the Mineral King part of the bill, in particular, faced new opposition.

The junior senator from California, S. I. Hayakawa, continued to oppose the inclusion of Mineral King in Sequoia National Park, and a vociferous ski industry supported his efforts. The opposition had placed a full-page advertisement in the *Washington Post* addressed to Congress and aimed directly at John Krebs. It stated that "Our current Congressman [Krebs] does not speak for us when he opposes development of a year-round recreational resort in Mineral King Valley." It listed signatures from hundreds of individuals.[101] The senior senator from California, Alan Cranston, had continued to support adding Mineral King to Sequoia National Park, but in testimony before a Senate subcommittee, he now said that he favored downhill skiing in Mineral King.[102]

In October, with no time remaining for a conference committee to iron out differences between House and Senate versions of the parks bill, Phil Burton transformed into a whirlwind of legislative energy. A *Washington Star* article called him a "one-man Conference Committee on parks."[103] He shuttled back and forth between House and Senate members, negotiating amendments to the bill and creating new, omnibus versions approved by the House through unanimous consent.[104] Finally, as time ran out, the bill faced a showdown in the Senate.

Senator Hayakawa introduced an amendment to take Mineral King out of the bill and require a one-year study. As an alternative, he wanted compensation for Disney. Hayakawa sought to take advantage of a procedure whereby the Senate would honor a request made by both senators from any one state,[105] and the ski association representatives thought they had secured Alan Cranston's agreement for such a delay.[106] However, Cranston, the Senate whip, disappeared from the Senate floor during the vote on the amendment offered by Hayakawa. While Cranston attributed his absence to the demands of other business, the ski association later accused him of a "double-cross"[107] and sent him a telegram saying that skiers would never forget this "day of infamy."[108]

The amendment was defeated, and the bill passed. Burton also rejected any compensation for Disney. Burton's bill then went back to the House, where Burton sought unanimous consent for its passage for a fifth and last time. However, a congressman from Louisiana, a state that received considerable federal subsidies for sugar, stood to object to Burton's bill. When he did, a furious Burton reportedly ran toward him yelling "There will never be another fucking nickel for sugar. I'll get you!" The congressman decided not to object, and the bill passed.[109]

On November 10, 1978, President Jimmy Carter signed the omnibus National Parks and Recreation Act of 1978.[110] Mineral King became a part of Sequoia National Park. The long battle had ended.

Epilogue

THE INFLECTION POINT

The dispute over Mineral King reflected dramatic changes in American attitudes toward and approaches to environmental issues. A sea change occurred between 1965, when the Forest Service released its prospectus to develop Mineral King, and 1978, when the dispute ended. Not only did the law evolve, government agencies, businesses, and environmental organizations transformed as they faced new situations. It was a remarkable period of ferment. During it, the fate of Mineral King, a spectacularly beautiful valley, hung in the balance.

The Supreme Court decision was a legal landmark that marks an inflection point in the development of environmental law. It "locked citizen standing into American jurisprudence and the daily operation of American environmental law,"[1] thereby signaling the emergence of lawsuits as an important means of raising environmental issues and challenging agency decisions. Surveys of environmental practitioners and academic experts, carried out thirty and forty years later, ranked the case as one of the most important environmental law decisions ever handed down.[2]

While the court rejected the club's attempt to provide broad interest-based standing, it recognized environmental harm as a basis for standing, showed how to establish the required "injury in fact," and allowed organizations to represent members who were among the injured. The effects of the decision were immediate. In the two years after the court handed it down, numerous cases cited *Sierra Club v. Morton* in finding that environmental plaintiffs had standing to sue, and in other cases standing was no longer contested. Relatively few decisions denied plaintiffs' standing.[3]

While the basic holding of the case has remained intact, a later, more conservative Supreme Court, led by Justice Antonin Scalia, did tighten the requirements for standing. In a 1993 case, *Lujan v. Defenders of Wildlife*, Justice Scalia articulated a threefold test for determining standing. First, there must be "injury in fact," which can be an environmental injury, the basic holding in *Sierra Club v. Morton*. However, the injury must be "concrete and particularized" and "actual or imminent," not "conjectural" or "hypothetical." Second, the injury must be caused by the illegal government action: the injury had to be fairly traceable to the challenged action of the defendant, and not to some other third party. Finally, it must be "likely"—in contrast to "speculative"—that a decision in the plaintiff's favor would redress the injury.[4]

These requirements demand greater proof to establish standing. They inhibit plaintiffs in some cases, such as those where the injury might occur over a lengthy period of time, where there was no close geographic nexus between the plaintiff and the place of injury, or where the effect of the illegal action was murky. After *Lujan*, the court seemed to back off slightly in a couple of cases, particularly *Massachusetts v. EPA*. In that 2007 case, Massachusetts was found to have standing to challenge the EPA's failure to regulate greenhouse gases even though the alleged injury was widespread and the remedy sought would have only a small effect in alleviating the injury.[5] Importantly, though, the cases subsequent to *Sierra Club v. Morton* illustrate that the Supreme Court possesses wide discretion to articulate the doctrine of standing, and that further limitations on standing by a conservative court could occur in the future.

The later tightening of standing in environmental cases also highlighted what was lost in the Mineral King case: the idea that a plaintiff should be able to sue and prevent environmental injury based solely on the public interest in securing adherence to the law. Instead, the law of standing rests on injury to the plaintiff, not simply injury to the environment. The rejected "interest theory" in the case would have gone some way toward recognizing standing without specific injury.

Still, the basic holding of *Sierra Club v. Morton* remains intact and enormously influential. It opened the gateway to modern environmental litigation. Throughout the 1970s and 1980s, environmental organizations expanded exponentially, and many of them made use of litigation to further their efforts.[6] In doing so, they have generally been able to meet even the tightened standing requirements.[7] The guiding principle established by *Sierra Club v. Morton* has remained steadfast for almost fifty years.

The changes reflected in the dispute over Mineral King extended well beyond the legal question of standing. The dispute arose when new information and ideas about the environment began to alter governmental decision-making. Among others, those forces included increased scientific understanding of how environmental effects occur, expanded knowledge about the long-term health effects of pollution, and emergence of a large citizen movement dedicated to protecting the environment. The use of the law as a tool for environmental protection intersected with these developments and magnified their effect.

In retrospect, one of the most surprising aspects of the Mineral King dispute was the Forest Service's seeming indifference to legal constraints upon its authority before the Sierra Club brought its suit. More understandably, the Disney company too seemed unconcerned about legal issues, such as the use of the dual permit system, until late in the process. After *Sierra Club v. Morton*, the law would now occupy an important place in what became a much larger, increasingly complex governmental system of environmental decision-making. Legal standards would be integrated into the decision-making processes employed by public agencies and businesses, which would pay much closer attention to those requirements.

This change would accompany the broadening of agency procedures to incorporate public input. As one study of the Mineral King dispute observed, when the Forest Service made its original 1965 decision, it "did not foresee the public awakening that was to occur a few years hence."[8] In that sense, the agency was caught unawares. The Forest Service's adamant refusal to hold a hearing on its Mineral King development would give way to vastly increased opportunities for public involvement. Law would establish the procedures by which agency action would become more regularized and open to public participation.

Another effect of the increased emphasis on legal constraints would be a change in the discretion available to agencies in their decision-making. Throughout the Mineral King struggle, the Forest Service saw itself as uniquely qualified, based on its assumed expertise, to decide the future use of Mineral King. As its own lawyer at the time put it, "The Forest Service feels that what's good for the Forest Service is good for the country; they're sure they're better able to make" these decisions about public lands than lay organizations.[9] This attitude, however, conflicted with the increasing perception that government agencies were not protecting the environment. The Forest Service's veil of expertise also was at odds with a public increasingly skeptical about deferring to government expertise, a development stemming in part from dissatisfaction with management of the Vietnam War.[10]

After *Sierra Club v. Morton*, agencies now would have to justify their decisions before courts. They would compile administrative records containing the materials that they had relied upon, documenting procedures that they followed, and explaining the reasons behind their decisions. In turn, these altered methods of agency decision-making would affect the exercise of discretion by the agencies. The evidence placed before agencies for their consideration would constrain the agencies' substantive choices.

Litigation also brought another significant result evident in the Mineral King litigation: delay as cases work their way through the courts. Agencies and permittees would find it difficult and risky to implement projects still under challenge in the courts. Delay would turn out to be an inevitable cost of opening the courts to ensure compliance with environmental laws.

The social and cultural ferment in which the Mineral King dispute played out was unique. When Walt Disney submitted his application to the Forest Service in 1965, he had no reason to anticipate that the future use of Mineral King would become the subject of endless headlines, or that the Disney company's actions would be relentlessly attacked. Similarly, the Forest Service could not have recognized then that its long-standing *modus operandi*—typified by unilateral decision-making and emphasis on maximizing use of forest resources—would be challenged. The Sierra Club also changed substantially during the period of the dispute, transforming from a small conservation group focused on outdoor activities to a national environmental organization.

As the dispute rolled on and these changes occurred, each of the organizations faced difficulties adapting. The Sierra Club's biggest problem had ethical overtones: it had endorsed a ski resort in Mineral King and, at a late date, reversed its position. Moreover, it did so after opposing skiing at San Gorgonio above the Los Angeles basin by pointing to Mineral King as an alternative. The club had what it believed were good reasons for the change in position on Mineral King, but it could not escape the charge that it had behaved at best inconsistently and at worst unethically. Its explanation—the original ski resort was much smaller than the one Disney would build—only partially worked. The club had simply changed its mind, and its reputation paid a price.

It had, however, decided to oppose Mineral King at a time when support for the project seemed overwhelming. The club had shown how, against long odds, it could alter public opinion and expose flaws in the Forest Service's processes. Without John Harper's passionate advocacy for the valley, and Mike McCloskey's understanding of how to mount a campaign of opposition, the Sierra Club would never have achieved the outcome it sought.

As for Disney, its work on the project was remarkable. Bob Hicks was an exceptionally able manager, and the Disney project is a tribute to his skills and to the Disney organization generally. Moreover, Disney often defended its project on the ground that it had merely responded to the Forest Service's prospectus, and this claim was largely accurate. The Forest Service was the principal instigator of the project.

The Disney personnel, however, failed to understand how anyone could see how its project, which was much larger than the Forest Service originally contemplated, could cause environmental damage. Disney also clung to the hope of a Mineral King development well beyond the point where it had any realistic chance of succeeding. The reason, of course, was loyalty to Walt Disney, an understandable and unobjectionable attitude. But times had changed. Who really knew whether Walt Disney would have been as adamant at that point?

Indeed, Walt Disney himself may well have also underestimated the constraints of building a project in a government-regulated environment of this type. One incident described by Bob Hicks suggests as much. Hicks reported that, on Walt Disney's last visit to Mineral King before his death, he pointed up to a parcel on Miner's Ridge and said, "I want the first ski lift up here next year." The Forest Service personnel immediately stressed to Bob Hicks that this action was not possible, as the service had not yet issued the long-term permit for the development. Hicks replied that "Walt will take care of it"[11] and moved on, but Hicks was anything but naive. He certainly knew that Disney's order could not be carried out.

The force of the environmental movement fundamentally challenged how the Forest Service operated. For much of this period, the agency would not even concede the need for a public hearing on the Mineral King project, relying instead on the dubious 1953 Chamber of Commerce gathering. While the court of appeals accepted the argument that this hearing was sufficient, that conclusion was unconvincing. Institutional imperatives—the service knew what was best in making public land decisions—were deeply ingrained and explain the agency's stubbornness. The Forest Service simply could not see the *point* of a hearing. The Forest Service did change after *Sierra Club v.*

Morton was remanded from the Supreme Court in 1972, substantially opening up its processes. But that change was very late in coming.

Even more important, the Forest Service repeatedly claimed that it had engaged in extensive planning for Mineral King before issuing its prospectus. The record, however, does not support that claim; its planning, to the extent it existed, was after the fact. The service had simply decided that Mineral King was suited for skiing and then rigidly implemented that idea. And, holding fast to the idea that "bigger is better," it enthusiastically signed on to the very large project that Disney proposed.

Finally, what about the ultimate outcome of the Mineral King dispute? The fundamental decision—whether to preserve Mineral King as part of a national park or use it as a world-class ski area—is essentially a choice between competing values. It is a political decision. Certain factors, however, shed light on that decision and suggest the ultimate outcome was appropriate.

The first factor was the administrative geography of Mineral King. By 1965, the valley was bounded by Sequoia National Park on three sides. As one description put it, the valley "jabs like a bent thumb into National Park land."[12] Because of this geographic arrangement, large-scale development of Mineral King would inevitably affect the park.

The biggest impact, and the one that generated the most controversy, was the need to transport skiers through the park. But other impacts would occur. For example, there was a likelihood that the anchors of some ski lifts for the Mineral King development would sit inside the park boundaries. In short, given the preexisting location of Sequoia National Park, building a very large ski project would inevitably affect the park, a land area that—by legal definition—was to be preserved.

Also important was the reason for this existing geographic arrangement. The Mineral King Valley had been left out of the park only because of old mining claims. Those claims, however, had long become dormant, and their economic value was nil, if it ever had been real. Thus, the historical reason for the valley's exclusion from the park no longer existed, and by 1965, that exclusion seemed to rest on questionable if not mistaken assumptions about the valley's mineral wealth.

Given this history, a logical argument inevitably gained traction: the historical "mistake" should be rectified by putting Mineral King in the park where it belonged. Even the skiing forces recognized that the geography of the Mineral King situation was "unfortunate": "It would be more comfortable for all concerned if it did not stick like a pig's foot into the gut of Sequoia National Park."[13]

A second, related factor concerned the road. In words that the Sierra Club often repeated, Walt Disney had said "I guess you might say it [the Mineral King development] won't ever be finished."[14] At some point, feared the Park Service, the new road would be too small to serve the ski development as it expanded. For example, the Park Service's respected consultant on the road, John Clarkeson, reported in 1968 that he "suspects that they [the California Highway Department] are designing the road with the idea of expanding it soon to four lanes." He also reported that "[h]is discussions with the Disney people back this up."[15] If the ski development later grew, as was likely, the pressure to expand the road through the park would become inexorable. Eventually, thought the Park Service, the road would essentially become a freeway through Sequoia National Park.

This likelihood meant that the Park Service and the Department of the Interior would necessarily be deeply suspicious of it, for a large road through a national park contradicted the park's core purpose. Their resistance was foreseeable from the outset.

Finally, a third factor that greatly influenced the outcome was the underlying question of how a development of the size proposed by Disney could "preserve" Mineral King. The Disney company had repeatedly promised that it could build the ski development while preserving Mineral King. Indeed, the company viewed the Mineral King development as the crowning achievement of its conservation efforts:

> The greatest chapter in the Disney Conservation Story is now being written. It is with Mineral King that our Company will prove more

> dramatically and emphatically than ever that preservation of natural beauty and resources need not be assured at the expense of enjoying that beauty by many people.[16]

Disney promised to meld both man and nature.

At the same time, however, Walt Disney equally emphasized the need to serve the burgeoning California population. As he said in an interview at the time, "[W]ith our population of about twenty-eight million in California, plus the tourists—we're going to have to build it big enough to take care of them."[17]

The sheer size of the project casts doubt on the assertion that it could be built and still preserve Mineral King. A large development would *inevitably* change Mineral King to such a degree that some substantial part of its natural attributes and beauty would be lost. Disney and the Forest Service never directly confronted that reality. They both viewed the valley through a very different lens than the Sierra Club, seeing "preservation" as aesthetic compatibility between the mountains and the resort.

If the development proposal had been smaller, the grounds for the Sierra Club's opposition would have been substantially weakened, and there might well have been some room for compromise. But the Forest Service's decision-making criteria automatically favored bigger over smaller, and when Robert Brandt and Walt Disney found themselves in fierce competition for the Forest Service approval, the result was an even larger facility. The large size, however, meant that it became increasingly difficult to justify the claim that the project would "preserve" Mineral King.

These factors suggest that the ski proposal faced considerable obstacles from the outset, even if all of them were not then fully apparent. They increased in intensity over time, and they largely explain the ultimate rejection of that proposal and the incorporation of Mineral King into Sequoia National Park.

Intertwined with these factors was the Sierra Club's lawsuit challenging the approval of the Disney development and the road. The suit stopped the momentum of the project, and it forced an examination of the Forest Service's decision-making from a new perspective: its legality. Without the Sierra Club's lawsuit, the fate of Mineral King almost certainly would have been different.

A new era had begun.

Acknowledgments

I read *Sierra Club v. Morton* in law school just after it was handed down. Intrigued, I visited the Mineral King Valley two years later and once again after that. In practicing law and teaching over a forty-five-year period, I represented the Sierra Club on several occasions. In one of them, standing was an issue, and it rekindled my interest in writing about *Sierra Club v. Morton*.

I did not realize how the project would be so contingent on the kindness and generosity of various individuals. Without the help of the people mentioned below, this book never would have been completed.

Loyola Law School Deans Victor Gold and Michael Waterstone provided financial support for the research, which led across the United States. I also greatly benefited from the support of the Fritz B. Burns Foundation, whose chair I hold. The research support I received from Loyola's library, headed by Dan Martin, was phenomenal. In particular, Caitlin Hunter, reference librarian, went far above and beyond the call of duty in researching other works on Mineral King and various strands of the background. Her support was unbelievable in its scope, and I cannot thank her enough. Later, Laura Cadra stepped in and was always willing to help, even on short notice, and went well out of her way to find photographs and answers to questions. Tiffani Willis, Tobe Liebert, Amber Madole, and Lisa Schultz kindly researched specific topics.

Others at the law school were also extraordinarily helpful. Pam Buckles somehow found ways to get interviews transcribed. Corinne St. Claire patiently helped me preserve the photographs of thousands of documents. Mel Banez, Thelma Wong Terre, Bridget Klink, and Liz Luk graciously handled a variety of sometimes challenging word-processing tasks. Caleb Borba, Alison Hahm, Kassandra Velasquez, Andreas Booher, and Stanford Faigin provided excellent student research assistance.

My colleague Sam Pillsbury encouraged me through the process of finding a publisher. Another colleague, Bob Brain, was always supportive and introduced me to his friend Paula Allen, who gave me much-needed advice.

My friend Lisa Hutton put me in touch with Shelley Alden Brooks, of the University of California at Davis, who helped me understand the perspective of a historian. Craig Jones at the University of Colorado shared his knowledge of the Sierra Nevadas.

In researching the book, the help of a group of individuals was critical. Louise Jackson, former head of the Mineral King Preservation Society, has encyclopedic knowledge of Mineral King and worked tirelessly to preserve its history. She went far out of her way to help my project, escorting me to Mineral King, reading a draft, helping with pictures, and putting me in touch with Bob Hicks and Pete Wyckoff, both of whom graciously met with me. Louise also led the way in preserving the papers of Bob Hicks, which are central to this book. Her friend Jana Botkin showed me around Mineral King one more time, and Laile Di Silvestro helped me to access the Hicks Papers. I am also very grateful to Ward Eldridge, the historian for Sequoia National Park, who guided me to and through the trove of documents on Mineral King in the park's possession. Susan Dearing went way out of her way to find a picture of her father, John Harper.

Mike McCloskey of the Sierra Club put up with two lengthy interviews and was always willing to answer my emails. Lee Selna and Jim Moorman, the club's lawyers, gave up their time to meet with me. Jack Gelin, the principal government lawyer at the court of appeals level, hosted me for a day in his house and helped me contact other individuals by phone. Others I met with in person included Joe Fontaine, John Hoffman, Harry Gesner, Doug Leisz, Jim Moorman, Lew Reid, Jim Stewart, Peter Strauss, Bruce Terris, and Tom Turner. For telephone interviews, I thank Don Allen, Greg Archibald, Michael

Bauernfeind, Terry Bray, Mary Ann Burtt, Jeanne Nienaber Clark, Jack Cox, Kelly Curtis, Rupert Cutler, MaryLu Everett, Michael Frith, John Fry, Albert Hill, Nancy Ingalsbee, William Jeffress, Scott Kruse, Jim Lake, Paul Locke, Ralph Mikan, Mathew Mitchell, Chuck Morse, Bud Pell, Sandy Quinn, John Rettenmayer, Tony Ruckel, John Schwartz, Larry Silver, Frank Ubhaus, John Watson, David Watts, Cynthia Wayburn, Harold Wexler, Ingrid Wicken, and Rosalind Wyman.

I quickly learned that finding the pertinent documents in depositories is impossible without the help of archivists. They are treasures. Some who helped me the most were Amy Reytar, Charles Miller, Bill Greene, Jennifer Mandel, Chris Livingston, Kevin Kern, Jonathan Waltmire, Adam Wallace, Jacqueline Sundstrand, Jeff Leich, Karen Miller, Sean Evans, Mona Ammon, Jason Howard, and Laura Russo. Ellen Byrne and Therese Dunn at the Sierra Club's Colby Library in Oakland, California, went out of their way to assist me. Maria Brandt effectively completed those research tasks when my time at Bancroft Library ran out, while Rich Arpi examined files at the Minnesota Historical Society. Others who aided me in finding information include Mike Traynor, Bill Tweed, Ellen Berkowitz, Suzanne Wilson, Bob Antonoplis, Toni Hope, Betsy Reifsnider, Aaron Isherwood, and Sarah Lu.

Individuals were willing to take on the task of reading my manuscript and giving me suggestions and corrections. One was Rachel Hooper, an extraordinarily talented environmental lawyer and great writer with whom I have had the privilege of working closely over the years. Rachel introduced me to her friend Thad Carhart, who encouraged me and put me in touch with Bob Wallace. Bob gave me the benefit of his more than forty years of experience in publishing to read my manuscript, offer comments, and encourage me. Brian Hembacher, for many years an environmental lawyer in the Los Angeles Office of the California Attorney General, also was kind enough to review it. Last, but certainly not least, Ken Manaster, my former professor and longtime coauthor, offered to read the manuscript without my asking, made very helpful suggestions, and was always encouraging. All authors should be as lucky as I was in receiving this help.

Charles Myers, at the University of Chicago Press, shepherded the project through. His guidance was outstanding and most appreciated. Caterina MacLean efficiently oversaw the production, while Kristen Raddatz was a marketing wizard. Susan Olin was a spectacular editor. Thanks also to Alicia Sparrow and Michaela Luckey for their administrative assistance and good humor, and to Bonny McLaughlin for indexing.

Finally, my wife Ann was indispensable in reading the manuscript, discussing the issues, making suggestions, helping with footnotes, and always encouraging me.

Notes on Sources and Abbreviations

The following sources, and their abbreviations, are used in the endnotes:

RBH Papers (Robert B. Hicks Papers), held by the Mineral King Preservation Society, Three Rivers, California.

NARA I—National Archives and Records Administration, College Park, Maryland. Documents principally reviewed were General Correspondence, 1906–1976, Office of the Secretary of Agriculture, Record Group 16; National Park Service Administrative Files, 1949–1971, Records of the Office of the Secretary of Interior, and General Correspondence of the Assistant Director for Design and Construction, 1965–1968, Record Group 79.

NARA II—National Archives and Records Administration, San Bruno, California. Documents principally examined were Central Files, Western Regional Office, National Park Service Service, 1925–1975, and Correspondence Files, 1967–1969; Sequoia National Forest Selected Historical Files, 1962–1969; and Sequoia-Kings Canyon National Park Correspondence and Subject Files, 1936–1977, Record Group 79. Additionally, the files for USDC ND CA SF Civil 81–2436, and Ninth Circuit CCOA #24966.

SNP Files—Sequoia National Park Mineral King Files, Mineral King Subject Files, held at the Ash Mountain Headquarters, Sequoia National Park.

OLF Papers—Orville L. Freeman Papers, held by the Minnesota Historical Society, St. Paul, Minnesota.

HP Papers—Harrison Price Papers, held by the University of Central Florida, Orlando, Florida.

GBH Papers—George B. Hartzog Jr. Papers, held by Clemson University, Clemson, South Carolina.

MKPS—Mineral King Preservation Society files, located in Three Rivers, California.

Dept. of Justice Files—DOJ File 90–1–14–191, General Records of the Department of Justice, held at the National Archives and Records Administration, College Park, Maryland.

All variations of Sierra Club records and the Philip Burton Papers are held by the Bancroft Library, University of California, Berkeley. Abbreviations for the Sierra Club records and related records are:

SCLDF Papers (Sierra Club Legal Defense Fund Papers). Documents principally examined from cartons 3, 4, 5, 6, and 7.

RJ Papers (Robert Jasperson Papers), housed at Bancroft Library, University of California, Berkeley. Documents principally examined from cartons 3, 7, and 8.

Sierra Club Members Papers. Documents principally examined from cartons 1, 52, 88, 93, 107, 121, 153, 183, 190, and 230.

Sierra Club Records. Documents principally examined from cartons 103, 106, 108, 109, 176, 161, 284.

GM Papers, George Marshall Papers, cartons 48 and 52.

All papers of the justices of the Supreme Court are held at the Library of Congress, Washington, DC, except for those of Potter Stewart, which are held at the archives of Yale University, New Haven, Connecticut.

Other archives researched include the Mineral King Collection, California State University, Fresno, California; the Harlan Hagen Papers and the Joe Fontaine Environmental History Collection at California State University, Bakersfield, California; the Ronald Reagan Presidential Library and Museum, Simi Valley, California; Mineral King Development Records, University of Southern California, Los Angeles, California; Annie R. Mitchell History Room at Tulare County Library, Visalia, California; Walt Disney Archives, Burbank, California; Stewart L. Udall Papers, University of Arizona, Tucson, Arizona; Thomas R. Hughes Papers, Minnesota Historical Society, St. Paul, Minnesota; Richard Sill Papers, University of Nevada, Reno, Nevada; S. I. Hayakawa Papers, Hoover Institution Archives, Stanford, California; Norman B. Livermore Jr. Papers, Edmund G. Brown Papers, and John L. Harper Papers, Bancroft Library, University of California, Berkeley; the Lyndon B. Johnson Presidential Library, Austin, Texas; Sierra Club Records, University of California, Los Angeles; and Sierra Club Records, San Diego State University, California.

The author has photographs of all archival documents cited.

Notes

Prologue

1. "Ecology: The New Jeremiahs," *Time* (Aug. 15, 1969): 38 ("Pollution may soon replace the Viet Nam war as the nation's major issue of protest"); Gladwin Hill, "Environment May Eclipse Vietnam as College Issue," *New York Times*, Nov. 30, 1969, 1 ("Rising concern about the 'environmental crisis' is sweeping the nation's campuses").
2. Kirkpatrick Sale, *The Green Revolution: The American Environmental Movement, 1962–1992* (New York: Hill and Wang, 1993), 19.
3. Thomas R. Wellock, *Preserving the Nation: The Conservation and Environmental Movements, 1870–2000* (Wheeling, IL: Harlan Davidson, 2007), 173.
4. "Issue of the Year: The Environment," *Time* (Jan. 4, 1971) ("In 1970, the cause that once concerned lonely crusaders like Rachel Carson became a national issue that at times verged on a national obsession").
5. "The Environment: A National Mission for the 1970s," *Fortune* (Feb. 1970).
6. Wellock, *Preserving the Nation*, 175; Benjamin Kline, *First Along the River: A Brief History of the U.S. Environmental Movement*, 3d ed. (Lanham, MD: Rowman and Littlefield, 2007), 81.
7. See, e.g., "Conservationists Sue to Halt Cross-Florida Canal," *New York Times*, Sept. 18, 1969; Harold M. Schmeck Jr., "Strict Ban on DDT Is Sought in Suits," *New York Times*, Dec. 30, 1969.
8. "The Scandal of Mineral King," editorial, *New York Times*, June 24, 1969; "Mineral King Folly," editorial, *New York Times*, Feb. 2, 1969.
9. Roger Rapoport, "Disney's War Against the Wilderness," *Ramparts* magazine (Nov. 1971): 26.
10. "Obstructionism at Mineral King," editorial, *Los Angeles Times*, Dec. 1, 1966.
11. Dave Smith, *Disney A to Z: The Official Encyclopedia*, 5th ed. (Los Angeles: Disney Editions, 2016), 779.
12. "Walt Disney Named Honorary Member," *Sierra Club Bulletin* (Apr. 1955): 3.
13. Rapoport, "Disney's War," 29 (quoting the Disney citation).
14. Walt Disney Productions, "Conservation: The Greatest Disney Story," undated, 1; MKPS (citing 37 "major awards and honors" for conservation).

15. Ryan C. Black et al. "Chief Justice Burger and the Bench: How Physically Changing the Shape of the Court's Bench Reduced Interruptions during Oral Argument." 43 J. S. Ct. Hist. 83 (2018).

Chapter 1

1. Pat Alder, *Mineral King Guide* (Glendale, CA: La Siesta Press, 1963), 5.
2. Russ Leadabrand, *A Guidebook to the Southern Sierra Nevada* (Los Angeles: W. Ritchie Press, 1968), 19.
3. Leadabrand, *Guidebook*, 29.
4. William R. Dudley, "Near the Kern's Grand Canyon," *Sierra Club Bulletin* (1903): 301, 302.
5. Mrs. Ray Buckman, "Back Country: Mineral King." *Kaweah Magazine (Aug. 1960)*: 3; Alder, *Mineral King Guide*, 7 (prison term).
6. Louise A. Jackson, *Mineral King: The Story of Beulah* (Three Rivers, CA: Sequoia Natural History Association, 2006), 10, 16; originally published as *Beulah: A Biography of the Mineral King Valley of California* (Three Rivers, CA: Westernlore Press, 1988).
7. "Mineral King," *Los Tulares*, Tulares County Historical Society (Sept. 1965): 1.
8. Buckman, "Back Country: Mineral King," 4.
9. "Mineral King." *Los Tulares*, 4.
10. *Id.*
11. Buckman, "Back Country: Mineral King, 4.
12. "Mineral King." *Los Tulares*, 2.
13. Douglas H. Strong, *From Pioneers to Preservationists: A Brief History of Sequoia and Kings Canyon National Parks* (Three Rivers, CA: Sequoia Natural History Association, 2000), 61.
14. Russ Leadabrand, "Let's Explore a Byway: Into Historic Mineral King," *Westways* magazine (Sept. 1963): 9.
15. John Muir, *The Yosemite* (New York: Century, 1912; reprint, Eugene, OR: Double-bit Press, 2020).
16. Jackson, *Mineral King*, 99.
17. The discussion of the development of Sequoia National Park is taken largely from the comprehensive history of the park by William C. Tweed and Lary M. Dilsaver, *Challenge of the Big Trees: The History of Sequoia and Kings Canyon National Parks*, rev. ed. (Staunton, VA: George F. Thompson, 2017), 75–76, 70. Technically, Congress created a smaller version of the park first, and then immediately expanded it.
18. *Id.* at 76–77.
19. *Id.* at 88, 102.
20. *Id.* at 116.

21. *Id.*
22. Walter Wells Jr., transcript, Statement of Walter Wells, *Hearings on Proposed Development of Mineral King Recreational Area*, Tulare County Public Library Records, March 13, 1953, 96 (describing the private land owned by his family in Silver City).
23. John Fry, *The Story of Modern Skiing* (Lebanon, NH: University Press of New England 2006), 33.
24. *Id.* at 46.
25. *Id.*
26. Emil R. Walter, "Lowell Thomas in Mineral King," *Sequoia Snow-Go*, Sequoia Ski-Club, Mar. 18, 1949.
27. "Snow Survey Party Ends Rugged Stay in Sierra," *Los Angeles Times*, May 5, 1948.
28. Forest Service, U.S. Dept. of Agriculture. *Mineral King-Sequoia National Forest—Winter Survey, 1947–1948*, July 1948, 12; Sierra Club Records.
29. Woodrow W. Todd, secretary-manager, letter to Mr. E. T. Scoyen, supervisor, Sequoia and Kings Canyon National Parks, Jan. 12, 1949; SNP Files.
30. "The Unbelievable 'Mineral King,'" *Western Ski Magazine* (Dec. 1946): 7–8.
31. Hugo Wolfe Frank, transcript, Statement of Hugo Wolfe Frank, *Hearings on Proposed Development of Mineral King Recreational Area*, Tulare County Public Library Records, March 13, 1953, 107 (quoting Friedl Phaifer [*sic*; Pfeifer]).
32. "Mineral King Is Undeveloped Gold Mine in Tulare County Backyard, Skier Says," *Visalia Times Delta*, May 14, 1947, 3.
33. Sierra Club Board of Directors, *Minutes*, Aug. 31, 1947, 9, at https://oac.cdlib.org/ark:/28722/bk000779m2v/?order=95&brand=oac4.
34. Lewis F. Clark, "Winter Sports in Mineral King," *Sierra Club Bulletin* (June 1949): 112, 115. The report also found that "[t]he terrain and snow conditions appear excellent for ski touring" (117).
35. Sierra Club Board of Directors, *Minutes*, Sept. 4, 1949, 6, at https://oac.cdlib.org/ark:/28722/bk000781v1h/?order=56&brand=oac4.
36. U.S. Forest Service. *Prospectus for a Proposed Resort and Ski Development at Mineral King, In Sequoia National Forest, California*, Nov. 1949; NARA II Forest Service Files.
37. U.S. Forest Service, California Region, press release, "Big Development Proposed for Mineral King Ski Area," Sept. 29, 1949, 1.
38. Arthur B. Ferguson Jr., and William P. Bryson, "Mineral King: A Case Study in Forest Service Decision Making," 2 Ecol. L.Q. 493, 1972, 503.
39. Earl Bachman, chief, Recreation Section, Division of Recreation and Lands, U.S. Forest Service, transcript, Statement of Earl Bachman, *Hearings on Proposed Development of Mineral King Recreational Area*, Tulare County Public Library Records, March 13, 1953, 31. See also Ferguson and Bryson, "Mineral King: A Case Study," 503.

40. Congressman Harlan Hagen, transcript, Statement of Harlan Hagen, *Hearings on Proposed Development of Mineral King Recreational Area*, Tulare County Public Library Records, March 13, 1953, 1; Harold Rainwater, transcript, Statement of Harold Rainwater, *Id.* at 3.
41. Hagen, *Id.* at 2.
42. "Throng Seen for Mineral King Skiing." *Los Angeles Times*, Mar. 15, 1953.
43. E. T. Scoyen, transcript, Statement of E. T. Scoyen, *Hearings on Proposed Development of Mineral King Recreational Area*, Tulare County Public Library Records, March 13, 1953, 198.
44. "Road, Avalanches Are Mineral King Problems," *Fresno Bee*, Feb. 3, 1953.
45. O. A. Tomlinson, regional director, memorandum to superintendent, Sequoia-Kings Canyon, Dec. 18, 1947.
46. Leslie H. Gould, transcript, Statement of Dr. Leslie H. Gould, *Hearings on Proposed Development of Mineral King Recreational Area*, Tulare County Public Library Records, March 13, 1953, 66–67.

Chapter 2

1. Stewart L. Udall, Foreword, *Wild by Law: The Sierra Club Legal Defense Fund and the Places It Has Saved* (San Francisco, CA: Sierra Club Legal Defense Fund, 1990), xi.
2. Neal Gabler, *Walt Disney: The Triumph of the American Imagination* (New York: Alfred A. Knopf, 2006), 276.
3. *Id.* at 514.
4. Bob Thomas, *Building a Company: Roy O. Disney and the Creation of an Entertainment Empire* (New York: Hyperion, 1998), 243 (noting "[t]he huge success of Disneyland").
5. Jeff Pepper, "New Heights: Mount Disney and Sugar Bowl," Walt Disney Museum, 2017, at http://www.waltdisney.org/blog/new-heights-mount-disney-and-sugar-bowl.
6. See Ethan Rarick, *Desperate Passage: The Donner Party's Perilous Journey West* (New York: Oxford University Press, 2008).
7. Brian E. Clark, "Sugar Bowl, Ski Slope with Ties to Walt Disney, Turns 75," *San Diego Union-Tribune*, Jan. 20, 2015.
8. Pepper, "New Heights: Mount Disney and Sugar Bowl."
9. *Id.*
10. "Third Man on the Mountain," Internet Movie Data Base at http://www.imdb.com/title/tt0053352/?ref_=fn_al_tt_1.
11. Alexandra K. Vicknair, "Mindsets, Motivations, Mickey Mouse, and the Mountains: The Social, Political, and Intellectual Foundations of the Mineral King Controversy" (2013), 67, at http://scholarworks.csustan.edu/handle/011235813/265.

12. "Walt Disney To Be Chief of Olympic Pageantry," *New York Times*, Nov. 5, 1958.
13. Robert Hicks, interview with the author, Monterey, CA, Oct. 14, 2014.
14. Harrison "Buzz" Price, *Walt's Revolution! By the Numbers* (Orlando, FL: Ripley Entertainment, 2003), 46.
15. Hicks, interview with the author.
16. John L. Harper, *Mineral King: Public Concern with Government Policy* (Arcata, CA: Pacifica Publishing, 1982), 75n4.
17. Meghan McCarthy McPhail, *A History of Cannon Mountain: Trails, Tales, and Skiing Legends* (Charleston, SC: History Press, 2011).
18. Roy Terell, "The Heroes of Squaw Valley," *Sports Illustrated* (Feb. 29, 1960).
19. Douglas Leisz, interview with the author, Placerville, CA, Mar. 9, 2017.
20. Robert B. Hicks, "Meeting with W. S. Davis, Assistant Regional Forester, in San Francisco—April 8, 1965." Memorandum to Royal Clark. Apr. 8, 1965, 2; RBH Papers.
21. "Slim" Davis, interview, "'Slim' Davis: The Forest Service View," *Western Ski Time* (Oct. 1968): 44; Arapahoe Basin, Colorado, at https://www.arapahoebasin.com/about/.
22. Price, *Walt's Revolution! By the Numbers*, 48.
23. Hicks, interview with the author.
24. Willy J. Schaeffler, *Report on Mineral King Project*, May 1960, 8; RBH Papers.
25. W. S. Davis, letter to Walter E. Disney, Feb. 26, 1965; NARA I Forest Service Files.
26. Harrison Price, "WDP Presentation on MK on Whether Studio Should Take Over Project," undated, 3; HP Papers.
27. Deposition of Robert Hicks. June 19, 1973, Sierra Club v. Hickel, No. 51,464 (N.D. Cal. 1969), 12.
28. Harper, *Mineral King: Public Concern with Government Policy*, 72.
29. Harry Gesner, interview with the author, Malibu, CA, Dec. 21, 2016.
30. Aljean Harmetz, "Janet Leigh, 77, Shower Taker of 'Psycho,' Is Dead," *New York Times*, Oct. 5, 2004.
31. Rosalind Wyman, telephone interview with the author, Los Angeles, CA, May 8, 2017.
32. Robert Hicks, Notes, "Bidding Considerations," draft, Aug. 2, 1965, 6; RBH Papers.
33. American Resort Consultants, Inc., *Development of Mineral King for Winter and Summer Recreation*, Jan. 3, 1965, 3, 4.
34. Hicks, Notes, "Bidding Considerations," 5.
35. Charles Wilkinson, "'The Greatest Good of the Greatest Number in the Long Run': TR, Pinchot, and the Origins of Sustainability in America," 26 Colo. Nat. Resources, Energy and Envtl. L. Rev. 69, 2015, 72.
36. W. S. Davis, assistant regional forester, "Plans—Mineral King Recreation Area," memorandum to forest supervisor, Sequoia National Forest, Dec. 8, 1964; NARA I Forest Service Files.

37. W. S. Davis, assistant regional forester, letter to Mr. Robert Brandt, president, International Productions, Inc., Jan. 22, 1965; NARA II Forest Service Files.
38. W. S. Davis, assistant regional forester, "Plans—Mineral King Recreation Area," memorandum to forest supervisor, Sequoia National Forest, Feb. 4, 1965; NARA I Forest Service Files.
39. W. S. Davis, assistant regional forester, letter to Edward A. Hummel, regional director, National Park Service, Feb. 5, 1965; NARA II Forest Service Files.
40. James B. Myers, acting regional director, National Park Service, "Proposal of a Winter Sport Area Involving Sequoia National Park," memorandum to director of National Park Service, Feb. 5, 1965; SNP Files.
41. W. S. Davis, notation on letter, Warren F. Hamilton, assistant regional director, to Mr. W. S. Davis, assistant regional forester, Feb. 18, 1965; NARA I Forest Service Files ("Mr. Hummel phoned and said they did not object to issuing of Mineral King prospectus. Letter will follow." Initialed "W D" with date 2–26–65.)
42. Edward A. Hummel, letter to W. S. Davis, assistant regional forester, Mar. 3, 1965; NARA II Forest Service Files.
43. Press release, National Forest News, California Region, Forest Service, Feb. 27, 1965; NARA II Forest Service Files.
44. Forest Service, U.S. Dept. of Agriculture, California Region, *Prospectus for a Proposed Recreational Development at Mineral King in the Sequoia National Forest*, Feb. 1965, 4, 8; NARA II Forest Service Files.
45. *Id.* at 5, 7.
46. *Id.* at 1, 5.
47. Sierra Club Board of Directors, *Minutes*, Nov. 12, 1949, at https://oac.cdlib.org/ark:/28722/bk000781v1h/?order=70&brand=oac4.
48. Edgar Wayburn, MD, *Your Land and Mine: Evolution of a Conservationist* (San Francisco: Sierra Club Books, 2004), 90.
49. Michael McCloskey, interview with the author, Portland, OR, June 5, 2017.
50. Harold K. Steen, *The U.S. Forest Service*, Centennial ed. (Durham, NC: Forest History Society, 2004), 282.
51. Sierra Club, *Articles of Association, By-Laws, and List of Members* (1892), 5, at https://books.google.com/books?id=f74UAAAAYAAJ&pg=PP8&source=gbs_toc_r&cad=2#v=onepage&q=accessible&f=false.
52. Michael P. Cohen, *The History of the Sierra Club: 1892–1970* (San Francisco: Sierra Club Books, 1988), 100, 190.
53. *Id.* at 80.
54. *Id.* at 339–40, 275; J. Michael McCloskey, *In the Thick of It: My Life in the Sierra Club* (Washington, DC: Island Press/Shearwater Books, 2005), xiii.
55. Wayburn, *Your Land and Mine*, 24 ("The double sponsorship requirement created an elite cadre").

56. Robert Wyss, *The Man Who Built the Sierra Club: A Life of David Brower* (New York: Columbia University Press, 2016), 39, 48.
57. *Id.* 180 (discussing the budgetary disputes).
58. Joseph Fontaine, interview with the author, Tehachapi, CA, Mar. 3, 2017.
59. Harper, *Mineral King: Public Concern with Government Policy*, 61.
60. *Id.* (reproducing memorandum to Advanced Planning Sub-Committee from John Harper, Sept. 4, 1962).
61. *Id.* at 64.
62. Conservation Committee, Kern-Kaweah Chapter, Sierra Club, *The Mineral King Basin: A Preliminary Report on the Character and Uses of This Portion of the Sierra Nevada, Tulare County, California*, 1964; Sierra Club Members Papers.
63. *Id.* at 2.
64. John M. Davis, superintendent, letter to John L. Harper, conservation chairman, Jan. 20, 1964; GM Papers.
65. Conservation Committee, Kern-Kaweah Chapter, Sierra Club. *The Mineral King Basin: A Preliminary Report on the Character and Uses of this Portion of the Sierra Nevada, Tulare County, California*, 1964, 12–13; Sierra Club Members Papers.
66. *Id.* at 13.
67. Harper, *Mineral King: Public Concern with Government Policy*, 71.
68. *Id.* at 76.
69. William E. Siri, president, "Mineral King Basin—Kern-Kaweah Report," letter to John L. Harper, Nov. 16, 1964; GM Papers.
70. George Marshall, "'The Mineral King Basin' Report," letter to John L. Harper, Dec. 3, 1964, 1–2; GM Papers, carton 48.
71. John Harper, letter to L. M. Whitfield, forest supervisor, Jan. 12, 1965, 2; NARA I Forest Services Files.
72. Joe Fontaine, interview by Ann Root, *Sierra Club Oral History Project* (1995), 21, at http://digitalassets.lib.berkeley.edu/roho/ucb/text/sierra_club_volunteer_leaders.pdf.
73. Sierra Club Board of Directors, *Minutes*, May 1–2, 1965, 12, at http://www.oac.cdlib.org/ark:/28722/bk0007b0j7k/?order=52&brand=calisphere.
74. Harper, *Mineral King: Public Concern with Government Policy*, 82.
75. Cohen, *History of the Sierra Club*, 342.
76. Will Siri, interview by Ann Lage, 1979, Sierra Club Oral History Project, 80, at https://archive.org/details/reflectsierracluboosiririch/page/80; McCloskey, interview with the author.
77. Bettina Boxall, "Martin Litton Dies at 97; Passionate Wilderness Conservationist," *Los Angeles Times*, Dec. 1, 2014.
78. Sierra Club Board of Directors, *Minutes*, May 1–2, 1965, 13, at http://www.oac.cdlib.org/ark:/28722/bk0007b0j7k/?order=52&brand=calisphere.

79. Siri, interview by Lage, 80–81, at https://archive.org/details/reflectsierraclub oosiririch/page/80.
80. Sierra Club Board of Directors, *Minutes*, May 1–2, 1965, 11, 13 (summarizing the "major points" on both sides), at http://www.oac.cdlib.org/ark:/28722/bk0007b0j7k/?order=52&brand=calisphere.
81. Cohen, *History of the Sierra Club*, 343.
82. Wallace Stegner, interview by Ann Lage, 1982, Sierra Club Oral History Project, 28, at http://digitalassets.lib.berkeley.edu/roho/ucb/text/stegner_wallace.pdf.
83. Mary Ann Burtt, telephone interview with the author, Los Angeles, CA, Feb. 15, 2019.
84. Siri, interview by Lage, 87, at https://archive.org/details/reflectsierraclub oosiririch/page/86.
85. David Brower, introduction, interview with Martin S. Litton, Sierra Club Leaders I, 1950s–1970s, 1982, iii, at http://digitalassets.lib.berkeley.edu/rohoia/ucb/text/sierraclubleaders01lagerich.pdf.
86. Sierra Club Board of Directors, *Minutes*, May 1–2, 1965, 14, at http://www.oac.cdlib.org/ark:/28722/bk0007b0j7k/?order=52&brand=calisphere.
87. https://vault.sierraclub.org/history/downloads/directors.pdf.
88. Edgar Wayburn, interview by Ann Lage and Susan Schrepfer, Sierra Club History Series, 1976–81, 43, at http://digitalassets.lib.berkeley.edu/roho/ucb/text/wayburn_edgar.pdf.
89. Sierra Club Board of Directors, *Minutes*, June 12, 1965, at https://oac.cdlib.org/ark:/28722/bk0007b0j7k/?order=71&brand=oac4.
90. Harper, *Mineral King: Public Concern with Government Policy*, 84.
91. McCloskey, interview with the author, Portland, OR, June 5, 2017.
92. John L. Harper, letter to the directors, Sierra Club, May 12, 1965, 1; Sierra Club Members Papers, carton 190.
93. John L. Harper, letter to Dr. William Siri, president, July 18, 1965, 1; Sierra Club Members Papers, carton 107.
94. William E. Siri, president, letter to John L. Harper, July 27, 1965, 1–2; Sierra Club Members Papers.
95. David Brower, letter to John L. Harper, May 20, 1965; Sierra Club Members Papers.
96. Ansel Adams, letter to John L. Harper, May 20, 1965; Sierra Club Members Papers.
97. John L. Harper, letter to Michael McCloskey, July 28, 1965, 1; Sierra Club Members Papers. See also Joe Fontaine, interview by Ann Root, 1995, *Sierra Club Oral History Project*, 21 at http://digitalassets.lib.berkeley.edu/roho/ucb/text/sierra_club_volunteer_leaders.pdf.

98. Michael J. McCloskey, memo to Will Siri, June 9, 1965, 1; Sierra Club Members Papers.
99. Robert Marshall, "Mineral King," memorandum to directors of the Sierra Club, Sept. 2, 1965, 1–2; GM Papers.
100. Frederick Eissler, *Report on Mineral King*, July 24, 1965, 1; Sierra Club Members Papers.
101. Sierra Club Board of Directors, *Meeting Minutes*, Sept. 11–12, 1965 at https://oac.cdlib.org/ark:/28722/bk0007b0j7k/?order=86&brand=oac4.
102. *Id.*
103. Sierra Club, press release, Sept. 14, 1964; Sierra Club Members Papers, carton 107.

Chapter 3

1. Omer Crane, "Fabled Mineral King Has Many Wouldbe [*sic*] Developers," *Fresno Bee*, Mar. 5, 1965.
2. Robert Brandt, "Re: Mineral King," letter to Eugene Wyman, Apr. 19, 1965; NARA II Forest Service Files.
3. Eugene L. Wyman, letter to the Honorable Orville Freeman, secretary of agriculture, June 30, 1965; NARA II Secretary of Agriculture Files. Brandt also wrote Freeman, reminding him of their earlier meeting; see Robert Brandt, letter to Orville Freeman, secretary of agriculture, June 28, 1965; NARA I Secretary of Agriculture Files.
4. Orville Freeman, secretary, letter to Robert Brandt, July 19, 1965; NARA II Forest Service Files; Orville L. Freeman, secretary, letter to Mr. Eugene L. Wyman, July 12, 1965; NARA II Forest Service Files.
5. Harry Gesner, interview with the author, Malibu, CA, Dec. 21, 2016.
6. Patrick Sisson, "Harry Gesner: An Architect, Maverick, and Modern Adventurer Riding the Waves," *Curbed*, https://www.curbed.com/2016/2/12/11029318/harry-gesner-architect-wave-house-sandcastle-house.
7. Gesner, interview with the author.
8. Gesner, interview with the author; Harry Gesner, "The Hall of the Mountain King," personal paper of Harry Gesner.
9. Jeanne Ora Nienaber, "Mineral King: Ideological Battleground for Land Use Disputes" (PhD diss., University of California, Berkeley, 1973), 41.
10. Robert Hicks, "Mineral King Bids," memorandum to Royal Clark, Mar. 1, 1965; HP Papers.
11. W. S. Davis, assistant regional forester, letter to Walter E. Disney, Feb. 26, 1965; NARA II Forest Service Files.
12. Robert Hicks, letter to Margaret A. Seaborn, Mar. 19, 1965; RBH Papers.

13. Mel Lieurance, recreation staff assistant, "Plans—Mineral King Recreation Area," memorandum to file, Apr. 1, 1965, 1–2; NARA II Forest Service Files; R. B. Hicks, "Meeting—Lawrence Whitfield and Mel Lieurance at U.S. Forest Service Office in Porterville—April 1, 1965," memorandum to Royal Clark, Apr. 1, 1965; HP Papers. Bob Hicks, "Bidding Considerations," memo to file (draft), Feb. 8, 1965, 8; RBH Papers.
14. H. A. Price and R. B. Hicks, "Preparation for the Application for Permit at Mineral King," memorandum to Royal Clark (draft), Apr. 7,1965, 1, 3; HP Papers.
15. Robert B. Hicks, memorandum to Royal Clark, Apr. 8, 1965, 1, 3; RBH Papers.
16. Robert B. Hicks, letter to Willy Schaeffler, ski coach, University of Denver, Apr. 14, 1965; HP Papers.
17. Pierluigi Serraino, "On the Work of Ladd and Kelsey, Architects," *Architecture for Sale Quarterly* (Spring 2015) at http://cargocollective.com/architectureforsale/The-Work-of-Ladd-Kelsey.
18. Robert B. Hicks, "Types and Estimated Size of Physical Facilities at Mineral King," memorandum to Thornton Ladd (Ladd and Kelsey), May 27, 1965, 3; HP Papers. See also Robert B. Hicks, letter to Thornton Ladd, Ladd and Kelsey, Architects, May 27,1965 (giving further instructions); HP Papers.
19. John M. Davis, superintendent, letter to Lawrence M. Whitfield, forest supervisor, Apr. 9, 1965; NARA I Files.
20. J. Michael McCloskey, *In the Thick of It: My Life in the Sierra Club* (Washington, DC: Island Press/Shearwater Books, 2005), 23–25.
21. *Id.* at 22.
22. Michael McCloskey, interview with the author, Portland, OR, June 5, 2017.
23. William E. Siri, president, letter to Mr. Charles Connaughton, regional forester, June 7, 1965, 1–2; NARA I Forest Service Files.
24. Sierra Club, press release, "Sierra Club Urges Hearing on Mineral King Area," June 10, 1965; Sierra Club Members Papers.
25. Chas. A. Connaughton, regional forester, letter to Dr. William E. Siri, July 1, 1965; Sierra Club Members Papers.
26. Rupert Cutler, "Sierra Club v. Hickel: Mineral King Valley" (PhD diss., part 1, Michigan State University, 1972), 247; Philip Burton Papers.
27. Michael McCloskey, assistant to the president for the president, letter to Mr. Edward Cliff, chief, Forest Service, Aug. 7, 1965, 3 (emphasis in original), 4; GM Papers.
28. *Id.* at 1.
29. Federal Highway Administration, "History of Scenic Road Programs," *Highway History*, at https://www.fhwa.dot.gov/infrastructure/scenichistory.cfm, 6. The Department of Commerce then housed the Bureau of Public Roads.

30. The President's Council on Recreation and Natural Beauty, *A Proposed Program for Scenic Roads and Highways*, 1966, Library of Congress Catalog Card Number 66–61527, iv–v.
31. Robert Brandt, "Re: Mineral King," letter to Eugene Wyman, Apr. 19, 1965, 2; NARA II Forest Service Files.
32. D. J. Steele, Division Engineer, Bureau of Public Roads, U.S. Department of Commerce, letter to William R. Bergren, June 15, 1965; GM Papers.
33. Bob Hicks, "Meeting with J. A. Legarra, Deputy State Highway Engineer, Sacramento—April 9, 1965," memorandum to Royal Clark, 2; HP Papers.
34. Harrison A. Price, letter to Honorable Hugh M. Burns, Oct. 30, 1963; HP Papers.
35. Hugh M. Burns, letter to Harrison A. Price, Apr. 28, 1964; HP Papers.
36. Hugh [unidentified last name], memo to Mike [McCloskey], July 16, 1965; RJ Papers. The memo stated that George Marshall, a Sierra Club board member, had heard that a bill on the governor's desk "would change the access road from a county road to a state highway, presumably so that it could be built to higher standards."
37. Michael McCloskey, assistant to the president, letter to Governor Edmund Brown, July 19, 1965; GM Papers.
38. John L. Harper, letter to Dr. William Siri, president, Aug. 18, 1965, 1; RJ Papers.
39. Walt Disney Productions, press release, "Disney to Submit Plans for Recreational Development of Mineral King," Aug. 18, 1965; RBH Papers.
40. W. S. Davis, assistant regional forester, "Plans—Mineral King," memorandum to Richard J. Costley, acting director, Recreation and Land, Aug. 24, 1965, 1; NARA II Forest Service Files.
41. "Sierra Nevada Resort Is Planned by Disney," *New York Times*, Aug. 23, 1965.
42. "Disney Plans Development in Sequoia National Park," *Los Angeles Times*, Aug. 20, 1965.
43. "Disney's Mineral King Proposal Challenged," *Los Angeles Times*, Aug. 31, 1965. This article erroneously placed the proposed ski resort in Sequoia National Park.
44. Dan Winston, "Mineral King Response Termed Greatest Ever"; SNP Files. The newspaper cannot be identified.
45. "Ski Resort of the Future," *Ski* magazine (Jan. 1966): 50 (quoting "one observer").
46. Walt Disney Productions, "Mineral King Project: Timetable for Events in Porterville, California, August 31, 1965"; HP Papers.
47. R. W. Feuchter, Forest Service, "Special Use Plans—Mineral King," memorandum to files, July 26, 1965; NARA I Forest Service Files.
48. Hicks later wrote to the Disney executives recounting a conversation with Congressman Harlan Hagen: "I told him that we had been advised not to do so [bring a trailer] but that Brandt had gone ahead and the Forest Service had said o.k. to him after he had prepared the display." Robert B. Hicks, memorandum

to H. A. Price et al., "Washington D.C. telephone conversation with Congressman Harlan Hagen from Tulare and Kings County," Sept. 23, 1965, 2; HP Papers.

49. "Ski Resort of the Future," 50.
50. "Disney and Others Talk Millions for Resort in an Isolated Valley of the Sierra Nevada," *Business Week* (Sept. 4, 1965): 40.
51. Superintendent, Sequoia and Kings Canyon, memorandum to regional director, Western Region, "Proposed Mineral King Development, Sequoia National Forest," Sept. 3, 1969; SNP Files.
52. Ron Taylor, "Mineral King Bids Overwhelm Officials," *Fresno Bee*, Sept. 1, 1965.
53. "Disney and Others Talk Millions," 40.
54. Omer Crane, "Disney's $35 Million Bid Earns Him Favorite's Role," *Fresno Bee*, Sept. 5, 1965.
55. Sequoia National Forest, Forest Service, "Mineral King Proponents," Aug. 31, 1965; NARA I Forest Service Files (listing the six applicants).
56. Dennis McLellan, "Ragnar Qvale, 86; Actor, Led Architectural Firm," *Los Angeles Times*, Oct. 2, 2001.
57. Douglas Martin, "Kjell Qvale Dies at 94; Married U.S. to Sports Cars," *New York Times*, Nov. 12, 2013.
58. Taylor, "Mineral King Bids Overwhelm Officials."
59. Crane, "Disney's $35 Million Bid Earns Him Favorite's Role."
60. Jeanne Ora Nienaber, "Mineral King: Ideological Battleground for Land Use Disputes" (PhD diss., University of California, Berkeley, 1973), 163.
61. John L. Harper, *Mineral King: Public Concern with Government Policy* (Arcata, CA: Pacifica Publishing, 1982), 87.
62. Walt Disney Productions, *A Proposal for the Development of Mineral King*, 1965; RBH Papers. Mineral King Recreational Development Co., *Proposal, Sequoia National Forest*, 1965 (copy in possession of the author).
63. Walt Disney Productions, *A Proposal for the Development of Mineral King*, 14.
64. *Id.*
65. *Id.* at 8 (emphasis in original).
66. Walt Disney Productions, press release, "Walt Disney Submits Application for Mineral King Recreation Development," Aug. 31, 1965; RBH Papers.
67. Mineral King Recreational Development Co., *Proposal, Sequoia National Forest*, 7, 5–6, 34–35, 57, 84.
68. *Id.*, Preface, Planning: Corporate and Finance.
69. *Id.* at 1–2, 18.
70. Walt Disney Productions, *A Proposal for the Development of Mineral King*, 11 ("Snow Safety"—"a carefully researched snow safety plan has to be carried out to control, avoid, and prevent major avalanches, snow slides, and snow creepage"); RBH Papers.
71. Forest Service, U.S. Dept. of Agriculture, California Region, *Prospectus for a*

Proposed Recreational Development at Mineral King in the Sequoia National Forest, Feb. 1965, 5; NARA II Forest Service Files.

72. W. S. Davis, assistant regional forester, "Plans—Mineral King Area," memorandum to Richard J. Costly, director, R&LU, WO. Sept. 3, 1965; NARA II.
73. Robert B. Hicks, "Trip to San Joaquin Valley September 8, 1965," memorandum to Walt Disney Productions, Sept. 15, 1965; HP Papers.
74. Richard J. Costley, director, Division of Recreation, letter to Michael McCloskey, Sept. 3, 1965; RJ Papers.
75. Cutler, "Sierra Club v. Hickel," 262.
76. Joe Fontaine, interview by Ann Root, 1995, *Sierra Club Oral History Project*, 21, at http://digitalassets.lib.berkeley.edu/roho/ucb/text/sierra_club_volunteer_leaders.pdf.
77. William R. Bergren, letter to George Marshall, Sept. 10, 1965; GM Papers.
78. Glen O. Robinson, *The Forest Service: A Study in Public Land Management.* (Baltimore: The Johns Hopkins University Press, 1975), 28; Nienaber, "Mineral King: Ideological Battleground," 40 ("the Forest Service is a 'decentralized' organization").
79. See David Stout, "Orville Freeman, 84, Dies; 60's Secretary of Agriculture," *New York Times*, Feb. 22, 2003; Minnesota Historical Society, Orville L. Freeman biography, http://collections.mnhs.org/governors/index.php/10004223.
80. A. W. Greeley, memorandum to Thomas R. Hughes, executive assistant to the secretary, "Mineral King"; NARA II. Tom Hughes, "Mineral King," memorandum to Art Greeley, Forest Service, Sept. 13, 1965; NARA II ("Before any final decision is made on this [Mineral King], get in touch with me").
81. Dr. Nienaber's nearly contemporaneous study describes the reaction of Forest Service personnel as mixed, with some saying that removing the final decision to Washington was logical since someone, probably the Sierra Club, would have appealed the decision to Washington in any event; "Mineral King: Ideological Battleground," 75. The regional forester, Charles A. Connaughton, later recalled that he had urged Freeman to make the decision; Charles A. Connaughton, interview by Elwood R. Maunder, 1976, "Forty-Three Years in the Field with the U.S. Forest Service," Forest History Society, Santa Cruz, California, 112, at https://foresthistory.org/wp-content/uploads/2016/12/Connaughton_Charles_A.pdf. The later actions by California personnel, however, indicate concern about retaining control over which applicant the secretary would ultimately choose.
82. A. W. Greeley, deputy chief, "Bids on Proposed Development at Mineral King," memorandum to Lester P. Gordon, inspector general, Sept. 22, 1965; NARA II Forest Service Files.
83. B. H. P., memorandum to Art [Greeley], Sept. 10, 1965; NARA II Forest Service Files.

84. Mary Carter Paint Co., letter to Mineral King Development Co., Sept. 15, 1965 (copy in possession of the author).
85. Notes from telephone call, "Information on Mineral King for Slim Davis," Sept. 30, 1965; NARA II Forest Service Files.
86. W. S. Davis, "Plans—Mineral King," memorandum to files, Sept. 15, 1965; NARA II Forest Service Files.
87. *Id.*
88. Jeremiah Stettler, "Renowned Avalanche Researcher Dies," *Salt Lake Tribune*, Feb. 4, 2007.
89. Phillip B. Lundstrom, "2310, September 9, 1965, Your Invitation to Meet," letter to U.S. Department of Agriculture, Forest Service, Attention Mr. W. S. Davis, Sept. 21, 1965; NARA II Forest Service Files.
90. W. S. Davis, letter to Phillip B. Lundstrom, director, Sept. 24, 1965; NARA II Forest Service Files.
91. Edward P. Cliff, chief, "Mineral King Development Proposal," memorandum to Secretary Orville L. Freeman, Sept. 30, 1965, 1; NARA II Forest Service Files.
92. *Id.* at 3.
93. Robert Hicks, "Bidding Considerations" (draft), Aug. 2, 1965; RBH Papers.
94. See Michael Barrier, "Walt's Goldwater Button: The Last Word, Maybe," at http://www.michaelbarrier.com/Essays/Walts_Goldwater_Button/WaltsGoldwaterButton.htm.
95. Hicks, "Bidding Considerations" (draft), 5.
96. Robert B. Hicks, letter to the Honorable Hugh Burns, California State Senate, Sept. 21, 1965; HP Papers.
97. Hicks, "Trip to San Joaquin Valley September 8, 1965."
98. Herbert Gold, "Nobody's Mad at Murphy," *New York Times Magazine* (Dec. 13, 1964).
99. Duke Norberg, "Senator Murphy," memorandum to Audrey Warren, Oct. 15, 1965; NARA II Forest Service Files.
100. "Brandt Rumored Top Contender," *Visalia Times-Delta*, Oct. 25, 1965.
101. "Brandt Rumored Top Contender"; Ron Taylor, "Brandt Shows Public His Mineral King Plans," *Fresno Bee*, Oct. 23, 1965.
102. Rosalind Wyman, telephone interview with the author, Los Angeles, CA, May 8, 2017.
103. Michelangelo Capua, *Janet Leigh* (Jefferson, NC: McFarland, 2013), 122.
104. Robert B. Hicks, letter to H. D. Thoreau, Hale Brothers and Associates, Sept. 21, 1965; HP Papers.
105. Ron Taylor, "More Delay Is Seen on Mineral King," *Fresno Bee*, Oct. 21, 1965.
106. Robert B. Hicks, "Mineral King," memorandum to "All Concerned," Oct. 15, 1965; RBH Papers.

107. Robert B. Hicks, "Willy Schaeffler's Telephone Calls," memorandum to "All Concerned," Oct. 18, 1965; RBH Papers.

108. Irvine H. Sprague, deputy director, letter to Thomas R. Hughes, executive assistant to the secretary, Oct. 22, 1965; Harlan Hagen Papers. Tom Hughes, memorandum to the secretary, Dec. 7, 1965 ("I have been in frequent contact with Governor Brown's man in Washington re Mineral King"); Thomas R. Hughes Papers. Associated Press, "Two Mineral King Bids Picked for Panel Review," *Los Angeles Times*, Oct. 28, 1965.

109. Tom Hughes, memorandum to the secretary, Oct. 25, 1965; Thomas R. Hughes Papers.

110. U.S. Dept. of Agriculture, press release, "Secretary's Committee to Review Recreation Proposals," Oct. 27, 1965; SCLDF Files. Associated Press, "Two Mineral King Bids Picked for Panel Review."

111. U.S. Dept. of Agriculture. telegrams to Chris Kuaisa, Mineral King Development Corporation, Ragnar C. Qvale and Associates, and D. Bollenbacker, Oct. 27, 1965; NARA II Forest Service Files. A sixth proposal had been rejected earlier for failing to meet the requirements of the prospectus.

112. Bob Hicks, "Mineral King," memorandum to Walt Disney et al., Oct. 28, 1965; HP Papers.

113. Robert B. Hicks, "Preparation for Washington Presentation on Mineral King," memorandum to "All Concerned," Oct. 29, 1965; RBH Papers.

114. U.S. Forest Service, "Opening Statement at Conference with Mineral King Proponents"; NARA II Forest Service Files.

115. [Unidentified author], U.S. Forest Service, notes on conference with Disney. Nov. 5, 1965; NARA II Forest Service Files.

116. Robert Hicks, interview with the author, Carmel Valley, CA, Oct. 16, 2014.

117. Associated Press, "Brandt Tells Mineral King Plans to U.S.," *Los Angeles Times*, Nov. 9, 1965.

118. Robert B. Hicks, notes, "Subject: Telephone Conversation with Slim Davis on Nov. 10, 1965"; RBH Papers.

119. *Id.* at 2.

120. W. S. Davis, assistant regional forester, "Plans—Sequoia (Mineral King Development Proposals)," memorandum to Arthur W. Greeley, deputy chief, Nov. 10, 1965; NARA II Forest Service Files. W. S. Davis, assistant regional forester, "Plans," memorandum to Arthur Greeley, deputy chief, Nov. 15, 1965; NARA II Forest Service Files.

121. Tom Hughes, memorandum to the secretary, Nov. 15, 1965; Thomas R. Hughes Papers.

122. Hicks, interview with the author.

123. Harrison A. Price and R. B. Hicks, "Preliminary Results on Investigations of Robert Brandt," memorandum to Walt Disney, Nov. 30, 1965; HP Papers.

124. Julian R. Blodgett and Associates, "Re: Robert 'Bob' Brandt [and] Mary Carter Paint Company, Inc." Nov. 30, 1965, 2; HP Papers.
125. A. W. Greeley, memorandum to Mr. Baker, Mr. Hughes, and Mr. Cliff, Dec. 1, 1965; NARA II Forest Service Files.
126. A. W. Greeley, deputy chief, "Analysis of Proposals to Develop Mineral King," memorandum to secretary's Review Committee on the Development of Mineral King, Sequoia National Forest, Dec. 1, 1965, 2, 4; NARA II Forest Service Files.
127. Roy O. Disney, president, letter to the Honorable Orville Freeman, Dec. 6, 1965; NARA II Forest Service Files.
128. Orville Freeman, secretary of agriculture, "Weekly Report," report to the president, Dec. 9, 1965, 2; Lyndon B. Johnson Presidential Library.
129. *Id.* at 3.
130. *Id.*
131. Robert Brandt, telegram to Harlan Hagen, Dec. 11, 1965; Harlan Hagen Papers.
132. Robert Brandt, telegram to the president, Dec. 15, 1965; Lyndon B. Johnson Presidential Library.
133. Thomas R. Hughes, executive assistant to the secretary, memorandum to Paul M. Popple, assistant to the president, Dec. 16, 1965; Thomas R. Hughes Papers.
134. Review Committee on the Development of Mineral King, Sequoia National Forest, "Analysis of Proposals to Develop Mineral King," memorandum to Orville L. Freeman, secretary, Dec. 15, 1965; NARA II Forest Service Files.
135. Tom Hughes, memorandum to the secretary, Dec. 15, 1965; Thomas R. Hughes Papers.
136. Orville L. Freeman, secretary, letter to Mr. Robert Brandt, president, Dec. 16, 1965; NARA II Files.
137. W. S. Davis, memo to file, July 8, 1960, quoted in M. Rupert Cutler, "A Study of Litigation Related to Management of Forest Service Administered Lands and Its Effects on Policy Decisions. Part Two: 'A Comparison of Four Cases'" (Ph.D. diss., Michigan State University, 1972), 166, at https://d.lib.msu.edu/etd/20976/datastream/FULL_TEXT/view/.
138. Harlan Hagen, letter to Robert Brandt, Dec. 14, 1965; Harlan Hagen Papers.
139. Edward P. Cliff, chief, by A. W. Greeley, "Mineral King. Development," memorandum to Thomas R. Hughes, Oct. 25, 1965, 2; NARA II Forest Service Files.
140. Walt Disney, letter to Orville Freeman; NARA I Secretary of Agriculture Files.

Chapter 4

1. Forest Service, U.S. Dept. of Agriculture, California Region, *Prospectus for a Proposed Recreational Development at Mineral King in the Sequoia National Forest*, Feb. 1965, 1, 3, 5; NARA II Forest Service Files.

2. Robert B. Hicks, "Trip to San Joaquin Valley September 8, 1965," memorandum to Walt Disney Productions, Sept. 15, 1965; HP Papers.
3. "U.S. Chooses Disney to Develop Sequoia Resort," *Los Angeles Times*, Dec. 18, 1965.
4. John McDonald, "Now the Bankers Come to Disney," *Fortune* (May 1966).
5. Robert Hicks, interview with the author, Carmel Valley, CA, Oct. 16, 2014.
6. "Mineral King Development Aide Is Named," *Fresno Bee*, Apr. 9, 1966.
7. U.S. Forest Service, Special Use Permit, para. 17, Jan. 10, 1966; Department of Justice Files.
8. Herbert Gold, "Nobody's Mad at Murphy," *New York Times*, Dec. 13, 1964.
9. Bob Hicks, "Summary of Meeting of Mineral King Committee, December 23, 1965," memorandum to Mineral King Committee, Dec. 24, 1965; HP Papers.
10. "Disney to Start Work on Sierra Ski Resort," *Los Angeles Times*, June 3, 1966.
11. Robert Hicks, "Discussion of Strategy for Road Commitment," memorandum (draft), Jan. 4, 1965; RBH Papers.
12. United Press International, "State Acts on Road Tie-in to Mineral King," Apr. 25, 1966.
13. "Outlook Seen Brighter for Mineral King Road," *Los Angeles Times*, Mar. 6, 1966.
14. California Highway Commission, agenda for meeting of April 20, 21, 22, 1966; box 31 bin 1742, California State Archives (showing 6:30 p.m. "Dinner: Host—Walt Disney Productions, Posey's—11th and O Streets, Sacramento").
15. "State Orders Mineral King Highway Plan," *Fresno Bee*, Apr. 22, 1966.
16. Harlan Hagen, letter to Walt Disney, Feb. 15, 1966; Harlan Hagan Papers. Walt Disney, letter to Congressman Hagen, Feb. 25, 1966; Harlan Hagen Papers.
17. Stanley A. Cain, "Mineral King Development Proposal, Sequoia and Kings Canyon," memorandum, May 3, 1966; GBH Papers.
18. Howard G. Baker, assistant director, Operations, "Mineral King Development Proposal, Sequoia and Kings Canyon," memorandum to regional director, Western Region, May 6, 1966; SNP Files ("Dr. Cain was not aware that there was an existing county road crossing the park").
19. Frank F. Kowski, superintendent, Sequoia and Kings Canyon, "Mineral King road project," memorandum to regional director, Western Region, May 17, 1966; SNP Files.
20. Frank F. Kowski, superintendent, Sequoia and Kings Canyons, "Mineral King road," memorandum to regional director, Western Region, July 22, 1966, 3; SNP Files.
21. Stanley A. Cain, assistant secretary for Fish and Wildlife and Parks, "Sequoia-Kings Canyon National Park," memorandum to Deputy Assistant Secretary [Clarence] Pautzke, Sept. 2, 1966, 1–2 (emphasis omitted); NARA II Park Service Files.

22. J. C. Womack, state highway engineer, letter to E. A. Hummel, regional director, National Park Service, Sept. 21, 1966, 3–4; SNP Files.
23. Edward A. Hummel, regional director, letter to J. C. Womack, state highway engineer, Oct. 18, 1966; SNP Files.
24. "Disney Seeking Public Backing on Resort Road," *Los Angeles Times*, Jan. 30, 1966.
25. Dan Winston, "Disney Says Operation Possible During 1971," *Visalia Times-Delta*, June 2, 1966.
26. Walt Disney Productions, *Walt Disney's Plans for Mineral King*, 1966; RBH Papers. Versions came in different colors, with some very slight differences in presentation.
27. *Id.* at 2.
28. *Id.*
29. Office of the Governor, "Mineral King Project, On-Site Review and Visit by Governor Brown," Sept. 19, 1966; Edmund G. Brown Papers.
30. Bob Jackson, "Walt Disney Biography," memorandum to Marty Sklar, Aug. 15, 1968, 4; RBH Papers.
31. Office of the Governor, "Mineral King Project, On-Site Review and Visit by Governor Brown," Sept. 19, 1966, 2; Edmund G. Brown Papers.
32. Office of Governor Edmund G. Brown, press release, Sept. 17, 1966, 2; RBH Papers.
33. Ron Taylor, "Brown Will Ask $25 Million For Road to Mineral King," *Fresno Bee*, Sept. 19, 1966.
34. Mike McCloskey, conservation director, letter to Ruth Shepherd, Jan. 26, 1966; Sierra Club Records Papers.
35. Lambert S. O'Malley, assistant administrator for Public Works, letter to Michael McCloskey, conservation director, May 2, 1966; Sierra Club Members Papers.
36. Michael McCloskey, conservation director, letter to the Economic Development Administration, U.S. Department of Commerce, Nov. 29, 1966; Sierra Club Members Papers. Lambert S. O'Malley, assistant administrator for Public Works, letter to Michael McCloskey, conservation director, Dec. 8, 1966; John L. Harper Papers.
37. Michael McCloskey, conservation director, letter to John Harper, chairman, Aug. 15, 1966; GM Papers.
38. Mike McCloskey, memo to members of the Mineral King Task Force, Mar. 3, 1966; GM Papers, carton 48 (noting in a "P.S." that "[t]he task force consists of two dozen people").
39. R. M. Jali, letter to board of directors, Sierra Club, Feb. 11, 1966; Sierra Club Members Papers.
40. John L. Harper, letter to "Dear Friends," Oct. 18, 1965, 2; SNP Files.

41. Joseph B. Fontaine, conservation chairman, Kern-Kaweah Chapter, Sierra Club, letter to the editor, "Sierra Club Stand," *Bakersfield Californian*, Dec. 10, 1966.
42. National Park Service, U.S. Dept of Interior, press release, "Hearings Scheduled for Wilderness Proposal for Parks"; GM Papers.
43. Chas. A. Connaughton, regional forester, "Wilderness and Primitive Areas (Sequoia and Kings Canyon National Parks)—Sequoia N.F.," memorandum to chief, Nov. 29, 1966; NARA II Forest Service.
44. Stewart M. Brandborg, executive director, "A Special Memorandum to Members and Cooperators: Sequoia and Kings Canyon National Parks Wilderness Hearings at Fresno, California, November 21 and 22, 1966," Nov. 11, 1966, 2; Sierra Club Records, San Diego State University.
45. Sierra Club Conservation Dept., "Hearings on Proposals to Protect the Wilderness of Sequoia and Kings Canyon National Parks on November 21–22, 1966," Nov. 11, 1966, 2–3; Sierra Club Records.
46. National Parks Association, "A Preliminary Wilderness Plan for Sequoia-Kings Canyon National Parks and the Surrounding Region," Nov. 21–22, 1966, 3, 9; GM Papers.
47. Sierra Club, "Statement of the Sierra Club on Proposals for Wilderness Areas within Sequoia and Kings Canyon National Parks," Nov. 21, 1966, 9; Sierra Club Records.
48. Wilderness Society, "Statement by the Wilderness Society in Support of the Establishment of Wilderness Areas within Sequoia and Kings Canyon National Park Presented by George Marshall at Public Hearings in Fresno, California," Nov. 21–22, 1966, 7; GM Papers.
49. Robert B. Hicks, letter to Frank F. Kowski, superintendent, Dec. 10, 1966, 2; Sequoia National Park Papers.
50. W. S. Davis, chief, Division of Recreation, memorandum to files, Nov. 21, 1966; SNP Files.
51. Donn B. Tatum, vice-president and administrative assistant to the president, Walt Disney Productions, statement before Hearing Commissioner John Preston, National Park Service, Fresno, California, Nov. 21, 1966; Phillip Burton Papers.
52. *Id.* at 2. Tatum stated that no opposition had been registered until after the secretary of agriculture chose Disney in December 1965. The Sierra Club's change in position came about six months earlier. But Tatum's statement was technically correct that the Sierra Club had never specifically advised Disney of the opposition.
53. *Id.* at 3, 4–5.
54. *Id.* at 6–7.
55. *Id.* at 7. See also, supplementing Tatum's testimony, Walt Disney Productions,

"Statement of Testimony from Walt Disney Productions to the United States Department of the Interior, National Park Service, Relative to Park Wilderness Proposals Sequoia and Kings Canyon National Parks California," "Exhibits from the Public," Nov. 21, 1966; NARA I Forest Service Files.

56. "Obstructionism at Mineral King," editorial, *Los Angeles Times*, Dec. 1, 1966.
57. "Scorecard," *Sports Illustrated* (Dec. 19, 1966).
58. John L. Harper, letter to Michael McCloskey, conservation director, Dec. 2, 1966; Sierra Club Members Papers.
59. See "Disney Project Has Bearing on Sequoia Plan," *Sacramento Bee*, Nov. 23, 1966; "Two Groups Fight Proposed Highway to Disney Resort," *Los Angeles Times*, Nov. 22, 1966.
60. See, e.g., "Disney MK Foes Speak," *Tulare Advance-Register*, Nov. 21, 1966.
61. See "Fight over Parks Land Designation," *San Francisco Chronicle*, Nov. 22, 1966; "Mineral King Park Views Widely Split," *San Jose Mercury*, Nov. 22, 1966; "Disney Enterprises Denies Plans for Another Disneyland," *Denver Post*, Nov. 22, 1966; "Mineral King Development," editorial, *Orange County (California) Register*, Nov. 28, 1966; "Park Service Enclosure Hearings End," *Riverside (California) Enterprise*, Nov. 23, 1966.
62. "Walt Disney, 65, Dies on Coast; Founded an Empire on a Mouse," *New York Times*, Dec. 16, 1966.
63. Neal Gabler, *Walt Disney: The Triumph of the American Imagination* (New York: Alfred A. Knopf, 2006), 631.
64. "Disney Aide Vows Push on Mineral King," *Fresno Bee*, Jan. 11, 1967.
65. See, e.g., Keith Schneider and Cornelia Dean, "Stewart L. Udall, Conservationist in Kennedy and Johnson Cabinets, Dies at 90," *New York Times*, Mar. 20, 2010. Thomas G. Smith, *Stewart L. Udall: Steward of the Land* (Albuquerque: University of New Mexico Press, 2017).
66. University of Arizona Library, *Stewart L. Udall: Advocate for Planet Earth*, at https://speccoll.library.arizona.edu/online-exhibits/exhibits/show/stewart-lee-udall/bio.
67. Stewart Udall, letter to Otis Chandler, Jan. 6, 1967; Stewart Udall Papers.
68. *Id.* at 2.
69. George B. Hartzog, director, National Park Service, "Mineral King Transportation Studies, Sequoia-Kings Canyon National Park," memorandum to secretary of the interior, Jan. 11, 1967; NARA II National Park Service Files.
70. Stewart L. Udall, secretary of the interior, to Alexander B. Trowbridge, acting secretary of commerce, Feb. 15, 1967; NARA II National Park Services Files.
71. Don Irwin, "Udall Bids for Monorail Route to Mineral King," *Los Angeles Times*, Mar. 12, 1967; Ron Taylor, "Udall Prefers Monorail for Mineral King Access," *Fresno Bee*, Mar. 13, 1967 (subheaded "Misinformed on State Plan?").
72. Walt Disney Productions, *Report on the Feasibility of Alternative Transportation Systems into Mineral King*, Mar. 14, 1967, 3, 8; NARA II Forest Service Files.

73. Donn B. Tatum, vice-president, Walt Disney Productions, letter to Honorable Stewart L. Udall, Mar. 16, 1967; NARA II National Park Service Files.
74. Edward P. Cliff, chief, "Special-Use Permit (Mineral King)," memorandum to Secretary Orville L. Freeman, Mar. 30, 1967; NARA II.
75. Orville L. Freeman, secretary, letter to Honorable Steward L. Udall, Apr. 14, 1967; Lyndon B. Johnson Presidential Library.
76. Kenneth Holum, acting secretary of the interior, letter to Mr. Gordon C. Luce, Apr. 18, 1967; NARA II National Park Service Files.
77. Kenneth Holum, acting secretary of the interior, letter to Donn B. Tatum, vice-president, Walt Disney Productions, Apr. 18, 1967; NARA II National Park Service Files.
78. William M. Blair, "Conservationists Fight Disney Resort Plan," *New York Times*, Mar. 13, 1967.
79. "State Board Oks Mineral King Highway," *Los Angeles Times*, Apr. 21, 1967; "State Commits Funds to Build Road to Resort," *Visalia Times-Delta*, Apr. 21, 1967.
80. P. J. Wyckoff, Mineral King staff specialist, "Plans—Mineral King," memorandum to files, Feb. 2, 1967; RBH Papers.
81. *Id.* at 3.
82. *Id.*
83. Walt Disney Productions, "World Record Foxtail Pines at Mineral King," *Mineral King News*, Feb. 1, 1967, 2; SNP Files. *See also* "Forest Rangers Find Rare Giant Foxtail Pine Trees in Mineral King," *Bakersfield Californian*, Feb. 2, 1967 (subheaded "Near Proposed Disney Village").
84. P. J. Wyckoff, letter to Robert Hicks, Mar. 17, 1967; SCLDF Papers.
85. *Id.* at 3.
86. *Id.*
87. *Id.* at 2.
88. Michael McCloskey, "Why the Sierra Club Opposes Development of Mineral King," *Sierra Club Bulletin* (Nov. 1967): 7. The document was originally drafted in May 1967 and selectively released then (Michael McCloskey, "Why the Sierra Club Opposes Development of Mineral King," May 8, 1967; Sierra Club Members Papers). It was then slightly edited and published in the November *Sierra Club Bulletin*.
89. *Id.* at 7–8.
90. *Id.* at 8.
91. *Id.*
92. *Id.* at 9.
93. *Id.* at 10.
94. "Mineral King," editorial, *National Parks* (July 1967): 2.
95. Bestor Robinson, letter to the editor, *National Parks* (Aug. 9, 1967).
96. Edward P. Cliff, chief, letter to Edward C. Crafts, director, May 16, 1967; George B. Hartzog Papers.

97. U.S. Dept. of Interior, news release, "Udall Establishes Bureau of Outdoor Recreation in the Interior Department," Apr. 2, 1962, at https://www.fws.gov/news/Historic/NewsReleases/1962/19620402.pdf.
98. Cliff, letter to Crafts, May 16, 1967, 3, 5.
99. Edward C. Crafts, director, Bureau of Outdoor Recreation, "Mineral King," letter to the secretary, May 17, 1967, 4; George B. Hartzog Papers.
100. Edward C. Crafts, director, Bureau of Outdoor Recreation, "Mineral King Road," memorandum to Assistant Secretary Anderson, June 9, 1967, 2, 3; George B. Hartzog Papers.
101. Stanley C. Cain, assistant secretary for Fish and Wildlife and Parks, "Mineral King," memorandum to the secretary, May 22, 1967, 3; NARA II National Park Service Files (emphasis omitted).
102. Orville Freeman, secretary, memorandum to John Baker, June 27, 1967; OLF Papers.
103. Stanley Cain, note to Under-Secretary Block, Nov. 20, 1967; NARA I Department of the Interior Files.
104. Stewart L. Udall, "The Face of Tomorrow," *West magazine*, *Los Angeles Times*, June 11, 1967.
105. *Id.*
106. *Id.*
107. W. S. Davis, chief, Division of Recreation, "Written Information—Sequoia N.F. Mineral King Road," memorandum to chief, June 13, 1967; NARA II Forest Service Files.
108. Stewart L. Udall, letter to Orville Freeman, Aug. 10, 1967, 2; NARA I Department of the Interior National Park Service Files.
109. *Id.* at 3. He suggested a "Selke Committee," which was a committee that Orville Freeman had appointed in 1964 to resolve issues concerning the Boundary Waters Canoe Area.
110. Walt Disney Productions, letter to Secretary Freeman, "Following Are Observations Made by Members of the Staff of Walt Disney Productions Regarding the August 10, 1967 letter from Secretary of the Interior Stewart L. Udall to Yourself," undated; NARA II Forest Service Files.
111. Richard J. Costley, memorandum to A. W. Greeley, Aug. 25, 1967 (noting also that Disney "will attempt to bring both [California] Senators to the meeting"); NARA II Forest Service Files.
112. "Disney Halts Mineral King Development," *Fresno Bee*, Sept. 29, 1967.
113. Orville L. Freeman, letter to Honorable Stewart L. Udall, Aug. 30, 1967, 2; NARA II Secretary of Agriculture Files.
114. Roy O. Disney, president, letter to the Honorable Stewart Udall, Sept. 21, 1967; NARA II Department of the Interior Files.

115. Roy O. Disney, president, Walt Disney Productions, telegram to the Honorable Stewart L. Udall, Oct. 11, 1967; NARA I Department of the Interior Files.
116. Senator Thomas H. Kuchel, "Mineral King: The Opportunity That Should Not Be Lost," *Western Ski Time* (Oct. 1967): 35.
117. John A. Baker, assistant secretary, memorandum to the secretary, Nov. 28, 1967; NARA II Secretary of Agriculture Files.
118. Phillip S. Hughes, deputy director, letter to Honorable Orville L. Freeman, Nov. 6, 1967; NARA II Secretary of Agriculture Files.
119. Mike McCloskey, conservation director, letter to members of the Mineral King Task Force, Nov. 22, 1967; GM Papers.
120. William M. Blair, "2 Cabinet Aides Clash Over Park," *New York Times*, Dec. 3, 1967.
121. Phillip Fradkin, "Impasse Stalls Mineral King Road," *Los Angeles Times*, Dec. 6, 1967. The article stated that Senator Thomas Kuchel had held a meeting the previous week that brought Udall and Freeman together. However, the memorandum from Freeman aide John Baker describes the meeting as only between Kuchel and Udall; see John A. Baker, assistant secretary, memorandum to the secretary, Nov. 28, 1967; NARA II Secretary of Agriculture Files.
122. John L. Harper, *Mineral King: Public Concern with Government Policy* (Arcata, CA: Pacifica Publishing, 1982), 135.
123. Jack Hope, "The King Besieged," *Natural History* (Nov. 1968): 53, 81.
124. Jeanne Ora Nienaber, "Mineral King: Ideological Battleground for Land Use Disputes" (PhD diss., University of California, Berkeley, 1973), 101; Michael McCloskey, interview with the author, Portland, OR, June 5, 2017 (noting Udall's uncertain position with Johnson); Thomas G. Smith, *Stewart L. Udall: Steward of the Land* (Albuquerque: University of New Mexico Press, 2017), 268 (detailing Udall's increasing misgivings about the Vietnam War).
125. Orville Freeman, diary entry, Dec. 8, 1967; OLF Papers.
126. *Id.*
127. Dept. of Agriculture, proposed press release, Dec. 19, 1967; NARA II Secretary of Agriculture Files (with footnote stating "USDA draft with modifications proposed by Secretary Udall").
128. Stewart L. Udall, secretary of the interior, letter to Honorable Orville L. Freeman, secretary of agriculture, Dec. 20, 1967; Stewart Udall Papers.
129. U.S. Department of Agriculture, press release, "Road to Mineral King Approved," Dec. 27, 1967; Stewart Udall Papers.
130. Eric Wentworth, "Disney Resort Project Wins Approval," *Washington Post*, Dec. 28, 1967.
131. William M. Blair, "Udall Yields and Opens the Way for a Resort in Sequoia Forest," *New York Times*, Dec. 28, 1967. See also "Udall Oks Road for Mineral King, Ends Deadlock," *Los Angeles Times*, Dec. 28, 1967.

132. Walt Disney Productions, "Statement from Roy O. Disney. Subject: Mineral King," Dec. 27, 1967; SNP Files.
133. Orville L. Freeman, letter to Roy O. Disney, Dec. 27, 1967, 2; NARA II Secretary of Agriculture Files.
134. Martin Litton, travel editor, letter to Honorable Stewart L. Udall, Dec. 27, 1967; Sierra Club Members Papers.
135. Stewart Udall, letter to Martin Litton, Jan. 2, 1968; Sierra Club Members Papers.

Chapter 5

1. Stanley A. Cain, assistant secretary for Fish and Wildlife, "Road to Mineral King," memorandum to Assistant Secretary Edwards, Director Hartzog, and Solicitor Barry, Jan. 4, 1968; George B. Hartzog Papers.
2. Stanley A. Cain, assistant secretary for Fish and Wildlife and Parks, "Mineral King Road," memorandum to director, National Park Service, Jan. 11, 1968; NARA II National Park Service Files.
3. Orville Freeman, diary entry, Mar. 1, 1968; OLF Papers.
4. Stewart L. Udall, handwritten note to Mr. Browning, Apr. 12, 1971; Sierra Club Members Papers. "Browning" is likely Peter Browning, whose article in *Harper's Magazine* about Mineral King had just appeared.
5. Howard W. Baker, associate director, National Park Service, "Mineral King," memorandum to assistant directors, Operations, Interpretation, and Design and Construction, WSC, Jan. 16, 1968; GBH Papers.
6. Associate solicitor, Parks and Recreation, "Mineral King Road," memorandum to director, National Park Service, Mar. 5, 1968; NARA II National Park Service Files.
7. See, e.g., M. M. Nelson, deputy chief, "Special Use Permits (Mineral King)," memorandum to record, Feb. 27, 1968.
8. P. J. Wyckoff, "Plans—Electricity to Mineral King," memorandum to files, Feb. 2, 1968; NARA I Forest Service Files.
9. John Clarkeson, president, Clarkeson Engineering Co., Inc., *Report on Road to Mineral King in Sequoia National Park, Three Rivers, California*, July 31, 1968; GBH Papers.
10. John Clarkeson, president, Clarkeson Engineering Co., Inc., *Supplement to Review of Proposed Mineral King Highway in Sequoia National Park*, undated [1968]; NARA II National Park Service Files.
11. M. M. Nelson, deputy chief, "Special Use Permits (Mineral King Road)," memorandum to record, Sept. 17, 1968; NARA II National Park Service Files.
12. "What Price Road?," editorial, *New York Times*, Jan. 24, 1968.
13. Alfred A. Knopf, letter to the president, Jan. 26, 1969; NARA II National Park Service Files.

14. Gary Soucie, telegram to Mike McCloskey, Jan. 3, 1968; SCLDF Files.
15. Orville Freeman, memorandum to John Baker, Feb. 21, 1968; OLF Papers.
16. John A. Baker, assistant secretary, memorandum to the secretary, Feb. 29, 1968; NARA II Secretary of Agriculture Files.
17. Ron Taylor, "Mineral King Faces New Attack," *Fresno Bee*, July 14, 1968.
18. John Rettenmayer, interview with the author, December 31, 2018.
19. Marilyn Senese, "Pickets March at Disney Studio," *Burbank Daily Review*, Mar. 5, 1969.
20. Tom Turner, *Sierra Club: 100 Years of Protecting Nature* (New York: Harry N. Abrams, 1991), 189.
21. Jack Hope, "The King Besieged," *Natural History* (Nov. 1968): 82.
22. John Rettenmayer and Albert Hill, "Summary of Mineral King Development," 2; RJ Papers.
23. Orville Freeman, letter to Stewart L. Udall, Sept. 27, 1968; NARA II Secretary of Agriculture Files.
24. Stewart Udall, letter to Orville Freeman, Oct. 16, 1968; NARA II Secretary of Agriculture Files.
25. Ray Hebert, "$710.4 Million Budget Adopted by State Highway Commission," *Los Angeles Times*, Oct. 23, 1968, 3.
26. "Road May Bear Disney Name," *Fresno Bee*, Sept. 25, 1968.
27. Superintendent McLaughlin to William Bowen, memorandum of telephone call, Sequoia and Kings Canyon National Parks, Dec. 20, 1968; SNP Files.
28. Hope, "The King Besieged," 52.
29. Jack Hope, letter to Mike McCloskey, Nov. 9, 1968, 1–2; RJ Papers.
30. *Natural History*, magazine press release, "Long Live the King!" Nov. 8, 1968; SCLDF Papers.
31. Robert B. Hicks, letter to Jack Hope, Nov. 1, 1968; NARA I Forest Service Files. Hicks also sent a cover letter to Hope that concluded "I look forward to a visit from you next time you are in California."
32. Hope, "The King Besieged," 53.
33. *Id.* at 53, 74.
34. Jeanne Ora Nienaber, "Mineral King: Ideological Battleground for Land Use Disputes" (PhD diss., University of California, Berkeley, 1973), 4.
35. Richard J. Costley, "F.S. & Disney Enterprises Meeting in L.A. re Mineral King," memorandum to deputy chief, Forest Service, Dec. 27, 1968, 4; NARA I Forest Service Files.
36. M. R. James, forest supervisor, "Term and Terminable Permits as Related to Mineral King Area," memorandum to regional forester, Feb. 4, 1969 (attaching land occupancy figures); SCLDF Files.
37. Costley, "F.S. & Disney Enterprises Meeting," 4–5.
38. *Id.* at 5.

39. Walt Disney Productions, *Master Plan Presentation of Walt Disney Productions' Mineral King Project*, Jan. 8, 1969; Sierra Club Members Papers.
40. Walt Disney Productions, Fact Sheet, "Walt Disney Productions' Master Plan for the Development of Mineral King in Sequoia National Forest," *DisneyNews*, apparently Jan. 27, 1969; SCLDF Files.
41. Walt Disney Productions, Fact Sheet, "Walt Disney Productions' Master Plan."
42. Walt Disney Productions, "Walt Disney Productions Outlines Master Plan for Mineral King," *DisneyNews*, Jan. 27, 1969, 2–3; RBH Papers.
43. Walt Disney Productions, "Mineral King Offers Recreational Potential Equal to Any in the United States," *DisneyNews*, Jan. 27, 1969, 2; RBH Papers.
44. *Id.* at 3.
45. *Id.*
46. Walt Disney Productions, "Mineral King Project: Example of Cooperation between Government and Private Enterprise," *DisneyNews*, Jan. 27, 1969, 4; RBH Papers.
47. Walt Disney Productions, Fact Sheet, "Walt Disney Productions' Master Plan," 8.
48. "Mineral King Public Recreation Area, Background Material—Basis for Master Plan Approval," 1969, 1; Sierra Club Members Papers. While this document does not state authorship on its face, its title and content are written from the perspective of the Forest Service.
49. W. S. Davis, chief, Division of Recreation, "Mineral King Master Plan," memorandum to Richard Costley, director, Division of Recreation, Jan. 9, 1969; NARA II Forest Service Files.
50. R. Lesler, "Mineral King Proposal," memorandum to R. J. Costley, Ray Housely, Jan. 16, 1969; NARA I Forest Service Files.
51. R. J. Costley, director of recreation, "Approval of the Plans Submitted by Disney Prod. for Development of Mineral King on the Sequoia N.F.," memorandum to the record, Jan. 27, 1968, 1–2; NARA II Forest Service Files.
52. M. R. James, forest supervisor, letter to E. Cardon Walker, executive vice-president, Jan. 21, 1969; NARA II Forest Service Files.
53. Jim Stewart, "Mineral King Press Conference," memorandum to "Those Concerned," Jan. 22, 1969; RBH Papers.
54. See, e.g., Walt Disney Productions, "Walt Disney Productions Outlines Master Plan"; U.S. Forest Service, "Mineral King Project Master Plan Approved," *Forest Service News*, Jan. 27, 1969; RBH Papers.
55. Walt Disney Productions, "Mineral King Project: Example of Cooperation," 5.
56. "Disneyland in the Snow," *People (Australia)* (Apr. 23, 1969): 27.
57. "Mineral King Folly," editorial, *New York Times*, Feb. 2, 1969.
58. See, e.g., "Does the Sierra Club Own the Mountains?" *Watsonville [California] Register-Pajaronian*, Feb. 19, 1969.
59. "To Guard and Preserve? Or Open and Enjoy?" *Time* (Feb. 7, 1969): 17.

60. Forest Service, U.S. Dept. of Agriculture, *Mineral King: A Planned Recreation Development*, Feb. 1969, 7; RBH Papers.
61. *Id.* at 1, 10, 7.
62. *Id.* at 6, 10.
63. *Id.* at 2.
64. *Id.* at 5, 9.
65. *Id.* at 12.
66. *Id.* at 5.
67. Sierra Club, *Mineral King at the Crossroads*, 1969, 3; Sierra Club Members Papers. While the brochure is undated, the written text, found in separate documents, is dated April 29, 1969. See Sierra Club, *Mineral King at the Crossroads: Will It Be Protected as Parkland? Or Become Another Over-developed Yosemite Valley?*; SCLDF Papers.
68. *Id.* at 1.
69. *Id.*
70. *Id.* at 7, 3.
71. *Id.* at 5.
72. *Id.* at 7–8.
73. Walter Ballenger, "Avalanche! A Memoir of Survival in Mineral King, California," *Quest* magazine (Feb.–Mar. 1979): 49, 50–51.
74. *Id.* at 51.
75. Bob Hicks, interview by Louise Jackson, July 31, 2013; MKPS.
76. Bob Hicks, "Mineral King Evacuation," memorandum to "All Concerned," Mar. 3, 1969, 2, 4; RBH Papers.
77. Ballenger, "Avalanche!" 49, 54.
78. David Beck, "Mineral King Accident," memorandum to Bob Hicks, Feb. 28, 1969, 5; RBH Papers.
79. *Id.* at 6.
80. Ron Taylor, "Record Snows, Avalanches Ruin Mineral King Buildings," *Fresno Bee*, Feb. 27, 1969.
81. *Id.*
82. "Slide Buries M-K Cabins," *Porterville Recorder*, Feb. 26, 1969.

Chapter 6

1. Jules Witcover, *The Year the Dream Died* (New York: Warner Bros. Books, 1997), 505.
2. Samuel P. Hays, *Beauty, Health, and Permanence: Environmental Politics in the United States, 1955–1985* (New York: Cambridge University Press, 1987), 54.
3. Terry H. Anderson, "The New American Revolution," in *The Sixties*, ed. David Farber (Chapel Hill: University of North Carolina Press, 1994), 184.

4. J. Michael McCloskey, *In the Thick of It: My Life in the Sierra Club* (Washington, DC: Island Press/Shearwater Books, 2005), xiii, 101.
5. Kirkpatrick Sale, *The Green Revolution: The American Environmental Movement, 1962–1992* (New York: Hill and Wang, 1993), 17.
6. McCloskey, *In the Thick of It: My Life in the Sierra Club*, xiii, 97–98.
7. Maurice Isserman and Michael Kazin, *American Divided: The Civil War of the 1960s* (New York: Oxford University Press, 2000), 120.
8. Phillip Shabecoff, *A Fierce Green Fire: The American Environmental Movement*, rev. ed. (Washington, DC: Island Press, 2003), 113.
9. Michael P. Cohen, *The History of the Sierra Club: 1892–1970* (San Francisco: Sierra Club Books, 1988), 436.
10. Michael McCloskey, interview with the author, Portland, OR, June 5, 2017.
11. Robert Wyss, *The Man Who Built the Sierra Club: A Life of David Brower* (New York: Columbia University Press, 2016), 260–61; Tom Turner, *David Brower: The Making of the Environmental Movement* (Oakland: University of California Press, 2015), 141.
12. Wyss, *The Man Who Built the Sierra Club*, 270–71.
13. Edgar Wayburn, MD, *Your Land and Mine: Evolution of a Conservationist* (San Francisco: Sierra Club Books, 2004), 125.
14. *Cohen, History of the Sierra Club*, 436 ("Conservation, thought McCloskey, required political expertise. It called for lawyers and experts in the practice of public policy").
15. John Henry Auran, "Special Report: Defend Your Right to Ski," *Skiing* (Oct. 1969): 62, 70.
16. Richard Leonard, interview by Susan R. Schrepfer, Sierra Club Oral History Series, vol. 1, 1975, 98, at https://archive.org/stream/richardmountain01leonrich/richardmountain01leonrich_djvu.txt.
17. Edgar Wayburn, interview by Ann Lage and Susan Schrepfer, Sierra Club History Series, 1985, 41, at http://digitalassets.lib.berkeley.edu/roho/ucb/text/wayburn_edgar.pdf.
18. Michael McCloskey, interview by Susan Schrepfer, Sierra Club Oral History Series, 1981, 176, at https://digitalassets.lib.berkeley.edu/roho/ucb/text/mccloskey_michael.pdf. See also Michael McCloskey, conservation director, letter to Kurt Bomke, Mar. 21, 1969; SCLDF Papers ("You are probably right that the Club has not fought the Disney development as hard as would have been desirable, but we are trying now to do as much as we can").
19. "Walter J. Hickel," Center of the American West, Oct. 15, 2003, at https://www.centerwest.org/wp-content/uploads/2011/01/hickel.pdf; Dennis Hevesi, "Walter Hickel, Nixon Interior Secretary, Dies at 90," *New York Times*, May 8, 2010.
20. McCloskey, interview with the author. (The suit was clearly "to delay" the proj-

ect. It was also "to buy time to build support for Congressional action; and to use the attendant publicity to build that support.")

21. McCloskey, interview with the author.
22. See, e.g., L. M. Whitfield, forest supervisor, letter to the editor, *Sierra Club Bulletin* (Jan. 2, 1968); SCLDF Papers.
23. Wyss, *The Man Who Built the Sierra Club*, 271.
24. Tom Turner, *Sierra Club: 100 Years of Protecting Nature* (New York: Harry N. Abrams, 1991), 186.
25. Cohen, *History of the Sierra Club*, 240 (terming the case the Sierra Club's "first legal suit").
26. National Parks Association, et al. v. Udall, __ F. Supp. ___, Civ. No. 3904–62 (D.D.C. 1963).
27. The history of the controversy over the Storm King facility is recounted in depth in Robert D. Lifset, *Power on the Hudson: Storm King Mountain and the Emergence of Modern American Environmentalism* (Pittsburgh: University of Pittsburgh Press, 2014).
28. Scenic Hudson Preservation Conference v. Federal Power Commission, 354 F.2d 608, 612 (2d Cir. 1965).
29. Tom Turner, *Wild by Law: The Sierra Club Legal Defense Fund and the Places It Has Saved* (San Francisco: Sierra Club Legal Defense Fund, 1990), 13.
30. Walter V. Hays, letter to Michael McCloskey, Mar. 10, 1967; SCLDF Papers.
31. Michael McCloskey, letter to John Harper, Jan. 22, 1968, quoted in John L. Harper, *Mineral King: Public Concern with Government Policy* (Arcata, CA: Pacifica Publishing, 1982), 137n20.
32. Conservation Law Society of America, Summary of Activities, 1967–1968; RJ Papers.
33. Robert Jasperson, letter to Michael McCloskey, Apr. 22, 1968; RJ Papers.
34. Robert Jasperson, letter to Phillip S. Berry, Feb. 5, 1969; SCLDF Papers.
35. McCloskey, interview with the author.
36. Leland Selna, interview with the author, Oakland, CA, July 2, 2015.
37. *Id.*
38. Wayburn, *Your Land and Mine*, 111.
39. Thomas R. Wellock, *Critical Masses: Opposition to Nuclear Power in California, 1958–1978* Madison: University of Wisconsin Press, 1998), 57–58.
40. Russ Leadabrand, "Mineral King: Go or No Go," *American Forests* (Oct. 1969): 35, 46.
41. The phrase apparently originated with Richard McArdle, the chief of the Forest Service between 1954 and 1962. See https://www.fs.usda.gov/Internet/FSE_DOCUMENTS/stelprd3791704.pdf ("The national forests are lands of many uses—and many users").
42. United States v. Midwest Oil Co., 236 U.S. 459 (1915).

43. W. S. Davis, chief, Division of Recreation, "Mineral King," memorandum to regional attorney, Feb. 13, 1969; NARA II Forest Service Files.
44. 16 U.S.C. § 1 (repealed).
45. 16 U.S.C. §§ 41 and 43.
46. 16 U.S.C. § 8 (repealed).
47. 16 U.S.C. 45(c) (transferred).
48. Jesse R. Farr, regional attorney, "Special Use Permit—Walt Disney Productions: Mineral King—Sequoia National Forest," memorandum to L. M. Adams, director, Forestry and Soil Conservation Div., OGC, Nov. 6, 1967; NARA I Forest Service Files.
49. Jesse R. Farr, regional attorney, "Special Use Permit—Walt Disney Productions: Mineral King—Sequoia National Forest," memorandum to regional forester, Attn: W. S. Davis, Dec. 11, 1967; NARA II Forest Service Files.
50. M. R. James, forest supervisor, "Sequoia National Game Refuge (Mineral King)," memorandum to regional forester, Feb. 4, 1969; SCLDF Papers.
51. Reorganization Plan No. II of 1939, 5 U.S.C. App. 1, 4 F.R. 2731, 53 Stat. 1431, Ch. 193 §4; 53 Stat. 813.
52. In an opinion dated June 10, 1941, the solicitor of the Department of Agriculture had concluded that the act transferred only limited functions to the secretary of the interior relating to the conservation of wildlife, game, and migratory birds that were previously exercised by a subagency known as the Bureau of Biological Survey; Opinion No. 3380, June 10, 1941.
53. 16 U.S.C. §497.
54. Office of the Secretary, Dept. of Interior, "Roadbuilding in National Parks: Adoption of Procedures," 34 Fed. Reg. 1405, Jan. 29, 1969.
55. Office of the Secretary, Dept. of Interior, "Roadbuilding in National Parks: Revocation of Procedures," 34 Fed. Reg. 6985, Apr. 26, 1969.
56. Commonwealth of Massachusetts v. Mellon, 262 U.S. 447, 488 (1923).
57. 354 F.2d 608, 615 (2d Cir. 1965).
58. McCloskey, interview with the author.
59. Robert W. Jasperson, letter to Phillip S. Berry, Feb. 5, 1969, 5; SCLDF Papers
60. Phillip S. Berry, interview by Ann Lage, 1988, Sierra Club Oral History Series ("[p]leading the case in that manner was the choice of the trial counsel"), 77, at https://archive.org/details/berrysierracluboophilrich/page/76/mode/2up; William G. Siri, interview by Ann Lage, 1979, Sierra Club Oral History Series ("I recall that some of us were puzzled and dubious but we felt we had to defer to the judgment of our lawyers"), 88, at https://archive.org/details/reflectsierracluboosiririch/page/n25/mode/2up.
61. McCloskey, interview with the author ("I suppose to a certain extent he [Selna] was given lots of leeway" and "I was clearly in the role of being the client and not the lawyer").

62. Berry, interview, Sierra Club Oral History Series, 1997, 77 (establishing a precedent on standing "was not our major goal at the beginning").
63. Robert Jasperson, letter to Phillip S. Berry, Feb. 5, 1969; SCLDF Papers.
64. Hon. Robert B. (Bob) Mathias, House of Representative. Cong. Record., Jan. 22, 1970 (quoting Bill Duncan, "Mineral King: A Resort in Limbo," *Long Beach Independent Press-Telegram*, Dec. 14, 1969), 20, 22.
65. Harold Wexler, interview with the author, February 17, 2017.
66. Robert W. Jasperson, general counsel, letter to Jack Hope, *Natural History* (June 11, 1969): RJ Papers.
67. Don Harris, "Mineral King: Breaking Down the Courthouse Door," at https://earthjustice.org/features/mineral-king-breaking-down-the-courthouse-door (noting that Selna agreed to take the case "at a sharply reduced rate").
68. McCloskey, interview, Sierra Club Oral History Series, 1981, 176. See also McCloskey, letter to Kurt Bomke.
69. Selna, interview with the author.
70. "Sierra Club Files Suit in Bid to Block Disney's Mineral King Development," *Wall Street Journal*, June 6, 1969.
71. Transcript, *CBS Evening News with Roger Mudd*, Apr. 12, 1969, 1; RJ Papers.
72. Edward P. Cliff, chief, Forest Service, "Mineral King Status Report," memorandum to the secretary, Feb. 12, 1969, 1–2; NARA II Forest Service Files.
73. "Disney Head 'Puzzled' at Sierra Uproar," *Anaheim Bulletin* (May 2, 1969).
74. Donn B. Tatum, "Mineral King #1," editorial rebuttal, KABC-TV Los Angeles, June 2 and 3, 1969.
75. E. Cardon Walker, executive vice-president, Walt Disney Productions, open letter, Apr. 25, 1969; NARA I Forest Service Files. The letter contains the handwritten notation that it was "sent to all Disney employees."
76. "Bad Publicity on Mineral King Irritates Disney Official," *Santa Ana Evening Register*, May 2, 1969, 2.
77. Joe Rosato, "Disney Firm Awaits Word on Roadway," *Visalia Times-Delta*, Apr. 6, 1969.
78. Sierra Club, transcript, Sierra Club press conference, June 6, 1969 (original in Bancroft Library; copy in author's possession).
79. Peter J. Wyckoff, letter to Robert Hicks, Feb. 12, 1969, 3; NARA II Forest Service Files.
80. W. S. Davis, chief, Division of Recreation, "Impact—Mineral King, Stage I," memorandum to forest supervisor, Sequoia National Forest, Apr. 25, 1969; NARA II Forest Service Files.
81. Sierra Club, press release, "Sierra Club Files Suit to Block Mineral King Development," June 5, 1969; Sierra Club Members Papers.
82. Gladwin Hill, "Suit Seeks to Bar Disney Forest Resort," *New York Times*, June 6, 1969; Philip Hager, "Sierra Club Suit Seeks to Block Mineral King," *Los Angeles*

Times, June 6, 1969; "Sierra Club Files Suit to Block Disney's Mineral King Development Plan," *Wall Street Journal*, June 6, 1969.

Chapter 7

1. Wolfgang Saxon, "Alfonso Zirpoli, Federal Judge, Is Dead at 90," *New York Times*, July 13, 1995.
2. United Press International, "William T. Sweigert: A U.S. Judge Since '59," *New York Times*, Feb. 18, 1983.
3. Robert Greenfield, *Bear: The Life and Times of August Owsley Stanley III* (Old Saybrook, CT: Tantor Media, 2017).
4. Ed Cray, *Chief Justice: A Biography of Earl Warren* (New York: Simon and Schuster, 1997), 138.
5. Mottola v. Nixon, 318 F. Supp. 538 (N.D. Cal. 1970) rev'd on other grounds 464 F.2d 178 (9th Cir. 1972).
6. Kapp v. National Football League, 390 F. Supp. 73 (N.D. Cal. 1974), vacated in part 1975 WL 959 (N.D. Cal. 1977), aff'd 586 F.2d 64 (9th Cir. 1978), cert. denied 441 U.S. 907 (1979).
7. W. S. Davis, chief, Division of Recreation, "Mineral King," memorandum to regional attorney, Feb. 13, 1969; NARA II Forest Service Files.
8. Pub. Law No. 465 §6.
9. *Id.*
10. Davis, "Mineral King," 2.
11. Clarence W. Brazee, "Mineral King Recreational Development," legal memorandum, 1969, 4; NARA II Forest Service Files.
12. U.S. Attorney General, opinion, "Permit to Construct Railroad Line Across Benecia Arsenal Military Reservation," 35 Op. Atty. Gen. 483, Nov. 27, 1928.
13. Bernard R. Meyer, associate solicitor, National Park Service, "Sierra Club v. Hickel et al.," memorandum to associate solicitor, Parks and Recreation, June 20, 1969, 2–3; SNP Files.
14. *Id.* at 3.
15. *Id.* at 5.
16. Brazee, "Mineral King Recreational Development," 10.
17. Untitled memorandum prepared by Disney lawyers, Mar. 12, 1969; NARA II Forest Service Files (listing legal authorities pertaining to the case).
18. Robert Hicks, oral history, June 17, 2013, MKPS.
19. Robert Hicks, oral history, Tulare County Treasures video, June 6, 2014.
20. "Mom v. Apple Pie," *Newsweek* (Feb. 10, 1969) ("When apple pie comes smack up against motherhood, it is plainly anybody's ball game").
21. David L. Warner, chief, General Litigation Section, unsent letter to Rodney W.

Hamblin, assistant U.S. attorney, June 19, 1969, Dept. of Justice Files, 2. The letter is marked "not sent."

22. Advertisement, "Hike-in to Mineral King"; Sierra Club Members Files.
23. Bob Ketchum, "Sierra Club Fights to Preserve Wilderness," *Western Outdoor News*, July 4, 1969.
24. Philip Fradkin, "Mineral King: Head-on Clash of Big Names," *Los Angeles Times*, July 7, 1969.
25. "Mineral King—a 'Boon to Many,'" editorial, *Bakersfield Californian*, July 3, 1969.
26. "Disney in the Middle," editorial, *Santa Ana Register*, July 28, 1969.
27. Ansel Adams, letter to Phil Berry, Aug. 27, 1969; Sierra Club Members Papers.
28. Bob Hicks, "Mineral King Planning," memorandum to Donn Tatum, Card Walker, and Ron Miller, July 7, 1969; RBH Papers.
29. John Wise, "Mineral King Planning," memorandum to Dick Irvine, July 17, 1969; RBH Papers.
30. Bob Hicks, "Revision of Mineral King Planning Memo Dated July 7, 1969," memorandum to Donn Tatum, Card Walker, and Ron Miller, July 23, 1969; RBH Papers.
31. "Board Okays Letter to Nixon on Road Delay," *Visalia Times-Delta*, July 1, 1969.
32. Daryl Lembke, "Sierra Club Attempts to Bar Mineral King Resort Permit," *Los Angeles Times*, July 2, 1969.
33. "Jurisdiction Key to Mineral King," *San Francisco Examiner*, July 2, 1969.
34. *Id.*
35. Lembke, "Sierra Club Attempts to Bar Mineral King Resort Permit."
36. Associated Press, "Sierra Club Attorney Claims Mineral King Has Green Light," *Bakersfield Californian*, July 2, 1969.
37. "The Mineral King Fight Begins," *San Francisco Chronicle*, July 2, 1969.
38. Associated Press, "Sierra Club Attorney Claims Mineral King Has Green Light."
39. "Jurisdiction Key to Mineral King."
40. Lembke, "Sierra Club Attempts to Bar Mineral King Resort Permit."
41. Thos. L. McKevitt, attorney, General Litigation Section, letter to Mitchell Melich, Esquire, solicitor, July 7, 1969; NARA I National Park Service Files; Bernard M. Meyer, associate solicitor, Parks and Recreation, Sierra Club v. Hickel, Civil No. 51464, memorandum to director, National Park Service, July 10, 1969; NARA II National Park Service Files.
42. Frank Ubhaus, interview with the author, Los Angeles, CA, Nov. 17, 2014.
43. Memorandum of Decision, Sierra Club v. Hickel, No. 51,464 (N.D. Cal. 1969), 1.
44. 16 U.S.C. §497.
45. Memorandum of Decision, Sierra Club v. Hickel, No. 51,464 (N.D. Cal. 1969) 4, citing 1948 U.S. Code Cong. & Ad. News, pp. 1337–1338; 1956 U.S. Code Cong. & Ad. News, 3334–36.

46. *Id.* at 5.
47. *Id.* at 6–7.
48. *Id.* at 7.
49. *Id.* at 8, 9.
50. Oddly, the Sierra Club's complaint had not directly raised the issue of authority for the transmission line. But the issue was discussed in the Sierra Club's brief. Plaintiff's Memorandum of Points and Authorities, Sierra Club v. Hickel, No. 51,464 (N.D. Cal. 1969), 30.
51. 16 U.S.C. §45(c).
52. Memorandum of Decision, Sierra Club v. Hickel, No. 51,464 (N.D. Cal. 1969), 10.
53. *Id.* at 11.
54. *Id.*
55. Complaint, Sierra Club v. Hickel, No. 51,464 (N.D. Cal. 1969), paragraph 3.
56. Memorandum of Decision, Sierra Club v. Hickel, No. 51,464 (N.D. Cal. 1969), 12.
57. *Id.*
58. *Id.* at 13.
59. *Id.*
60. Ubhaus, interview with the author.
61. Mike McCloskey, memorandum, Aug. 5, 1969; Richard Sills Papers (noting that "The Government asked that the club be required to post a $75,000 bond").
62. Associated Press, "No Bond Required in Mineral King Suit," *Bakersfield Californian*, Aug. 5, 1969; "Sierra Club Wins Again in US Court," *Visalia Times-Delta*, Aug. 5, 1969.
63. Leland R. Selna Jr., letter to J. Michael McCloskey, Esq., Aug. 5, 1969; Sierra Club Members Papers.
64. Preliminary Injunction, Sierra Club v. Walter J. Hickel, Civil No. 5164 (N.D. Cal.).

Chapter 8

1. Gladwin Hill, "Sierra Club Wins a Round in Disney Resort Fight," *New York Times*, July 27, 1969. See also Associated Press, "U.S. Court Injunction Holds Up Mineral King Resort Permits," *Los Angeles Times*, July 24, 1969, 3.
2. Walt Disney Productions, *DisneyNews*, July 30, 1969; NARA I Forest Service Files.
3. *Id.* at 2.
4. *Id.*
5. "Disney Won't Drop MK Resort Project." *Tulare Advance-Register*, July 26, 1969, 1.
6. United Press International, "Resort Plan Foes Weigh Costs If Beaten in Court," *Fresno Bee*, Aug. 1, 1969.
7. Hill, "Sierra Club Wins a Round."
8. Walt Disney Productions, "'What's Up at Mineral King,' a Presentation by Rob-

ert B. Hicks at the California State Chamber of Commerce Panel Meeting on Natural Resources—Travel and Recreation," Dec. 7, 1967, 6; RBH Papers.

9. Walt Disney Productions, *DisneyNews*, "Nationally Recognized Conservationists To Advise Walt Disney Productions on Mineral King," Nov. 6, 1969, 1–3; NARA I Forest Service Files.
10. Within the club, the attitude toward Robinson was mixed. For example, some saw him as an "overly willing compromiser" in the battle over Dinosaur National Monument; see Michael P. Cohen, *The History of the Sierra Club: 1892–1970* (San Francisco: Sierra Club Books, 1988), 181. With respect to Mineral King Valley, he supported the Forest Service's aims (Cohen, *History of the Sierra Club*, 249–50).
11. Walt Disney Productions, *DisneyNews*, Nov. 1969; NARA I Forest Service Files (sending to editors "a previously released statement written by Horace M. Albright, a member of Walt Disney Productions' newly announced Conservation Advisory Committee" and originally published in the *New York Times* on July 26, 1969).
12. Walt Disney Productions, Fact Sheet, "Walt Disney Productions' Master Plan for the Development of Mineral King in Sequoia National Forest," undated; SCLDF Papers.
13. Burton Peterson, note to Michael McCloskey, Nov. 6, 1969.
14. Doug Pfeiffer, "Memo from the Editor," *Skiing* (Sept. 1969).
15. "Mineral King: Court Action Threatens All Recreation Development on Public Lands," *Western Ski Time* (Oct. 1969): 14, 15.
16. John Henry Auran, "Defend Your Right to Ski," *Skiing* (Oct. 1969): 62, 64.
17. *Id.* at 80.
18. E. Lewis Reid, interview with the author, San Francisco, CA, 2017.
19. Russ Leadabrand, "Mineral King: Go or No Go," *American Forests* (Oct. 1969): 35, 44.
20. Donald Harris, memorandum to Sierra Club Legal Committee Members, July 25, 1969; RJ Papers.
21. "Club Wins More Than Injunction in N.Y. Court," *Sierra Club Bulletin* (Aug. 1969): 3.
22. "President's Message: A Report to the Members and a Plea for Help," *Sierra Club Bulletin* (Sept. 1969): 22.
23. Leland R. Selna Jr., "Mineral King," letter to J. Michael McCloskey, chief of staff, Sept. 26, 1969; Sierra Club Members Papers.
24. R. Frederic Fisher, "Legal Fees/Mineral King," letter to J. Michael McCloskey, chief of staff, Oct. 9, 1969, 2; Sierra Club Members Papers.
25. Dick Leonard, "Mineral King Litigation," letter to Phillip S. Berry, president, Nov. 5, 1969, 3; RJ Papers.
26. Paul Locke, "Sierra Club v. Walter J. Hickel, et al. Civil No. 51464—Mineral

King," letter to Department of Justice, Attn. David R. Warner, chief, July 28, 1969; Dept. of Justice Files.

27. See, e.g., Robert H. Whaley, attorney, "Sierra Club v. Walter J. Hickel, et al.," memorandum to Thomas McKevitt, attorney, July 25, 1969; Dept. of Justice Files.
28. Raymond C. Coulter, acting solicitor, Dept. of Interior, letter to Honorable Shiro Kashiwa, assistant attorney general, Aug. 12, 1969; Dept. of Justice Files.
29. Howard V. Campbell, "Sierra Club v. Walter J. Hickel, individually and as Secretary of the Interior, et al., Civil No. 51464, N.D. California," memorandum to Neil Brooks, assistant general counsel, Aug. 22, 1969, 3, 20; Dept. of Justice Files.
30. Shiro Kashiwa, assistant attorney general, "Appeal of Citizens Committee, et al. v. Volpe, et al., 69 Civ. 295, S.D. N.Y., and Sierra Club v. Hickel, Civ. No. 51464, N.D. Cal.," memorandum to Erwin N. Griswold, solicitor, Sept. 11, 1969; Dept. of Justice Files (noting, in the attached, detailed analysis, that "[t]he General Litigation Section of the Division, and the Departments of the Interior and Agriculture, all recommend appeal").
31. Peter L. Strauss, "Sierra Club v. Hickel—Appeal Recommendation," memorandum to the solicitor general, Sept. 19, 1969, 3; Dept. of Justice Files.
32. *Id.*
33. Erwin N. Griswold, solicitor general, "Re: Sierra Club v. Walter J. Hickel, et al.," memorandum: Appeal Authorized as to Standing, Sept. 24, 1969; Dept. of Justice Files.
34. Donn B. Tatum, letter to Honorable Clifford M. Hardin, Sept. 22, 1969; NARA II Secretary of Agriculture Files.
35. *Id.* at 2.
36. *Id.*
37. *Id.*
38. *Id.* at 3.
39. Janet Wasco, *Understanding Disney* (Malden, MA: Polity Press, 2001), 145–51.
40. Robert DeRoos, "The Magic Worlds of Walt Disney," *National Geographic* (Aug. 1963): 159.
41. "Walt Disney Named Honorary Member," *Sierra Club Bulletin* (Apr. 1955): 3.
42. A. W. Greeley, associate chief, letter to Donn B. Tatum, president, Oct. 3, 1969; NARA II Forest Service Files.
43. Shiro Kashiwa, assistant attorney general, "Requesting a Conference Concerning the Limitations on Appeal Authorized in Sierra Club v. Walter J. Hickel, et al., No. 51464, N.C. Cal.," memorandum to Mr. Erwin N. Griswold, solicitor general, Sept. 29, 1969; Dept. of Justice Files.
44. Erwin N. Griswold, solicitor general, "Re: Sierra Club v. Walter J. Hickel," mem-

orandum: Appeal Authorized on All Issues, Sept. 30, 1969; Dept. of Justice Files. Griswold handwrote in at the bottom: "Superseding earlier determination authorizing appeal on standing only."

45. Clifford M. Hardin, secretary of agriculture, letter to Donn B. Tatum, president, Nov. 13, 1969; NARA I Secretary of Agriculture Files.
46. Donn B. Tatum, president, letter to Clifford M. Hardin, secretary, Dec. 1, 1969; NARA I Secretary of Agriculture Files.
47. "Mineral King Not a Private Preserve," editorial, *Los Angeles Times*, June 11, 1969.
48. Clifford M. Hardin, letter to Mrs. Otis Chandler, Nov. 28, 1969; NARA I Secretary of Agriculture Files.
49. For the full text, see the *Frank McGee Report*, National Broadcasting Company, Aug. 24, 1969; Sierra Club Members Papers.
50. "Mineral King Project Shouldn't Be Blocked," *Visalia Times-Delta*, June 19, 1969.
51. "The Scandal of Mineral King," editorial, *New York Times*, June 24, 1969.
52. "Saving Natureland," editorial, *Christian Science Monitor*, June 11, 1969.
53. "Hollywood in Sequoia," editorial, *St. Louis Post-Dispatch*, June 9, 1969; "Enlarged Threats to the Sequoias," editorial, *Kansas City (Mo.) Star*, June 16, 1969.
54. Arnold Hano, "Protectionists vs. Recreationists—The Battle of Mineral King," *New York Times Magazine* (Aug. 17, 1969).
55. *Id.* (emphasis in original).
56. *Id.* (emphasis added).
57. Jacques Gelin, interview with the author, Rockville, MD, Mar. 17, 2015.
58. Brief for the Appellants, Sierra Club v. Walter J. Hickel (No. 24966), U.S. Court of Appeals for the Ninth Circuit, filed Dec. 1, 1969.
59. *Id.* at 6.
60. *Id.* at 16.
61. *Id.* at 19.
62. *Id.* at 8, citing Massachusetts v. Mellon, 262 U.S. 447, 488 (1923).
63. *Id.* at 9–10.
64. *Id.* at 17.
65. Motion to Accelerate Oral Argument of Appeal, Sierra Club v. Walter J. Hickel (No. 24966), U.S. Court of Appeals for the Ninth Circuit, filed Dec. 1, 1969; NARA II. It attached a declaration from Edward P. Cliff, the chief of the Forest Service, outlining the background of the project.
66. Order Granting County of Tulare Leave to File Amicus Curiae Brief, Sierra Club v. Walter J. Hickel (No. 24966), U.S. Court of Appeals for the Ninth Circuit, filed Dec. 15, 1969; note of court personnel indicating that order was filed December 2 "granting Far West Ski Assn. leave to file amicus curiae brief on behalf of appellant"; NARA II.
67. Brief for Appellee, Sierra Club v. Walter J. Hickel (No. 24966), U.S. Court of Appeals for the Ninth Circuit, filed Jan. 19, 1970, 48.

68. *Id.* at 8, 9, 54.
69. Brief of Amicus Curiae on Behalf of United States Ski Association [and] Far West Ski Association Urging Reversal, Sierra Club v. Walter J. Hickel (No. 24966), U.S. Court of Appeals for the Ninth Circuit, filed Dec. 29, 1969, 2.
70. *Id.* Appendix: U.S. Forest Service, Tabulation of Term-Revocable Permits, May 5, 1969.
71. *Id.*
72. Reply Brief for Walter J. Hickel, Secretary of the Interior, et al., Appellants, Sierra Club v. Walter J. Hickel (No. 24966), U.S. Court of Appeals for the Ninth Circuit, filed Feb. 6, 1970, 1.
73. Federal Judicial Center, biography of Frederick George Hamley, at https://www.fjc.gov/history/judges/hamley-frederick-george.
74. Obituary, "John F. Kilkenny, 83, Retired Federal Judge," *Seattle Times*, Feb. 21, 1995; Personnel of the Court, Jan. 1993, at https://digitalcommons.law.ggu.edu/cgi/viewcontent.cgi?article=1625&context=ggulrev.
75. Federal Judicial Center, biography of Ozell Miller Trask, at https://www.fjc.gov/history/judges/trask-ozell-miller.
76. Gus Muehlenhaupt, acting assistant regional director, Cooperative Programs, "Sierra Club Injunction Against Mineral King Developments," memorandum to acting regional director, Feb. 9, 1970; SNP Files (memorandum from Park Service employee summarizing the oral argument which he attended). See also Philip Fradkin, "U.S. Appeals Mineral King Ban," *Los Angeles Times*, Feb. 15, 1970.
77. Leland Selna, interview with the author, Oakland, CA, July 2, 2015.
78. Leland Selna Jr., "Sierra Club—Mineral King," letter to H. Donald Harris, Esq., Mar. 17, 1970; SCLDF Papers.
79. McClatchy Newspaper Service, "Disney: No Plans to Drop Mineral King," *Fresno Bee*, Feb. 4, 1970.

Chapter 9

1. Sierra Club v. Hickel, 433 F.2d 24 (9th Cir. 1970).
2. *Id.* at 29, 30.
3. *Id.* at 30–31, distinguishing Scenic Hudson Preservation Conference v. Federal Power Commission, 354 F.2d 608 (2d Cir. 1965), cert. denied, Consolidated Edison Co. of New York, Inc. v. Scenic Hudson Preservation Conference, 384 U.S. 941, 86 S.Ct. 1462, 16 L.Ed.2d 540 (1966); Office of Communication of United Church of Christ v. F.C.C., 123 U.S.App.D.C. 328, 359 F.2d 994 (1966); and Road Review League v. Boyd, 270 F. Supp. 650 (S.D.N.Y. 1967).
4. The "aggrieved" or "adversely affected" language is traceable to the Adminis-

trative Procedure Act, which authorized judicial review where this requirement was met; 5 U.S.C. § 702.

5. Association of Data Processing Service Organizations, Inc. v. Camp, 397 U.S. 150, 90 S.Ct. 827, 25 L.Ed.2d 184 (1970).
6. Sierra Club, 433 F.2d at 33.
7. 433 F.2d at 35, 36.
8. *Id.* at 36.
9. *Id.* at 37.
10. *Id.* at 38 (Hamley, Circuit Judge, concurring).
11. *Id.*
12. "U.S. Court Upsets Order Blocking Mineral King Bid," *Los Angeles Times*, Sept. 18, 1970.
13. "Disney Firm Asks Sierra Club Cooperation," *Visalia Times-Delta*, Sept. 18, 1970.
14. "Sierra Club Will Appeal Ruling on Disney Project," *New York Times*, Sept. 20, 1970.
15. Peter Browning, "Mickey Mouse in the Mountains," *Harper's Magazine* (Mar. 1972): 65, 68.
16. I. William Berry and Robert Lochner, "Mineral King Scores an Upset," *Ski Holiday* (Dec. 1970): p. 15.
17. Walt Disney Productions, "Statement by Donn B. Tatum, President, Walt Disney Productions," Sept. 17, 1970; SNP Files.
18. M. M. Nelson, "Mineral King," memorandum to Mr. Cliff, Jan. 14, 1970; NARA II Forest Service Files.
19. Ricard Bergholz, "Murphy Reaffirms His Support for Mineral King Plan," *Los Angeles Times*, Oct. 18, 1970.
20. The Public Land Law Revision Commission had recently completed a comprehensive review of the public land holdings. The federal government owned one-third of the nation's land, and over 75 percent of those lands were included within the jurisdiction of the Ninth Circuit. Public Land Law Review Commission, *One Third of the Nation's Land: A Report to the President and the Congress*, June 1970, 327.
21. H. Donald Harris Jr. and R. Frederick Fisher, cochairmen for the legal committee, "Report of Legal Committee on Litigation," letter to Phillip S. Berry, Esq., president, July 23, 1969, 3; Sierra Club Members Papers.
22. Gladwin Hill, "Conservationists See Gains in U.S. Courts," *New York Times*, Oct. 19, 1970.
23. Hill, "Conservationists See Gains."
24. R. Frederic Fisher, "Environmental Law," *Sierra Club Bulletin* (Jan. 1971): 24, 28.
25. Stanley R. Harsh, assistant general counsel, letter to Shiro Kashiwa, assistant attorney general, Oct. 7, 1970; Dept. of Justice Files (recommending opposition

to the stay and that if the stay is granted, it be conditioned "on the giving of security").

26. James W. Howell, "Service Approval of New Road to Mineral King," memorandum to Acting Superintendent Raftery, Oct. 5, 1970; SNP Files.
27. Report of the Study Group on the Caseload of the Supreme Court, 57 F.R.D. 573, 580 (1972).
28. See, e.g., Russell E. Butcher, "Environmentalists Go To Court," *American Forests* (June 1971): 29, 30.
29. 425 F.2d 97 (2d Cir. 1970).
30. Sierra Club v. Hickel, 433 F.2d 24, 33 fn. 9 (9th Cir. 1970).
31. Petition for a Writ of Certiorari, Sierra Club v. Walter J. Hickel, U.S. Supreme Court No. 70–34, filed Nov. 5, 1970, 10.
32. Petition for a Writ of Certiorari, 11.
33. Leland Selna, interview with the author, Oakland, CA, July 2, 2015.
34. Petition for a Writ of Certiorari, 22–35.
35. Dennis Hevesi, "Walter Hickel, Nixon Interior Secretary, Dies at 90," *New York Times*, May 8, 2010.
36. Ron Taylor, "Mineral King Faces Further Legal Delays," *Fresno Bee*, Feb. 23, 1971.
37. Walt Disney Productions, *DisneyNews*, Feb. 22, 1973; RBH Papers.
38. "Soaring Cost for Mineral King Road," *San Francisco Chronicle*, Feb. 24, 1971.
39. Bill Stall, "Mineral King Highway Cost Hits $38 Million," *Sacramento Bee*, Feb. 23, 1971.
40. Fred A. Strauss, letter to Jim Stearns, director, California Department of Conservation, Feb. 25, 1971; SNP Files.
41. Art. III §2 U.S. Constitution.
42. See Laurence H. Tribe, *American Constitutional Law*, 3d ed. (New York: Foundation Press, 2000), 1:386 ("Standing issues are . . . perhaps most frequently found in challenges by private plaintiffs to governmental actions").
43. Louis L. Jaffe, *Judicial Control of Administrative Action* (Boston: Little, Brown, 1965), 459.
44. 397 U.S. 150, 154 (1970).
45. See, e.g., William C. Tweed and Lary M. Dilsaver, *Challenge of the Big Trees: The History of Sequoia and Kings Canyon National Parks*, rev. ed. (Staunton, VA: George F. Thompson, 2017), 95 (the club's second outing in 1902 into the Sierra Nevadas was into Kings Canyon, where a permanent camp was established) and 199–205 (the club's work in the development of Kings Canyon); Tom Turner, *Sierra Club: 100 Years of Protecting Nature* (New York: Harry N. Abrams, 1991), 120; Michael McCloskey, memorandum to Lee Selna, Oct. 28, 1970; SCLDF Papers.
46. Complaint, Sierra Club vs. Walter J. Hickel, No. 51464 (N.D. Cal.) paragraph 3.
47. Brief for Petitioners, Sierra Club v. Rogers C. B. Morton et al., U.S. Supreme Court No. 70–34, filed May 8, 1971, 8.

48. Edward Lee Rogers, "Re: Sierra Club v. Hickel, 9th Cir., No. 24966," letter to Leland R. Selna Jr., Oct. 8, 1970; SCLDF Papers.
49. Bruce Terris, interview with the author, Washington, DC, Mar. 18, 2015.
50. James Moorman, interview with the author, Washington, DC, Mar. 18, 2015.
51. Brief for the Wilderness Society, Izaak Walton League of America, and Friends of the Earth as Amicus Curiae. Sierra Club v. Rogers C. B. Morton et al. U.S. Supreme Court No. 70–34, filed 14 June 1971, p. 63.
52. Tom Turner, "Who Speaks for the Future?," *Sierra Magazine* (July/Aug. 1990): 30, 67 ("Moorman appealed to Lee Selna to embrace the standing arguments articulated in the friend-of-the-court briefs, but Selna was firmly committed to the original approach").
53. Selna, interview with the author.
54. H. Donald Harris, cochairman, Sierra Club Legal Committee, "Re: Sierra Club v. Hardin (Disney)," letter to James Moorman, Esq., Center for Law and Social Policy, Apr. 21, 1971, 2; SCLDF Papers.
55. Jacques Gelin, interview with the author, Rockville, MD, Mar. 17, 2015.
56. 42 U.S.C. §4342 (establishing the three-person council).
57. Erwin N. Griswold, solicitor general, "Re: Sierra Club v. Morton No. 939, October Term, 1970," letter to Russell E. Train, Esq., chairman, May 26, 1971; Dept. of Justice Files.
58. Morton Hollander, chief, Appellate Section, Civil Division, "Re: Sierra Club v. Morton (S. Ct. No. 939, Oct. T. 1970)," memorandum to Edmund B. Clark, chief, Appellate Section, Land and Natural Resources Division, June 1, 1971; Dept. of Justice Files.
59. Shiro Kashiwa, assistant attorney general, Land and Natural Resources Division, "Sierra Club v. Morton (S. Ct. No. 939, Oct. T. 1970)," memorandum to the solicitor general, June 4, 1971; Dept. of Justice Files.
60. Erwin N. Griswold, solicitor general, "Re: Sierra Club v. Morton No. 939, October Term, 1970," letter to Russell E. Train, Esq., chairman, June 7, 1971, 1–2; Dept. of Justice Files.
61. David Watts, telephone interview with the author, Los Angeles, CA, Apr. 10, 2015 (discussing the Forest Service's concerns: even before the Court of Appeals decided the case, "everybody said that if they had standing in this case, we've got problems all over the United States with the Sierra Club. And so the idea of standing became very, very critical at that juncture").
62. Brief for Respondent, Sierra Club v. Rogers C. B. Morton et al., U.S. Supreme Court No. 70–34, filed Aug. 27, 1971, p. 9.
63. *Id.* at 10.
64. *Id.* at 9, 17 (citing brief for the Wilderness Society, Izaak Walton League of America, and Friends of the Earth as *amicus curiae*, 54–57, 62–63).
65. *Id.* at 31.

66. *Id.* at 23–24, 24.
67. Scenic Hudson Preservation Conf. v. Federal Power Commission, 354 F.2d 608 (2d Cir.1965).
68. Brief of the County of Tulare as Amicus Curiae, Sierra Club v. Rogers C. B. Morton et al., U.S. Supreme Court No. 70–34, filed Aug. 23, 1971, 10.
69. *Id.* at 6.
70. *Id.* at 6.
71. *Id.* at 2.
72. "Nader Joins Mineral King Critics," *Fresno Bee*, Aug. 26, 1971.
73. Roger Rapoport, "Disney's War Against the Wilderness," *Ramparts* (Nov. 1971): 27, 33.
74. Peter Browning, "Mickey Mouse in the Mountains," *Harper's Magazine* (Mar. 1972): 65, 69.
75. Bob Hicks, "Extending a Train to Mineral King," interoffice communication, April 8, 1971; RBH Papers.
76. Bob Hicks, "Train Access to Mineral King," interoffice communication, Dec. 30, 1971, 1; RBH Papers.
77. Michael McCloskey and Albert Hill, *Mineral King: Mass Recreation Versus Park Protection in the Sierra* (San Francisco: Sierra Club, 1971). The brochure text was included in *Patient Earth, ed.* John Harte and Robert H. Socolow (New York: Holt, Rinehart and Winston, 1971).
78. *Id.* at 8, 5, 10.
79. *Id.* at 3.
80. Tom Turner, *Wild by Law: The Sierra Club Legal Defense Fund and the Places It Has Saved* (San Francisco: Sierra Club Legal Defense Fund, 1990), 19.
81. Sierra Club Legal Defense Fund, "Active Docket," Oct. 26, 1971; RJ Papers.
82. Edward P. Cliff, chief, letter to Honorable Don R. Clausen, Nov. 19, 1971; Ronald Reagan Law Library Files.
83. United Press International, "Justice Hugo Black Dies at 85; Served on Court 34 Years," Sept. 25, 1971.
84. Lesley Oelsner, "Harlan Dies at 72; On Court 16 Years," *New York Times*, Dec. 30, 1971.
85. Leo Rennert, "Mineral King Fate Is Up to Two New Justices," *Fresno Bee*, Oct. 17, 1971.
86. Leland R. Selna Jr., letter to H. Donald Harris, Esq., Oct. 19, 1971; SCLDF Papers.

Chapter 10

1. The audio recording of the oral argument is available at https://www.oyez.org/cases/1971/70-34. A transcript of the hearing is available at https://www.supremecourt.gov/pdfs/transcripts/1971/70-34_11-17-1971.pdf. Quotes used in

this chapter have been corrected, where necessary, to more accurately reflect the actual words used.

2. See, e.g., "A Dam in Kentucky Opposed by Douglas Delayed 6 Months," *New York Times*, Jan. 21, 1968.
3. M. Margaret McKeown, "Supreme Court Justice William O. Douglas Was Not Just a Legal Giant, But Also a Powerful Environmentalist," *Seattle Times*, Aug. 16, 2018. See also Adam M. Sowards, "Protecting American Lands with Justice William O. Douglas," *George Wright Forum* 32, no. 2 (2015): 165.
4. William O. Douglas, *A Wilderness Bill of Rights* (Boston: Little, Brown, 1965).
5. See, generally, Adam M. Sowards, *The Environmental Justice: William O. Douglas and American Conservation* (Corvallis: Oregon State University Press, 2009).
6. "Memo on WOD and the Sierra Club," Jan. 27, 1971; William O. Douglas Papers, Library of Congress.
7. *Id.*
8. *Id.*
9. Bob Woodward and Scott Armstrong, *The Brethren: Inside the Supreme Court* (New York: Simon and Schuster, 1979), 174.
10. Transcript, Sierra Club v. Morton (No. 70–34) (Nov. 17, 1971), 4–5.
11. *Id.* at 6–7.
12. *Id.* at 10–11.
13. *Id.* at 11.
14. 425 F.2d 543 (D.C. Cir. 1969).
15. *Id.*
16. *Id.* at 12.
17. *Id.* at 13.
18. *Id.* at 15.
19. *Id.* at 16.
20. *Id.* at 19–20.
21. *Id.* at 21, 22.
22. Ira E. Stoll, "Ginsburg Blasts Harvard Law," *Harvard Crimson*, July 23, 1993; "At the Supreme Court: A Conversation with Justice Ruth Bader Ginsburg," *Stanford Lawyer*, Nov. 11, 2013.
23. Transcript, Sierra Club v. Morton (No. 70–34) (Nov. 17, 1971), 23.
24. *Id.* at 25.
25. *Id.*
26. *Id.* at 26.
27. *Id.* at 27.
28. *Id.* at 29.
29. *Id.*
30. *Id.*
31. *Id.* at 33, 34–35.

32. *Id.* at 36.
33. *Id.* at 37.
34. *Id.*
35. *Id.* at 39. See J. Rafferty, memorandum of telephone call, Nov. 11, 1971; SNP Files (noting a call from "Watts" [presumably lawyer David Watts] "looking for benefits to the Park as a result of the road" and advising "no apparent benefits other than easier and faster response to forest fires").
36. *Id.* at 40.
37. *Id.* at 42.
38. *Id.* at 44.
39. *Id.* at 44, 45.
40. William O. Douglas, conference notes, Sierra Club v. Morton, No. 70–34, Nov. 19, 1971; William O. Douglas Papers.
41. Harry Blackmun, conference notes, Sierra Club v. Morton, No. 70–34, undated; Harry A. Blackmun Papers.
42. Douglas, conference notes, Sierra Club v. Morton.
43. *Id.*
44. Blackmun, conference notes, Sierra Club v. Morton.
45. Douglas, conference notes, Sierra Club v. Morton.
46. Harry A. Blackmun, pre-argument memorandum on Sierra Club v. Morton, Secretary. No. 70–34, 2.
47. Douglas, conference notes, Sierra Club v. Morton.
48. 401 U.S. 402, 404 (1971).
49. See http://www.naacpldf.org/thurgood-marshall; NAACP v. State of Ala. ex rel. Patterson, 357 U.S. 449 (1958) (standing to attack an Alabama statute requiring unincorporated associations to produce membership lists).
50. See Roger Goldman and David Gallen, *Thurgood Marshall* (New York: Carroll and Graf, 1992), 80 (discussing the intricacies of standing involved in challenging state enforcement of restrictive racial covenants).
51. Memorandum re Sierra Club v. Morton, 70–34; Thurgood Marshall Papers. See also Robert B. Percival, "Environmental Law in the Supreme Court: Highlights from the Marshall Papers," 23 Envtl. L. Rptr. 10606 (1993) (discussing the law clerk's memorandum).
52. Douglas, conference notes, Sierra Club v. Morton.
53. Potter Stewart, First Draft Opinion, Sierra Club v. Morton, No. 70–34, circulated Feb. 14, 1972, 1, 3–4; Potter Stewart Papers.
54. *Id.* at 4, 5.
55. 5 U.S.C. §702.
56. Association of Data Processing Service Organizations, Inc. v. Camp, 397 U.S. 150, 152–53 (1970).
57. Stewart, First Draft Opinion, Sierra Club v. Morton, 7.
58. *Id.* at 7–8.

59. *Id.* at 8.
60. *Id.* at 12, citing NAACP v. Button, 371 U.S. 415, 428 (1963).
61. *Id.* 12–13 and n. 16 ("the 'trap' does not exist").
62. *Id.* at 12n15.
63. Charles F. Wilkinson, "Justice Douglas and the Public Lands," in *"He Shall Not Pass This Way Again": The Legacy of William O. Douglas*, ed. Stephen L. Wasby (Pittsburgh: University of Pittsburgh Press, 1990), 244 ("The dissent in *Sierra Club v. Morton* . . . has had no effect at all on the law of standing").
64. William O. Douglas, Eighth Draft Dissent, Sierra Club v. Morton, No. 70–34, circulated Feb. 14, 1972; William O. Douglas Papers.
65. Christopher Stone, "Should Trees Have Standing? Towards Legal Rights for Natural Objects," 45 So. Cal. L. Rev. 450 (1972). See M. Margaret McKeown, "The Trees are Still Standing: The Backstory of *Sierra Club v. Morton*," 44 J. Sup. Ct. History 189 (2019).
66. Douglas, Eighth Draft Dissent, Sierra Club v. Morton, 2–3.
67. *Id.* at 4.
68. *Id.* at 5.
69. *Id.* at 7.
70. *Id.* 8–9.
71. *Id.* at 11.
72. Thurgood Marshall, "Re: No. 74-34—Sierra Club v. Morton," memorandum to Justice Potter Stewart, Sierra Club v. Morton, No. 70–34, Feb. 17, 1972; Thurgood Marshall Papers.
73. "Sierra Club Effort to Bar Disney Complex at Mineral King Is Set Back by High Court," *Wall Street Journal*, April 20, 1972.
74. William J. Brennan Jr., "Re: No. 74-34—Sierra Club v. Morton," memorandum to Justice Potter Stewart, Feb. 15, 1972; William J. Brennan Jr. Papers.
75. William J. Brennan Jr., Second Draft Dissent, No. 74-34—Sierra Club v. Morton, circulated Mar. 30, 1972; William J. Brennan Jr. Papers. The first draft was kept as an internal document and not circulated to the court.
76. *Id.* at 3.
77. William J. Brennan Jr., Third Draft Dissent, No. 74-34—Sierra Club v. Morton, circulated Mar. 31, 1972; William J. Brennan Jr. Papers.
78. Byron White, memorandum re: No. 70–34 Sierra Club v. Morton, April 1, 1972; Byron R. White Papers.
79. Woodward and Armstrong, *The Brethren*, 164n*.
80. See, generally, Peter Manus, "The Blackbird Whistling—The Silence Just After: Evaluating the Environmental Legacy of Justice Blackmun," 85 Iowa L. Rev. 429 (2000).
81. Linda Greenhouse, *Becoming Justice Blackmun* (New York: Times Books, 2005), 31.
82. Harry A. Blackmun, H.A.B. memorandum re No. 70–34—Sierra Club v. Morton, Secretary, Nov. 15, 1971; Harry A. Blackmun Papers.

83. Harry A. Blackmun, First Draft Dissent. No. 74–34—Sierra Club v. Morton, circulated Mar. 30, 1972, 1; Harry A. Blackmun Papers.
84. *Id.*
85. *Id.* at 2 (quoting majority opinion).
86. *Id.* at 3.
87. *Id.*
88. *Id.* at 5.
89. *Id.* at 5.
90. Harry A. Blackmun, letter to Professor Scot Powe, Apr. 28, 1972; Harry A. Blackmun Papers. Chief Justice Burger had warned him "not to wear his heart on his sleeve" in another case; see Greenhouse, *Becoming Justice Blackmun*, 114.
91. William J. Brennan Jr., Fourth Draft Dissent, No. 74–34—Sierra Club v. Morton, circulated Apr. 11, 1972; William J. Brennan Jr. Papers.
92. William Jeffress, telephone interview with the author, Los Angeles, Nov. 7, 2014. Mr. Jeffress was law clerk to Justice Stewart at the time and the principal clerk working on the case.
93. Potter Stewart, Fourth Draft Opinion, Sierra Club v. Morton, No. 70–34, circulated Apr. 11, 1972, 8; Potter Stewart Papers.
94. *Id.* at 14.

Chapter 11

1. Louise Nichols, Conservation Dept., Sierra Club, letter to John W. Rettenmayer, Jan. 24, 1972 (noting that Selna "returned from Washington quite optimistic about the court's decision").
2. John P. MacKenzie, "Sierra Club Asks Wider Power to Sue," *Washington Post*, Nov. 18, 1971.
3. Ron Taylor, "Sierra Club Vows to Continue Fight Against Mineral Kings [*sic*]." *Fresno Bee*, Apr. 20, 1972.
4. Sierra Club, press release, "Sierra Club Sees Mineral King Decision as a Technical Rebuff, Not the Final Chapter," Apr. 19, 1972; Sierra Club Members Papers.
5. Taylor, "Sierra Club Vows to Continue Fight."
6. United Press International, "Club Eyes New Mineral King," *Bakersfield Californian*, Apr. 21, 1972.
7. Taylor, "Sierra Club Vows to Continue Fight."
8. U.S. Forest Service, press release, "Supreme Court Decision on Mineral King," April 19, 1972; SNP Files.
9. "Club Sees Invitation by Court to Refile Its Plea," *Los Angeles Times*, Apr. 20, 1972.
10. Thomas J. Foley, "Sierra Club Loses High Court Bid to Block Ski Resort," *Los Angeles Times*, Apr. 20, 1972.

11. "The Sierra Club Loses on Mineral King," *San Francisco Examiner*, Apr. 19, 1972. See also United Press International, "Sierra Club Loses Suit on Disney Plan," *Los Angeles Herald Examiner*, Apr. 19, 1972.
12. John P. MacKenzie, "Ecologists Lose Suit but Win," *Washington Post*, Apr. 20, 1972.
13. Foley, "Sierra Club Loses High Court Bid."
14. William M. Blair, "Supreme Court Sets Aside Suit of Sierra Club to Block Resort," *New York Times*, Apr. 20, 1972.
15. William O. Douglas, "Who Speaks for Nature's Voiceless," *Los Angeles Times*, Apr. 23, 1972.
16. Sierra Club, press release, "Sierra Club Sees Mineral King Decision as a Technical Rebuff."
17. Elizabeth Fullenwider, Conservation Dept., Sierra Club, letter to Elaine McAndrews, June 9, 1972.
18. "Sierra Club Effort to Bar Disney Complex at Mineral King Is Set Back by High Court," *Wall Street Journal*, Apr. 20, 1972.
19. Sierra Club, press release, "Sierra Club Sees Mineral King Decision as a Technical Rebuff," 2.
20. Tom Turner, "Mineral King: Did We Win or Lose?" *Not Man Apart* (June 1972): 7, 10.
21. 42 U.S.C. §4332(C).
22. W. S. Davis, chief, "Mineral King Environmental Statement," memorandum to Ray Housely, director of recreation, Jan. 26, 1972; NARA II Forest Service Files.
23. Forest Service, Region Five, U.S. Dept. of Agriculture, *Environmental Statement, Mineral King, A Planned Year-Round Recreation Development, Sequoia National Forest, California*, draft, Jan. 1972, 21; NARA II Forest Service Files.
24. Russell P. McRarey, acting deputy chief, "Mineral King Environmental Statement (Your Memo 1/26)," memorandum to regional forester, R-5, May 3, 1972, 1–2; NARA I Forest Service Files.
25. Earl L. Butz, secretary, letter to Honorable Rogers C. B. Morton, secretary, June 20, 1972; NARA II Secretary of Agriculture Files.
26. Walt Disney Productions, *DisneyNews*, remarks by E. Cardon Walker, president, Walt Disney Productions, Visalia, California, May 3, 1972, 3–4; Sierra Club Records.
27. *Id.* at 6–7.
28. *Id.* at 5, 7.
29. *Id.* at 5.
30. *Id.* at 2–3.
31. *Id.* at 7–8
32. Walter A. Williams, "News Conference—Mineral King Proposal," memorandum to superintendent, May 17, 1972, 1; SNP Files. Williams stated that he

attended the press conference, and his memorandum to the superintendent of Sequoia and Kings Canyon National Parks set forth a detailed synopsis of what had transpired.

33. Walt Disney Productions, *DisneyNews*, remarks by E. Cardon Walker, 9.
34. *Id.*
35. Earl Wallace, "County Officials See Sierra Club as Loser," *Visalia Times-Delta*, May 4, 1972 (noting that "Disney has arranged for full page advertising to appear in major daily newspapers across the state tomorrow telling the firm's story").
36. Walt Disney Productions, advertisement, "I Remember Because I Was There with Walt Disney at Mineral King," *San Francisco Examiner*, May 8, 1972.
37. *Id.*
38. Williams, "News Conference—Mineral King Proposal," 2.
39. Walt Disney Productions, advertisement, "I Remember.".
40. Williams, "News Conference—Mineral King Proposal," 1.
41. Bob Hicks, "Train Access to Mineral King," interoffice communication, Dec. 30, 1971, 1; RBH Papers.
42. Williams, "News Conference—Mineral King Proposal," 1.
43. Douglas R. Leisz, "Statement of Douglas R. Leisz, Regional Forester, Visalia, California," May 3, 1972, 1; SCLDF Files.
44. Forest Service, Region 5, "Mineral King Reaches a Turning Point," *California Log*, May 10, 1972, 2.
45. Leisz, "Statement of Douglas R. Leisz," 3.
46. Merle E. Stitt, acting director, Western Region, letter to Edward Savage, May 11, 1972, 1; SNP Files.
47. Daniel J. Tobin Jr., acting director, Western Region, letter to Edward Savage, May 23, 1972; SNP Files.
48. Earl Wallace, "Mineral King Railway Proposed," *Visalia Times-Delta*, May 5, 1972.
49. Donn B. Tatum, chairman of the board, letter to Calvin E. Baldwin, county counsel, May 31, 1962, 1–2; RBH Papers.
50. Robert B. Hicks, letter to John A. Leisure, forest supervisor, Mar. 28, 1975, 3; NARA I Forest Service Files (if Park Service authority existed to grant the permit, "it apparently would have to be revocable, thereby undoubtedly prohibiting any private financing of an access system").
51. See, e.g., Walt Disney Productions, letter to Secretary [Orville] Freeman, "Observations Made by Members of the Staff of Walt Disney Productions Regarding the August 10, 1967 Letter from Secretary of the Interior Stewart L. Udall to Yourself," undated [1967], 4; NARA II Secretary of Agriculture Files.
52. Roy O. Disney, president, letter to Stewart L. Udall, secretary of the interior,

Sept. 21, 1967, 3; NARA II National Park Service Files (citing two previous Disney reports studying those possibilities).

53. Williams, "News Conference—Mineral King Proposal," 3.
54. "New Developments on Mineral King," editorial, *Los Angeles Times*, May 7, 1972.
55. *Id.*
56. E. Cardon Walker, president, Walt Disney Productions, letter to the editor, *Los Angeles Times*, May 13, 1972.
57. Ron Taylor, "Disney May Cancel Mineral King Plans," *Fresno Bee*, May 14, 1972.
58. Sierra Club, press release, "Sierra Club Will Still Oppose Mineral King Development," May 3, 1972; SCLDF Files.
59. Sierra Club, minutes, Annual Organizational Meeting of the Board of Directors, May 6–7, 1972, 19.
60. Sierra Club, transcript, Sierra Club press conference, June 6, 1969 (original in Bancroft Library; copy in author's possession).
61. Sierra Club, minutes, Meeting of the Annual Organizational Meeting, 19.
62. *Id.* at 20.
63. *Id.*
64. Sierra Club, staff report, "Mineral King: The Battle Goes On," *Sierra Club Bulletin* (May 1972): 26.
65. Notice of Motion and Motion to Amend Complaint, Sierra Club v. Morton, No. 51464 WTS (N.D. Cal. 1969), June 2, 1972, 1–2.
66. *Id.* at 3–5.
67. Defendants' Memorandum of Points and Authorities in Opposition to Plaintiffs' Motion to Amend the Complaint, Sierra Club v. Morton, No. 51464 WTS (N.D. Cal. 1969), June 22, 1972, 3.
68. Plaintiff's Reply Memorandum in Support of Motion to Amend the Complaint, Sierra Club v. Morton, No. 51464 WTS (N.D. Cal. 1969), June 29, 1972, 5.
69. Memorandum of Decision on Plaintiff's Motion for Leave to Amend Complaint, Sierra Club v. Morton, No. 51464 WTS (N.D. Cal. 1969), July 6, 1972, 2.
70. James W. Moorman, "Re: Mineral King," memorandum, July 28, 1972; Sierra Club Members Papers.
71. Plaintiffs' Memorandum of Points and Authorities in Opposition to Defendants' Motion to Dismiss the Amended Complaint, Sierra Club v. Morton, No. 51464 WTS (N.D. Cal. 1969), Aug. 29, 1972, 3.
72. *Id.* at 30.
73. *Id.* at 31–33.
74. James W. Moorman, interview by Ted Hudson, Sierra Club Oral History Series, 1994, 75, at https://archive.org/details/attorneyenvironmentoomoorrich/page/75.
75. Memorandum of Decision, Sierra Club v. Morton, No. 51464 WTS (N.D. Cal. 1969), Sept. 12, 1972, 2–3.

76. *Id.* at 3.
77. James W. Moorman, "Mineral King," memorandum to Sierra Club and Sierra Club Legal Defense Fund officers, Sept. 14, 1972; SCLDF Files.
78. John D. Hoffman, "Re: Mineral King," letter to Professor Christopher Stone, Sept. 3, 1974, 2; SCLDF Files.
79. "An OK for Mineral King Road Ban," *San Francisco Chronicle*, May 19, 1972.
80. "Mineral King Road: Assembly Votes to Kill Half of Proposed Route," *Fresno Bee*, May 31, 1972. See also United Press International, "Vote to Ban Road into Mineral King," *San Francisco Chronicle*, May 31, 1972.
81. Norman B. Livermore Jr., interview by Ann Lage and Gabrielle Morris, Sierra Club Oral History Series, 1981–82, 78, at http://digitalassets.lib.berkeley.edu/roho/ucb/text/livermore_norman.pdf.
82. N. B. Livermore Jr., letter to Donn Tatum, Aug. 2, 1972; Norman B. Livermore Jr. Papers.
83. George B. Hartzog Jr., "Mineral King," memorandum to assistant secretary for Fish and Wildlife and Parks, Aug. 15, 1972; George B. Hartzog Papers.
84. Livermore, interview, Sierra Club Oral History Series, 1981–82, 81.
85. *Id.* at 81, 82.
86. Ford B. Ford, assistant secretary for resources, letter to George B. Hartzog Jr., Aug. 30, 1972; George B. Hartzog Papers.
87. Ronald Reagan, press release, "Mineral King," Aug. 18, 1972; Sierra Club Records.
88. United States Ski Association, press release, "Mineral King," Aug. 23, 1972; MKPS.

Chapter 12

1. Peter J. Wyckoff, "Environmental Statement, Mineral King," memorandum to Bob Hicks, Aug. 1, 1972, 1–2; RBH Papers.
2. Bob Hicks, "Telephone Conversation with Pete Wyckoff, July 17, 1972," inter-office communication to file, July 17, 1972; RBH Papers.
3. Forest Service, U.S. Dept. of Agriculture, "Minutes of Inter-Agency Meeting Regarding Mineral King Environmental Statement," undated, 5; NARA I (noting that many in the government group thought that the target date for completion in about a year "was optimistic").
4. M. R. James, forest supervisor, "Mineral King Environmental Statement," memorandum to regional forester, July 18, 1972; SNP Files.
5. Earl L. Butz, secretary, letter to Rogers C. B. Morton, secretary of the interior, Dec. 26, 1972; SNP Files.
6. Nathaniel P. Reed, assistant secretary of the interior, letter to Earl L. Butz (ad-

dressee unidentified on letter itself), Feb. 1, 1973, 1; NARA I Secretary of the Interior Files.

7. *Id.* at 2.
8. Nathaniel P. Reed, memorandum to Associate Director Bulett, quoted in John C. Raftery, acting superintendent, Sequoia and Kings Canyon, "Mineral King Transportation Analysis," memorandum to regional director, Western Region, from acting superintendent, Sequoia and Kings Canyon, Sept. 21, 1973; SNP Files.
9. Bob Hicks, "Proposed Compromise for Development of Mineral King," interoffice communication, July 3, 1973, 1; RBH Papers.
10. Robert B. Hicks, letter to W. S. Davis, Feb. 13, 1973, 2–3; NARA I Files.
11. *Id.* at 3.
12. W. S. Davis, chief, Division of Recreation, letter to Robert B. Hicks, Feb. 16, 1973; NARA.
13. Alan M. Voorhees and Associates, Inc., *Mineral King Transportation Analysis*, June 1973; NARA I.
14. U.S. Forest Service, "Multimodal Access to Mineral King," 1973, 1; RBH Papers.
15. Robert B. Hicks, letter to Douglas R. Leisz, regional forester, Oct. 13, 1973; RBH Papers.
16. Philip Fradkin, "Planned Mineral King Resort Appears Doomed," *Los Angeles Times*, Oct. 23, 1973.
17. John C. Raftery, acting superintendent, Sequoia National Park, "Mineral King Transportation Analysis," memorandum to regional director, Western Region, Sept. 21, 1973; SNP Files (noting that "[w]e believe that the right-of-way now in use is not owned by the County").
18. M. R. James, forest supervisor, letter to Mr. Raymond Sherwin, Apr. 27, 1973, 2; NARA II Forest Service Files.
19. J. M. McCloskey, "Notes of Conference with Supervisor, Sequoia National Forest, May 31, 1973."
20. "Minutes of Sierra Club–Forest Service Meeting," May 31, 1973, 5; Sierra Club Records. While authorship is unclear, the content seems to indicate that it was a Sierra Club document distributed to all in attendance, including Forest Service personnel.
21. See, e.g., Philip Fradkin, "Disney Studying Lake Near Truckee for Sierra Resort," *Los Angeles Times*, Sept. 3, 1974; "Disney Eyes Tahoe Area Site; Mineral King Resort 'Not Out,'" *Fresno Bee*, May 16, 1974.
22. United Press International, "Sierra Club, Disney Reveal Project Accord," *Los Angeles Times*, Dec. 19, 1974.
23. See, e.g., Robert A. Jones, "How Disney Resort Plans Went Awry," *Los Angeles Times*, Mar. 22, 1978.

24. A. E. Hall Jr., chief, Fisheries Habitat Branch, "Mineral King Environmental Impact Statement: Fish and Wildlife," Mar. 29, 1973; NARA II Forest Service Files.
25. Peter J. Wyckoff, "Mineral King Preliminary Draft Environmental Statement," letter to Robert Hicks, May 29, 1974; NARA I Forest Service Files.
26. Douglas R. Leisz, regional forester, letter to W. S. Davis, undated; NARA II Forest Service Files.
27. Michael McCloskey, "Preliminary Draft Mineral King Environmental Statement," letter to John Leasher [*sic*; correct spelling is Leasure], forest supervisor, July 16, 1974, 5; SCLDF Files.
28. Ronald J. Cayo, letter to Laurens H. Silver, Esq., Sept. 18, 1973; SCLDF Papers.
29. Robert B. Hicks, letter to John Leasure, supervisor, Sequoia National Forest, July 25, 1974, 8; NARA I Forest Service Files.
30. Jim Stewart, "Mineral King Draft Environmental Statement," interoffice communication, Oct. 25, 1974; RBH Papers.
31. *Id.* at 1–2.
32. *Id.* at 2.
33. *Id.* at 3, 2.
34. *Id.* at 5–6.
35. The Solicitor's Office within the Department of the Interior had examined this issue. Under the 1973 decision of the United States Court of Appeals for the District of Columbia Circuit in Wilderness Society v. Morton, 479 F.2d 842 (D.C. Cir. 1973), cert. denied 411 U.S. 917, there was a strong argument that a short-term permit had to be revocable in fact, not just in theory. See associate solicitor, Conservation and Wildlife, "Sierra Club v. Morton, Civil No. 51464 WTS (D.N.D. Cal., filed June 5, 1969); A Reexamination of the Revocability Requirement for the Special Use Permit To Be Issued by the National Park Service," memorandum to assistant secretary, Fish and Wildlife, undated draft (likely 1973 or 1974 from content); SCLDF Papers.
36. *Id.* at 7.
37. Philip Fradkin, "Mineral King Valley Development Backed," *Los Angeles Times*, Jan. 13, 1975.
38. Ron Taylor, "Study Pictures Outsize Resort," *Fresno Bee*, Jan. 12, 1975.
39. U.S. Forest Service, "Analysis of Mineral King Comments Is Completed," *Forest Service News*, May 23, 1975; Sierra Club Records.
40. Resources Agency of California, "Re: Draft Environmental Statement, Mineral King Recreational Development," letter to Douglas R. Leisz, regional forester, Mar. 28, 1975, 2.
41. Nathaniel Reed, assistant secretary of the interior, letter to [Douglas] Leisz, Apr. 4, 1975,1–2; SCLDF Papers.
42. King Patrick Leonard, division head, Environmental Section, Tulare County

Planning Department, letter to Douglas R. Leisz, regional forester, Mar. 6, 1975, 6; SCLDF Papers.

43. Robert B. Hicks, letter to John A. Leasure, forest supervisor, Mar. 28, 1975, 3, 4–5; NARA II Forest Service Files.

44. John A. Leasure, forest supervisor, "Preparation of Mineral King Final Environmental Statement," memorandum to regional forester, May 28, 1975; NARA II Forest Service Files (summarizing a proposed revision to the Mineral King project proposal agreed to at a meeting of May 14).

45. John A. Leasure, forest supervisor, "Meeting with Walt Disney Productions Concerning Mineral King Proposal," memorandum to regional forester, May 27, 1975; SCLDF Papers.

46. Peter J. Wyckoff, letter to Charles A. Baker, Dec. 8, 1975; NARA II Forest Service Files ("[W]e have spent considerable time working with [Disney] on a modified development proposal").

47. Michael McCloskey, executive director, "Conversation with Jim Stewart at Walt Disney Productions," memorandum to Larry Silver, SCLDF, Dec. 11, 1975, 1–2; SCLDF Papers.

48. U.S. Forest Service, *Sequoia National Forest News*, news story version, "Revised Mineral King Development Proposal Announced," Feb. 26, 1976; NARA II Forest Service Files. U.S. Forest Service, *Sequoia National Forest News*, feature story version, "Revised Mineral King Development Proposal Announced," Feb. 26, 1976; Sierra Club Members Papers.

49. Joan Sweeney, "Skiing: Forest Service Proposes Cut in Visitors to Mineral King," *Los Angeles Times*, Mar. 11, 1976.

50. Sierra Club, press release, "Mineral King Project Would Damage Sequoia National Park and Wildlife Refuge," Apr. 1, 1976; Sierra Club Members Papers.

51. Jack Cavanaugh, "Polly Lauder Tunney, 100, Fighter's Widow, Dies," *New York Times*, Apr. 15, 2008.

52. Jean Merl, "John Tunney, California Senator Who Worked for Environmental Protection and Civil Rights, Dies at 83," *Los Angeles Times*, Jan. 12, 2008.

53. George L. Baker, "M-K Development Opposed by Cranston," *Fresno Bee*, Apr. 15, 1976.

54. Claire Dedrick, secretary for resources, letter to Douglas R. Leisz, Sept. 16, 1976; SCLDF Papers.

55. Office of Congressman John Krebs, news release, Mar. 15, 1976; Tulare County Library, Mineral King Archives.

56. Office of Congressman John Krebs, news release, Mar. 15, 1976, 6; Tulare County Library, Mineral King Archives.

57. See, e.g., Doug Hoagland, "Harrell Raps Krebs' Mineral King Stand," *Visalia Times-Delta*, Mar. 16, 1976.

58. Associate director, National Park Service, "H.R. 6882—Addition of Mineral King Valley to Sequoia National Park," memorandum to legislative counsel, Mar. 1, 1976; NARA II National Park Service Files.
59. National Park Service, Dept. of the Interior, *Feasibility Report, Mineral King, California*, 43; SCLDF Files.
60. Associate director, National Park Service, "H.R. 6882," 1, 3.
61. James Moorman, "Mineral King," memorandum to John Hoffman, Larry Silver, and Mike McCloskey, Aug. 18, 1976, 2; Sierra Club Members Files.
62. John Hoffman, interview with the author, Corte Madera, CA, Jan. 18, 2019.
63. Doug Hoagland, "Sierra Club Lawsuit Dismissed," *Visalia Times-Delta*, Mar. 16, 1977.
64. John D. Hoffman, "Re: Mineral King," memorandum to Sierra Club Conservation Administration Committee, Apr. 7, 1977; SCLDF Papers.
65. "Sierra Club Shelves Mineral King Suit," *Fresno Bee*, May 31, 1977.
66. Ron Taylor, "Mineral King Compromise," *Fresno Bee*, July 8, 1977.
67. Robert A. Jones, "Mineral King Resort Proposal Resurrected," *Los Angeles Times*, Sept. 19, 1977.
68. Skiers to Keep Mineral King Natural, "Recent Conversation with James Stewart of Disney," Newsletter #6, Oct. 7, 1977; Ed Pell, "Notes of Conversation with Jim Stewart, Disney VP, 9/23/77," undated; UCLA Sierra Club Files.
69. George L. Baker, "Interior Opposes Newest Proposal for Mineral King," *Fresno Bee*, Nov. 24, 1977.
70. Doug Hoagland, "New Mineral King Plan Unveiled," *Visalia Times-Delta*, Jan. 12, 1978; United Press International, "U.S. Offers Scaled-Down Resort Plan," *Los Angeles Times*, Jan. 13, 1978.
71. Larry E. Moss, "On Mineral King and the Kern Plateau," *Sierra Club Bulletin* (Oct. 1973): 43, 46.
72. John Jacobs, *A Rage for Justice: The Passion and Politics of Phillip Burton* (Berkeley: University of California Press, 1995), 352–53.
73. Judith Robinson, *You're in Your Mother's Arms: The Life and Legacy of Congressman Phil Burton* (San Francisco: M. J. Robinson, 1994), 403.
74. *Id.* at 406.
75. Carl Cannon, "Wheeler-Dealer for the Powerless," *Washington Post*, Apr. 17, 1983.
76. Ben Pershing, "A Look Back at Congress' Most Memorable Leadership Battles," *Roll Call*, June 19, 2014, at https://www.rollcall.com/news/record-shows-leadership-elections-make-and-break-political-careers (discussing the 1976 race for majority leader).
77. Nancy Ingalsbee, telephone interview with the author, Los Angeles, May 18, 2017.
78. Nancy Ingalsbee, testimony, "House of Representatives Subcommittee on

National Parks and Insular Affairs—Hearing October 27, 1977," 3; Sierra Club Records.

79. Mary Ann Eriksen, "Testimony of Mary Ann Eriksen, Southern California Representative, Sierra Club, and Southern California Vice President, Federation of Western Outdoor Clubs on H.R. 1771, The Addition of Mineral King to Sequoia National Park," Oct. 27, 1977, 3; Sierra Club Records.
80. "Statement of United Brotherhood of Carpenters and Joiners of America Before Subcommittee on National Parks and Recreation. House Interior Committee H.R. 1771-Mineral King," Oct. 27, 1977, 2; Sierra Club Records.
81. Jerome Waldie, "Testimony of Jerome Waldie representing Friends of the Earth on H.R. 1771 before Subcommittee on National Parks and Insular Affairs, Committee on Interior and Insular Affairs," Oct. 27, 1977, 2; Sierra Club Records.
82. T. Mark O'Reilly, "Statement of T. Mark O'Reilly, Director of Public Relations, United States Ski Association," undated; Sierra Club Records.
83. David Beck and Susan Beck, letter to Honorable John Krebs, Oct. 22, 1977, 2; UCLA Sierra Club Records.
84. Subcommittee on National Parks and Insular Affairs, transcript of proceedings, Hearing Held Before Subcommittee, Oct. 27, 1977, 70. List of Witnesses, Subcommittee on National Parks and Insular Affairs, Oct. 17, 1977, 2.
85. "Statement of John Krebs, Member of Congress, Before the U.S. House of Representatives Subcommittee on National Parks and Insular Affairs," Oct. 27, 1977, 9; Sierra Club Records.
86. "Statement of John Krebs, Member of Congress, Before the U.S. House of Representatives Subcommittee on National Parks and Insular Affairs," Oct. 27, 1977, 9, 6; Sierra Club Records.
87. Senator Alan Cranston, "Statement by Senator Cranston Before the House Interior Committee Parks and Recreation Subcommittee on H.R. 1771," Oct. 27, 1977, 3.
88. Walt Disney Productions, "Statement for the Interior and Insular Affairs Committee—National Parks and Insular Affairs Subcommittee—Hearings on H.R. 1771 Presented by James L. Stewart—Vice President, Corporate Relations, Walt Disney Productions." Oct. 27, 1977; Sierra Club Records.
89. Transcript, testimony of James Stewart, Hearing before the Subcommittee on National Parks and Insular Affairs of the Committee on Interior and Insular Affairs, Oct. 27, 1977, 102.
90. John Fogarty, "Sharp Debate over Mineral King's Future," *San Francisco Chronicle*, Oct. 28, 1977.
91. J. Y. Smith, "Outspoken U.S. Senator S. I. Hayakawa Dies at 85," *Washington Post*, Feb. 28, 1992.
92. Gladwin Hill, "Carter Plan Opposes a 'Disneyland North,'" *New York Times*, Jan. 26, 1978.

93. Dept. of the Interior, news release, "Administration Recommends Incorporation of Mineral King into Sequoia National Park," Jan. 26, 1978; SNP Files.
94. M. Rupert Cutler, "Statement of M. Rupert Cutler, Assistant Secretary for Conservation, Research and Education, Before the Subcommittee on National Parks and Insular Affairs, House of Representatives, Relating to H.R. 1771 and H.R. 1772 Which Would Transfer the Mineral King Valley of the Sequoia National Forest, Calif., to the Sequoia National Park," Jan. 26, 1978, 3; SNP Files.
95. William J. Whalen, "Statement by the Department of the Interior Before the Subcommittee on Parks and Insular Affairs, House Committee on Interior and Insular Affairs, on H.R. 1771 and Other Bills Concerning the Mineral King Valley, California," Jan. 26, 1978; SNP Files.
96. Hot Sheet, U.S. Forest Service, California Region, "Administration Supports Mineral King's Addition to Sequoia National Park," Jan. 27, 1978; NARA II Forest Service Files.
97. "Disney Raps Action on Mineral King," *San Francisco Chronicle*, Feb. 16, 1978; see also "Disney Chief Hits Mineral King Decision," *Los Angeles Times*, Feb. 16, 1978.
98. Edmund G. Brown Jr., governor, letter to John H. Krebs, member of Congress, Feb. 14, 1978; SNP Files.
99. Jacobs, *A Rage for Justice*, 352, 365.
100. Paul Houston, "House Oks Parks Measure; Burton Tactics Criticized," *Los Angeles Times*, July 13, 1978.
101. Advertisement, "Mr. President, Senators and Members of Congress, as Citizens of California's 17th Congressional District, We Want You to Know," *Washington Post*, Apr. 28, 1978.
102. Senator Alan Cranston, "Statement by Senator Alan Cranston Before the Senate Energy and Natural Resources Committee Subcommittee on Parks and Recreation in Support of S.88, A Bill to Add Mineral King to Sequoia National Park," Apr. 28, 1978, 3; Samuel I. Hayakawa Papers.
103. Roberta Hornig, "Rep. Burton Out to Save Parks Bill: He's a One-Man Conference Committee," *Washington Star*, Oct. 12, 1978.
104. Jacobs, *A Rage for Justice*, 374.
105. Doug Underwood, "Mineral King Downhill Skiing Axed," *Visalia Times-Delta*, Oct. 13, 1978.
106. Ingalsbee, interview with the author.
107. United States Ski Association, "Cranston 'Walks Out' on Skiers," *Far West Ski News*, Oct. 17, 1978.
108. Ingalsbee, interview with the author.
109. Jacobs, *A Rage for Justice*, 377.
110. Seth S. King, "President Signs a Bill for Record Spending of $1.2 Billion on 100 Parks, Rivers, Historic Sites and Trails," *New York Times*, Nov. 12, 1978.

Epilogue

1. Oliver Houck, "Unfinished Stories," 2002, 73 U. Colo. L. Rev. 867, 909.
2. James Salzman and J. B. Ruhl, "New Kids on the Block—A Survey of Practitioner Views on Important Cases in Environmental and Natural Resources Law," 2010, 25 Nat. Resources & Env't 45 (ranking the case seventh); James Salzman and J. B. Ruhl, "Who's Number One?" Nov.–Dec. 2009, Env't Forum (ranking it eighth in a 2009 survey and fourth in a 2001 survey). In the 2009 survey, academics ranked it fourth while practitioners ranked it third.
3. A search on Westlaw reveals that between 1972 and 1975, ninety-five environmental cases cited the *Sierra Club v. Morton* decision. Of those, seventy-three mentioned standing. Fifty-nine of those cases found that the plaintiffs had standing to sue; fourteen did not. During the same period, forty-one cases in the state courts cited the case.
4. 504 U.S. 555, 560–61 (1992).
5. 549 U.S. 497, 524 (2007).
6. David B. Spence, "Paradox Lost: Logic, Morality, and the Foundations of Environmental Law in the Twenty-first Century," 20 Colum. J. Envtl. L. 145, 168 (1995) (citing growth in environmental organizations in the 1980s ranging from 9 percent to 67 percent annually).
7. See Christopher Warshaw, and Gregory E. Wannier, "Business as Usual? Analyzing the Development of Environmental Standing Doctrine Since 1976," 5 Harv. L. & Pol'y Rev. 289 (2011).
8. Jeanne Nienaber, "The Supreme Court and Mickey Mouse," *American Forests* (July 1972): 31.
9. Russell J. Mays, Office of General Counsel, U.S. Department of Agriculture, interview by Rupert Cutler, Aug. 14, 1970, quoted in M. Rupert Cutler, "Sierra Club v. Hickel: Mineral King Valley" (undated draft), Lyndon B. Johnson Presidential Library.
10. See David Halberstam, *The Best and the Brightest* (New York: Random House 1972).
11. Bob Hicks, interview by Louise Jackson, May 22, 2013, 6; RBH Papers.
12. "Interest Revives in Mineral King," *Visalia Times-Delta*, Jan. 30, 1953.
13. John Henry Auran, "Special Report: Defend Your Right to Ski," *Skiing* (Oct. 1969): 63 (quote from a sidebar entitled "Is Mineral King an Ecological Issue?").
14. Walt Disney Productions, *Walt Disney's Plans for Mineral King*, 1966; RBH Papers.
15. Deputy assistant director, Interpretation, National Park Service, "Mineral King Study by Dr. Clarkeson," memorandum to chairman, Road Committee, June 10, 1968; NARA II National Park Service Papers.

16. Walt Disney Productions, "Conservation: The Greatest Disney Story," undated, 4; RBH Papers.
17. Richard Hubler, *Biography of Walt Disney*, unpublished draft, 613; from the Richard Hubler Collection, Howard Gotlieb Archival Research Center, Boston University.

Bibliography

This list includes both books cited and others consulted but not cited.

Alder, Pat. *Mineral King Guide*. Glendale, CA: La Siesta Press, 1963.

Brooks, Karl Boyd. *Before Earth Day: The Origins of American Environmental Law, 1945–1970*. Lawrence: University of Kansas Press, 2009.

Cannon, Jonathan Z. *Environment in the Balance: The Green Movement and the Supreme Court*. Cambridge, MA: Harvard University Press, 2015.

Cohen, Michael P. *The History of the Sierra Club: 1892–1970*. San Francisco: Sierra Club Books, 1988.

Cray, Ed. *Chief Justice: A Biography of Earl Warren*. New York: Simon and Schuster, 2008.

Einberger, Scott R. *With Distance in His Eyes: The Environmental Life and Legacy of Stewart Udall*. Reno: University of Nevada Press, 2018.

Farber, David, ed. *The Sixties*. Chapel Hill: University of North Carolina Press, 1994.

Fellmuth, Robert C. *Politics of Land Ralph Nader's Study Group Report on Land Use in California*. New York: Grossman Publishers, 1973.

Flippen, J. Brooks. *Conservative Conservationist: Russell E. Train and the Emergence of American Environmentalism*. Baton Rouge: Louisiana State University Press, 2006.

Fry, John. *The Story of Modern Skiing*. Lebanon, NH: University Press of New England, 2006.

Gabler, Neal. *Walt Disney: The Triumph of the American Imagination*. New York: Alfred A. Knopf, 2006.

Galub, Arthur L. *The Burger Court 1968–1984*. Millwood, NY: Associated Faculty Press, 1986.

Godfrey, Anthony. *The Ever Changing View: A History of the National Forests in California, 1891–1987*. California: USDA Forest Service, 2005.

Goldman, Roger, and Gallen, David. *Thurgood Marshall*. New York: Carroll and Graf Publishers, 1992.

Greenfield, Robert. *Bear: The Life and Times of August Owsley Stanley III*. Old Saybrook, CT: Tantor Media, 2017.

Greenhouse, Linda. *Becoming Justice Blackmun*. New York: Times Books, 2005.

Griswold, Erwin N. *Ould Fields, New Corne: The Personal Memoirs of a Twentieth Century Lawyer*. St. Paul: West Publishing, 1992.

Halberstam, David. *The Best and the Brightest*. New York: Random House, 1972.

Harper, John L. *Mineral King: Public Concern with Government Policy*. Arcata, CA: Pacifica Publishing, 1982.

Harte, John, and Socolow, Robert H., eds. *Patient Earth*. New York: Holt, Rinehart and Winston, 1971.

Hays, Samuel P. *Beauty, Health, and Permanence: Environmental Politics in the United States, 1955–1985*. New York: Cambridge University Press, 1987.

Hirt, Paul W. *A Conspiracy of Optimism: Management of the National Forest Since World War Two*. Lincoln: University of Nebraska Press, 1996.

Isserman, Maurice, and Kazin, Michael. *America Divided: The Civil War of the 1960s*. New York: Oxford University Press, 2000.

Jackson, Louise A. *Mineral King: The Story of Beulah*. Three Rivers, CA: Sequoia Natural History Association, 2006; originally published as *Beulah: A Biography of the Mineral King Valley of California*. Three Rivers, CA: Westernlore Press, 1988.

Jacobs, John. *A Rage for Justice: The Passion and Politics of Phillip Burton*. Berkeley, CA: University of California Press, 1995.

Kline, Benjamin. *First Along the River: A Brief History of the U.S. Environmental Movement*. 3rd ed. Lanham, MD: Rowman and Littlefield, 2007.

Lazarus, Richard. *The Making of Environmental Law*. Chicago: University of Chicago Press, 2004.

Leadabrand, Russ. *A Guidebook to the Southern Sierra Nevada*. Los Angeles: W. Ritchie Press, 1968.

Lifset, Robert D. *Power on the Hudson: Storm King Mountain and the Emergence of Modern American Environmentalism*. Pittsburgh: University of Pittsburgh Press, 2014.

MacDonald, James B., and Conway, E. John. *Environmental Litigation*. Madison: University of Wisconsin Extension, 1972.

Maltz, Karl. M. *The Coming of the Nixon Court: The 1972 Term and the Transformation of Constitutional Law*. Lawrence: University Press of Kansas, 2016.

McCloskey, J. Michael. *In the Thick of It: My Life in the Sierra Club*. Washington, DC: Island Press/Shearwater Books, 2005.

McPhail, Meghan McCarthy. *A History of Cannon Mountain: Trails, Tales, and Skiing Legends*. Charleston, SC: History Press, 2011.

Miller, Char. *Gifford Pinchot and the Making of Modern Environmentalism*. Washington, DC: Island Press/Shearwater Books, 2001.

Muir, John. *The Yosemite*. New York: Century, 1912; reprint, Eugene, OR: Doublebit Press, 2020.

Pearson, Byron E. *Still the Wild River Runs: Congress, the Sierra Club, and the Fight to Save the Grand Canyon*. Tucson: University of Arizona Press, 2002.

Price, Harrison "Buzz." *Walt's Revolution! By the Numbers*. Orlando, FL: Ripley Entertainment, 2003.

Rarick, Ethan. *Desperate Passage: The Donner Party's Perilous Journey West*. New York: Oxford University Press, 2008.

Robinson, Glen O. *The Forest Service: A Study in Public Land Management*. Baltimore: The Johns Hopkins University Press, 1975.

Robinson, Judith. *You're in Your Mother's Arms: The Life and Legacy of Congressman Phil Burton*. San Francisco: M. J. Robinson, 1994.

Ruckel, H. Anthony. *Voices for the Earth*. Denver: Entrada Press, 2014.

Sale, Kirkpatrick. *The Green Revolution: The American Environmental Movement, 1962–1992*. New York: Hill and Wang, 1993.

Schrepfer, Susan. *The Fight to Save the Redwoods*. Madison: University of Wisconsin Press, 1983.

Shabecoff, Phillip. *A Fierce Green Fire: The American Environmental Movement*. Rev. ed. Washington, DC: Island Press, 2003.

Sheffer, Victor B. *The Shaping of Environmentalism in America*. Seattle: University of Washington Press, 1991.

Smith, Dave. *Disney A to Z: The Official Encyclopedia*. 5th ed. Los Angeles: Disney Editions, 2016.

Smith, Thomas G. *Stewart L. Udall: Steward of the Land*. Albuquerque: University of New Mexico Press, 2017.

Sowards, Adam M. *The Environmental Justice: William O. Douglas and American Conservation*. Corvallis: Oregon State University Press, 2009.

Steen, Harold K. *The U.S. Forest Service*. Centennial ed. Durham, NC: Forest History Society, 2004.

Stradling, David, ed. *The Environmental Movement, 1968–1972*. Seattle: University of Washington Press, 2012.

Strong, Douglas H. *From Pioneers to Preservationists: A Brief History of Sequoia and Kings Canyon National Parks*. Three Rivers, CA: Sequoia Natural History Association, 2000.

Thomas, Bob. *Building a Company: Roy O. Disney and the Creation of an Entertainment Empire*. New York: Hyperion, 1998.

Turner, James Morton. *The Promise of Wilderness: American Environmental Politics Since 1964*. Seattle: University of Washington Press, 2012.

Turner, Tom. *David Brower: The Making of the Environmental Movement*. Oakland: University of California Press, 2015.

———. *Sierra Club: 100 Years of Protecting Nature*. New York: Harry N. Abrams, 1991.

———. *Wild by Law: The Sierra Club Legal Defense Fund and the Places It Has Saved*. San Francisco: Sierra Club Legal Defense Fund, 1990.

Tweed, William C., and Dilsaver, Lary M. *Challenge of the Big Trees: The History of Sequoia and Kings Canyon National Parks*. Rev. ed. Staunton, VA: George F. Thompson, 2017.

Udall, Stewart L. Foreword, *Wild by Law: The Sierra Club Legal Defense Fund and the Places It Has Saved*. San Francisco: Sierra Club Legal Defense Fund, 1990.

Wasby, Stephen L., ed. *"He Shall Not Pass This Way Again": The Legacy of William O. Douglas*. Pittsburgh: University of Pittsburgh Press, 1990.

Wasco, Janet. *Understanding Disney*. Malden, MA: Blackwell Publishing, 2001.

Wayburn, M. D., Edgar. *Your Land and Mine: Evolution of a Conservationist*. San Francisco: Sierra Club Books, 2004.

Wellock, Thomas R. *Critical Masses: Opposition to Nuclear Power in California, 1958–1978*. Madison, WI: University of Wisconsin Press, 1998.

———. *Preserving the Nation: The Conservation and Environmental Movements, 1870–2000*. Wheeling, IL: Harlan Davidson, 2007.

Witcover, Jules. *The Year the Dream Died*. New York: Warner Books, 1997.

Woodward, Bob, and Armstrong, Scott. *The Brethren: Inside the Supreme Court*. New York: Simon and Schuster, 1979.

Wyss, Robert. *The Man Who Built the Sierra Club: A Life of David Brower*. New York: Columbia University Press, 2016.

Yarbrough, Tinsley E. *Harry A. Blackmun: The Outsider Justice*. New York: Oxford University Press, 2008.

Index